THE SCRAPBOOK
in AMERICAN LIFE

Patricia P. Buckly

Patricia P. Barker

THE SCRAPBOOK
in AMERICAN LIFE

~~~~~

EDITED BY

**Susan Tucker, Katherine Ott, and
Patricia P. Buckler**

~~~~~

TEMPLE UNIVERSITY PRESS PHILADELPHIA

Temple University Press
1601 North Broad Street
Philadelphia PA 19122
www.temple.edu/tempress

⊖The paper used in this publication meets the requirements of the American
National Standard for Information Sciences—Permanence of Paper for Printed Library
Materials, ANSI Z39.48-1992

Text design by Kate Nichols

Library of Congress Cataloging-in-Publication Data

The scrapbook in American life / edited by Susan Tucker, Katherine Ott,
and Patricia P. Buckler.
p. cm.
Includes bibliographical references and index.
ISBN 1-59213-477-7 (cloth : alk. paper)—ISBN 1-59213-478-5 (pbk. : alk. paper)
1. Photograph albums—United States—History. 2. Photographs—Conservation and
restoration—United States—History. 3. Scrapbooks—United States—History. 4. Popular
culture—United States. I. Tucker, Susan, 1950– II. Ott, Katherine. III. Buckler, Patricia.

TR465.S393453 2005
973--dc22
2005052875

*On the title page : Album by Louise Hovey in 1880s from Division of Domestic Life,
National Museum of American History, Smithsonian Institution;
accession no. 232.559, catalog no. 61.293, photograph no. 79-11535*

2 4 6 8 9 7 5 3 1

~~~~~~

TO THE MEMORY OF RODRIS ROTH

(1930–2000)

FOR HER PIONEERING WORK

ON EPHEMERA

Contents

〜〜〜〜

PART II. Books of the Self

Acknowledgments

〜〜〜〜

THIS ANTHOLOGY was nurtured over long years by many people. First of all, to Steven Zeitz, Jim Burant, Lucinda Manning, and Catherine Johnson, thanks are owed for their insightful work in introducing us to new aspects of scrapbook history. Steven Zeitz forced Katherine to take ephemera seriously as a topic for scholarship when he organized a stimulating conference on that subject in the hot summer of 1994. The ripples from that Philadelphia Area Consortium of Special Collections Libraries (PACSCL) event, where Katherine stepped tentatively into the enticing geography of ephemera, eventually led to the doorsteps of Susan and Pat. Once the three of us found one another, there was no turning back. Jim Burant supported our work when it was only a dream, and his friendship and collegiality remain inspirations to us. Ellen Gruber Garvey, Deborah Smith, and Georgen Gilliam, too, came forward early in our gatherings and provided assistance. L. Rebecca Johnson Melvin's excellent exhibition at the University of Delaware Library, entitled *Self Works*, proved a seminal example of the treasures hidden in archives.

Olivia Primanis, Jane Rutherston, and Joan Schwartz, through their insights into conservation and archival theory, also helped us. Thanks to the Newcomb Foundation for Susan's grants to compile an online bibliography and time line on scrapbooks and in turn alerting us to the complex history of ephemera. To Rebecca Black and Danielle Bias for compiling these entries and for working with Susan, special thanks. Purdue University gave Pat a summer faculty-research grant, and Purdue University North Central gave her a sabbatical to finish the research.

For their reading of various versions of the introduction and chapters, we thank Rosanne Adderley, Elspeth Brown, Rosalind Hinton, Jan Paris, David Serlin, Kate Weber, Beth Willinger, and Helena Wright. Nancy Gwinn, director of Smithsonian Institution Libraries, took some of our assertions about collections to the research libraries community and ran interference for us as people responded. The enthusiastic replies helped refine our analysis as well as reaffirmed our beliefs about the significance of ephemera. Special thanks go to a fellow parent, Julian Yochum, who fortuitously had a pen available in the carpool line when the opening sentence of the introduction started to roll forth.

Thanks to the Smithsonian Books editors who first believed in the project. Mark Hirsch, now at the National Museum of the American Indian, brought our idea for an anthology to the press, and Jeff Hardwick and Emily Sollie kept the faith as we worked to put it all together. In addition, Katherine's colleague Eric Jentsch was ever willing with the scanner, and Ron Brashear, at the Dibner Library, answered odd manuscript questions with aplomb. Gretchen Smith Mui served as an able and friendly editor.

The closing of the Smithsonian University Press in the fall of 2004 sent our manuscript hither and fro. We were pleased that it landed with Temple University Press. Janet Francendese, William Hammell, Jennifer French, and Gary Kramer worked to make the book come to life. Special thanks to Janet for her welcoming words throughout the publication process and to Bobbe Needham for editing gracefulness.

For their unfailing intellectual and moral support, as well as their knowledge of the collections they serve, we thank the librarians and archivists who have helped us over the years: Chris Cotrill and Jim Roan, National Museum of American History; Susan Strange and Vanessa Broussard-Simmons, Archives Center, National Museum of American History; Sheila O'Neill, formerly at the National Library of Medicine; Brenda Square, the Amistad Collection at Tulane University; Rebecca Hankins, Texas A&M University Library; and Florence Jumonville, Earl K. Long Library, University of New Orleans. We have dedicated this volume to the late Rodris Roth. During her career as a curator at the Smithsonian Institution's National Museum of American History, Rodris led the way in studying and interpreting domestic life in all its richness, including scrapbooks. The breadth of her interests was matched only by her generosity to colleagues and other scholars.

Finally, we thank partners, children, family, and friends who made space in their lives for a book that seemed never ending, especially Franny, Antoine, Linda, Karen, Kay, and Warren.

[KATHERINE OTT, SUSAN TUCKER, AND

PATRICIA P. BUCKLER]

~~~~~

An Introduction to
the History of Scrapbooks

~~~~~

JOHN DANZER is a remarkably productive man, but he is not sure if that is a good thing or a bad thing. Danzer, an artist and a designer of garden furniture, has been making scrapbooks for more than twenty years. His compiling system is efficient and systematic: he clips material and passes it to an assistant, who organizes it into albums. Danzer readily admits that his energy for clipping and saving is hard for even his friends to grasp. The scrap-covered walls of one of the rooms in his upstate New York house rival the wall of Joe Orton's London flat depicted in the film *Prick Up Your Ears* (1987) or John Forbes Nash Jr.'s garage hideaway in *A Beautiful Mind* (2001). Probably many contemporary scrapbook makers respond to scenes of cut scraps plastered across walls or overflowing bulletin boards with a mixture of horror, attraction, and self-recognition. For Danzer, his albums and their assemblage are invaluable both in his artistic process and in working with clients. Yet there is another, ineffable element to Danzer's scrapbook intensity that he shares with kindred souls dating back several centuries.

As do all things in this world, scrapbooks have a history. This anthology explores the history of scrapbook making—its origins, uses, changing forms, and purposes as well as the human agents behind the books themselves. The excess of fragments that burst the bindings and bulge the pages makes scrapbooks a pleasurable feast for both makers and consumers. Scrapbooks are one of the most enduring yet simultaneously changing cultural forms of the last two centuries, similar in their development to the pen or even the clavichord, the earliest musical keyboard instrument: the task and

[1]

function remain constant, while the form and structure alter under the influence of aesthetics and new materials. Despite the popularity of scrapbooks, placing them within historical traditions has never been undertaken until now.[1] This book examines scrapbooks and their makers, the artifacts saved within their covers, their readers, and U.S. culture. It does not explain how to make scrapbooks or improve assemblage techniques but instead explores the curious history of what others have done in the past and why these splendid examples of material and visual culture have such enduring appeal.

Selves in Books

The prolific Danzer and other scrapbook makers have countless forebears. In 1881, when Monte Grover, a Wyoming prostitute, pasted published poetry into her scrapbook, she followed a common practice of using clippings to construct an idealized life by isolating a set of values that she found around her. She preserved marks of her inner identity and her best self within a scrapbook (see Carol Bowers, in this volume). People today, more than one hundred years later, find their identities recorded and inscribed in bureaucratic files and data banks; their official human identities are found in X rays, birth certificates, driver's licenses, and DNA samples. But a scrapbook represents a construction of identity outside these formalized and authoritative records. It is the self that guides the scissors and assembles the scraps.[2]

At the same time, scrapbooks are not transparently autobiographical. Rather, a compiler often hopes that the mass assembling of individual examples will reveal the whole, as William Dorsey may have intended in compiling his monumental work of three hundred scrapbooks on people of color (see Susan Tucker, in this volume). Another compiler may use a scrapbook as a vehicle for encompassing information too diffuse to otherwise discern patterns. Ted Langstroth, a collector of all manner of printed material in the early twentieth century, gathered scraps into albums as a whale skims for krill along the surface of the ocean; he also acquired and reworked the albums of others.[3] Some makers create scrapbooks to contribute to their community, to provide a public service; such scrapbooks include the books on Mormon Church activities that have been donated over the years to the University of Utah library's special collections.

The scrapbooks of Charles Hemstreet, a professional scrapbook compiler of the 1930s, provide yet another cautionary note about inferring too much about the compiler's interior life, or autobiography, from examination of the work. Clients sent him clippings, which he organized into books, sometimes for fees as high as $21,000. His work included scrapbooks on the Wallis Simpson–Duke of Windsor romance and World War II cartoons about France published in the United States.[4]

For others, scrapbooks are an autobiographical form but with a twist. The compiler envisions himself or herself through the images positioned on the page.[5] Scrapbooks resemble a movie or a photograph in that they all capture "lived time" in a material form. Yet scrapbooks leave far more to the imagination. The makers express themselves with every swipe of glue yet ultimately remain free, elusive, and hidden. The adolescent girl in her bedroom, the Gilded Age doctor in his study, the boy in front of the television—all are obscured from sight. The scrapbook, as a private stage setting, remains similarly obscured.[6]

While autobiographical in origin, scrapbooks are not confessional, as diaries are. Scrapbooks may be compared to anecdotes—they represent collections of personal materials and are understandable in the same way that such stories, as a specific literary genre, are understood. Real events do not present themselves as complete tales, so creating sustained narratives from scraps is difficult. Scrapbooks can be a method of resolving the conflicting claims between the real and the imaginary or remembered.[7] They preserve the pieces but without reliance on the chronology that situates entries in a diary. If flawed as reflections, scrapbooks can function as supplements to individual identity. For example, the maker may incorporate contradictions that cannot be expressed otherwise, substitutes for expressions of the self not allowed elsewhere.[8]

Gertrude Mace compiled a scrapbook (see Figure I.1) that preserved expressions of hope for her son. Ron Mace, who became an influential architect and a founder of Universal Design, contracted polio as a child and was hospitalized for several months in 1950. His mother compiled an album of all the get-well cards nine-year-old Ronnie received. The cards are full of hope, encouragement, and positive thinking; as a group, they embody a mother's prayers for a seriously ill child. Read against Mace's later achievements and the searing critiques of similar sentiments by the disability rights movement, the cards dramatically exemplify contemporary cultural exhortations to grin and bear it, to triumph over adversity.

Scrapbooks, then, are a material manifestation of memory—the memory of the compiler and the memory of the cultural moment in which they were made. Scrapbooks represent individual and group identity in cultures increasingly dependent on reading, visual literacy, and consumption of mass-produced goods. They display artifacts and ephemera that track the migration of ideas and commodities up and down the cultural hierarchy of capitalism. They hold historical accounts in print and images that tell how events and lives were understood and told to others, how individuality spars with the public and the commercial. At the same time, they are but partial, coded accounts—very small tellings of memory. Scrapbooks contain abundant hieroglyphics for the researchers who can decipher them, yet their often-enigmatic contents can stymie even the most patient scholar.[9]

As with most things, scrapbooks hold different value for different people. Historians tend to judge each one individually, usually as part of biographical work and sometimes in isolation from historical and economic context. Anthropologists treat them as folk culture; art historians, as receptacles for prints and photographs. When scrapbooks are added to archives and libraries, they bring with them complex preservation problems.[10]

Figure I.1. *Page of get-well cards from the scrapbook of greeting cards kept by Ron Mace's mother. Mace, who was hospitalized with polio in the early 1950s, went on to become the founder of Universal Design.* (Courtesy Ronald Mace Collection, Division of Science, Medicine, and Society, National Museum of American History, Smithsonian Institution)

Scrapbooks and albums share their origins with traditions of collecting, display, and exhibition and the development of print and book styles. The disparate ancestral strands snake their way into the modern scrapbook through the centuries and the histories of memory, education, libraries, publishing, art, and even home videos. Writings and images have been used to represent memory since the beginning of history, and often these were prized and collected. However, the time line for scrapbooks and albums begins in earnest with the elements of classical learning.

The Genealogy of Memory Keeping

To the early Greeks, places in the mind—*koinoi topoi*—were used as memory aids for recreating events, information, and knowledge. Once such topoi were committed to memory, a person could mentally revisit them to retrieve information,

comfort, or facts for debate. These topoi (the root of the word *topic)* thus performed a function similar to that of scrapbooks, which came much later, in that both relied on the retention of data—one in the mind, the other on the physical page. Topoi, like scrapbooks, were places in which to find things. Memory was essential to rhetoric, an idea taken up by Cicero and Quintilian. Quintilian's *Instituto Oratorio* (ca. AD 90) instructs students in ways to preserve and record memory.[11] One name for the tablet on which they might write was *album* (from the Latin word meaning "white," designating the tablet on which public records were inscribed). Medieval society enhanced this practice, expanding methods for keeping material markers of memory. Pilgrims collected devotional objects and souvenirs, sometimes attaching them to pages of Bibles and other religious texts.[12] Scribes produced emblem books, with bound pages of drawings accompanied by interpretations in verse of the complex allegorical images.

In Europe in the thirteenth century came the gradual introduction of paper and, two centuries later, the revolutionary art of printing. These, in turn, led to the next iteration of the album. In the early Renaissance, while the efforts of individuals to preserve thoughts for private learning continued, efforts to teach others through the collection of images for more public use began. Giorgio Vasari (1511–74), who wrote about hundreds of artists in his *Lives of the Most Eminent Italian Architects, Painters, and Sculptors* (1551), advocated keeping works of art in albums, a method that influenced protomuseums and libraries.[13] Robert DeCandido has written about artists and collectors who preserved prints in this way. Such albums constituted the backbone of every collection, or "cabinet," of the period.[14]

The fledgling practice of compiling albums is also illustrated by Samuel Pepys (1633–1703), who kept his collection of bookplates in a scrapbook entitled "Vulgaria." Pepys also compiled two albums of ephemera on London and Westminster. Today, a large proportion of the twenty million prints in the Bibliothèque Nationale continues to be kept in this compiled manner.[15]

Such albums were often stored in a *Wunderkammer*, or cabinet of curiosities—a specially constructed bureau, gallery, or room in which albums were displayed along with objects as diverse as stuffed monkeys, botanical specimens, statuary, jewelry, paintings, and varied exotica. The *Wunderkammer* and *Kunstkammer* were the earliest recognizable versions of the modern museum and figured significantly in traditions of assemblage and display, for in them wealthy elites amassed their cultural capital. The taste for cabinets originated in the seventeenth century and continued into the nineteenth, although in an attenuated, middle-class form. Similarly, the albums kept in the *Wunderkammer* evolved, over many generations, into scrapbooks, the equivalent of a poor family's cabinet of curiosities. These were the books created not so much to serve the memory as to enact rituals of consumption and the hoarding of treasure.[16] And where monarchs once commissioned works and wielded their patronage to control the works' content, scrapbooks were self-commissioned (and on occasion, commercial), giving the ego free reign.

In the era of the *Wunderkammer*, fragments of memory were also gathered into a kind of album or blank book called a commonplace book, in which elites and aspiring elites gathered words for speeches, writing, and conversation and displayed their learned acquisitions. The commonplace book was both a memory aid and a notebook for personal growth, the progeny of the early Greeks' places in the mind.[17] In 1642 Thomas Fuller explained that keeping a commonplace book could serve as an aid to memory and as a "way of preserving learning and putting it to effective use."[18] John Locke's *A New Method of Making Common-Place Books*, published posthumously in 1706, brought structure to the popular blank-book format by adding subject headings, places for references, and an index. According to Locke, excerpts should be short and contain an argument, written as a summary in the margin.[19] These self-made anthologies were kept by schoolboys and statesmen alike.

The twin practices of gathering and arranging textual fragments in notebooks became institutionalized in the curricula of schools. "Gathering and framing" occupied the time of such notable figures as Francis Bacon, Samuel Johnson, William Byrd II, Thomas Jefferson, and Robert Herrick.[20] Published versions of the commonplace books of famous men abounded.[21] As printed matter became more accessible, personal commonplace books came to resemble scrapbooks, with clippings and artifacts tipped in and overlaid on one another.[22]

In the late eighteenth century, another variation in book format edged albums closer to modern scrapbooks. In 1775 James Granger published a biographical history of England designed with blank pages on which the owner could affix prints.[23] Granger and subsequent editors urged book owners to collect engravings to enhance the pages of their books. A Grangerized, or extra-illustrated book, came to mean a printed, bound book with illustrations, letters, autographs, or other materials added later—personalized, that is, by each owner. These combinations of printed book and manuscript reached the zenith of their popularity in the nineteenth century. Occasionally, the owner of a Grangerized book would tip in illustrations unrelated to the text, making for strange and interesting hybrid volumes.

Color Printing and Other New Technologies

The success of color-printing technologies in the late eighteenth and nineteenth centuries meant that the general public now had cheap and plentiful color images at their disposal. Printed ephemera for use in albums appeared in the early nineteenth century. First developed by the German Alois Senefelder, lithography took the world by storm and revolutionized styles of visual perception. Senefelder's work was followed by the successes of others in color printing, notably Godefroy Engelmann in Paris in the 1830s. Quickly thereafter, small color scraps—the leftover pieces from larger printing jobs—seemed too precious to be discarded and too valuable to be given away. Marketed first in Germany, these die-cut glossy printed paper images were salvaged by bakers who used them for wrapping special breads—Easter bread, for instance, wrapped in a paper showing a spring scene. From the late 1830s onward, collectors sought such chromolithographs. The fad of collecting them fueled the printing industry, and the fad of compiling them in a scrapbook or scrap album inspired another product.[24]

Color scraps, or chromos, found an enthusiastic market in the owners of blank friendship books, passed around among nineteenth-century Americans. A transformation of the Dutch and German *album amicorum* (almost always called by its Latin name) of the seventeenth and eighteenth centuries, the friendship album was a place for inscribing autographs, poetry, prose, and wishes from friends. Pre–Civil War friendship albums were homemade and sewn together by the maker, a local bookbinder, or a stationer. The contents combined mass-produced sources and friends' words and autographs.[25]

Other printing inventions and improvements in engraving, letterpress, and lithography brought ever more paper collectibles. Throwaway printed paper artifacts—ticket stubs, advertising cards, candy wrappers, and more—became a part

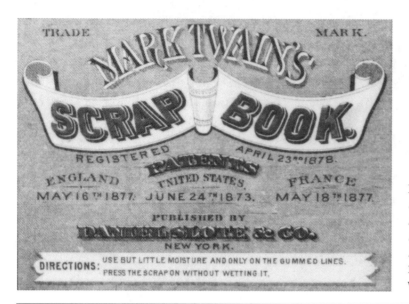

Figure I.2. *An example of a Mark Twain scrapbook album (late nineteenth century), showing Twain label.* (Courtesy American Heritage Center, University of Wyoming)

of everyday life. Books to hold such paper became the preoccupation of many young people and an inducement to free or inexpensive collecting.

By 1835 the use of scrapbooks was common enough to warrant a Hartford, Connecticut, publisher to issue for two years a periodical entitled *The Scrapbook,* which described the hobby of scrapbooks as keeping a blank book in which pictures, newspaper cuttings, and the like were pasted for safekeeping. Stationers sold sheets for enthusiasts to cut and paste, newspapers offered pages for clippings, and merchants offered trade cards. Holiday cards, such as valentines, were made from these various sources and pasted into such albums. Indeed, by the late 1860s cheap chromolithography made colored images available to every household and had found its way into practically every scrapbook or album.[26]

Commercial scrapbooks were marketed widely throughout the nineteenth century and included such titles as *Shipment's Common Sense Binder* (ca. 1825) and *The Ideal Patented Scrapbook* (ca. 1830). Always eager for a money-making scheme, Mark Twain patented a successful scrapbook in 1873 and subsequently marketed his scrapbooks through Daniel Slote of New York.[27] With characteristically inflated prose, Twain praised his album as the "only rational scrapbook the world has ever seen"[28] (see Figure I.2). A unique feature of Twain's design related to the method for attaching scraps to the page: the book came with pages already coated with mucilage. Other patentees claimed that their products had such improvements as gummed pages, interleaves, stronger bindings, and more durable and flexible photographic papers that made pictures much easier to manipulate.[29]

An Educational and a Moral Tool

The universal public education movement and its emphasis on order and repetition—two values embedded in the making of commonplace books—proved a boon for scrapbooks. Master educators encouraged teachers to keep their own anthologies of clippings and artwork for instruction. From the 1860s to the 1930s, the training of kindergarten teachers included making albums with geometric paper designs. Because textbooks were scarce, such homemade books were critical to many schools. Nineteenth- and early-twentieth-century educators also promoted scrapbooks as a means of teaching art skills.[30] In 1873 the entrepreneur Louis Prang obliged with his introduction of chromo cards for children, marketing them as simple designs of "great sweetness" and "beautiful art bits." Similar art products flourished well into the twentieth century and supplied schoolchildren across the United States with inspirational and functional materials.[31]

Such practices were equally commended to parents, who were exhorted to use scrapbook making as a means of converting their children from feral creatures to good citizens.[32] Writing in the 1880s, E. W. Gurley stressed scrapbook creation in promoting family harmony and solving the problems of both idleness and unfocused reading. "Would it not be a pleasant picture of a farmer's family gathered around the fireside of a winter's evening overhauling a bundle of papers selected for this purpose?" he asked. Noting his own penchant for compiling, he attributed the desire for scrapbooks to the growth of newspapers, "from 2 in the times of Franklin to over 8000 in 1880." "We all read, but are we all well informed?" he asked and answered no. The problem could be solved if "we read for a purpose, look for something and keep it when found, and in no other form can it be so well preserved as in the pages of a good scrapbook."[33]

Each family member could make his or her own book—the father on farming, the mother on the home, the boys on horses or cattle, the girls on poetry or stories. Besides learning how to create domestic harmony and how to be good spouses, scrapbook makers were also improving their visual literacy and training the mind's eye. They practiced graphic design, interpreted advertising conventions, and absorbed such iconic cultural images as the U.S. flag, Uncle Sam, barefoot boys with fishing poles, Niagara Falls, and floral bouquets.[34]

Although ideally all family members were included in the scrapbook-making circle, much album making fell to the female gender. From the early nineteenth century to the present, girls and women were seen as the most frequent compilers. Todd Gernes has shown that girls and women came to be associated with friendship albums, for example, and Tamar Katriel and Thomas Farrel report that people who were shown a century-old scrapbook described its maker as a "she."[35] Compiling scrapbooks of trade cards was also associated with girls (see Ellen Gruber Garvey, in this volume). In general, scrapbook and album making was considered a female activity, linked to traditional female concerns of holding families together and pre-serving nostalgic items.[36]

However, this may well be a misperception, a product of the language used to define male and female activity and the gender fault line between leisure and work.[37] A number of essays in this volume (those by Katherine Ott, Susan Tucker, and James Kelley) speak of albums and scrapbooks in the lives of men. When lab books, ledgers, and other professional scrapwork forms are included, the gender gap shrinks. In addition, a number of early antiquarians and learned men compiled scrapbooks as part of their life's work; collection, not publishing, was their goal. Charles Poulson, for example, saved every reproduced photograph and watercolor of Philadelphia he could find and then willed albums of these items to the Library Company on his death in 1866. Artists' scrapbooks are yet another large category of works that includes many examples by men.[38]

The Culture of Capitalism

Scrapbook and album making captured the culture of capitalism in the desires to pos-sess objects and understand oneself through possessions. An 1872 book entitled *The Happy Nursery* urged that children be taught to value paper products as tokens of affection (see Meredith Eliassen, in this volume). Assembled into scrapbooks, these tokens spoke of all "the best and warmest" feelings learned within the home. And, of course, colorful trade cards became the bonus for purchasing a product.

The scrapbook reached maturity at the same time that industrial capitalism was reaching its first peak. The world of the late nineteenth century exploded with pos-sibilities—consumer goods, mail-order catalogs, streetcars that could transport a per-son across communities and bring strangers to one's door, half-tone images of far-flung places and people. As caches for the booty of capitalism, scrapbooks fit seamlessly into the rituals of consumption and etiquette that helped new members of the middle class identify one another.[39] Scrapbooks supported consumers in the second half of the nineteenth and the early twentieth century as they manipulated cutouts of furniture, packaged food, store-bought clothing, and other mass-produced items.[40] They fed dual, opposing impulses: one, to grab and hoard what one could before it moved out of reach; and two, to select the exact thing and discard the rest. Not surprisingly, the thousands of trade cards printed during the 1880s and 1890s ended up in scrapbooks and the rubbish pile.

Not only was scrapbook making a hobby recommended by the arbiters of middle-class taste; the album itself became a commercial product—a mass-produced object marketed, without irony or improbity, as unique and individualized. Homemade scrapbooks, although they never became extinct, were eventually marginalized by the commercial gift-book trade.[41] Late-nineteenth-century ledger design branched out to accommodate buyers of commonplace books. These blank books, revised with headings and illustrations, made them a popular present for students. Still other publishers mass-marketed blank books with title pages and headings for religious and school prizes, debutantes, brides, and even death notices, to name but a few of the purposes for such books.[42]

The Photography Revolution

The coming-of-age of scrapbook albums also depended on popular acceptance of photography. The invention of photography in 1837 forever altered the making of scrapbooks and albums. Not only were there photographs to be entered into scrapbooks, but also the forms of scrapbooks themselves became more varied and abundant. The period 1850–1910 brought a variety of patented photograph albums alongside more polished versions of commonplace books and scrapbooks.[43] In the early 1850s, Louis Blanquart-Evard introduced albumen printing paper and assembled albums of photographs for his customers in France.[44]

In 1850 Mathew Brady issued *The Gallery of Illustrious Americans*, an album of twelve lithographic portraits based on photographs.[45] Available on a subscription basis, the portraits were an early version of today's pseudoscrapbooks, albums that offer an intimate view of a celebrity or show readers the lives of the rich and famous through photographs and imitation handwritten entries. Such books have thrived for a long time. Even a cursory library search will call up numerous titles, including *A Scrapbook Containing Photographic Portraits of British Notables* (1863), *A Sportsman's Scrapbook* (1928), *My Guidance Scrapbook: Vocations* (1931), *I Am a Woman Worker: A Scrapbook of Autobiographies* (1936), *Cecil Beaton's Scrapbook* (1937), *A Fox Hunter's Scrapbook* (1945), *Britain at Arms: A Scrapbook from Queen Anne to the Present* (1953), *The Marx Bros. Scrapbook*, by Groucho Marx (1973), *General Hospital: The Complete Scrapbook* (1995), and *Princess Diana—Forever in Our Hearts: A Scrapbook of Memories* (1997). Publications such as these carried the scrap ideology into homes around the world.

As publishers observed the substantial market for blank books, they considered how to adapt them to accommodate photographs. Studies by book conservators show that albums used for photograph mounting appeared as early as 1850. Richard Horton shows that a common, unstubbed blank book was first used in the United States for photographs in the 1850s, while Jane Rutherston found that the bulk of British patents for albums and scrapbooks dated from 1860 to 1900.[46] As early as 1861, photography journals had urged their readers to collect their multiplying *carte-de-visite* images into albums produced especially for this purpose. The *carte-de-visite* album had become an established institution by the 1870s, and albums for cabinet photographs were to remain popular until World War I.[47] Both Elizabeth Siegel and Sarah McNair Vosmeier echo in their essays in this volume an 1864 proclamation by *Godey's Lady's*

Book: "Photograph albums have become not only a luxury for the rich but a necessity for the people. The American family would be poor indeed who could not afford a photograph album." Rapidly joining the family Bible on the parlor table as proof of middle-class gentility, the photograph album quickly established its own conventions, its own rules for maintenance and domestic display, and practices that continue to shape collections of family pictures today. From the beginning the scrapbook and the album were interchangeable in function. Although scholars and conservators have devoted more attention to the photograph album, perhaps the more public of the two, many of these books were used also to hold scraps and other memorabilia.[48]

Albums for photographs alone appeared, but often photograph albums also contained at least some paper ephemera and handwritten notes. New paper and printing production technology increased the amount of paper products available for newspaper illustration and for photographs themselves. Publications such as *Frank Leslie's Illustrated News* and *Harper's Weekly* overflowed with images. In the late 1880s, when Kodak introduced the lighter-weight print papers and rolled film that ushered in the snapshot era, cutting reached new heights, and scrapbooks and photograph albums became more mixed in format.[49]

Private and Unique

Neither albums nor scrapbooks are exactly books. Certainly as a genre they are rarely found in lending libraries. Most often, scrapbooks are created and kept in private, for a limited few to see. They are eccentric and idiosyncratic, making them impossible to pick up and read as one would a published book. The meaning found in any particular scrapbook depends on the nimble skills of the reader.[50] Even when they are similar to books, with leaves and bindings, the content is different. Nor does the existence of innovations such as e-books matter a whit to the content of scrapbooks, although e-zines and blogs share many commonalities with scrapbooks. In form, many scrapbooks more closely resemble the junk drawer found in kitchens and desks. Some scrapbooks spend their entire existence unbound, in shoe boxes or other staging areas, awaiting the day when the gatherer will become a compiler.

Scrapbooks represent a mass-cultural form, but individually each is unique, authentic, and not easily reproducible. Walter Benjamin's classic essay "The Work of Art in the Age of Mechanical Reproduction" speaks to this point. The humble scrapbook's aura of authenticity lives on, even after its contents cease to make sense to the reader.[51] Consequently, scrapbooks are perhaps most similar to the artist's book, that one-of-a-kind creation with pages read as compound pictures.[52] The meaning of every selected image or object has an implied relationship to everything else in the volume. Keith Smith has described the process of comprehending artist's books: "Referral sets the order of viewing. Binding maintains the order. Turning pages reveals the order."[53] Above all, as with artist's books, the experience of reading a scrapbook is intensely physical and sensual. The pages must be touched to be turned, and the turning creates movement between objects and amasses visual stimulation. Caring for, handling, and playing with scrapbooks activate the same emotions enjoyed in experiencing art.

Other precursors and cousins to the modern scrapbook require further exploration of the unique within the mass produced. Sewing quilts from scraps of fabric is similar, although commonly associated with group work rather than that of individuals.[54] Mention of almanacs, catalogs, and fancy craft paper cutting, such as Chinese paper cuts, should also be included as of potential importance, as should the composition techniques of mosaics and stained-glass windows.[55]

Although it would be impossible to list the many types of scrapbooks, some of the most common ones are single-purpose albums, single-theme or single-topic albums, and single-material albums. Single-purpose albums might be created for a special celebration—a birth, a teaching portfolio, or a school project, for example. Single-theme or single-topic albums might concentrate on a private individual's life and times or the life of a celebrity, such as a movie star or sports hero. The scrapbooks Julian Black kept on the boxer Joe Louis fit into the category of the single-theme album, as do scrapbooks of photographs of flowers, bird species, or trips (see Figures I.3 and I.4); scrapbooks of favorite comic strips; and albums recording significant events such as wars, earthquakes, presidential elections, or world's fairs.[56] *The Simple Art of Scrapbooking* has tips for making thirty types of single-theme scrapbooks, including relatively recent concerns such as retirement.[57] Collections of stamps, postcards, trade cards, wine labels, or matchbooks are examples of single-material albums. The paper dollhouses Beverly Gordon writes about in this volume are probably in a class of their own.

Perhaps the most consulted scrapbooks in libraries and archives are those about the theater. These include single-format albums that focus on playbills, photographs, drawings, or ticket stubs, as well as albums devoted to one star, a particular theater, a performing company, or genre.[58] One of the most stunning examples of scrapbook extravagance is the three-album set of scrapbooks devoted to Diaghilev's Ballet Russe, compiled by his earliest London patron, Lady Ripon. These albums are oversized (28 by 22 inches) and, as a group, offer a visual tour of the productions that made the Ballet Russe the phenomenon it was. Although some of the photographs and prints might be found elsewhere, the compilation itself provides a singular overview and enables a viewer to experience the impact of the whole. Most significant, the three-volume set includes a series of pen-and-ink, pencil, and watercolor portrait sketches of Vaslav Nijinsky by Jean Cocteau.[59]

Rupture and Reassemblage

If the historical development of scrapbooks is clear, how then do we read these fragments as cultural artifacts? Scrapbooks are a pleasure to make and examine, but what guidance is there for those who want to analyze them and use them as evidence for

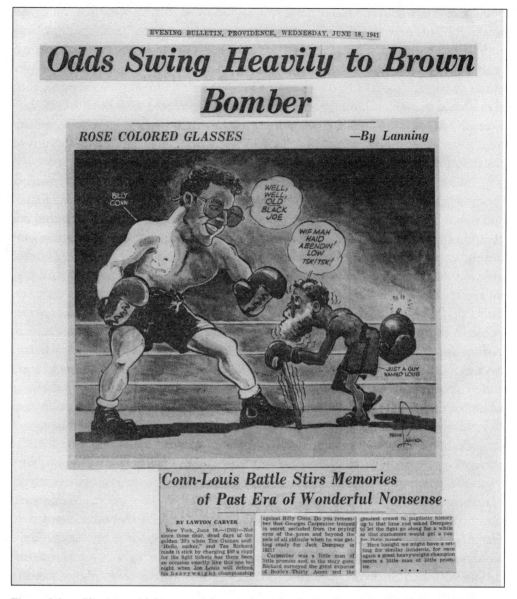

Figure I.3. *Clippings with heavy racial overtones, from Joe Louis scrapbook, 1941.* (Courtesy Julian Black Scrapbooks of Joe Louis, 1935–44, Archives Center, National Museum of American History, Behring Center, Smithsonian Institution)

understanding history? Numerous works analyze illustrated books and their expository images.[60] Certainly scrapbooks are rich in material culture, but they are not like published books and images. Published works are the product of many people, from the author, editor, and designer to the printer and marketer. Where does one begin with the unpublished, highly personal scrapbook?

Figure I.4. *Page from a "Mrs. Kendrick's" motoring trip to the Grand Canyon and points west in the 1930s.* (Courtesy Scrapbook Collection, Archives Center, National Museum of American History, Behring Center, Smithsonian Institution)

As prime examples of material and visual culture, scrapbooks lend themselves to analysis with interdisciplinary tools. A material and visual culture approach examines the relationship between text or artifact and its social world. In this regard, if scrapbooks can be distilled to one overarching interpretive theme, it is that of rupture. Scrapbooks shuffle and recombine the coordinates of time, space, location, voice, and memory. What could be more emblematic of the fractured narratives of modernity than scrapbooks?

In museum-exhibition practice, one of the basic psychological truths is that the viewer usually believes that what he or she is looking at is natural, authentic, true. The problem is that everything gets its meaning from its context, which is partly supplied by the viewer and partly by the curator and designer. Everything in an exhibit has been removed from its primal environment and artificially reconstituted. The same rupture occurs in scrapbooks, which are, after all, assembled from scraps. Consequently, the first thing that the serious critic must do is let go of the notion that any part of what is under analysis is free of manipulation. As with objects in exhibitions, the contents of scrapbooks undergo double and triple readings: as themselves, as fragments on a page, and as objects related to whatever the viewer brings to them. Susan Pearce has looked at the rupture (although she does not use the term) that is the foundation of collecting. She divides collecting into three categories: systematics, the construction of a collection to represent an ideology; fetishism, the removal of the object from its historical and cultural context and its redefinition by the collector; and souvenir gathering, in which the object is prized for its power to carry the past into the future.[61]

Albums and scrapbooks present examples of all three categories, but above all they manipulate meaning through rupture and the reconstruction that follows. They shift from the real to the imaginary realm, often with no sign that any change has occurred. The contents fracture chronology; events that occurred weeks or decades apart seem, when placed side by side on a page, to happen simultaneously or in reverse order.[62] Displacement and rupture appealed to late-nineteenth- and early-twentieth-century sensibilities. A hallmark of expositions of the era was the bricolage of cultures, cut from sites around the world and installed on the urban fairgrounds of Chicago, St. Louis, Cincinnati, and San Francisco (see Jennifer A. Jolly, in this volume).[63] In addition, the popular middle-class pastime of collecting—the single-minded hunt for objects of desire—helped turn rupture and reassemblage into a commonplace.[64] Reassemblage provided one way to turn fracture into harmony and create unity out of differences.

Collage: The Scrapbook's Art Form

Collage and its variant, montage, reached prominence during the time that scrapbooks first enjoyed great popularity. The common sense of Marcel Duchamp's generation that made understandable his controversial Ready-Mades, commonplace objects transformed into sculptures, also stoked the fragmentation of the visual world of the early twentieth century. Repetition, mass reproduction, and appropriation of public materials for private interpretation punctuated the avant-garde art scene at the turn of the century. These tactics were grounded in mundane experience, not imposed by the scions of high culture. They sprang up from workers in industry and toilers in urban life.[65]

In the 1850s and 1860s, Hippolyte Bayard, Eugene Appert, Henry Peach Robinson, Oscar Rejlander, and others experimented with photomontage, a process that allowed twentieth-century artists to creatively manipulate images. By the early twentieth century, the informal and highly personal scrapbook had infiltrated the public domain in the form of collage, described by art historians as among the first truly modern art forms.[66] Amateur photographers used similar techniques to add to albums and scrapbooks. Scrapbook makers and artists grasped the idea of a fragmented world and expressed it through a scrap aesthetic. The arrangement of items in both collage art and scrapbooks functioned in much the same manner. As Diane Waldman notes in *Collage, Assemblage, and the Found Object*, collage has layers of meaning.[67] Both creative forms reflected the modernist characteristics of rupture and multifaceted interpretation. Scrapbooks relied on the assemblage of images borrowed from diverse origins, often discovered by chance and reconstituted to create an entirely new context and meaning.

The convergence of the dissimilar to produce meaningful association was of revolutionary significance. The collage technique consciously sought to cross boundaries among and between genres and media. High-art collage contrasted with the scrapbook's low-art collage, which contained the private side of identity, the nonpolitical and nonideological. The collage of the scrapbook more overtly juxtaposed the scraps of found or used objects with the memories of the compiler. The viewer must seek the hidden rhyme that connects the elements on the page.[68]

Montage, an assemblage form closely tied to scrapbooks and collage, is an "aesthetic practice of combination, repetition, and overlap."[69] Montage reached its golden era in the interwar years with cinema and photography. The juxtaposition of unexpected yet familiar images provided the visual syntax for montage. Yet, as with the history of collage, scrapbooks receive little recognition as the ubiquitous mass visual and material form that buoyed the public art of montage.[70] Melissa A. Johnson's discussion of Hannah Höch in this volume is a welcome corrective.

The rise of the middle class frames the era of the classic scrapbook. From the mid- to the late-nineteenth century, many forms of manufacturing consolidated into the blunt force of industrial capitalism. Commodity capitalism, a tributary of this ocean of power, swelled from factories into department stores and mail-order catalogs full of mass-produced consumer goods. The wages for many workers increased and stabilized enough to underwrite the dominance of a middle class of citizens. The ideology of the middle class included the obligation to consume and display goods. Yet the scrapbooks of these avaricious Victorian consumers prove that they were not passive or defenseless in the face of advertising and the proliferation of goods. Trade cards were cut up to suit the compiler's needs—flowers or animals were removed, product identities snipped away—demonstrating that commerce was not a sacred cow.[71]

Scrapbooks existed at the crossroads of print culture and commodity capitalism. Seemingly without compunction, compilers ransacked commercial images and plundered paper products to suit themselves.[72] Compilers, through the continual action of separation and reconstitution, undermined the alienation that often characterized social relations under capitalism. Objects may have originated in the prevailing and impersonal marketplace, but individuals converted the unfamiliar into the familiar by cutting up the materials of capitalism and turning them into gifts to themselves. Compilers personalized their clippings and infused them with individual meaning outside the arena of market exchange.[73]

Consumer demand for visual material in the last third of the nineteenth century also brought a renaissance of printing and book design. Attention to the handicraft of bookmaking characterized the Arts and Crafts movement. William Morris and the Kelmscott style looked backward to early printed books and medieval and Gothic manuscripts for inspiration. Mass-marketed scrapbooks often borrowed the hand-sewn bindings, cloth pages, and embossed vine-and-castle imagery of this style.

Ephemeral Ephemera

One of the most challenging characteristics of scrapbooks is that they are ephemeral. In fact, they exemplify ephemera made from other ephemera. Ephemera is simply a form carrying graphic or prose information that was meant to survive only for the life span of an event, meeting, or brief period of relevance. The term *ephemera* encompasses a wide range of materials—conference agendas, menus, tickets, leaflets, bills and invoices, labels, calendars, greeting cards, score cards, trade cards, and coupons. Ephemera are created with their demise assumed.[74]

Most scrapbooks and their ephemeral content do not last and provide only a fleeting usefulness. They disintegrate and crumble. The leaves fall out. The enclosures drop off the page. Archivists, the most conscientious embalmers of primary materials, tend to neglect them because they are conservation nightmares. None of the solutions available will correct all the problems. Sometimes an archivist must destroy a scrapbook—take it apart—to save it.[75]

Ephemera are beloved by collectors but, curiously, spurned by many serious scholars. They are seldom studied or analyzed. Consequently, their value is not widely appreciated. Few scholars comprehend how to use ephemera as evidence.[76]

Ephemera have been called "raw, unedited history—the purest kind," as well as "the other half of history: the half without guile."[77] To some extent, ephemera do reveal culture makers with their guard down, in all their glorious and unrestrained excess: the brilliant crassness of popular culture, which both attracts and repels. But this characterization somewhat overstates the extent to which ephemera are extracultural, less grounded in their historical context than, say, a novel or a film. It is certainly true that ephemera are among the least understood and most dismissed components of archival holdings. Even many of the early collectors of and writers on ephemera, the so-called friends of the genre, saw these mundane items meant for fifteen minutes of fame as emblematic of the decline of taste.[78]

The Stigma of Mass Culture

The stigma attached to mass culture led earlier students of ephemera into dead-end disquisitions on good and bad typography, bombastic language, and poor composition at the expense of serious analysis about why and how the styles developed and thrived. The collection, storage, and cataloging of ephemera remain often haphazard and arbitrary, and the professional literature, rather sparse. Some librarians, archivists, and museum professionals, as well as scholars, find scrapbook content more amusing than serious. Yet archivists, special collections librarians, and collectors also tend to be the stalwart protectors of scrapbooks. Scholars too are slowly starting to take an interest in ephemera and their use as more than an occasional book illustration or exhibition brochure.[79]

One of the biggest obstacles to using ephemera and scrapbooks as primary source material is that they usually arrive devoid of context, with no attribution, provenance, history, or biographical information. Ephemera just exist. There is seldom any listing of items within scrapbooks.[80] Apart from research libraries, few institutions have the reference tools necessary to support intensive research, such as city and company directories, dictionaries of engravers and artists, or books on iconography and symbols. If a university library has some of these resources, they are likely to be housed, unless they are available online, at scattered locations around the library system—in the business, art, or medical branches. All this makes it frustrating and fatiguing to try to argue *from* ephemera as well as with them. In addition, most library information access and indeed most academic scholarship rely on the written word as the point of departure and as the foundation for analysis. This tends to make interpretation of images, objects, and mass culture a poor and maligned cousin in the scholarship hierarchy.

Ephemera look the way they do partly because there are few editorial or administrative constraints on them. Producers have no jury or peer review to pass judgment on their taste or truthfulness, only a printer paid to get the product out. Consequently, ephemera often display more drama and hyperbole than do other kinds of primary sources. Yet ephemera have nobility. Their very transitoriness makes them all the more precious.

One of the great poets of the nineteenth century used ephemera in her writing process. Emily Dickinson scissored out images and texts from journals and mailed them to friends. She wrote her poems on household detritus—on the backs of bags, bills, chocolate wrappers, and old shopping lists and along the margins of newspapers and flyers—and refused to publish them.[81] Her motivation for elevating ephemera may have been a perverse tactic to keep her poetry out of circulation. Or she may have been influenced by the prevalent bourgeois ethos of waste not, want not. Lydia Maria Child, in her popular 1832 book *The Frugal Housewife*, recommended that old letters be saved so that they could be written on again—on the back. Child prodded readers to gather up fragments of time as well as materials, to waste nothing.[82]

Another aspect of the life of ephemera has to do with their circulation through the market—their life cycle within capitalism.[83] Objects change categories many times during their existence. Materials once treasured are given away, become rubbish, or end up stored in a museum. Much of the content of scrapbooks, because it is incomprehensible, exists in a timeless limbo—significant but without value.[84]

The mundane nature of scrapbooks can also be read in a more subversive way. In *The Practice of Everyday Life*, Michel de Certeau wrote at length about the manipulation and use of popular culture by those who consume it but do not control or make it. His analysis of the processes of consumption of culture by common people highlights such everyday activities as reading, talking, walking, and cooking, which he analyzed as creative tactics that people use to maintain control over their lives in the face of the power of the state and society.[85] De Certeau's "unrecognized producers, poets of their own acts," might easily include scrapbook makers.[86] They circumvent publishing, bypass copyrights, and freely cannibalize printed sources. Scrapbook makers avoid the external editing process that would squeeze their creations into narrative and prose forms acceptable to mass audiences. Instead, each album is a rogue and a renegade that both parries with and parallels popular forms.

Guy Debord takes a less positive view of such activities in *Society of the Spectacle*.[87] Debord places spectacle at the core of modern experience. Although he used a hatchetlike manifesto to deliver his argument, when viewed with memory books in mind, a sketchy scrapbook epistemology emerges. For Debord, modern society lacks quality because of the dominance of the commodity form. Life becomes an immense accumulation of spectacles: representations of events not directly experienced or lived. As a result, images are detached from context and eventually merge into a common stream of unreality, the heart of spectacle. Spectacle, then, defines relationships among people. It is a social relationship mediated by images, such as those material manifestations earnestly gathered into albums. In both de Certeau's and Debord's frameworks, scrapbooks mediate one's personal circumstances within capitalistic society. Debord's view of human endeavor is a sobering counter to de Certeau's. Yet both throw light on the link between scrapbook making's appeal and the ideological contexts that support the collection of ephemera.

Scrapbooks have been a central storehouse for U.S. memory. Yet, as David Lowenthal cautions in *The Past Is a Foreign Country*, we must not assume that the material before us reflects a timeless past—that our contemporary analysis perfectly captures past eras or that the material under analysis was once part of a static, undynamic era.[88] We can only speculate about the worldviews of compilers who worked long before the world had experienced nuclear weapons, *Brown v. Board of Education*, Walt Disney, the diminution of religion, AIDS, the Internet, or even aspirin or fluoride in the water supply. The least problematic use of scrapbooks is perhaps similar to what Roy Rosenzweig and David Thelen in *The Presence of the Past* describe as the task of public historians: to link the fragments of individual memory, vague bits of knowledge, and the desire for community, to a shared past.[89] Rosenzweig and Thelen also report that such activities as creating albums and going to museums are among the main ways people understand and connect with their own individual histories. The authors found that history associated with grand narratives was not of much interest to people, yet their interviewees felt the pull of the past. This past implied a more personal or famil- ial connection, while history signified the big, official narrative in which the individ- ual was overlooked or lost. In this regard, then, scrapbooks can be understood to reflect the past rather than history.[90] And, like memories, scrapbooks lack closure. They often stop and become silent without forewarning.

Scrapbooks are once again surging in popularity.[91] In the 1990s and early 2000s, home videos, individual and family Web pages, and, most significant, the immensely popular hobby of scrapbooking are serving the need to order life and pre- serve memory first recognized centuries ago. As one popular magazine article noted: "From elite Manhattan bookbinders to mall-based scrapbook stores, America seems to be cutting and pasting, as never before. We're attending Memories Expos, and going to 'crops' (quilting bees for clip artists). We're inviting neighbors over for pres- entation by Creative Memories (like Tupperware parties for scrapbookers). We're spending $300 million annually on scrapbook materials, according to the Hobby Industry Association, which estimates that one out of five US households has a scrapbook fanatic."[92]

As was true for the late nineteenth century, the other heyday of scrapbook and album makers, this is a time of changing technology, with nostalgia and retrospection popular, memoirs a favorite literary form, and a world that seems awash with paper. When one can easily download illustrations and digitize or even improve the quality of older photographs, the appeal of making one's own book is strong. As Mihaly Csik- szentmihaly notes in "Why We Need Things," artifacts seem to reproduce themselves, increasing in complexity as they go along. Human intervention makes for greater and greater complexity of function.[93] The *Wall Street Journal* noted in the late nineties that a Finnish company offered twenty-four different types of scrapbook scissors.[94] In 1996 Creative Memories trained more than forty-nine thousand consultants to sell scrapbook ware and teach scrapbooking techniques.[95]

Adaptations of scrapbooks are visible in contemporary culture as well. Home movies and videos are a combination of memory bank, popular form, diary, pho- tograph album, and scrapbook. From the cheap 8-millimeter films that hit the post- war market to the digital mixes of today, family movies usually lack an obvious plot. They are fragments of experience, sometimes edited according to a recognizable logic but more often simply strings of disparate images with fractured chronology at unconnected locations. Like scrapbooks, home movies turn experience into visual memories of significance for the makers but become harder to read the further one moves away from the creators. Like scrapbooks, they commemorate significant occasions—a birth or a baptism, weddings, celebrations, and travel. And they are all fragments clipped from the context or sequence that would provide fuller understanding.[96]

"The Sims" (short for *simulations*) have captured the imagination of thousands of computer-game and Internet players who exchange chitchat in coffee shops, classrooms, and homes.[97] Nineteenth- and twentieth-century paper dollhouses fostered similar play with the surprisingly ordinary. Rodris Roth examined twenty-five examples from one collection and found only the typical, unastonishing scenarios of mundane life.[98] Perhaps those imaginary paper sets, lacking in complex fantasies, anticipated the mass appeal of "The Sims."

Such contemporary aspects make scrapbooks and albums a rich resource for scholars interested in popular culture. By the same token, the scrapbook's short life, their chaos of oblique signs known only to compilers, and the frequent lack of any recognizable context make for challenges that often doom the memory book to oblivion and place it at the bottom of conservation treatment programs in libraries. For these reasons, the insights of those who have studied particular albums and scrapbooks become even more important.

A Forecast of This Book

This book is divided into two sections: Part I, "Manuscripts of Learning and Knowing"; and Part II, "Books of the Self." "Manuscripts of Learning and Knowing" considers scrapbooks and albums intended primarily to support learning and transfer knowledge. They have been used to reinforce a particular point of view. "Books of the Self" includes essays that examine evolving individuals who collected materials more directly about their private selves. These were used to aid in individual and group accumulation of memories and in identity, growth, and survival.

Part I begins with Katherine Ott's essay, which places the scrapbook in its most prolific period—the turn of the twentieth century, when the work of physicians was being contested, as well as elevated to authoritative status. Ott's physicians became enthusiastic compilers of texts that would enable them to practice medicine and claim a place within the wider community of professionals.

Emily Wharton Sinkler began her scrapbook of cooking receipts, household formulas, and medical remedies in 1855, and for three generations on her South Carolina plantation, ledger pages carried knowledge from one generation to the next. The scrapbook was continued by her daughter-in-law and later by her granddaughter, who began to add her recipes in 1914. Their entries had rules and codes, implied exchanges with the outside world and that of the plantation, and built community ties. In her essay, Anne Sinkler Whaley LeClercq, a descendant, interweaves biography and memory to interpret the recipes recorded in the family's scrapbook.

From biography and newspaper clippings, Patricia P. Buckler shows in her contribution how mementos preserved in the scrapbook kept by a Baltimore woman, along with her letters, reconstructed the more formalized, published accounts of the Mexican War (1846–48).

Jennifer A. Jolly compares the private memories and public history in Gertrude Raddin's scrapbook of the 1893 World's Columbian Exposition in Chicago with what the fair's organizers intended visitors to take away. Jolly also examines the way one person's scrapbook allows access to three levels of history: the events, people, and objects present at the fair; the cultural role of the scrapbook itself; and the writing and recording of history.

How individuals learned of the nearby and faraway through scrapbook making is also explored by Ellen Gruber Garvey in her essay on trade card collecting. Garvey analyzes the prescriptive literature that promoted trade card scrapbooks for the wholesome benefits of thrift, learning, and self-reliance. She also looks at the 1880s advertising phenomenon of cards colorfully imprinted with merchants' names and wares and their relation to industrialization and progress.

Beverly Gordon examines another type of scrapbook—the paper dollhouse book—for its ability to convey social and artistic meanings. The rooms in these books were elaborate collages of pasted-in pictures of furniture and other household objects set against backdrops of wallpaper, fringed paper rugs, and crepe-paper curtains that depicted the world of wealth and well-being that consumption might bring.

Collections, collages, and historical discourse also inform Melissa A. Johnson's exploration of the Weimar-era scrapbook of the German artist Hannah Höch. Johnson examines how Höch presented issues both personal and public that were central to German cultural identity and the concept of modernity during the years of the Weimar Republic (1918–33), especially the perceived Americanization of German culture *(Amerikanismus)*. Höch was an avid, near-obsessive clipper of magazine images, a process that influenced her revolutionary work in photomontage.

Part II, "Books of the Self," begins with Carol Bowers's analysis of the scrapbook of Monte Grover (1865–1905), a prostitute. The securing of a haven for one's private self must have seemed very important to Grover as she struggled to market herself to her clientele. Using court records, clippings, and the scrapbook, Bowers uncovers the time Grover reserved for private interests and relationships and reveals the self Grover imagined but never attained.

A more successful evolution of self was allowed young Willa Cather, who made her scrapbook by sewing pieces of cotton cloth and binding them with a fabric cover. Jennifer L. Bradley's essay interprets how Cather's scrapbook provides a complex and intricate look at the author's childhood. Bradley also notes how this scrapbook reappears in Cather's 1918 novel *My Ántonia* as the picture book Jim Burden makes for Yulka and Ántonia.

In her contribution, Meredith Eliassen has chosen twelve photographs from the library of San Francisco State University to illustrate the gathering of personal memorabilia by children. Especially notable is an image from a series of scrapbooks made by Japanese American students confined to an internment camp during World War II. The internees described their experience in words and pictures, designed to be distributed to chapters of the American Junior Red Cross.

Friendships, of course, were the focus of many scrapbooks, and Sarah McNair Vosmeier's essay explores the networks of affection found in early photograph albums. Using albums and other materials such as census records, local history sources, and letters, Vosmeier focuses on the exchange of photographs, the balance of power between the sexes, and the complicated world of friendship and courtship in the 1860s.

African Americans who documented themselves and their relationships in scrapbooks leave ephemera especially rich in clues as to how racial division was manifested on paper and in images. Susan Tucker's essay looks at the photograph album of Fletcher Henderson, a jazz pianist who captured the decade of his youth, 1910–20, and the scrapbook of Juanita Page Johnson, a Chicago high school student in the 1920s. Tucker also touches on the scrapbooks of abolitionists; the scrapbooks of William Dorsey, whose more than three hundred scrapbooks helped build the collection of the American Negro Historical Society; and the albums assembled by W.E.B. DuBois for the Paris Exposition of 1900.

James Kelley explores the relationships of Grace Hall-Hemingway and Kathleen Bradshaw-Isherwood to their famous sons, Ernest Hemingway and Christopher Isherwood, arguing for a matrilineal interpretation of the sons' works through an in-depth look at the mothers' albums.

Elizabeth E. Siegel examines professional advice on how to keep personal photograph albums and finds a reciprocal relationship between commerce and the home. Ultimately what was at stake for album producers, the popular press, and album owners, she concludes, were definitions of family, society, and country.

L. Rebecca Johnson Melvin's essay tells of seven scrapbooks made by her mother as a preteen in a small town in Kentucky during the Depression. This impressionable young girl gathered scraps about life far away: opera stars of radio broadcasts, the English king and queen's visit to North America, the birth and growth of the Dionne quintuplets, and other subjects. Through her scrapbooks she defined her interests and her aspirations to become part of a distant world.

In sum, scrapbooks exhibit a complicated verbal, material, and visual chronicle of changing U.S. society, yet the story each album tells is chaotic and ambiguous. They invite rereading. Readers can temporarily impose a logical pattern on a scrapbook's contents, but any interpretation is bound to be as inconstant and ephemeral as the scrapbooks themselves. In fact, no scrapbook can present meaning without the collaboration of a reader, yet no reader (aside from the scrapbook maker) knows enough to interpret any scrapbook authentically and definitively.

The appeal of scrapbooks may well lie in this very ambiguity, which is enhanced because they offer both permanency and fluidity. The images and print fixed to the page will outlast their creators. Because the objects themselves were usually not meant for such permanency—that is, were ephemeral—their immortality looms even larger. Their fluidity derives from the freedom of later readers to imagine any story they wish in connection with a whole scrapbook or a single artifact pasted inside it. By matching each unique response to each unique volume, the scrapbook satisfies a typical American impulse to honor creativity and enterprise while experiencing the joy of discovery.

PART I

~~~~~~~

Manuscripts of
Learning and Knowing

[KATHERINE OTT]

I

~~~~~

Between Person and Profession

~~~~~

The Scrapbooks of Nineteenth–Century
Medical Practitioners

ONE OF THE MOST COMMON MISCONCEPTIONS about scrapbook keeping is that it is now and always has been an activity dominated by girls and women. The contemporary stereotype of feminine scrapbook keepers leaves out the countless boys and men who have kept multidimensional laboratory books, ship and travel logs, science notebooks, newspaper clippings books about businesses, and even conventional scrapbooks. Both stamp collecting and coin collecting are common hobbies for men, and when a wider definition of scrap assemblage is used, men are as prolific as women in filling books with ephemera to document their transit through the world. Men's books are overlooked because they are often an adjunct to paid and professional work rather than a private, domestic activity. The nineteenth- and early-twentieth-century books assembled by medical practitioners, mostly males in a male-dominated profession and world, make an intriguing contrast to the typically domestically oriented albums compiled by females—the former, subdued and stately; the latter, bursting with color and movement.

Physicians' scrapbooks are distinct partly because of the prominence of medicine within the hierarchy of professions. Scrapbooks of medical practitioners are characteristically celebratory while also presenting an air of sobriety and resolve. Unlike other scrapbooks commonly found in special collections, medical albums do not have as a primary purpose amusement, entertainment, or hobby, nor do they emphasize artistic visual display and plenitude of material. There is often a strong and self-conscious element of performance and self-fashioning in physician scrapbooks.[1] They are personal monuments to a life, an institution, or a career, compiled by the subject or by a spouse, a devoted employee, or other interested person. They have a strong flavor of timelessness, universality, and justification of a life. They are primers for statecraft and oratory, similar in motivation and enactment to the Renaissance commonplace book.[2]

The scrapbooks of medical practitioners provide an intimate glimpse into the personal lives of individuals and augment or expand biographical information contained in letters and manuscripts. More important for the purposes of this essay, when read collectively the scrapbooks elaborate a shared work culture among physicians by capturing less formal (though no less self-conscious) expressions of professional identity. They add a new dimension to the visual field of medicine.

Next to artists, architects, and illustrators, physicians probably constituted the profession most reliant on the graphic exchange of information. Physicians were steeped in both popular and professional conventions of visual display.[3] In nineteenth-century textbooks, information was typically conveyed by means of ornate text fonts, often with several designs intermingled. The printing was small and dense with engravings and woodcuts sprinkled throughout. Textbooks contained few photographs until well into the twentieth century, when halftones began to appear regularly. The images in medical textbooks, as in other genres of technical manuals, had sparse explanations. Often a solitary figure or plate number, corresponding to a number buried within the text and sometimes several pages distant, might be the only identification accompanying the image. Readers were expected to either share the author's erudition or search the text for related information and make their own inferences. At other times a short phrase, for example, "Chart V.—Relapsing Fever (Murchison)," attends an image of spiking lines on a graph or a blurred halftone of an X ray, with no other guidance for analysis.[4] The intended pool of readers was small and exclusive.

Yet visual display and visual interpretation were essential to nineteenth- and early-twentieth-century medical training.[5] Physicians-in-training observed patients during grand rounds or at the shoulder of a preceptor. They pored over atlases with magnificent chromolithographs and memorized the Latin names for body parts by studying anatomical charts, as well as preserved specimens, dissected cadavers, and their own sketches.[6] Teachers stressed to their students the need to habituate themselves to careful observation of the signs presented by their patients' bodies.

Physicians' highly visual world of bodies and pathologies casts the interpretation of their scrapbooks in a different light from those of young girls. The enterprise of cutting and pasting and thinking about meaning was shared by both groups, but physicians put their handiwork to different use and held different structures with which to interpret their production.

Case Records and Documentation

Some physicians used scrapbooks as elaborated case records.[7] The Philadelphia ophthalmologist William F. Norris (1839–1901) was such a scrapbook keeper. The son of a prominent Philadelphia surgeon, Norris graduated from the University of

Pennsylvania Medical School in 1861 and went off to serve as a U.S. Army surgeon during the Civil War. After an extended study trip to Europe, he settled in as a professor of ophthalmology and otology at the University of Pennsylvania. Like most physicians of his day, Norris was a visual and tactile learner and interested in the graphic recording of information. He was animated by the application of photography to medical practice and experimented in microphotography.[8] His visual sophistication and eclecticism were apparent in his scrapbook. The book contained drawings of pathological orbits (eye sockets) and tissue by several artists, as well as photographs of children with socket tumors (called glioma or retinoblastoma). His scrapbook served as an atlas of ophthalmology, and that title appeared along the spine. Perhaps Norris's natural curiosity about sight, vision, and graphic data led him into ophthalmology. In any event, his carefully composed photographs of ophthalmic patients were a rarity of their time as far as content and composition. His album was a working document and a reference tool. It contained notations in several different hands, indicating that it was used by more people than just Norris. The album performed double duty, as a teaching tool and as a kind of business ledger, where the business was cataloging and working on the human body.

Another physician, Joseph Carson (1808–76), created a kind of nineteenth-century virtual version of a book he published commercially.[9] Carson, who received his medical degree from the University of Pennsylvania in 1830, was a professor of materia medica (pharmacology) at the Philadelphia College of Pharmacy and at the University of Pennsylvania.[10] In 1869 he published *A History of the Medical Department of the University of Pennsylvania*, and many of the original documents on which he based his book he glued into scrapbooks.

These scrapbooks capture an unusual relationship to professional identity. For the learned Carson, fascinated with the history of his craft, past and present intermingled. He collected paper ephemera related to legendary medical practitioners of decades past, as well as to medical education and practice. He juxtaposed original documents with pages from the published text (see Figure 1.1). His albums contain lecture-admission tickets, receipts for dues, and letters from famous doctors, along with their portraits. Carson's packed albums served both as a reference tool for the history he recorded and as paper-and-gum monuments to the towering figures of his profession. Carson was particularly interested in eighteenth-century University of Edinburgh faculty members, such as William Cullen, Thomas Cooper, and Alexander Munro, and he included copper-plate portraits of them and admission tickets to their numerous anatomy lectures. As a means to position himself closer to his personal heroes and to recreate memorable public events, Carson's albums are much like the celebrity scrapbooks kept by young people about their favorite actors and musicians.

Carson's scrapbooks also manipulated time and space. As with many scrapbooks, they not only transgress chronology but also often find it irrelevant.[11] In some of his albums the ordering of events shifts from strictly chronological or sequential to emotional and back again, as items are later added or removed. The documents—disparate

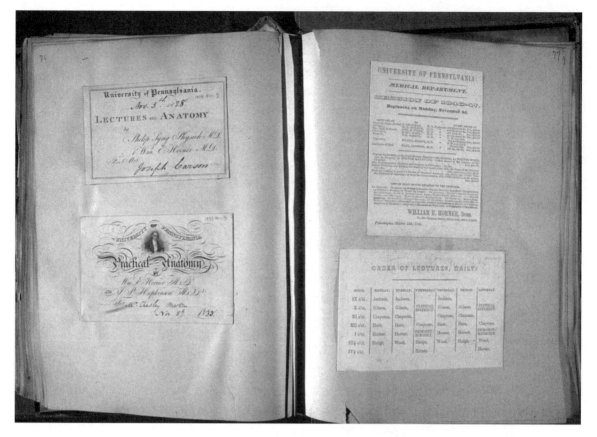

Figure 1.1. *Joseph Carson broke linear time and shuffled geography within the pages of his scrapbook. Shown here are lecture admission coupons that span several years. Carson also used his scrapbook to supplement his History of the Medical Department of the University of Pennsylvania (1869).* (Courtesy College of Physicians of Philadelphia)

examples of ephemera related to medical practice in Pennsylvania—are largely unrelated to the text. With these juxtapositions the compiler compressed history: a promissory note from 1706 appears opposite a clipped printed page from 1869. Although these items are separated by 150 years, the reader encounters the two contemporaneously. Events that are otherwise unrelated, as well as geographically dispersed, are brought together in an artificial relationship fabricated through the taste and judgment of the compiler. Tinkering with the physics of experience was a popular Victorian pastime.[12] Victorians were, after all, the people who fooled with time and space by inventing photography, cinema, and science fiction.[13]

Some sixty years later, William Wadsworth (1868–1955), another Philadelphia physician, kept similar but far more humble celebrity albums. Wadsworth's albums consisted of loose-leaf binders with cutout portraits of doctors glued to the pages.

Arranged alphabetically, some pages have several images of the same doctors; other pages have only one picture. His album is reminiscent of the late-nineteenth-century "mug books" printed by groups and associations and containing pictures of local luminaries accompanied by a short glowing paragraph about each person's contributions to the success of whatever they all shared in common, whether the anniversary of a town, establishment of a congregation, or laying of a factory's cornerstone. Then, as now, people were eager to celebrate milestones in a collective endeavor. The official history of these institutions was presented as page after page of the faces ("mugs") of the pillars of the community.[14] Wadsworth recorded and celebrated his fellow physicians, both his contemporaries and those from the past, by simply saving their pictures. He did not add any commentary or identify why the doctors were important or appealed to him (other than an occasional clipping added to the page). Nor did he include reprints of their published work.

Wadsworth's second album contains medical scenes excised from magazines and journals, such as copies of paintings and drawings. It was an intensely personal collection, similar to an emperor's hoard—a pile of precious but undifferentiated treasure. Yet it has the look and feel of an amateur stamp collector's album, the work of an enthusiast unconcerned with pretense. Until the 1960s and 1970s, the main historians of medicine and collectors of medical artifacts were physician hobbyists—that is, men interested in the history of their craft and with sufficient subject knowledge to judge intellectually what was worth documenting. Physician collectors continue to preserve and retain many of the best collections of medical artifacts, some of which rival public holdings in museums.

The scrapbooks of George Milbry Gould provide other possibilities for understanding what physicians saw when they made and looked at professional scrapbooks. Gould (1848–1922) was a multitalented and energetic man who followed his intellectual inclinations into religion, printing, medicine, poetry, psychology, and medical lexicography. He left six scrapbooks devoted to a multiplicity of topics, including ophthalmology, headaches, motion pictures and eyestrain, insanity, and suicide.[15] Gould was born in Maine but grew up in the rolling Appalachian foothills of southern Ohio when slavery was bitterly contested and the underground railway funneled escapees north to Canada. He was a drummer boy in the war, worked in a print shop, traveled in Europe, and then served as a Unitarian minister after graduating from Harvard Divinity School in 1874. At the age of forty, Gould received an MD degree from Jefferson Medical College in Philadelphia. He then practiced for a few years as an ophthalmic surgeon. Gould is remembered primarily for his ophthalmic publications and his best-selling medical dictionary. But he wrote another book, seldom mentioned in his obituaries, that was widely influential among those interested in disability. With Walter Pyle, he published the exhaustive *Anomalies and Curiosities of Medicine*, which, with 968 pages and more than three hundred illustrations, remains one of the most complete catalogs of disability and body differences of the nineteenth and twentieth centuries.[16] Gould's scrapbooks allow modern readers to see behind his obsession as well as gain a deeper understanding of the aesthetics of medical graphic display. Not much is known about Gould's personal style and charm (or lack thereof). His writings on philosophy, poetry, and biography reveal that he was highly literate and inquisitive. As a preacher, he must have been aware of the conventions of public speaking and performance. At one time he owned a book shop and likely came across some of the numerous works on elocution published in the mid–nineteenth century. The wide-ranging examples that appear in *Anomalies* and his skill in lexicography perhaps give a clue to Gould's passion for gathering and saving the ephemeral bits of information he encountered.

Physician Marguerite Cockett carefully compiled her scrapbook in chronological order.[17] Before entering the Woman's Medical College, from which she graduated in 1905, Cockett (1878–1954) studied nursing and displayed some talent in sculpture. In her scrapbook she preserved letters of recommendation from her high school for admission to the Woman's Medical College, postcards, and membership cards in professional associations.[18] The contents, unlike those of the scrapbooks of most other women but in line with those of her male physician counterparts, were all related to her profession, including items concerning her ambulance service in World War I. Cockett's identity and private thoughts were, understandably, a reflection of her life's work. Her scrapbook chronicles the incremental achievements along her path to the goal of medical practice.

Cockett's album is not unique in this. Many medical practitioners' albums are keepsakes for their honors, degrees, certificates, and invitations to professional events. Their makers catalog physicians with whom they socialized and what they ate while attending the precursors of today's continuing medical education courses and listening to colleagues explain new techniques. Others stuff their albums with clipped reviews of their publications and notices of their lectures.

At the extreme edge of the spectrum of scrapbooks as vehicles of ego and memory is that of Sir William Arbuthnot Lane (1896–1943).[19] A colorful, controversial surgeon at Guy's Hospital in London, Lane specialized in fractures, cleft palates, and the operative treatment of constipation. Well known for his surgical skill, Lane probably performed the first ileocolostomy. His biographer, who had trained under him, defended Lane's rather free use of the knife, commenting: "If Lane unwisely removed the colon, thank goodness it was Lane doing the surgery."[20] In his scrapbook of journal and newspaper clippings by and about him, Lane marked through all text not directly related to him. Remarkably for a surgeon, many of the clippings in his album were literally torn from journals rather than razored or carefully scissored out.[21]

Military Physicians

The physician compilers retold their lives in book form, chronicling both their profession and their place within it. An emphasis on profession is not unique to medicine, to be sure—the scrapbooks of professionals resemble those of public figures, especially those in the performing arts, in that they attempt to impose form and order on a life by staying close to a core narrative. In this way scrapbooks turn a mere existence into a life. In the focus on career building, vivid and often striking juxtapositions occur. For example, the second scrapbook made by Frank Keefer (1865–1954), a career army surgeon who served as assistant surgeon general for the years 1927–29, elides his army life and personal life without comment.[22] After retiring from the military, he headed the Washington, D.C., chapter of the American Red Cross until 1942. In Keefer's second scrapbook, a compilation of his official career, his wedding announcement is tipped in along with other orders of the day.[23] The implication is that taking a wife was as much a duty detail and career obligation as inspecting a facility or serving on a court-martial jury.

The first of Keefer's scrapbooks is the official record, traced through copies of general orders, promotions, and transfers. The second covers the same years but includes other materials and Keefer's handwritten commentary on what he experienced. In the pages of his scrapbooks, the reader catches glimpses of the mundane life of an army doctor. To qualify for his 1890 commission, Keefer passed examinations in science, anatomy, physiology, therapeutics, materia medica, medicine, hygiene, surgery, obstetrics, and bacteriology as well as literature, Latin, French, and German. He owed $1.69 for surgical instruments purchased in Philadelphia, and he received a letter of reprimand because he was late in arriving at his new post at Fort Stanton, New Mexico, in 1893.

Keefer served tours of duty in the Philippines during the Spanish-American War and returned a few years later. In the Philippines he organized and was in charge of an ambulance company, oversaw sanitary inspections, and observed the rebellion after the war, all of which he chronicles in the second album. The contents are a mix of photographs and clippings from magazines about the Philippines. One page that Keefer entitled "Sketches found in a Spanish Barrack, Manila, Aug. 13, '98," includes drawings of a woman. It is a modern irony of reading other peoples' scrapbooks that just as Keefer was a plunderer of objects left behind in a hastily abandoned barracks, historians now intellectually plunder these remnants for evidence of something long lost. Keefer corrected locations and spellings and added terse comments to the published captions. For a *Harper's* article entitled "Hospitals of Manila" that he clipped, he changed "Tagalo" to "Tagalog" in one caption, and under the photograph of a woman he crossed out "beggar" and wrote "native woman."[24]

An example of unexpected richness in Keefer's scrapbook is a cartoon of Lieutenant General Robert Lee Bullard (1861–1947). The cartoon, probably drawn with affection and humor by a fellow staff member, depicts Bullard early in his military career, the posts where he served, and the native peoples and subordinates with whom he interacted. Ethnic caricatures surround Bullard and serve as a burlesque, depicting his extensive career and his elevation through his mastery over others. Bullard was born and raised in Alabama. As a boy he changed his name from William to Robert Lee, a gesture of allegiance to the "Lost Cause."[25] On his way up in the ranks, Bullard served at various posts in the Southwest (he was part of at least one campaign against the Apache) and later commanded a regiment of African American Alabamans. Bullard's life experience makes the whole scrapbook—as well as the cartoonist's intentions and people, like Keefer, who came within Bullard's orbit—all the more layered with potential meanings.[26]

Like Keefer's scrapbook, the World War I memory book of William Middleton (1890–1975) includes a combination of official military papers and personal mementos.[27] Middleton received his medical degree from the University of Pennsylvania in 1911 and spent most of his professional career working for the Veterans Administration or on the faculty of the University of Wisconsin Medical School. As a young doctor barely launched in private practice, Middleton served first with the British Expeditionary Forces and then, from 1917 to 1919, with the American Expeditionary Forces. He was in Belgium and France, at the battle of the Marne and at Meuse-Argonne, where he no doubt witnessed the horrors of war surgery, including the ravages of mustard gas, shrapnel wounds, loss of limbs, and typhus.[28] His haunting scrapbooks have a matter-of-factness and innocence that war poets such as Joyce Kilmer and Rupert Brooks captured with a searing calm. Included is a typed list, reproduced in such quantity that only the period strikes remain sharp and clear, of what to take to war ("2 Jackets, 1 pr leggings, 3 Shirts, 6 Collars, 1 Pistol," and so on), as well as instructions if bringing one's own horse. There are military-issue Christmas and New Year's cards; photographs of bombed-out ruins, mobile hospitals, soldiers, and one image identified simply as "Johnny's Grave"; postcards of France; coins secured with tape; and journal entries about such things as his induction, gas attacks by "the Hun," and his comrades. Middleton also pasted in booklets on how to deal with flies, vermin, cases of scabies, and symptoms of gas poisoning, as well as mileage vouchers, war-risk insurance forms, and a bread-ration ticket that he pinched from Dijon. The juxtaposition of foreign coins and greeting cards with instructions on how to use a respirator present the mundane absurdity of war more clearly than can a shelf full of religious and ethical tracts. Middleton survived the war—and also left a scrapbook of a 1933 Hawaiian junket he took with his wife.

Silent Endings

In addition to their sometimes unusual subject matter, physicians' scrapbooks are unlike more consciously "popular culture" ones, such as those composed of trade-card collections or vacation-travel memorabilia, in the way they begin and end. Medical scrapbooks are akin to diaries and journals in that they often begin with fanfare, solemn pronouncement, or the marking of some occasion. But they end with serendipity, by chance, or in tragic silence: the compiler graduates, goes on to other projects, dies, or otherwise disappears. There is seldom closure or conclusion, just a series of blank pages. Others' albums end when the vacation or the semester ends.

But medical scrapbooks conclude like the scrapbooks kept by a tuberculosis patient in Saranac Lake, New York. They ceased when she ceased.

But before the albums trail off, we can discern other forces at work that subtly influence the reading of the volumes. Among the most poignant aspects of scrapbooks is the recurring element of heteroglossia, the presence of many voices. First are the voices of the compiler who began the album and the compiler who finished it—perhaps different people or the same person, years later, writing in a feeble hand. Laura Heath Hills (d. 1960), for instance, assembled items and made an album as a medical student; much later, probably in preparing the album for donation to the Medical College of Pennsylvania, she penned captions for the items.[29] The notes of the archivist along the edge of a photograph add the voice of yet another generation and orientation to the album's contents. Anonymous archivists who leave notes about missing photographs or dates and other recovered information also have a strong presence in scrapbooks. Their bracketed metanarratives make the scrapbooks all the more complex and collaborative.

Unspoken Attitudes

Another voice is one the compiler expropriates by means of the transfixed text. In his album, James Thorington compiled clippings related to the movement among ophthalmologists at the turn of the century to stop optometrists and opticians from using pharmaceuticals in their practice and from performing minor surgery.[30] Thorington (1858–1944) was an active member of the Philadelphia community of ophthalmologists that included William Norris, William Thomson, George de Schweinitz, and George Gould, several of whom, as noted here, kept scrapbooks. Thorington designed retinoscopic instruments and took an interest in the politics of his profession.[31] The clippings he preserved in his scrapbook record the debates over control of the profession. Thorington did not need to add his editorial comments to the scraps he pasted in: the third-party prose of the items, such as a letter from an Elmira, New York, colleague excoriating against an optometrist with "no education" and a patent medicine maker, reflected Thorington's position. Opposite this is a letter from someone whom Thorington no doubt viewed as an unscrupulous optometrist, offering to pay Thorington a commission for any "eye strain" patients he might refer to the cad's care. Thorington gathered numerous pieces of information and evidence about the outrageous and objectionable behavior of optometrists—in his words, the "so-called [optometrist], which is a newfangled name for optician." He continued by drawing the facetious parallel that to allow such nonophthalmologists to move beyond employing simple optics in their practice makes as much sense as allowing "truss makers [to] treat hernia or splint makers [to] treat fractures, provided that they can pass an examination in physics." The lay public and most other medical practitioners were not aware of these turf battles in the practice of ophthalmology and eye care, yet they continued throughout much of the twentieth century. The animus of the early years has been lost or remains only as unsubstantiated anecdote. The bits of ephemera Thorington preserved help recreate the heated internal debates between opticians and optometrists and their rivals, ophthalmologists.

When read alongside Thorington's album, the ephemera in the scrapbook of John Sargent, a Philadelphia physician who graduated from Jefferson Medical College in 1876, reinforces the significance of Thorington's preserved remnants. Sargent's album, for example, contains a scrap about the indiscriminate use of atropine eye drops.[32] Atropine, derived from the belladonna plant, was used to dilate the eyes. One brochure written by an optometrist recounts the case of a young woman who, following the use of atropine eyedrops, became irrevocably insane and was eventually committed to an asylum. In another reported case of atropine poisoning, a nine-year-old boy was nearly killed by the overstimulation produced by the drug. The lesson to be derived from these examples was that one did not need dangerous eyedrops to be able to examine eyes. The handful of cautionary cases, distilled in the brochure from a much larger pool of reports and hearsay, can be read as a marshaling of the most persuasive arguments for convincing turn-of-the-century patients and practitioners. The ultimate consequences of inattention or noncompliance were insanity or death.

Sargent's album appears to be a family scrapbook and contains primarily non-medical materials. It was assembled in a product patented by Mark Twain, with gummed pages and interleaves for easy assembling.[33] Not a strictly professional book, it chronicled the breadth of his interests through newspaper clippings and letters. Mixed in with the family materials is a clipping about his delivery of conjoined twins and a letter from a physician asking for an appointment to view them (see Figure 1.2).

As organized repositories of knowledge, scrapbooks are uniquely able to take readers into these physicians' lives and practices in ways that printed prose cannot. As productions and performances of culture, they capture the exuberance of events and reveal unspoken attitudes and hidden assumptions about aspects of medical training and practice. For example, students at the Medical College of Pennsylvania practiced pelvic exams and obstetrics with a chamois doll baby that they nicknamed Nicodemus, and images of the doll appear in several students' albums.[34] The image of Nicodemus in the scrapbook of Elizabeth Reifsnyder, who graduated from the Woman's Medical College in 1896, is striking, for it appears on a page with Chinese women and their babies (see Figure 1.3).[35] Reifsnyder was a medical missionary in Shanghai at the turn of the last century, at about the time the Rockefeller Foundation was funding medical training missions in China and religious missionary work there was peaking.[36] Reifsnyder was part of a constant flow of Woman's Medical College graduates to China, funded largely by the Ladies Medical Missionary Society. The first WMC graduate to take up foreign work went in 1869, and eventually some 230 WMC physicians went abroad for a time.[37] The peculiar placement of Nicodemus on a page with photographs of live babies may signify that Reifsnyder saw her

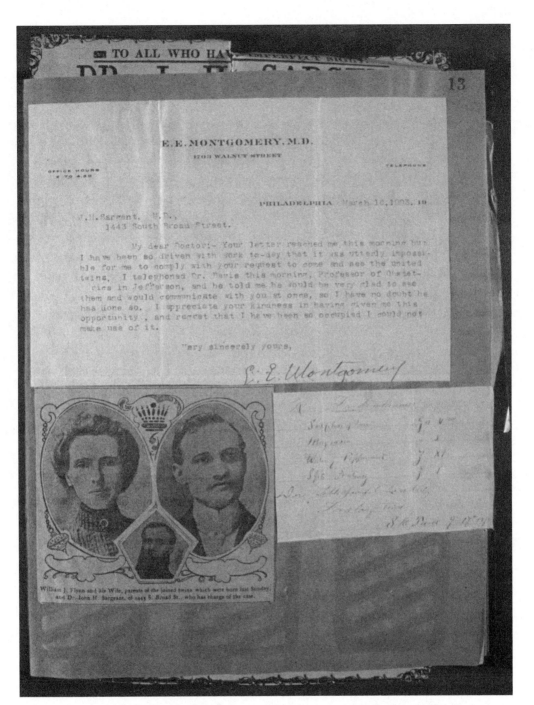

Figure 1.2. *John Sargent's scrapbook shows ephemera related to the conjoined twins whom he delivered, including a letter from a colleague interested in viewing the children.* (Courtesy College of Physicians of Philadelphia)

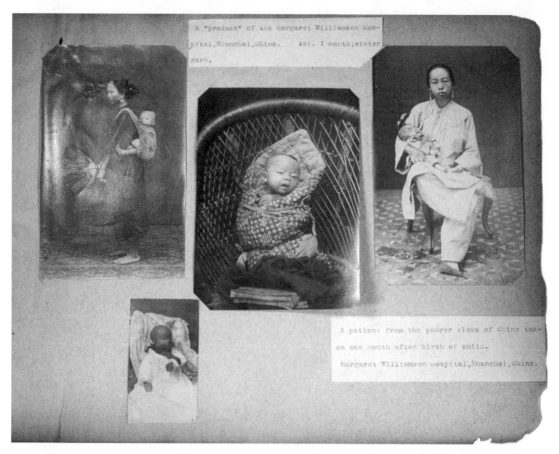

Figure 1.3. *Elizabeth Reifsnyder, who worked as a medical missionary in Shanghai in the early twentieth century, kept a scrapbook of her medical education and experience. Along with photographs of Chinese mothers and their children, this page shows a photograph of the doll baby with which Reifsnyder and other students at her medical college practiced obstetrical procedures.* (Courtesy Archives and Special Collections on Women in Medicine, Drexel University College of Medicine)

tenure in China primarily as a continuation of her medical training: she practiced with Chinese babies just as she had with Nicodemus. The lighthearted caption above the image of Chinese babies reads, "A product of the Margaret Williamson Hospital," indicating that new babies were a work product for Reifsnyder. In Reifsnyder's scrapbook, as in others, the careful viewer can glean what is seldom spoken.

WHAT EMERGES from the scrapbooks kept by these doctors are traces of public topics that reverberated in their personal lives, from an illustrious anatomist's lectures to trench warfare, from turf battles over specialties to imperialist medical missions. The narrator who would have looked over the reader's shoulder and excitedly pointed to the page, explaining it all, is long gone. So we are left with our imagination and our desire to connect with the past. These physicians' scrapbooks retrieve the density of life. Preserved in the layers of ephemera and photographs are the back notes and undertones of their existence. They take us elsewhere and here at the same time.

2

~~~~~~

Daily Life on a South Carolina Plantation, 1855–1983

~~~~~~

A Scrapbook Memory from Three Generations of Women

AS DISCUSSIONS OF CULINARY history today often state, women have always cooked. That we know less about their roles in the kitchen than about male chefs' doings should come as no surprise, but the many family scrapbooks tell of the care women took with this work. Consider this recipe: "Boil a chicken with the giblets until tender. Set aside until cold, then cut into pieces 1/2 inch square. Put into a stewpan with pepper, salt, 3 hard-boiled eggs chopped fine, a teacup of the broth the fowl boiled in, a coffee cup of cream and a piece of butter rolled in flour the size of an egg. Set on the fire and simmer for 10 minutes. Then add a teacup of wine and serve." This recipe, entitled "Chicken Terrapin," is 150 years old. It does not age. It was a sure-fire finger licker then and can still be used today, one stubborn constant amid a century and a half of tumult.

Here is another recipe, labeled "Brandy Peaches": "Pick out the fairest peaches. Peel very thin and throw into cold water. One and 1/2 pints of water to 3 pounds of sugar will boil 8 pounds of peaches. When cold put into jars and fill the jars with whiskey or brandy." If you do not like that one right off, have a second helping; you will.

Another recipe, "Sweet Potato Pone," is distinctive: "One quart grated potato, 1/2 pint molasses, 10 ounces butter, 3 eggs. Cream butter and sugar, add eggs. Add grated potato gradually with molasses."

These enduring jewels are but three of the many old-fashioned recipes preserved intact and verbatim from a scrapbook of recipes kept and maintained by three generations of South Carolina women. The story of that cooking inheritance follows. It is the story of three tough, smart Southern women and their legacy.

To the early-twenty-first-century mind, there is something of a paradox in the idea that bright, tough women lived in contentment practicing the feminine arts of cooking, sewing, and mothering in the paternalistic slave culture of the antebellum South. The prevailing historiography is typified by such works as Anne Firor Scott's *The Southern Lady* and Drew Gilpin Faust's *Mothers of Invention*. Here the view is expressed that white women in the antebellum South were subordinate, controlled creatures of a paternalistic, patriarchal society. Typical is Faust's assertion that "women's associations and organizations had not blossomed in the antebellum South. . . . Slaveholding southern women thought of themselves primarily as part of a hierarchical family or household, with their most significant connections tying them in relationships of dominance and dependence to their husbands, children, and slaves rather than to other white women." In a similar vein Scott states: "The social role of women was unusually confining there [in the South], and the sanctions used to enforce obedience peculiarly effective." The image and reality of the Southern lady, according to Scott, was of a submissive, obedient paragon of virtue. Scott quotes Augustus Baldwin Longstreet to underscore her point: "Men found intelligence in woman a quality that in general distressed more than it pleased. When they did not openly condemn, they treated it with insulting condescension." Scott concludes: "Women, along with children and slaves, were expected to recognize their proper and subordinate place and to be obedient to the head of the family. Any tendency on the part of any of the members of the system to assert themselves against the master threatened the whole, and therefore slavery itself."[1]

Emily Wharton Sinkler, her daughter-in-law Anne Wickham Porcher Sinkler, and her granddaughter Anne Sinkler Fishburne were vibrant, energetic, and fully involved in a multifaceted community and plantation life. They were determined, creative, and independent. And yet they survived and thrived in a patriarchal society where their roles were surely tightly circumscribed.

A partial explanation for their happiness and fulfillment may be the fact that they were essential to the economic and social well-being of the plantations of which they were an integral part. The evidence for this view of self-fulfillment and self-awareness is abundant in the culinary scrapbook they kept over three generations. There they recorded their practices and revealed the methods and means by which they organized and controlled the plantation's social life. They husbanded the resources of these large plantation communities, including preserving and storing food supplies and creating and disbursing medical remedies. They were ingenious in devising remedies for diseases and discomforts from pneumonia, whooping cough, and digestive complaints. They worked with the region's medical doctors to maintain the health and hygiene of their communities. They were, in fact if not in title, the managers of a large and important part of plantation life. They were respected and revered by family and servants alike for their critical roles, which were quite comparable to the role of chief operation officer and board member of a small business corporation today.

The image that emerges of women's life in Upper St. John's Parish, South Carolina, and in particular in the Sinkler family is one of equality and independence in a community that was proud of its self-reliance. Women were partners with their husbands in the plantation community, and their intelligence and creativity were admired. When women were widowed or their husbands incapacitated, the entire responsibility for the management of the plantation often devolved to them.

The scrapbook provides evidence that these women and their women slaves and servants were pioneers of sorts: they learned how to make do in a rural, isolated environment, they invented alternatives for everyday necessities, and they managed and husbanded the plantation's resources. The scrapbook shows the significant role of the caretaker in the antebellum South, generally a woman, to the health and hygiene of the plantation population.

Scrapbooks were a method of codifying the common law for governance of much of the daily life of the plantation. They became the means for the mistress of the plantation to organize household information and make ready use of it to supervise and complete daily chores. Because there were no ready-made household products and no prepackaged foods or even medicines, the mistress of the house had to write down these formulas for ready access. The scrapbook became the easy medium for recording and organizing this information. The preservation of unique food lore and traditions was one way that generations were bound together by the best customs and heritage of the past. The written-out practices were passed on from one generation to the next, their vibrancy assured by the daily search for improved or different methodologies and the dutiful recording of new ideas, recipes, and remedies into the ever-evolving, burgeoning scrapbook.

The three women of the Sinkler family who kept a cooking and medical scrapbook from 1855 to 1983 shared similar life paths. They were female caregivers on a rural, remote cotton plantation. Each received an informal education at home that inculcated the skills of the feminine arts—literature, languages, writing, reading aloud, sewing, and music. Each developed a rapport, based on necessity, with their largely African American household and kitchen servants. Each lived in a structured, paternalistic society in which many of the major decisions were made by husbands, fathers, and brothers. Despite the Civil War and a span of 150 years, their worlds were remarkably similar. The battered and used scrapbook tells their story.

A Compendium of Household Knowledge

Emily Wharton Sinkler initiated a scrapbook of cooking recipes, household formulas, and medical remedies in Charleston in 1855. This scrapbook, measuring seven inches high and six inches wide, was an eclectic, multisource compendium bringing

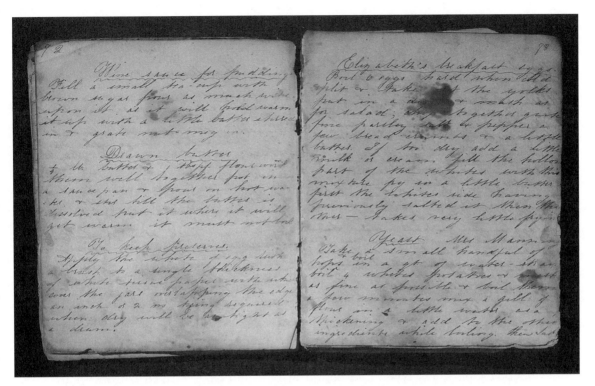

Figure 2.1. *The receipt and remedy book begun in Charleston, South Carolina, in 1855 by Emily Wharton Sinkler and maintained until 1983 by her granddaughter Anne Sinkler Fishburne.* (Courtesy Anne Sinkler Whaley LeClercq)

together cooking recipes, household formulas, and medical remedies from a wide variety of sources (see Figure 2.1). From 1848 to 1875 Emily was the mistress of Belvidere, a cotton plantation located in Upper St. John's Parish on the banks of the Santee River. Emily lived between the comfort and elegance of Charleston and the privations of a remote, self-sufficient, antebellum rural plantation.

The scrapbook was Emily's guide and resource as she struggled to secure provisions for a large plantation community. She organized it with an alphabetical index so that she could easily keep track of her entries. The scrapbook had numerous handwritten paste-ins, including letters with cooking recipes from Emily's friends and family, as well as many newspaper clippings dealing with medical remedies and culinary practices. The names given to the entries reflect a faithful recording of Emily's network of friends and family—"Dr. Morris' Prescription for Sorethroat," "Dr. Meigs Nutgalls," "Elizabeth's Breakfast Eggs."

Emily handed down her scrapbook to her daughter-in-law, Anne Wickham Porcher Sinkler, who had married Emily's youngest son, Charles St. George Sinkler. After their marriage in 1883, Anne and Charles became the owners of Belvidere, which prospered under their care until Anne's death in 1919. Anne added a number of her own recipes, household formulas, and medical remedies. She used Emily's index and format. She was particularly interested in cures for drunkenness, reflecting her difficult struggle with a husband who had became addicted to liquor, paregoric, and opium.

The scrapbook went next to Anne's daughter, Anne (Nan) Sinkler Fishburne, who used the book extensively, making many of her own additions. Nan added many loose-leaf fold-ins, including three for blackberry wine. She became the mistress of Belvidere on her mother's death in 1919 and continued to manage the plantation for her impaired father until 1940, when it was destroyed by the Santee-Cooper Project, which created Lake Marion and Lake Moultrie. Nan's recipes called for ingredients unavailable to her mother and grandmother, such as gelatin instead of Cooper's isinglass and baking soda instead of soda saleratus, and she also used different words to describe measurements, such as a "half-cup" rather than a "gill." Nan's storeroom was legendary for its relishes, preserves, pickled fruits, and preserved vegetables.

After Belvidere was flooded, Nan carried her grandmother Emily's and her mother Anne's scrapbook to her farm in Pinopolis, South Carolina, where she lived until 1983. The scrapbook had another life when Nan undertook a church project to produce a faithful replica entitled "Old Recipes from Old St. John's," which included every recipe from the scrapbook, as well as some additional recipes. Nan's cookbook replica was typed and bound in blue-and-white-striped cotton. Many copies were sold to make money for Trinity Episcopal Church in Pinopolis.

The scrapbook has been reproduced in total in *An Antebellum Plantation Household, Including the South Carolina Receipts and Remedies of Emily Wharton Sinkler*.[2] Today, the original is brittle, the result of the acidity of the paste used to attach household remedies gathered from local news sources. The paper itself is of remarkably fine rag content; the binding is of string. In places the ink is blurred, so deciphering the writing is difficult. Yet Emily's cutout recipes and home remedies from an array of newspapers have survived. In a letter home she described the scene in 1842 at Eutaw, her first South Carolina home, where all were reading papers sent south by Emily's Philadelphia family: "Who thought of sending me the *Ladies Register*? It is the very thing I wanted. Do you know it contained the most charming receipts which Eliza and I are going to try." Both Anne and Nan added paste-ins and letters from their day, as well as additional culinary and medical recipes.

What can studying the scraps of women's lives teach people today about history? Can we infer something of women's roles as caregivers on large plantations as they went about concocting remedies for whooping cough, asthma, diarrhea, and drunkenness? Can we imagine the quality of their interactions with slaves and servants as they prepared elaborate desserts that included ladyfingers and whipped cream? Can we envision the pace of their lives as they supervised the making of one hundred pounds of soap or prepared lime for preserving eggs? Can we wonder about their efforts to maintain their style and demeanor as they concocted methods for washing ribbons or cleaning and starching collars, cuffs, false sleeves, and petticoats?

Above all, the variety and eclecticism of the sources reveal patterns of social communication in the southern United States of the mid–nineteenth century. The diversity of sources indicates that rural, pre–Civil War South Carolina was vitally connected to the world at large. The range of newspaper and periodical clippings shows ready communication between the rural South and Philadelphia, New York, and Paris. Folded into the middle of the scrapbook is Fleishmann and Company's yeast advertisement entitled the "Vienna Model Bakery" from the Centennial Exhibition, held in Philadelphia in 1876. Methods of communication were changing as the country turned to steamships and railroads and the first telegraphs provided nearly instantaneous communication.

This scrapbook provides insight into the culinary and medical knowledge of the nineteenth and early twentieth centuries. It is a faithful index of the health problems and remedies of the plantation household, including a large African American community, as well as an amalgam of holistic folk remedies. It also includes household formulas for making soap, ink, starch, washing compounds, and much more. In this way it is similar to numerous household guides that appeared in the nineteenth century, such as Anne Cobbett's *English Housekeeper,* published in London in 1851. Cobbett's book has many household remedies—"To Destroy Bugs," "Blacking for Shoes," and "To Take Oil from Stone or Boards"—that Emily followed. Cobbett's ingredients—sweet oil, unslacked lime, pearl ash, rottenstone, silver caustic, gum arabic, and corrosive sublimate—all appear in Emily's household remedies.

Recipes

The scrapbook's cooking entries show the influences of French Huguenot cooking, the low country's rice culture, Virginia's use of cornmeal in breads and spoon breads, and Emily Wharton Sinkler's own Northern traditions of cooking with potatoes and buckwheat flour. Her culinary concoctions also reflect the cooking traditions of African slaves, such as flavoring soups and vegetables with salt pork, deep frying meats, and using hominy and cornbread.

The sources for the recipes are many: the plantation's cooks, named Chloe, Rachel, Satira, Dinah, Cat, and Louisa; neighbors and friends such as the Gaillards, Porchers, and Mannings, to whom many of the recipes are attributed; and family members such as Mary Wharton, who sent German recipes from the Philadelphia newspapers, and Elizabeth Allen Sinkler, who managed the house at the Eutaw plantation.[3]

Emily Wharton relied on several print cookbooks as the basis for many of her own recipes. Her brother-in-law Seaman Deas Sinkler had given her a French cookbook, and she had other contemporary cookbooks, such as Sarah Rutledge's *The Carolina Housewife,* first published in 1831, and Mary Randolph's *The Virginia House-wife,* first published in 1847. Emily attributed several of her recipes to Randolph, including "Vermicelli," "Salad Dressing," "Cosmetic Soap," "To Make Soap," and "Old Fowl Soup." Many of Emily's recipes have the same names as those in *The Carolina Housewife*: "Indian Cakes," "White Fricassee," "Sauce Piquante," "Potatoes a la Lyonnaise," "Maitre d'Hotel Potatoes," "Charlotte of Apples," "Plum Pudding," and "Sweet Potato Pone."

The scrapbook shows the meticulous nature of its original compiler, Emily Wharton Sinkler. The frontispiece carries the inscription: "Emily Sinkler, 1855, Charleston." She created an alphabetical index at the end that carefully notes the page and name of each entry. The original book contained seven major sections: meats (pages 1–6), miscellaneous (pages 7–13), vegetables (pages 14–24), desserts (pages 25–42), bread and warm cakes (pages 43–70), miscellaneous (pages 71–90), and medical receipts (pages 91–106). Anne and Nan followed this arrangement, adding their own entries in the appropriate category and noting them in the index.

Each section contains a trove of practical, resourceful, ingenious advice. The meats section, which includes recipes for duck stew and venison pastry, shows the availability of low-country game. The plantation had turkeys, chickens, sheep, and cows, and thus it is not surprising that there are recipes for roasting a turkey, making English mutton sausages, and using beef leftovers in stews and pies. There are two recipes for "Bouilli Beef" that use beef bouillon and meat stewed for many hours. "Beef Scrapple" combines the simmering of beef bones with Indian meal to make a breakfast cake.

The vegetables section shows plantation adeptness in pickling and preserving to make the most of seasonal produce. Tomatoes are preserved in soy or in ketchup and put up whole in stone jars. Emily's Philadelphia heritage is evident in her extensive use of potatoes. There are more than ten recipes for using potatoes, including potato puddings, potato bread, potato cheese, potato croquettes, Irish potatoes, and, of course, boiled potatoes. There are also the more Southern recipes for yams and sweet "Spanish" potatoes.

In rural South Carolina, sugar and sweets were purchased at a premium. Puddings were made from locally grown ingredients such as blackberries, and plums were served with a wine or a sugar-based sauce. Custards and creams were made from sugar, cream, and eggs available on the plantation.

The bread and warm cakes section shows the influence of the traditional Southern use of cornmeal and rice. Indian meal from ground corn was used in such warm spoon breads as "Bannocks," "Indian Cakes," and "Baked Indian Pudding," the last of which was sweetened with another local ingredient, molasses. The importance of the Southern rice culture is seen in such specialties as "French Rice Pudding," "Rice Cakes," "Rice Scones," and "Rice Bread."

Medical Remedies

The scrapbook has remedies for a variety of diseases, from consumption to alcoholism. The remedies provide an indication of the common ailments of the nineteenth and early twentieth centuries—scarlet fever, malaria, whooping cough, consumption, and many more diseases no longer prevalent in the United States. In the nineteenth century and well into the twentieth, there were no antitoxins or vaccines for tetanus or diphtheria; neither were there antibiotics for pneumonia, measles, and whooping cough. Quarantine was the only practical method of dealing with contagious diseases.

The fear of disease and epidemics dictated the routine of family life. Mosquito-borne diseases such as malaria and yellow fever caused such symptoms as fevers, chills, jaundice, and debilitation. In Emily's day, malaria was attributed to the bad air of the swamps and not to mosquitoes, a connection not made until 1880 by the French physician Charles Laveran. During the summer and early fall, the Sinklers left the plantation for the mountains or the beach.

The scrapbook also has remedies for catastrophic diseases such as typhoid and lockjaw (tetanus) and for more mundane ailments such as dysentery and sore throat. The medical remedies rely on blackberry cordials and blackberry wines made at Belvidere. Possible prescribers of these remedies include the Sinkler family doctors— Dr. Francis Peyre Porcher, Dr. Henry Rutledge Frost, and Dr. Francis Kinloch Huger. In addition, the scrapbook contains medical clippings from a wide range of newspapers.

The medical remedies used in the mid–nineteenth century included purging therapies using the lance and leech, calomel, tartar emetic, and arsenic. Doctors set out to bleed, blister, and salivate patients. Thus it is not surprising that one of Emily's remedies, "For cold with fever in Children," called for the following: "Calomel or mercury and chalk, 1/2 grams; rhubarb, 1 oz.; ipecac, 1/4 grams. The above each in powder. Give one every four hours in a little syrup till a laxative effect is produced, then employ quinine if the fever continues. Sweet spirits of nitre and paregoric may be given at night. Mustard applications morning and evening."

However, many of the remedies used for common stomach complaints are not so unusual today. Emily's "For Dysentery" called for "one tablespoon common salt, mixed with 2 tablespoon vinegar. Pour upon it 1/2 pt hot water." Her "For Diarrhea" is the typical mother's brew: "Take a freshly killed chicken. Boil in 2 or 3 qts. Water for several hours and drink the broth freely." Another cure for stomach ailments called for "three tablespoons Fennel seed, 2 oz. Soot from a wood fire, a dessert spoon of powdered Rhubarb. Boil these in a pint of water down to a half-pint. When cold, add a wine glass of brandy and sweeten with loaf sugar."

From Cleaning Products to Fashion

Emily, Anne, and Nan devised a whole range of cleaning fluids and insecticides that they used at Belvidere. Some were copied from Cobbett's *English Housekeeper*, while others are from newspapers of the time. Still others were probably local concoctions. These include formulas for making hair wash and hair dye, soap, ink, paste, and insecticides; for copying and preserving flowers and ferns; and for sewing patterns, including feather stitching.

Women's fashions in the late 1840s and 1850s were of the Second Empire mode. Napoleon III and Empress Eugenie revived the French court, and the fashion-conscious empress set the style: gowns of silk accessorized with laces, ribbons, fringes, feathers, and flowers. Women wore voluminous skirts and accessorized everyday dresses with collars and cuffs. These styles were epitomized in *Frank Leslie's Ladies' Gazette*, to which Emily subscribed. She also relied on the Paris fashion magazine *La Brodeuse*, which provided embroidery patterns. Her many ribbons had to be properly washed; she advised: "Make a lather of clean white soap, the water as warm as you can bear your hands. Soap may be applied where there are grease spots on the wrong side. As soon as washed have ready a hot iron and press them out. While wet pressing on the wrong side. To stiffen dip in gum Arabic."

While the scrapbook reveals much about the lives of Emily, Anne, and Nan, much more is known about their lives from their letters and family stories and anecdotes. Each of these women kept up countless correspondences with friends, family, and neighbors, all of which reveals much about the daily pattern of their existence. Surprisingly it tells little about the quality of their married relationships or their hopes and aspirations. But we can learn something of those lives by reading between the lines.

Emily Wharton Sinkler

Emily Wharton Sinkler (1823–75) was the first keeper of the scrapbook. The evidence from the scrapbook shows that Emily was a diligent homemaker. She devised recipes for cooking game. She created household formulas for soaps, candles, insecticides, and much more. She concocted inks and pastes. She was a master of sewing and hand stitching. She was a superb horticulturist, designing and planting a garden that bloomed with flowers and blossomed with fruit and vegetables for the table. She was resourceful, ingenious, and determined that her South Carolina family would continue in the style and customs that she had known in Philadelphia. Most of all, she was aware of the need for a permanent record of her recipes, formulas, and remedies.

Emily Wharton married Charles Sinkler of Eutaw Plantation on September 8, 1842, at St. Stephen's Church in her hometown of Philadelphia. They sailed immediately for Charleston and by November 1842 were living with Charles's parents at Eutaw Plantation in Upper St. John's Parish on the Santee River. In January 1848, Emily and Charles moved the short distance across Eutaw Springs to Belvidere, located on the cypress- and oak-lined Santee River. Captain James Sinkler, the son of a Scots immigrant, had secured a land grant to Belvidere in 1770. In 1785 Captain Sinkler's wife, Margaret Cantey Sinkler, built the Belvidere house.

As was typical of a plantation house in Upper Saint John's, the two-story frame house stood high off the ground on six substantial brick arches. Its welcoming central brick staircase led to a wide, covered front porch. There was no central hall. Instead, one entered the dining room or the living room through huge individual doors directly off the porch. Each of these rooms had a fireplace. Behind the parlor was a large library. On the second floor were four large bedrooms off a central hall. In the attic were an additional bedroom and a storeroom. Behind the dining room was a large pantry that was kept securely locked. Steep stairs led down and outside to the kitchen building. Nearby in the yard were a milk house, a smokehouse, and a cook's cabin. At Belvidere, Emily was the mistress of a large house, a family, and an extended household of more than 195 slaves. The slave row was at some distance from the main house and included about fifteen whitewashed frame cabins, each with a central fireplace. A whitewashed frame church formed the core of the slave row.

Emily settled into life on the banks of the Santee Swamp in the deepest, darkest reaches of the Santee River. The dark cypress trees and the deep black water of Eutaw Springs were strange to her, as were the hoot of the night owl and the cry of the blue heron. Her city-trained ears longed for the clamor of her native Philadelphia with its cobblestone streets and clatter of horse-drawn drays, surreys, and barouches. As she wrote in a letter home: "I have had quite enough of green trees and roosters and am panting for brick walls and noise."

Emily's days were timed to the rising sun, the full red moon of October, and long, sunny autumn afternoons when she would walk along the sandy carriage entrance beneath the gray-green, mossy live-oak trees. She loved the company of Elizabeth Allen Sinkler, her sister-in-law, whom she called Eliza. Accompanied by barking terriers and swift gray hounds, they would take a fast walk to the big boiler at Eutaw Springs. Legend had it that a young Eutaw Indian had drowned there trying to find the source of the upswelling, and Emily thought she heard his call in the sighing of the pines. She learned to distinguish the wild scream of the Eutaw peacocks from the howl of low-country wildcats and Carolina panthers.

Emily's husband, six years her senior, had enlisted in the U.S. Navy after his graduation from the College of Charleston in 1832. An avid hunter, he awakened most mornings at 4 A.M. to go duck or turkey hunting, and his success with the gun provided ample game for the Belvidere house. Thus it is not surprising that Emily's cookbook has entries for duck stew and venison pastry. Here is how Emily prepared venison: "Take the meat from a breast or shoulder of venison. Cut into pieces about 2 inches square. Crack the bones and put them with all the trimmings of the meat into a stew pan with pepper and salt and stew for two hours. Strain this and put the meat into this broth with 3 gills of port wine, 2 onions cut in slices, a few pieces of butter the size of an egg. Let the meat stew in this till half-done. Then take out meat and put in a deep dish and pour over enough of the gravy to cover it, with a teaspoon of flour stirred in. Cover with pastry and ornament the top. Cook on a slow fire. Before it is sent to the table add the juice of a lemon and 1/2 gill of port wine to the remainder of the gravy."

Charles Sinkler's commitment to farming kept him busy year-round from dawn to dusk. In one letter Emily confided to her brother Henry that "the weather is quite warm enough to satisfy any reasonable person, planters and farmers not included, of course. For those worthy individuals incorporate themselves so thoroughly in the feelings of their crops that instead of enjoying the cool nights and morning and a blanket at night they are thinking of the shivering cotton which tho it warms others unfortunately cannot warm itself." Not only was cotton the principal cash crop; it was also the source of yarn for their sheets, clothes, and much more that the self-sufficient plantation community required.

Emily became the consummate housekeeper, known for her hospitality, and friends often came and stayed for a week or more. She enjoyed putting on dinner parties, ending each with a flourish of three desserts. In winter, dinner parties at Belvidere were served before a huge, roaring open fire in an elegant dining room. In one letter Emily described her menu for a wedding party: "We had soup, boiled turkey and celery sauce, roasted haunch of venison and tongue for first courses; Charlotte Russe, epergne of custard and apple snow; I can see your incredulous look when you come to Charlotte Russe, but you may spare it for it was perfectly successful. Every thing was right about it even to the ladies fingers around it."

Emily soon learned that the low country was not for the squeamish or those afraid of rats, cockroaches, ants, bedbugs, fleas, and other such vermin. Her scrapbook had remedies for each of these pests. This is what she did about ants: "Procure a large sponge; wash it well; press it very dry; by so doing it will leave the small cells open; lay it on the shelf where they are most troublesome; sprinkle some white sugar lightly over it 2 or 3 times a day and take a bucket of hot water to where the sponge is; carefully drop the sponge into the boiling water and you will slay them by thousands; squeeze the sponge and begin again." As for fleas and bedbugs, she counseled putting a few drops of wormwood on a handkerchief or a piece of folded muslin and placing it in the bed haunted by the intruders.

Cleanliness was a challenge for Emily's household. Soap was a much-prized commodity for personal hygiene and washing. Emily had four household formulas for soap. Here is one of them: "Take 6 pounds of potash, and 4 pounds of lard and $1/4$ pound of rosin. Beat up the rosin and mix all well together. Set it aside for five days. Then put the whole into a ten-gallon cask of warm water and stir twice a day for ten days. At the end of which time you will have 100 pounds of soap."

Emily also supervised the washing of clothes. She and the household slaves were kept busy starching lawn; doing up ribbons, collars, and cuffs; and pressing the full-skirted dresses of the day. Petite and beautiful, Emily favored blue silks and cambric for her dresses. She devised all manner of washing formulas to keep her whites white, blacks black, and muslins and silks in shiny perfection. Emily advised: "Whoever will soak clothes from twenty-four to thirty six hours before washing them will find that they can do without patent washing fluids and save nearly all the wear of clothes by rubbing too."

Emily had learned many of her home remedies from her African American slaves, from her brother-in-law Seaman, and perhaps from her doctors. Her prescription for asthma was this: "Take the leaves of the stramonium or Jamestown weed dried in the shade, saturated with a pretty strong solution of saltpeter, and smoked so as to inhale deeply the fumes."

Emily restored the old garden at Belvidere, which became known throughout the Santee area. She scoured the countryside for cuttings and root clippings and collected plants from her friends and neighbors. Her rose garden included many fine old Bourbon roses such as Cloth of Gold and Souvenir de Malmaison. She kept and annotated a copy of *North American Botany; Comprising the Native and Common Cultivated Plants North of Mexico*, by Amos Eaton and John Wright, first published in 1840. Emily's scrapbook contains planting secrets such as the following: "At night put your seeds in a cup and pour scalding water enough on to cover; soak until morning, then plant 1/2 an inch thick in light rich loam. Cover the spot with a piece of board which must not be removed until 48 hours after planting." She decorated her house with dried flowers. Her formula for drying ferns was this: "The most perfect and beautiful copies imaginable of ferns may be made by thoroughly saturating them in common porter [a dark beer made from malt] and then laying them flat between white sheets of paper, more pressure than of an ordinary book, and let them dry out."

Emily reigned as the mistress of Belvidere Plantation for twenty-seven years. On February 10, 1875—Ash Wednesday—she was killed in a buggy accident.

Anne Wickham Porcher Sinkler

Emily's scrapbook treasure was passed on to her daughter-in-law Anne Wickham Porcher Sinkler (1860–1919). Anne was the daughter of Mary Fanning Wickham of Virginia (she was born at Hickory Hill Plantation, just outside Richmond) and Julius Porcher of St. Julien's Plantation in Upper St. John's Parish. Mary Fanning's mother had been Lucy Carter, a daughter of Robert Carter of Shirley Plantation. Mary Fanning named her daughter Anne, and her family and friends called her Annie. The Porchers were neighbors and friends of Emily and Charles Sinkler. Still, it was a matter of chance that Emily's youngest son, Charles St. George Sinkler, known as Charlie, met, fell in love with, and married the lovely, auburn-haired Anne.

Charlie and Anne were children of the Civil War. Charlie had been born in 1853. Anne, born on September 14, 1860, had lost her father in the Battle of Missionary Ridge. Anne's mother, who after her husband's death moved to New York City to live with her sister Lucy Carter Byrd, died when Anne was about fifteen years old. Anne continued to visit her Porcher cousins at Walworth and St. Julien's Plantation in Eutawville, South Carolina, and her friendship with Charles Sinkler developed during those visits. The warmth of their relationship is revealed in the more than one hundred love letters sent between New York and Eutawville. (Anne kept Charles's letters, dated May to December 1883, and they are in the safekeeping of the author.)

Charlie and Anne were married in New York City on December 5, 1883. Anne took over Emily's housekeeping and gardening duties and continued to record her formulas, recipes, and remedies in Emily's scrapbook. It is possible to distinguish Anne and Emily's handwriting; among other things, their *x*'s are completely different.

Anne was a self-disciplined person, thoughtful of the welfare and feelings of others. Like Emily she had lived in both the North and the South. She had a warm and generous personality. A pretty woman, she had a wonderful head of curly auburn hair and a lovely figure. She seemed to have had a working knowledge of the medicines used in her day—calomel, salts, castor oil, fever medicines, iodine, and disinfectants. In the Belvidere house she had a locked closet where she had a full supply of these medicines and plenty of clean bandages. Anne supervised the health and welfare of the plantation community. She also saw that manners and courtesies were learned and adhered to by both whites and blacks. It was said that she had a firm hand in a velvet glove.

Anne continued the flower and vegetable garden that Emily had begun. Under her watchful eye, the gardener (called Daddy Lewis) cultivated plants and performed various tasks. They made a successful team. One of their gardening rules was to never plant seeds until after Easter—one could not count on the weather until after the full moon at Easter. Several other rules of thumb guided them. If it rained, the weather would not clear until the wind went around and blew from the northwest. If there was rain during the night, it would not stay clear. A halo around the moon meant it would rain within three days. Rain before 7:00 A.M. meant it would clear before 11:00 A.M. Cloud formations known as mares' tails heralded rain. An unusually brilliant day was a weather breeder—that is, the next few days would be unsettled. Daddy Lewis and Anne's specialties included their asparagus bed and their fragrant, shell-pink Duchess roses.

Anne's rolls, bread, and rice cakes showed her love of baking. Her rice cakes called for one to "mix 4 spoonfuls soft boiled rice, 1 spoonful butter—2 eggs and 1 gill milk together. Stir in rice flour [and] form into little round cakes and bake." Her Virginia corn bread recipe, which may have come from her mother, called for "rubbing a piece of butter the size of an egg into 1 pt corn meal; make into a batter with some new milk and 2 eggs, add some yeast. Set by the fire for an hour; butter some pans and bake." Anne's sponge cake was the envy of the neighborhood. In cryptic style her recipe called for "10 eggs, their weight in sugar and the weight of 6 in flour. Just before putting in the pan, squeeze in juice of 1 lemon."

Chickens and eggs were staples at Belvidere. Anne devised methods to preserve eggs in limewater. She noted that "gypsum or sulfate of Lime or Lime Water will keep eggs for 6 months or more" and that "to keep eggs one need only immerse in boiling water enough to count 20 at a rapid rate." Anne's "Fricassee Chicken" was made thus: "Cut up the chicken; put in a saucepan with 1 pt water, 1 onion cut small, a little mace, pepper, and salt. Boil 20 mins. Take out the chicken, strain gravy in a bowl; put in saucepan about 2-oz butter mixed with a large spoonful of flour. Put in the pieces of chicken, stir till hot, and then add the gravy. Add a gill of cream and 2 eggs well beaten and a little chopped parsley. Stir till it almost boils."

Anne also used eggs in her salad dressing. She had access to the family cookbooks and attributed her salad dressing to Mrs. Randolph. She made it in this way: "Boil two fresh eggs ten minutes, put them in water to cool, then put the yolks in a soup plate, pour on them a table spoonful of cold water, rub them with a wooden spoon until well dissolved; then add two spoonfuls of oil. When well mixed, put in 1 teaspoonful of salt and one of made mustard; when all these are united and quite smooth, stir in two spoonfuls of vinegar. Put it over the salad which must be cut up."

During Anne's time as mistress at Belvidere Plantation, the kitchen continued to be located in an outbuilding. Cooking was no easy task—some was done on an open fire and some on a wood-burning stove. Stocking it with the right type of wood was an art. Special boxes for oak, hickory, and pine were restocked each day, and Anne supervised the cutting and sorting of the wood.

Anne and Charlie had three daughters: Emily (b. 1884), Anne (b. 1886), and Caroline (b. 1895). Shortly after Caroline's birth, General Sinkler (who received this title as a member of the South Carolina Militia) developed a high fever that destroyed his short-term memory. He also became addicted to alcohol, paregoric, and opium. Anne searched the newspapers for a remedy to his addictions. The scrapbook contains several methods for curing drunkenness. One called for the use of ipecacuanha taken in half-drachma doses as an emetic; another called for the preparation of a tonic that would act as a stimulant: "sulfate of iron, 5 grains; magnesia, 10 grains; peppermint water, 11 drachmas; spirit of nutmeg, 1 drachma; take the above twice a day."

During her later years, Anne became very deaf and used a horn for hearing. She died of a tumor of the spleen in 1919, when she was fifty-nine years old.

Anne Sinkler Fishburne

On her mother's death, Anne (Nan) Sinkler Fishburne (1886–1983) took on the duties of supervising planting at Belvidere.[4] Nan, a petite, green-eyed beauty, fell in love with William Kershaw Fishburne, called Kershaw by all, a dashing young doctor from Walterboro, South Carolina. They were married at Belvidere Plantation on April 14, 1910, when Nan was twenty-three and Kershaw (who had vowed to remain a bachelor if he were not married by his thirtieth birthday) two days shy of thirty. They moved to a small summer village, Pinopolis, located on a high point in the Wasmasaw Swamp. But Nan continued to supervise and farm at Belvidere for her widowed father.

Nan had grown up on Belvidere Plantation. By the time she was two years old, she had her own pony. She accompanied the stablemen who took the cows out to the grazing fields in the morning and brought them in for the afternoon milking. She would remain at the stable yard to see the milking, and it was not long before she learned to milk. She wanted to know how to do everything around the plantation. Among many other things, she was taught how to tell a mule's age by pulling up its lip and inspecting its teeth carefully. All dogs thought life was sublime as long as they were with Nan. They knew she saved tidbits from her meals for them, and they followed her wherever she and her pony went.

Nan took part in the milking routine at Belvidere. Each morning's milking would be taken in big buckets from the stable yard to the milk house, a small white square building with a pointed roof close to the kitchen house, and delivered to a woman called Maum Hetty, who had complete charge of the milk. The milk was poured into wide shallow enamel pans and put into the safe, a set of screened shelves on legs, three feet from the floor. After two or three hours the cream would rise to the top of the milk, forming a floating, creamy yellow blanket. Later in the day this luscious blanket would be skimmed—some put into a butter churn and some saved for rich desserts. Each day a saucer of warm milk was put outside on the step for Nan's cat. Here also Nan learned the process of making butter the way it had always been done by her grandmother and mother. Their scrapbook contains the recipe "Orange County Butter," which describes a process that took thirty-six hours.

Nan grew up enjoying life in the kitchen house. Placed so as to minimize the danger of fires, the kitchen house was ten feet from the milk house and thirty feet from the outside rear stairs of the big house. During Nan's younger years Dinah managed the kitchen. Secure in her position, she was reportedly a wonderfully consistent cook. The kitchen was a popular place for all ages. There would often be an extra sweet potato on the hearth or a few leftover waffles and always some coffee or tea down by the fire. When mealtime came, Dinah's dishes would be put on two trays and covered with big silver domes to keep the food hot. They would be carried by one of the kitchen helpers up the back stairs to the pantry and delivered to the head butler, called Daddy Ischum, who had a flair for making all proceedings in the dining room seem festive and elegant. The dining room was sunny, and during the winter there was always a fire in the large fireplace. Members of the family gathered there to read, write, or chat in front of a comfortable fire. A servant was always on call to bring in wood, run errands, or attend to whatever was needed.

Nan grew up observing her mother's activities, so it is not surprising that she continued the family's dining traditions. Breakfast was a full meal—fruit in season, followed by hominy, eggs, bacon, and sausage, and then waffles and home syrup. Nan learned to make delicious crisp waffles. The recipe for them is in the scrapbook and is entitled "Sweet Waffles." It calls for six eggs, one-fourth pound butter, one and one-half pounds flour, one pint milk, one-half pound white sugar, and one teaspoon cinnamon. Nan updated this recipe in her "Old Recipes from Old St. John's": "2 cups flour, 2 tsp. baking powder, 1 small tsp. salt, 1 teaspoon sugar, 1 egg, 1 large tblsp. Lard, with milk enough to make a creamy batter, and thin enough to pour from a pitcher."

Nan also learned to garden under the careful eye of her mother and Daddy Lewis. The garden was a combination flower and vegetable garden. In season there were individual squares devoted to vegetables—asparagus, carrots, collards, lettuce, spinach. There was also a hotbed for mushrooms.

The Belvidere Plantation garden included a scuppernong grapevine arbor, and Anne learned to make wine from these grapes, which ripened in September, as well as from blackberries. The scrapbook has three recipes for making blackberry wine: "Lady's Book Blackberry Wine," "Cousin Dolly's Blackberry Wine," and "Mrs. Porcher's Blackberry Wine." Each summer Nan spread the word through her cook, Cat, that she would pay for blackberries, and all the neighborhood children would bring in pints, gallon jars, and baskets of fruit. Having gathered the ripest berries, Nan would have them mashed. To a gallon of the fruit she would add a gallon of water and three pounds of brown sugar. The strained liquid would be poured into French brandy casks and allowed to stand for six months. Any guest who came to Nan's house was served a glass of this delicious wine in one of her green Venetian wineglasses.

Nan believed that a garden nourished the soul. She loved the garden's constant change—plants unfurling, light and shade from the moving sun, and her wind harps playing their soughing song in the huge pines. She loved to tell the story of the overbooked, rich American men on safari. As they marched posthaste for the shooting, they suddenly heard a deathly silence behind them. Looking back, they saw their porters sitting serenely on the ground. When they inquired as to the problem, the head porter said that they were waiting for their souls to catch up with them—the pace had been so frenetic that their souls had been left behind. Nan felt that her garden was a surcease from being overscheduled, from the hurry and worry of the world. She found peace in what she called the whole system of the garden—the trees, flowers, breeze, insects, birds, lizards, and butterflies. She felt that everything in this system was changing, evolving, developing on schedule with a very big pattern that is enveloping us all. In creating her garden Nan knew that she was helping nurture the system, helping bring it to full beauty and vigor. And in return the abundance of beauty and serenity nurtured her.

Like Emily and Anne before her, Nan maintained the Belvidere garden both for its flowering beauty and its vegetables. She loved to tell the story of her older sister, Emily Sinkler Roosevelt, who on her visits back home from Philadelphia would say as she stepped off the train: "Miss Anne, man, have you got my stand of spinach started?" Nan raised every type of vegetable, from green peppers, cucumbers, and tomatoes to sweet potatoes in the Belvidere garden.

In 1940, as part of the Works Progress Administration, the federal government impounded the Santee River to create a hydroelectric system with Lake Moultrie and Lake Marion. Unfortunately, Belvidere was in the path of this development. Nan saw to the dismantling of Belvidere board by board. Some of its finest woodwork was moved to various family houses in Pinopolis.

Nan and Kershaw had established a thirteen-acre farm in Pinopolis. Initially they lived in the summerhouse of Ophir Plantation with a full pack of Kershaw's hounds. Gradually Nan filled this farm with a camellia garden, a rose garden, and a wild swamp garden full of swamp azaleas, bay trees, and bamboo. Nan believed that her garden was an extension of her home—in essence, rooms to be enjoyed and sat in. She had seating arrangements for playing bridge, others for reading aloud.

Nan and Kershaw had fields for cotton and oats and a huge vegetable garden, where they raised prize garden crops. Nan's pantry was loaded with jars of her fig preserves, green tomato pickle, blackberry jam, tomato catsup, and tomato soy, to name a few. Without their vegetable garden, Nan said, they would have had a limited diet. As on the plantation, now in Berkeley County there were no stores from which vegetables could be bought. The stores had only sacks of rice, flour, salt, and sugar. So gardening was an essential everyday endeavor.

Nan continued to maintain the scrapbook. Many of her entries were on pieces of paper that were simply inserted into the book. Her "Sweet Pickle Peaches" required one to "weigh 4 lbs. of sugar and pour on it 2 quarts of vinegar. Then add 1 oz of cloves, 1 oz of cinnamon, and put it on the fire. As soon as it comes to a boil have ready 8 lbs. of clingstone peaches pared. Let them boil for 15 minutes, and then put them in a jar and pour the syrup over them hot and seal up." These delicious peaches were often served as a side relish with pork or ham.

Interestingly, Nan updated Grandmother Emily's version of "Mango Pickle." Neither version uses mangos—Emily's version uses green peppers, while Nan's uses green cantaloupes—but both are delicious. Here is Nan's version: "Slit green cantaloupes on one side and put them in strong salt and water. On the 3rd day after take them out and without bruising or breaking them get out the seeds and pulp. Then wipe them and place them in jars and pour boiling vinegar over them. They can be stuffed afterwards whenever convenient." Nan's mango stuffing was thus: "1 lb. White mustard seed, 1/2 lb. Black mustard seed, 1/4 lb. Celery seed powdered, 4 tablespoonfuls of black pepper, 2 tablespoonfuls powdered Allspice, 6 tablespoonfuls grated horse radish, 6 tablespoonfuls powdered ginger, 5 onions, green peppers chopped. Put 8 tablespoons of brown sugar and sweet oil and make it the consistency of mush. After the mangoes are stuffed and laid in the jar pour boiling vinegar over them."

Kershaw and Nan's home became the "big house" for their children, Emily and Anne, and their grandchildren. I was one of those grandchildren and spent all my weekends with them in the country. Sunday dinner was always a marvel, and most of the delicious concoctions were right out of the scrapbook. There was always "Satira's Corn Pie," scalloped tomatoes, and sweet potato pudding, while the meat dish would be fried chicken, ham balls, or country sausages. Nan especially loved desserts, and her "Floating Island," made of custard with egg-white peaks on top, was a real delicacy.

T HUS THE SCRAPS from the lives of three women were preserved for more than 150 years in this small family cookbook and remedy book. The scrapbook provided a handy tool for preserving the lore of one generation for the next. When

Anne took over the household duties at Belvidere, she had Emily's formulas, recipes, and remedies to rely on. It is clear that she added her own as time went by. Anne trained her own daughter, Nan, in the ways of women. The socialization process was probably not an overt one. Nan simply learned the lore of her family from her mother, Dinah the cook, and Daddy Lewis the gardener. Nan used the scrapbook to organize her own activities. She had great reverence for the values and customs of her Belvidere heritage. She preserved them by replicating them faithfully in "Old Recipes from Old St. John's," her reproduction of the culinary items in the scrapbook. As she said in the foreword to that small volume: "As the swift shuttle of thought brings before me scenes from the past, there are none that I more love to recall than those which have St. John's Berkeley for a background. United to one another as we were by the ties of blood and tradition, the outstanding feature of our neighborhood was the true spirit of hospitality sitting with gladness. The exchange of delicacies and first fruits of the season was one of the gracious and kindly customs and much skill went into the concocting of dishes sufficiently delectable to tempt the most jaded palate."

[PATRICIA P. BUCKLER]

3

〜〜〜

Letters, Scrapbooks, and
History Books

〜〜〜

A Personalized Version of the Mexican War,
1846–48

I N 1832, WHEN she was about twelve, Ann Elizabeth Buckler of Baltimore started a scrapbook and continued it until 1855, when she was about thirty-five. Ann Lizzie, as she was known to family and friends, used her scrapbook as a kind of autobiographical composition, telling her story through a combination of pasted-in items and handwritten explanatory comments. Her entries include poems, writings, clippings, sketches, watercolors, and other mementos. Included among these items are some tokens of the war between the United States and Mexico that was fought between 1846 and 1848, gifts of returning soldiers who were friends of the family. The story behind these Mexican War souvenirs is the particular focus of this essay, a story worth telling not only because of what it relates about the life of the scrapbook's creator but also because it provides a look at the intersection of private life and public affairs at a pivotal time in U.S. history.

This story can be reconstructed in part because Ann Elizabeth was not only a scrapbook maker but also a faithful letter writer, whose correspondence with an uncle living abroad during this period has also been preserved. These letters convey news of the extensive Buckler family, as well as the writer's personal feelings on subjects ranging from the romantic prospects of various friends and relatives to the effects of the European famine on the Baltimore commodities market. They also contain war news, some doubtless acquired from newspapers and some from close friends and relatives in the military.

Ann Elizabeth usually wrote to her uncle William Buckler—her father's brother, who lived in Canton, China—in tandem with her aunt Elizabeth Buckler, William's sister. They wrote at the same time because letters were usually prepared to take advantage of the pending departure of a ship in port. Although both Ann Lizzie and Aunt Elizabeth touch on much of the same news, their attitudes and opinions about the same events, especially in reference to the Mexican War, contrast sharply. The younger woman embraces the popular, patriotic enthusiasm for the campaign, while the older woman is disgusted by the public's excited approval of events that take such a severe toll in human suffering and death. Reading these letters together provides dramatic insight into the differences between these two women of different generations, living during the same period, members of the same household.

When considered in concert with the scrapbook entries, these letters reveal more clearly Ann Lizzie's personality, as well as her attitude toward private and public matters. Furthermore, placing the two sets of letters and the scrapbook entries into the context of the times allows a far more complete and textured picture of her life to emerge. In other words, these discrete pieces of life writing and personal records convey much more information when viewed as parts of a larger discourse that is autobiographical yet also historical. The resulting gestalt exposes the richly mediated interrelationship between private lives and public events. Any compilation of memorabilia, pictures, letters, clippings, and so forth, bound into a self-contained volume such as a scrapbook, can constitute an individual, unique memoir. However, an individual scrapbook's meaning becomes more completely realized when supplemented by strata of letters, family history, public history, and contemporaneous newspaper accounts.

The Scrapbook's Family

The scrapbook's maker, Ann Elizabeth Buckler, was born in 1820, the oldest child of Dr. John Buckler, a well-known Baltimore physician, and Eliza Slone Buckler. John Buckler was one of eight children, including the much younger Thomas, who also became a physician. A third son, William, who represented the family's interest in the China trade, lived in Canton for years at a time. The family also included five daughters—Elizabeth, Anne, Jane, Mattie, and Hannah—about whom much less is known.

John and Eliza Buckler had, in addition to Ann Elizabeth, five children—William, James, Mary, Riggin, and Leslie. Ann Lizzie married a naval officer, Henry Rolando, and they had four children, two sons who died in childhood and two daughters who never married. All six are buried in Greenmount Cemetery in Baltimore. Over the years since its creation, the scrapbook has been handed down through generations of the Buckler family, eventually coming into the keeping of my father-in-law, Humphrey Warren Buckler Jr., a great-great-nephew of its maker, and after his death to my husband and me. The scrapbook seems originally to have had between 100 and 110 pages of souvenirs with some additional blank pages remaining in the back. The pages measure $13\frac{1}{2}$ inches high by 11 inches wide and are made of paper the texture of construction paper. The paper pages have deteriorated, making them fragile and difficult to handle. The cover boards, while not leather, seem to have been printed in a faux leather pattern. Over time some pages and pictures have been removed and framed but are still in the family. Other pages became loose and, along with other items that appear never to have been pasted in, have remained pressed between the bound pages.

Among the hundreds of individual items collected in the scrapbook are ten objects related to the Mexican War: a pen-and-ink drawing of Governors Island, an island off the tip of Manhattan that was the location of a military installation where troops trained for the Mexican War; seven handmade playing cards labeled "Mexican cards taken from Arista's camp after the battle of Chipultepec (Col. Magruder)"; a segment of red cloth pinned to a piece of paper, with the notation, "A piece of the flag from the Castle of San Juan d'Ulloa Given me by Allan McLane U.S.N"; and an engraved invitation to the Grand Inauguration Ball for Zachary Taylor and Millard Fillmore on March 5, 1849, inscribed, "The honor of Dr. Buckler & Ladies Company is Requested."

Women's Art as Memoir and History

That a few scrapbook entries and letters carry the primary surviving impressions—indeed, as far as one can tell, the only impressions—that these two women recorded of historical events is perfectly consistent with the customary practice of the antebellum era, 1820–60. Women were tied to home and family and seldom wrote for publication or expected recognition from outside the family circle. They used domestic or decorative arts as outlets for creative expression and as vehicles to chronicle and reflect on their daily experiences.[1] Women compiled and composed diaries, scrapbooks, albums, journals, letters, and other bits of personal memorabilia to leave a memory or record of themselves for ensuing generations, apparently knowing full well that no other evidence of their lives was likely to remain. These women wrote to gain for themselves some of the "security, authority, legitimacy and identity" that historian David Thelen refers to in his introduction to *Memory and American History*. They wanted to compose memories establishing not only that they existed but also that they acted and thought in certain ways. They seemed to recognize that by composing their own remembrances they could shape the images of themselves that were left behind. Thelen sees such memory-making activities as an important source for modern readers to understand "how individuals, ethnic groups, political parties, and cultures shape and re-shape their identities—as known to themselves and to others."[2] Memory, as Thelen concludes, is constructed, not reproduced. Most significant, the way memories are constructed lets us explore how "individuals connect with larger-scale historical processes."[3] Thelen's argument forestalls problems with the types of evidence used: the emphasis is placed on the authenticating qualities of the memories, rather than the personal or "unofficial" nature of the sources.

Modern scholars have disagreed sharply about the value of manuscripts versus artifacts in conveying cultural or historical truth. William Hesseltine dismissed artifacts as having only "illustrative value"; they were mute when it came to providing "meaningful information," he maintained, and they failed to present "cause and effect, event and consequence, situation and response." In an opposing argument presented in his classic essay "American Studies: Words or Things?" John A. Kouwenhoven argued that historians place too much value on words to the neglect of things: "We have, in fact, based our ideas of America primarily upon ingenious verbal generalizations that are sometimes laughably and sometimes tragically unrelated to actualities." Taking an intermediate position, Wilcomb E. Washburn held that a material culture study that focused exclusively on the artifact and ignored the written word would be essentially incomplete. He objected to the "unjustifiable theoretical distinction between manuscripts and museum objects . . . because it confuses the particular vehicle of an idea with the idea itself. The specific fact may be either in the form of a written document—a manuscript—or a material artifact or 'manufact.'" Furthermore, he contended, it is a historian's duty to treat the manuscript and manufact as "equivalent in meaningfulness." Both are necessary "companion keys to the past."[4]

Because scrapbooks themselves span the line between text and artifact, the addition of letters, which are exclusively verbal, must be viewed in this "companion key" light. Scrapbooks and letters share many self-expressive qualities, but there are some differences that are fruitful to examine, such as the conditions of composition, the intended audience, and the document's projected durability. Scrapbooks can be studied like other artifacts of material culture, using Thomas J. Schlereth's definition of material artifacts, because they are objects "made or modified by humans consciously or unconsciously, directly or indirectly," that "reflect the belief patterns of individuals who made, commissioned, purchased, or used them, and, by extension, the belief patterns of the larger society of which they are a part." They offer evidence of the "values, ideas, attitudes, and assumptions" of the society in which they were produced.[5]

The personal memento scrapbook, in particular, combines cultural conventions with unique individual choices in a manner that captures both the personal and the social realities of a person's life. For instance, the individual who composes a scrapbook or album does so over time, building a multifaceted yet singular item that represents the self. Jerome Bruner defines "life narrative" as a kind of storytelling influenced by learned processes that enable the individual to "structure perceptual experience, to organize memory . . . [to] purpose-build"—that is, to reconstruct life in a manner that enables the individual to become the "story told."[6] As expressive discourse, the scrapbook expresses an individual's personality through manipulation of the world in which the self is grounded.[7] The scrapbook maker uses the situation at hand to construct a separate reality that is rooted in his or her cultural matrix. The personal memento scrapbook combines language with visual and associative artifacts to represent the personality of its composer or encoder. It actively incorporates scraps or fragments of the maker's external reality into an expression of the individual self.

Turning the pages reveals the scrapbook maker's interests, activities, and experiences; through a scrapbook, the person records events and interests, explores ideas, comes to grips with the present and visualizes the future. When reading a personal memento scrapbook, the reader sees a narrative composition that is deliberately and carefully fashioned to reflect a particular vision of the maker's life and self.

At the same time, that vision is portrayed according to the cultural conventions of its maker's time and place and, therefore, must be interpreted in light of its cultural context. Taken together, the words and artifacts symbolize the scrapbook maker's personal and cultural identity—communicating wants, needs, aspirations, and values.[8] The context also dictates the author's sense of audience, the awareness that the volume might be viewed by a variety of others—friends, family, acquaintances, visitors, and perhaps, eventually, people who were not yet born when the book was made. A scrapbook, therefore, must be created with the intention of preserving its contents and conveying its memories forward over time. It embodies some hope of permanence. It locates its maker in historical time and place and shows the context in which its author's life is rooted while it reveals an individual's hopes and dreams, loves, friendships, grief, faith, and joy. Scrapbooks seem to embody Estelle Jelinek's argument that women's autobiographical writings emphasize "the personal and concrete over the intellectual and abstract."[9] Explanatory notations attached to the souvenirs found in scrapbooks are brief or nonexistent. Their significance is almost exclusively associative: those who know what they represent, know what they represent; those who do not, do not.[10]

Letters, Diaries, and Journals

Although the scrapbook may be seen as an autobiography or memoir composed over time, for spontaneity and brevity one must turn to the letter, diary, or journal. Although scrapbooks are usually compiled chronologically closer to the actual events they reflect than are memoirs, they are generally assembled at a date somewhat later than the event and, therefore, incorporate reflections that are more distanced from events than are letters. According to Joanne E. Cooper, letters, diaries, and journals tend to have an "immediacy not found in memoirs . . . ; diaries and journals reflect more directly the author's views and circumstances than events recalled, reshaped and recorded years after they have taken place." Cooper further notes that "letters, while they share some features with journals and diaries (significantly the characteristic of immediacy), differ in that they are addressed to a specific person. Both the tone and form of the chronicle are then coloured by the audience and the writer's degree of intimacy to that audience."[11]

The ideal combination of immediacy and reflection, then, would come from the integration of these remembering genres—diaries, journals, and letters for the raw reactions and feelings of the writer; scrapbooks, albums, and memoirs for the time-sifted and contemplatively considered reconstruction and interpretation of past experiences. By studying both Ann Elizabeth Buckler's letters and her scrapbook, readers can see through one lens into her observations and emotions at the moment of experience or immediately thereafter, while scrutinizing through another lens her more distant and reflective reactions recorded somewhat later. Combining these viewpoints provides a far deeper and more compelling understanding of Ann Elizabeth as an individual situated in a specific time and place.

Scrapbooks as Intertext

The significance of any scrapbook resonates beyond the immediate circumstances of its composition, because the manner in which a scrapbook constructs meaning from other texts makes it more than a simple artifact. A scrapbook is quite literally an *intertext,* an item whose plurality of texts points to a culture's prior texts while creating a dialogue of its own with its contemporary cultural context and the cultures of future readers. The concept of intertextuality, first articulated by Julia Kristeva and influenced by the work of Mikhail Bakhtin, states that no text stands alone as the exclusive imaginative offspring of a single author; every text is informed by other texts, whether they have been read by the author or the reader or even if they exist in a cultural context not expressed in words: "A literary work is not simply the product of a single author but of its relationship to other texts and to the structures of language itself."[12] In fact, intertexts are not necessarily literary but include all signifying practices ranging from historical documents to table settings. Kristeva theorizes a "three-dimensional textual space whose three 'coordinates of dialogue' are the writing subject, the addressee (or ideal reader), and exterior texts." She describes this textual space as intersecting planes having horizontal and vertical axes: "The word's status is thus defined horizontally (the word in the text belongs to both writing subject and addressee) as well as vertically (the word in the text is oriented towards an anterior or synchronic literary corpus) . . . each word (text) is an intersection of words (texts) where at least one other word (text) can be read [;] any text is constructed as a mosaic of quotations; any text is the absorption and transformation of another."[13]

The scrapbook is the ideal object for intertextual investigation, because its connection with other texts is visible on its pages. It is literally composed of texts and quotations, intermingled to express metatextual meanings. Kristeva further asserts that a reader can be engaged appropriately with a text only through the use of "something outside the text able to make it into a meaningful whole."[14] Although scrapbooks are sometimes compiled by single individuals (the scrapbook author), they are highly referential, so much so that no clear-cut individual interpretation is possible. Thus the vertical axis that infuses the present text with other texts opens a space for an unlimited number of connections and associations. The items collected in the Buckler scrapbook refer to earlier times (the events of the war that yielded the relevant artifacts are in the past) and also look forward to the future (the same items will inform future readers of those same events). Other texts associated with this scrapbook—letters, family records, newspaper accounts, historical annals, and other external reports surrounding the same event—provide the necessary codes that will more fully contextualize the individual's dialogue with contemporary events.

Although the scrapbook's multitude of texts signifies unlimited possibilities for dialogue with a preexisting body of texts (cultural context), the interplay among these texts can be at best speculative. In examining the Buckler scrapbook and its related documents, one can designate probable meanings for discrete elements and suggest connections among them, but definitive interpretation is impossible. Therefore, although the following discussion of the dialogue among texts and artifacts may seem true and accurate, it remains just one of many conversations that could be suggested by these same materials.

The Dialogue among Texts and Artifacts

The earliest dated letter, written at "Fort Columbus Governors Island August 22" (1846), was written by Ann Elizabeth Buckler to "Mr. William Buckler Via Marseilles Canton, China," and is postmarked December 2, 1846; it was received January 24, 1847. A partial transcript follows:

Fort Columbus Governors Island August 22

My dear Uncle

Ever since I have been here I have been looking out for a vessel for Canton but as I can hear of none, I thought I would write to you by Overland mail. We (that is Lizzie Frick myself) have been here two weeks, as usual have had a most delightful visit. The island is very gay there being here now about 1800 men. To be sure 800 of them are the California regiment which gives the Col a great deal of trouble As they are volunteers they seem to have no idea of discipline & are continually fighting & deserting, however the Col by letting them see they are under his command and, that he will be obeyed, has got them into some kind of order. The officers are quite gentlemanly but of course very green. George Pendleton is a Lieut in one of the companies yesterday saw McHenry Hollingsworth who is also a Lieut. . . .

My letter has just been interrupted by the band playing for guard mounting so of course I had to stop until they were done. I never could do anything while music was going on. We have a delightful band which plays twice a day The other [evening?] a large party of us went out to boat. We had the band in a large boat with us which made it delightful. The evening was beautiful & I enjoyed it exceedingly. . . . Colonel J. Magruder has come home from Texas with a pair of mustaches six inches long. He looks quite savage. He is on the recruiting service, but last I heard of him he was quite [illegible] no doubt from the number of dinners & suppers given to him at the club since his return.[15]

A complementary item to this letter is the drawing of Governors Island in Ann Elizabeth's scrapbook (see Figure 3.1).

Neither the scrapbook nor the existing letters give specific indications as to the circumstances that brought Buckler and her cousin Lizzie Frick to New York, but it becomes clear in reading the letters that they are visiting the family of Colonel James Bankhead, a career army officer stationed at Governors Island whose family is mentioned frequently in the letters of both Ann Elizabeth and her aunt Elizabeth. She does mention that, as of the letter's date—August 22, 1846—she has been at the base for two weeks and that this is not her first stay ("as usual have had a most delightful visit"). The summer of 1846 was a busy one at Fort Columbus: the U.S. Congress had declared war on Mexico on May 13 of that year, and both regular and volunteer troops were undergoing training on Governors Island.

Governors Island and the War

The island had a long history of military service, having been first fortified in 1624 by settlers of the Dutch West India Company. A star-shaped, dry-moated fortification was partly built by the U.S. government by 1794 and was completed by 1801. The drawing of Governors Island in the

Figure 3.1. *The top picture on this page of the Buckler scrapbook shows Governors Island, New York, where Ann Elizabeth wrote one of her letters to Uncle William.* (Courtesy Patricia P. Buckler)

scrapbook shows what may be the edge of the fort with a large flag unfurled above it, but the most prominent feature is another still-existing structure known as Castle Williams, a fort 210 feet in outer diameter with walls 8 feet thick and 40 feet high. Castle Williams is located in the island's historic district, along with other buildings already on the site when Ann Elizabeth Buckler visited. Among the other structures on the island were an 1840 Federal-style manor house that served as quarters for the commanding general; Block House, an 1839 Greek Revival building used as the post hospital; and the Governor's House, built in 1708 and rebuilt as a Georgian-style manor house in 1805. Ann Lizzie no doubt also saw the South Battery, constructed in 1812 to defend Buttermilk Channel, the strip of water between Governors Island and Brooklyn.[16]

The "delightful band" of Governors Island mentioned in this letter apparently joined General Winfield Scott in Mexico. In his biography of Scott, John S. D. Eisenhower describes the landing at Tampico on February 18, 1847: "Soldiers lined the banks to cheer their commander, and a band brought from Governors Island, New York, played martial tunes."[17]

Ann Lizzie's references to "the Col" Bankhead, come chiefly in connection with his work as commander of the "California Regiment," a regiment of New York State volunteers recruited and "charged with a colonization as well as a military mission, . . . carefully selected at least that was the intention to provide the nucleus of a 'mighty Anglo-American population' on the shores of the Pacific."[18] In fact, the undisciplined behavior of the volunteers that Ann Lizzie noted in her letter was characteristic of this unit even after it arrived in California in March 1847 under Colonel J. D. Stevenson. The men of this regiment "began to 'sow wild oats,'" "were not disposed to work on the fortifications," and were "insubordinate." Although they were expected to remain as settlers after the close of the war, a number deserted the army to hunt for gold.[19] Colonel Bankhead, however, served in Mexico with the Second Artillery under General Scott. The son of James Bankhead, an officer in the American Revolution, Colonel Bankhead was a career officer, having been appointed a captain in the Fifth Infantry on June 18, 1808. By 1846 he had risen to the rank of colonel of the Second Artillery.[20]

The Buckler letters mention the Bankheads again when Ann Lizzie writes from Baltimore on February 25, 1847: "The Bankheads are to be here the 2nd of March to spend three months. . . . I do not think they have heard from the Col lately, but I see by the papers that his regiment is at Tampico, & I suppose he is there too. People seem to think the war will not be over for many years."

Bankhead continued with Scott to Vera Cruz, which was taken by U.S. forces after a brief siege on March 29, 1847. Afterward, Bankhead was dispatched to Washington, bearing the flags of the fortress of San Juan de Ulloa and the city of Vera Cruz, as well as a "whole sheaf of captured regimental colors, and twelve handsome cannon."[21] Ann Lizzie mentions in her letter of April 28: "Col Bankhead is expected every day, he is coming home with despatches & all the flags & trophies taken at Vera Cruz & Tampico." She continues: "He is very fortunate in being sent home & is besides ordered to his old station on the Island which pleases the girls. I suppose Lizzie and her Mother will go North with the col, but I shall try hard to keep Nora, who loves Balt."

Perspectives on the War

Like those of many other cities, Baltimore's celebration of the victories included an illumination, described by Ann Lizzie in the same letter to her uncle.

> We had a magnificent illumination last Wednesday in honor of the victories. It was the most beautiful thing of the kind, I ever saw. The whole city was one blaze of light Burnums Hotel was superb a sperm candle in each pane of glass. It took 2100 for the windows alone the front of the porch was decorated with transparencies representing the different battles. Our windows looked very prettily with flowers, candelabras, & the Chinese lanterns. I walked nearly over town, got mashed almost to death in the crowd, & got home about 12 o'clock. I have altogether been quite dissipated for the last week.

Ann Lizzie's enthusiasm for the victories and her participation in the celebration highlights the difference between herself and her aunt. The younger woman's acquaintance with military families such as the Bankheads and the participation of her own friends, including Allan McLane and John B. Magruder, probably contributed to the pride and patriotism she clearly felt in response to the victories in Mexico. While she exclaims to Uncle William about the decorations in the Baltimore home, her aunt Elizabeth sees the same events in an opposite light.

When Aunt Elizabeth mentions the victory at Vera Cruz and Bankhead's part in it in her letter to William, also dated April 28, she expresses disgust at the great celebrations that took place in Baltimore after the victory:

> The whole town crazy last week about the illumination for victory, very brilliant & the streets crowded, I was *mad* and scolded to see our windows filled with flowers and candles when I knew how many lives had been sacrificed at Vera Cruz, poor Mrs. Bankhead was the picture of woe for several days, crying all the time at the doleful letters from the Col, he had been sleeping on the ground without any pillow but an old coat for 2 nights wet with dew & only a few crackers, she began to rejoice when she heard Vera Cruz & Alvarado were taken & that he was coming home in the [illegible] with the Mexican Flags & spoils taken, Nora did not like public papers announcing

that he was sent home by Gen. Scott on account of infirm health they think he is perfectly well but I fear they will find him altered for the worse in 4 months He must have suffered from exposure & privations of every kind it is said that he is ordered back to Governors Island.

Mrs. Bankhead's impression of conditions at Vera Cruz (as reported by Aunt Elizabeth in her letter) are supported by historical accounts. George Ballantine, a young Briton in one of David Twiggs's regiments, recorded that each man was prepared for the landing at Vera Cruz with "two days' rations in his haversack, and each man carried a full canteen of water, a blanket, or, as a substitute, his greatcoat; the rest of his clothing and possessions were to remain aboard the vessel he was leaving."[22]

Colonel Bankhead was a member of General Scott's inner circle, known as the "little cabinet," that was charged with working out every detail of military operations. He was promoted to brevet-brigadier-general for conspicuous gallantry at Vera Cruz on March 29, 1847. When an expedition proceeded in 1848 from Vera Cruz to Cordoba and Orizaba, General Bankhead was instructed to occupy those towns and clamp down on the guerrillas who terrorized the road to the interior. As with the California volunteers on Governors Island, Bankhead insisted on discipline among his troops. He ordered respectful treatment of the locals, prohibited plundering and other lawless behavior, and protected the people's rights to practice their Catholic religion.[23] At the time of his death in Baltimore in 1856, Bankhead had charge of the military department of the east.[24]

In addition to Colonel Bankhead, other family friends were at the battle of Vera Cruz, and one of these friends, Allan McLane, provided Ann Lizzie with a souvenir for her scrapbook: "A piece of the flag from the Castle of San Juan d'Ulloa Given me by Allan McLane U.S.N." (see Figure 3.2). In a letter written by one of her uncles, Dr. Thomas Buckler, to her uncle William, dated November 30, 1845, Ann Lizzie is discussed as a possible match for McLane. At least, he says, "the McLanes" are anxious to make a "match for her with Allen of the Navy." A midshipman at the time of the Mexican War, McLane served in the Home Squadron under Captain John Henry Aulick, who was second in command to Commodore Matthew Perry. At Vera Cruz, Scott had borrowed some heavy guns from the U.S. Navy, which were hauled ashore from the blockading ships and manned by seamen.[25] According to Charles L. Dufour, the guns were dragged three miles through sand and water until they were in position.[26] N. C. Brooks writes:

Figure 3.2. *At the top left of this page of the Buckler scrapbook is pinned a piece of red fabric with the notation: "A piece of the flag from the Castle of San Juan d'Ulloa Given me by Allan McLane U.S.N."* (Courtesy Patricia P. Buckler)

GALOPPE, AMAZON AND TIGER.
Descriptive of Hunting in South Africa.

THE GREAT EXHIBITION.
God Save the Queen ! !

FINALE.

A series of the flag from the
Battle of San Juan & Ulloa
given one by Allan Mclane

A WARNING FOR GREEDY BOYS.

FOND MOTHER.—Why, Georgy! what are you crying for? Such a good boy, too, as you have been all day!
GREEDY BOY.—I've eaten so much T-t-tur key, that I can't eat any P-p plum-pudding at all!

CAPITAL IDEA FOR COLD WEATHER.

The naval battery which opened its fire on the 24th, under the command of Captain Aulick, was erected within 700 yards of the walls of the city, and such was the secrecy and celerity with which the work was performed by the night labours of two thousand men, that its proximity was not discovered by the besieged until the intervening chaparral was suddenly cut away from before it by some daring volunteers headed by Midshipman Allan McLane, a descendant of the brave Revolutionary officer of the same name, and, to the great astonishment of the enemy, it stood boldly developed with its guns mounted, and the men at their stations.[27]

In one volume of a five-volume scrapbook on the Mexican War housed at the Historical Society of Pennsylvania in Philadelphia, this incident is mentioned in a newspaper clipping containing the transcription of a dispatch from Captain J. H. Aulick and addressed to Commodore M.C. Perry:

It is due to Midshipman Allan McLane that I should not omit to mention that on a call for volunteers to cut away some brushwood which obstructed the view to a battery on which we wished to direct our fire, he sprung through an embrasure followed by two men (William Cavanaugh, seaman—the name of the other I have not been able to ascertain), and amidst a shower of balls quickly removed the obstruction, for which gallantry I complimented them on the spot. . . . (From the Washington Union, Saturday night, April 10)[28]

That a piece of the flag is preserved in the Buckler scrapbook reflects more than the family's personal interests. The attitude at home in the states toward the Mexican War was heavily influenced by the press, which "molded the popular perceptions of the conflict." It was "the first major event in American history to be reported by the penny press," and it was the first conflict in which the press employed professional war correspondents. The reporters, often volunteer soldiers themselves, glamorized the war for the U.S. public, creating battlefield heroes and fashioning a new concept of patriotism. The newspapers portrayed Americans as superior to other nationalities not only in military strength but also in moral character, and attributed to Americans "a much higher degree of patriotism" than any other people. "It became a familiar refrain: the great advantage enjoyed by America's fighting men over their Mexican foes was their superior devotion to cause and country, their patriotism."[29]

The war served to crystallize the "American quest for national identity." The general public was kept well informed about this war because the cheap publication costs and mass circulation of U.S. newspapers coincided with innovative reporting techniques—the telegraph and the pony express—to provide fast, if not always accurate, information. Furthermore, because the Mexican War was the first to make broad use of volunteer soldiers, the general public felt closely connected with the war effort and had a greater stake in its outcome. Patriotic symbols such as the U.S. flag, the bald eagle, and national songs played new roles in the way average Americans looked at their own country and its enemies. The Mexican War was the first war in which soldiers fought under the Stars and Stripes rather than regimental and unit flags, and thus the flag, in particular, became an important icon of democratic principles and of the nation's destiny and mission. Soldiers competed for the honor of carrying the national flag into battle or being the first to raise it over a captured fortress or city. The right to raise the flag over the fortress of San Juan de Ulloa was so hotly contested that a soldier and sailor did it jointly. "To the volunteers the honor was especially dear for it mingled national pride with state loyalty and proved the patriotism of the citizen-soldier."[30]

Nevertheless, the annexation of Texas and the war with Mexico were controversial in many parts of the country, particularly in the Northeast, where abolitionists believed that adding the southwest territories to the Union would increase the power of Southern slave-holding states. New England's antislavery leaders were the most vocal, urging their followers to refuse to cooperate with the government and even, at times, wishing for the success of Mexican troops. Pacifists also actively opposed the war, and the clergy of the Northeast—especially the Unitarians, Congregationalists, and Quakers—preached against it.[31] Many Americans, however, believed in the concept of manifest destiny and favored expanding the nation's boundaries to the Pacific. In fact, as a result of this war, the United States acquired not only Texas but also California, Nevada, Utah, most of Arizona and New Mexico, and parts of Colorado and Wyoming. The piece of the flag from San Juan de Ulloa that is preserved in the Buckler scrapbook is thus rich in symbolism. Not only does it represent the family's close connection with the war at the individual, personal level, but also it embodies the nation's own emergent identity and its newly felt conviction of its manifest destiny.

Ann Lizzie and her family paid close attention to politics and kept abreast of issues of the day. With an uncle in Canton, their interest in the China trade probably points to a practical commitment to U.S. expansionism. West Coast ports under U.S. control would likely facilitate commerce with the Far East. Other correspondence not directly connected with this war shows that Ann Lizzie herself traveled to China, kept a detailed journal of her trip (now lost), and applied to become U.S. consul to Shanghai:

> After much trouble I have not succeeded in obtaining the appointment of consul for Shanghai. But a Mr. Lyon has it he is very rich & very peculiar & has an idea that he will be able to travel about the country. The secretary of state said he was sorry but that the appointment had been made by Mr. Polk a personal friend of Mr. Lyon. He also requested permission to keep my little description of Shanghai which I made up from memory & my Journal but I declined giving it to him.

Other news in this letter, dated February 26, 1847, deals with the purchase and commissioning of ships, the sale of products imported from the Far East, the holding of stock in a new railroad, and other business ventures. The character of Ann Lizzie that comes across in her scrapbook and letters is that of a shrewd, energetic businesswoman with a cosmopolitan view of the world, a contradiction of the widely held idea that all nineteenth-century women limited themselves to domestic affairs and left business and professional activities to men.

"Prince John" Magruder

The next scrapbook souvenir and corresponding letter references involve Colonel John Bankhead Magruder, who contributed the group of seven handmade playing cards labeled "Mexican cards taken from Arista's camp after the battle of Chipultepec (Col. Magruder)" and now in the scrapbook. In her letter from Governors Island on August 22, 1846, Ann Lizzie mentioned Colonel Magruder as one of the many acquaintances she met there.

John Bankhead Magruder, the nephew of James Bankhead, was also an artillery officer and served under Robert E. Lee. Magruder graduated from West Point in 1830 and served in the Mexican War in its early stages in 1846. By the time Ann Lizzie was visiting Fort Columbus in the summer of 1846, he was captain of the First Artillery and on recruiting service. He returned to Mexico to participate in the siege of Vera Cruz. Magruder saw quite a lot of action: the battles of Palo Alto, May 8, 1846; Resaca de la Palma, May 9, 1846; the siege of Vera Cruz, March 9–29, 1847; Cerro Gordo, where he was brevetted to major, April 18, 1847; LaHoya, June 20, 1847; and Ocalaca, August 16, 1847. He participated in the assault and capture of Mexico City, beginning with the storming of Chapultepec on September 13, 1847, where his "field battery, 1st artillery . . . had . . . some spirited affairs against superior numbers, driving the enemy from a battery in the road, and capturing a gun."[32] Magruder's name is on the list of those wounded during the attack on Chapultepec, and he was brevetted to lieutenant colonel for gallant and meritorious conduct during that battle. He was engaged in the assault and capture of Mexico City on September 13–14.[33]

A photograph of Magruder shows him with a mustache very like the one Ann Lizzie describes in her letter. Magruder was a colorful figure who was nicknamed "Prince John" because of his courtly manner and style of entertainment, his lordly air, and his "brilliant ability to bring appearances up to the necessities of the occasion." Magruder married Esther Henrietta Von Kapff in Baltimore in 1831, and they had three children: Isabel, Kate, and Henry.[34] Magruder's relationship with the Baltimore Bucklers for the period of the war remains ambiguous, although, of course, the family of his uncle, James Bankhead, is mentioned frequently in the letters. There had to have been enough connection for Magruder to have given Ann Lizzie the playing cards retrieved from the enemy's bivouac. Eventually, too, the Magruders and the Bucklers became quite close. Magruder's daughter, Isabel, became the first wife of Dr. Riggin Buckler, one of Ann Lizzie's younger siblings.

After the Mexican War, Magruder was stationed at Fort McHenry, Baltimore, during 1848 and 1849. Between the Mexican War and the Civil War, Magruder served at various posts in Texas, Louisiana, Kansas, California, Rhode Island, and Washington, D.C. He is reported to have fought in the first and only duel in Los Angeles. He resigned on April 20, 1861, to join the Provisional Confederate Army, where he was appointed brigadier-general on June 17, 1861. Early in the Civil War he distinguished himself as a brilliant officer, but he lost ground in the Richmond area battle against McClellan, thus disappointing Lee, who transferred him to command the district of Texas, New Mexico, and Arizona in 1862.[35] His mates considered him "a born soldier": "He would fight all day and dance all night. He wrote love songs and sang them, and won an heiress rich beyond comparison." Magruder continued to lead a colorful life even after the defeat of the Confederacy. He joined the army of the Mexican emperor, Maximillian, and died in Texas. He is buried in Galveston.[36]

Taylor and Arista: Heroes and Adversaries

Although the scrapbook notation refers to the battle of Chapultepec, published histories of the war refer to the capture of Arista's camp after the battle of the Rio Grande near Matamoros in 1846: "His [Arista's] camp is said to have been brilliantly furnished, and the victors enjoyed a repast prepared beforehand by the Mexicans in sure anticipation of a triumph. Large supplies of ammunition, small arms, and the private service and equipage of the general were captured by our army."[37] Another published account reported:

When the Mexicans saw the fall of this veteran regiment [Tampico Regiment], panic seized them. Horse and foot, breaking their ranks, and crowding on each other, rushed towards the Rio Grande, in swimming which lay their only hope of escape. At the head of the pursuit rattled the flying artillery, pouring in its bloody fire. The infantry followed at a run, cheering as it advanced. About two hundred yards from the ravine the Americans reached the deserted camp of the Mexicans. Here beeves were killed, campfires were lighted, and meals were cooking, so little had the enemy expected such a result to the day's struggle. In the midst of the tents stood the gorgeous pavilion of Arista. It contained treasures of plate, hangings, and other luxuries, equal to a satrap's. The spoil of the camp was prodigious. Three standards, eight pieces of artillery, an immense quantity of ammunitions, with the arms and equipments of seven thousand men and two thousand horses fell into the hands of the victors.[38]

An even more specifically relevant reference is found in a scrapbook of newspaper clippings located at the Historical Society of Pennsylvania. Headed "The Battle on the Rio Grande," it is signed by "Correspondent of the North American" and is dated Matamoras, May 26, 1856: "We are enjoying ourselves here in Matamoras and waiting to recruit our horses, and for the fresh arrival of troops. We got a great deal of public property in the city. Among the tobacco distributed among the troops, were a good many Spanish playing cards: I am going to keep a pack for you as trophies of the war."[39]

Knowing U.S. war heroes and receiving war souvenirs from them was glamorous enough, but the association with the Mexican general Mariano Arista must also have been exciting. Arista was commander of the Mexican forces that fought Zachary Taylor in the first battles of the Mexican War, May 4–7, 1846, at Matamoros and the battle of Resaca de la Palma. According to Fayette Robinson in *Mexico and Her Military Chieftains from the Revolution of Hidalgo to the Present Time*, Don Mariano Arista was a close confederate of the populist hero and leader of Mexico, Antonio López de Santa Anna, going back to the 1820s. Arista, one of Mexico's ablest commanders, was considered one of the best cavalry officers in the world.[40]

However, the disaster at Matamoros was blamed on Arista, who was made the "scapegoat for the sorry situation throughout Mexico."[41] He was tried by courtmartial and dismissed from the army in early July. By the end of that month, the Mexican government headed by Mariano Paredes had fallen, and by September 15 Santa Anna had returned from exile to great popular acclaim and had assumed command of the Army of Mexico. Santa Anna played the most prominent military role until the capture of Mexico City by General Scott's troops a year later.[42]

After the conclusion of the war, however, Arista became minister of war and marine during President José Joaquín de Herrera's second term. Under Herrera's direction, Arista reformed Mexico's military and helped transform the government into a modern state. He was elected president of Mexico and took office on January 15, 1851, succeeding Herrera. According to Thomas Cotner: "The general was evidently the favorite among the people. He had gained the reputation of helping to formulate many of the strong national measures of the Herrera administration . . . he enjoyed the support of the administration [and] held the approval of a majority of the moderate liberals in Congress."[43]

The playing cards from Arista's camp resonate at many levels. They were apparently among the more common souvenirs brought back from the war and were associated with highly regarded commanders on both sides. Arista's rout was a coup for the Americans, and his defeats by Zachary Taylor at Matamoros and Resaca de la Palma were so one-sided that they were said to have guaranteed Taylor's election to the presidency. According to Brainerd Dyer's biography of Taylor, when the news of the general's triumph reached the United States, "the American People hailed him as a military genius. . . . Old Rough and Ready became the hero of the people." Furthermore, Congress adopted resolutions thanking Taylor for his service and the "fortitude, skill, enterprise, and courage, which have distinguished the recent brilliant operations on the Rio Grande" and authorized the striking of a special gold medal.[44]

The interconnections between the Mexican hero, Arista, and the U.S. hero, Taylor, surface in the letters and scrapbook of the Buckler women. In a letter to William Buckler dated April 28, 1847, Aunt Elizabeth mentions Taylor's triumphs:

> It is thought Old Taylor will be our next President he is not more than 45 years every paper is filled with accounts of his bravery & mercy at the same time shown to the poor mexicans, he is idolized by his aides & all the officers, he was marching on towards the city of Mexico the last accounts, said at the head of 16000 men, many must die from the climate as the heat was intense a month ago.

The military fame Taylor won during the first year of the war with Mexico thrust him into the political limelight; he was acclaimed by newspaper editors, politicians, and the populace at large. In June 1848 he reluctantly accepted the Whig Party's nomination for president and was elected, with Millard Fillmore as his vice president, in November of that year. The Mexican War transformed both the victorious general, Taylor, and the loser, Arista, into politicians. Both served as presidents of their respective countries and would have done so simultaneously if Taylor had not died in office in July 1850.

According to Brainerd Dyer, two inauguration balls were held in Washington on March 5, 1849, to celebrate President Taylor's accession to the presidency,

> one at Jackson hall, the other in a large new ballroom on Judiciary Square near the City Hall. In spite of a ten-dollar admission charge this hall was packed by three thousand celebrating Whigs. A future president who attended the latter ball was Abraham Lincoln, ardent supporter of Taylor in the election campaign and one of the congressional managers of the ball. Lincoln seems to have enjoyed the affair far more than did the guest of honor, for he remained until three or four o'clock in the morning.[45]

Rounding out the Mexican War souvenirs in the Buckler scrapbook is the invitation to Taylor's Grand Inauguration Ball at Judiciary Square. Lincoln's name is indeed on the list of managers, along with those of many other recognizable politicians and military officers, including Winfield Scott and Robert E. Lee. This invitation, inscribed "The honor of Dr. Buckler & Ladies Company is Requested," is pasted inside one of the end boards of the scrapbook. Its socially correct address, mentioning only the male head of the household by name, reinforces the idea that women in the nineteenth century were seldom acknowledged as individuals, only as adjuncts or accessories to men.

I N A POIGNANT WAY, this final artifact brings my argument back to the idea of women creating their own records of their lives through their homely compositions of diaries, letters, journals, and scrapbooks. As Jean V. Matthews explains: "Sexual identity was perceived as dependent upon clearly defined kinds of activity."[46] Although going to war was out of the question for Ann Lizzie Buckler, supporting the war and collecting souvenirs from the soldiers who did fight were allowable. A woman could even marry a war souvenir, so to speak: Ann Lizzie was romantically linked to one officer and eventually married another, Henry Rolando, a naval officer who served on the sloop *Germantown* at the second incident at Tabasco, June 16, 1847.

Although society restricted women to the sphere of the home, they were deeply interested in the political, social, religious, and economic affairs of their day. Judging by their letters and scrapbook notations, the Buckler "ladies" read newspapers avidly, talked with family, friends, and acquaintances about the war, and were concerned about its effects on the battlefront as well as the home front. They cleared a small space for themselves in the overwhelming flow of historical events by collecting artifacts that signified their connectedness with the affairs of their time. In their private writings, they expressed their opinions about issues of the day, leaving a record of their beliefs. In other words, as the men were creating and recording history in the public arena, women such as Ann Lizzie and her Aunt Elizabeth were leaving their own marks.

Matthews writes of the general female restlessness of the nineteenth century that demanded for women "greater opportunity for self-expression and personal growth together with a higher degree of recognition of their personalities."[47] A close reading of Ann Lizzie's scrapbook and her letters shows that she shared this restlessness. She was not simply an attachment to the men in her life but an intelligent, vital, and active woman who conducted business, expressed opinions both political and social, traveled the world, and felt confident enough in her own abilities to apply for a job as U.S. consul to Shanghai. Besides the Mexican War souvenirs, her scrapbook is filled with poetry and prose clippings, hand drawings, and painted pictures of family and friends, as well as of far-off places, including woodblock prints from nineteenth-century Japan. Cartoons of political and social satire abound, along with sentimental notes regarding her mother and sister and brothers. One wonders whether Ann Lizzie thought about the future when she glued her souvenirs to the page. Perhaps she planned to share her memories with any children she might have. Whatever inspired her authorship, she created a text that communicates with readers many years later and inspires us to have a conversation about her life.

[JENNIFER A. JOLLY]

4

~~~~~

History in the Making

~~~~~

A Columbian Exposition Scrapbook

I N 1893 GERTRUDE RADDIN visited the World's Columbian Exposition in Chicago's Jackson Park.[1] During her visit Raddin collected souvenirs, advertising cards, and images of the exposition's attractions. Later she created a personal record of the exposition, assembling her scraps and adding newspaper articles documenting its prominent position in the public sphere. The scrapbook she produced is now housed in the Northwestern University Archives in Evanston, Illinois.

A carefully clipped newspaper article folded into the scrapbook's opening pages suggests a theme with which to approach the study of Raddin's Columbian Exposition scrapbook. The article, entitled "All Wanted Relics: Thousands Flock to the Reopening of Jackson Park," describes "relic hunters" who, following the exposition's conclusion, returned to the fairgrounds to plunder its former attractions. Whether Raddin herself returned to the exposition after its close is not known; however, her scrapbook is evidence that she too was, in a sense, one of the relic hunters. She visited the exposition, collected evidence of her path through Jackson Park, and assembled the relics of her experience in a scrapbook.

When Raddin clipped this article, she may have instinctively recognized how well this evocation of relics captured not only her own desire to preserve evidence of her experience but also a popular component of the exposition itself. The Columbian Exposition, informally known as the Chicago World's Fair, displayed numerous relics, particularly ones related to the history of Columbus, that blended nostalgia with history and created the atmosphere that characterized the exposition: history as spectacle. The term *relics* also evokes fairgoers' craze for mementos and illustrates the mindset of many after the exposition's close: its temporality fueled the popularity of souvenirs, and the closer they were to original—that is, if they were taken directly from the site—the more successfully they captured an authentic exposition experience.[2]

Scrapbooks of the Columbian Exposition allowed fairgoers like Raddin to integrate their souvenirs with newspaper clippings and commentary to create personalized narratives of the fair, thus representing their experience there. Scrapbooks also serve as relics for the historian: they evoke historical distance to effect nostalgia, substitute for the historical commentator who acquired the contents and made the scrapbook, and provide what Thomas Schlereth refers to as an "encounter of the third kind."[3] Yet more revealing, scrapbooks reinforce the fact that historical documents, and written histories in general, are constructed by individuals and for individuals to provide orientation in a larger, public scheme.

Gertrude Raddin's scrapbook allows access to three levels of history: first, the events, people, and objects present at the World's Columbian Exposition and their impact; second, the cultural role of the scrapbook itself; and third, the writing and recording of history. This multilevel approach is possible because scrapbooks, in their creation and subsequent reading, represent the intersection of a specific referential origin, a historical social practice (with both public and private elements), and the need for a self-consciously critical approach to deciphering the array of information they present.[4] Raddin's scrapbook provides a unique opportunity to explore these issues in relation to the themes that form the core of the album: Columbus as a historical figure, the notion of progress, and the exposition's aftermath and effects.

Gertrude Raddin, Scrapbook Maker

Little is known of Gertrude Raddin apart from the traces of her personality left behind in her scrapbook.[5] She was the eldest daughter of a boot and shoe merchant and had a younger sister and brother. Her family moved to Evanston, Illinois, from Massachusetts when she was a girl or young woman, sometime before 1880. They were neither poor nor wealthy; they had a few servants but also took in boarders. Raddin likely lived a sheltered life within her family and church community. She never married and, although thirty-five at the time of the fair, probably still lived in the family home. Raddin was a long-time member of the First Methodist Church and the Daughters of the American Revolution, and both of these institutional identities are evident in her scrapbook.

Raddin likely made one or more day trips south to Chicago to the Columbian Exposition together with her brother, Charles; his wife, Belle; and perhaps other family members. One can imagine Belle, who made scrapbooks on other occasions, encouraging Gertrude to save and collect materials while at the fair or clip out articles that interested her.[6] Evanston was close enough to Chicago to receive constant news of the exposition and be caught up in its excitement. Even when the family was not at the fair, talk of its themes could have been integrated into daily life, perhaps through daily newspaper articles or church sermons.

After the exposition closed, Gertrude and Belle sat down together to assemble their scrapbooks, most likely at the family home. Perhaps Charles or their sister, Alice, added their comments. Belle Raddin collected so much material for her scrapbook that she created two albums, one showing an overview of their visit and another focusing on the Fine Arts Building. They are replete with articles about the fair, dense collages, and, perhaps reflecting Belle's interest in art history developed while a student at Northwestern, reviews and biographies of artists who exhibited at the fair.

In contrast to Belle's, Gertrude's album is spare, arguably sparse. Sometimes only one or two items are positioned on a page, defying the Victorian aesthetic of "cluttered eclecticism" that characterized many late-nineteenth-century scrapbooks.[7] The scrapbook's major themes form a skeletal frame, with random material interspersed in and among these core ideas. Its layout suggests a designer with a limited or austere aesthetic sense, who perhaps had never been exposed to the many books and magazines providing instruction in scrapbook construction.[8] All the items are carefully clipped out, many with their original labels. But the arrangements are often awkward and visually naïve, as if Gertrude were learning to assemble a scrapbook for the first time. Finally, unlike her younger scrapbook-making companion, Gertrude did not have university training; for her, the Methodist Church provided a public, institutional counterweight to the fair's commercial and promotional mechanisms and narratives.

Gertrude Raddin created a scrapbook that bears traces of her familial interactions; her involvement with the church; her exposure to the press, the public, and ephemera circulating at the fair; and her thirty-five years of personal experience. It is a distinctive record of the Columbian Exposition that demonstrates how she integrated the private, social, and public domains of her life to produce and reproduce narratives dealing with Columbus as a historical figure, the progress of civilization, and the fair's effects and aftermath.

Columbus, Source of Spectacle

Pasted on the frontispiece of Gertrude Raddin's scrapbook is a color lithograph of the shield of Columbus, comprising four sections: Isabella's castle, representing the Kingdom of Castille; Ferdinand's lion, representing the Kingdom of Leon; a land-and-sea formation, representing the New World; and five anchors, representing Columbus. This shield sets the stage for the first theme of the scrapbook, as well as

Figure 4.1.   *A two-page spread in Gertrude Raddin's Columbian Exposition scrapbook contrasting an unidentified peasant in the re-creation of Columbus's room at La Rabida and the administration, electrical, and U.S. government buildings from the Court of Honor at the Exposition.* (Courtesy Northwestern University Archives)

for the exposition: the history of Columbus and the discovery of America. Originally planned for 1892, the World's Columbian Exposition commemorated the arrival of Columbus in America with a visual cornucopia of pictures, souvenirs, statues, replicas, and performances.[9] The displayed replicas of Columbus's ships—the *Niña, Pinta,* and *Santa Maria*—were quite popular and are referenced in various other scrapbooks of the exposition. La Rabida, a replica of the Spanish convent where Columbus stayed, housed relics and paintings of Columbus; it too is reproduced in Raddin's scrapbook.[10] As Karal Ann Marling suggests, the rickety caravels and La Rabida all served as quaint, slightly exotic reminders of the progress in U.S. industry, from its European origins to its emerging position of prominence.[11] Such a comparison is demonstrated in Raddin's scrapbook in a double-page spread that juxtaposes cards illustrating the magnificent, elaborate buildings of the White City with a view of the modest interior of La Rabida (see Figure 4.1). These life-size historical recreations, along with the innumerable Columbian relics, the staged historical events and performances, and the prominent statues of Columbus throughout the grounds, added to the aura of history as spectacle, suitable for consumption by the spectators.[12]

Guy Debord has argued that within the "society of the spectacle," history is transformed into a spectacle to render it consumable. The Columbian Exposition's relics and performances serve as examples of what he considers one key function of the spectacle: they bury history in culture by appearing to preserve intact the culture of the past.[13] By witnessing the fair's spectacular events, spectators could consume history on an emotional and personal level. The seeming ability to access the culture of the past through dramatization and the display of relics, although illusory, was further codified in the mass production of souvenirs that proliferated at the exposition. Such public events and mass-produced imagery helped make up for a lost social unity by sponsoring the mass circulation of and exposure to spectacular history. For critical theoreticians such as Debord, one role of spectacle in society is to preserve the status quo and class power.[14]

Columbus dominates Raddin's album. She had access to the vast amount of ephemera produced by fair organizers that incorporated the Columbus theme—from guidebooks, picture books, and pamphlets to colorful advertising cards, tickets, and souvenirs with scenes from Columbus's life. The fourth page of the scrapbook is filled with guidebook pictures of five epochs of his life. The scenes depict a bearded Columbus meeting with Ferdinand and Isabella, plotting his course, sitting in chains, rejoicing at the sight of land, and arriving on shore. Another scene reproduced twice in the scrapbook is the "Apotheosis of Columbus," a colorful advertising card for beef extract showing a clean-shaven Columbus surrounded by a series of coats of arms as he reveals America, depicted as a devout kneeling native, to an imagined audience.[15] Raddin cut up this card, preserving the grouping but removing the product and "Apotheosis" labels, and pasted it above another image of a bearded Columbus with his sword lowered and a newspaper drawing of Captain Anderson, who sailed the replica Viking ship (pictured on the opposite page of the scrapbook) to the United States for the fair. These images could have served as references to any number of Columbian events staged on floats and in performances, which in turn served as spectacular references to the historical past. The role of the exposition's events, spectacles, and the Columbian souvenirs collected for the scrapbook was to incorporate the viewer and the scrapbook creator into the exposition's culture, to mark their presence as spectators and consumers. As Susan Stewart notes in her discussion of souvenirs, the memory of the body (being at the fair) is replaced by the memory of the object (the scrap included in the book), and the object bears the trace of the authentic experience.[16]

However, a close investigation of the scrapbook reveals that Raddin's experience of the exposition was most likely not governed by blind consumption of spectacles and relics. A scrapbook represents the intersection of the personal and the public: it includes materials from the public sector that have been carefully selected and reorganized to express the interests and concerns of its maker. Raddin's personal take on the history of Columbus has an individualized twist, and the scrapbook is the forum that allowed her to articulate this in a personal but also a social space.[17] Judy Sund has argued that although the quadricentennial celebration of Columbus's voyage stirred debate regarding the negative consequences of his journey, the dominant imagery of the explorer remained that of hero and genius and was carefully monitored. Further, his presentation made great use of religious conventions and overtones, as the "Apotheosis of Columbus" advertising card and the five epochs of the "Life of Columbus" pictures attest. However, the images of Columbus included in Raddin's scrapbook are edited, visually diverse, and interspersed with alternative explorer heroes such as the Vikings. Further, Raddin sets the Columbian imagery of the scrapbook into an explicitly moral and historical context by bracketing the scrapbook with a pair of articles discussing Columbus's status as a historical figure and hero.[18] She thus marks out her own distinctive response to the spectacle of the fair and the presentation of Columbus, using mass-produced imagery and published texts.

A good Methodist, Raddin seems to have taken great interest in the moral debates revolving around Columbus that were instigated by the celebration of the Columbian quadricentennial. On the third page of her album, Raddin pasted a newspaper article entitled "The Facts about Columbus," by the Reverend James Mudge, DD, who discusses Columbus's moral character. Defining heroes as those who transcend the vices of their time, he promotes a history that makes Columbus neither a hero nor a saint. Instead, history should recognize Columbus's achievements but not lose sight of his moral shortcomings—his years as a pirate, his greed, his treatment of the natives of America. Rather than look to Columbus as a hero-discoverer of America, he argues, Americans should celebrate heroes such as the "great Englishman" (Mudge likely refers to George Vancouver, who explored the island of Vancouver in 1793) whose centennial was to be celebrated later in the month.

The final article in the scrapbook, "No Canonization for Columbus," reflects a similar view of Columbus's misbegotten status as a heroic icon. It contributes to the debate on the moral character of historical figures (and to this end also discusses the question of the moral character of George Washington). The central issue for this author, however, is the question of canonization. The article declares that Columbus is not and does not deserve to be a saint, primarily because of his extramarital relations and illegitimate children. In a slightly ambiguous conclusion, the article states that Columbus should receive credit for what he deserves but that the Catholic Church would be tarnished if it took seriously proposals to canonize him.

By framing the scrapbook within these two discussions of Columbus, Raddin identifies the importance of these discussions within her experience and memories of the fair and suggests a theme through which to approach the rest of the scrapbook.[19] Raddin's choice of imagery taken from the fair is celebratory and maintains a central position in the scrapbook, yet the articles counter the highly praiseworthy and devout presentation of Columbus available to her. The prominent position of the two articles suggests that the maker and the reader begin the scrapbook's narrative with questions regarding Columbus's moral and historical position and revisit the debate at the close of the book.

Through the Columbus theme Raddin managed to represent one of the exposition's historical themes in her own terms. She was able to signify her presence at the fair and her experience of the perhaps awe-inspiring Columbian relics and exhibitions while also asserting the importance of the debates regarding both Columbus's status in history and the social and moral role granted to historical figures. This personal history of the Columbian Exposition thus can be taken as negotiation of and resistance to the spectacular history presented there: it rejects the uniformity of Columbian imagery, remembers the fair as an event inspiring great debate, and asserts the individual's historical judgment.

The Progress of Civilization

According to the *Official Directory* of the World's Columbian Exposition, its purpose was to commemorate the discovery of America by exhibiting the "resources of the United States, their development, and the *progress of civilization* in the world [italics added]."[20] As commentators have pointed out, this theme of progress pervaded the exposition, from its layout and design to its contents and object lessons.[21] Chief among the supposed evidence of progress adopted by the fair designers were the contrasts between the tribal groups and villages displayed on the Midway Plaisance and the imperial grandeur of the Court of Honor and its contemporary industrial and cultural exhibits. As with the Columbian relics, the distancing effect created by exposure to nonindustrial and traditional cultures distinct from urban Chicago evoked nostalgia at the same time that it exaggerated U.S. progress and achievement and inspired patriotic pride. The central theme of the Columbus story was progress. A staple of historical narrative, progress represented the historical process leading from the time of Columbus's discovery of America to the nation's international status as host of the 1893 World's Fair.

In Raddin's scrapbook, multiple discourses on the notion of progress and civilization parallel the motif of Columbus's discovery of America. The album's fifth page has an article describing the Women's Building, a central theme of which reflects a common line of feminist discourse from the time of the Columbian Exposition: one way women gained public recognition at the fair, and in U.S. society more generally, was as domesticators of the world—women's domestic roles were metaphorically and literally transferred from the home to the rest of the world.[22] In this article, the Women's Building is seen to represent, through the object lessons contained within the building itself, the centrality of women's contributions toward making

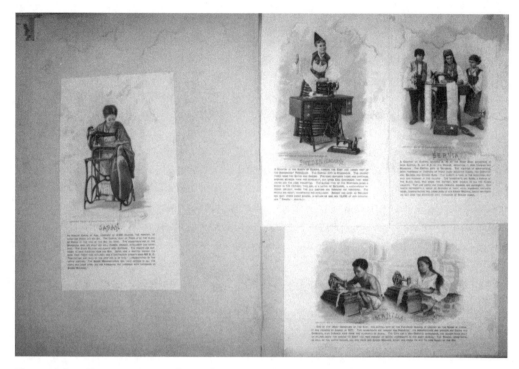

Figure 4.2. *Singer sewing machine advertising cards in Gertrude Raddin's Columbian Exposition scrapbook.* (Courtesy Northwestern University Archives)

the world a better, more civilized place. The inclusion of this article within the scrapbook suggests that such a conception of women resonated with Raddin; perhaps as a white, Christian woman she also was able to imagine her public and domestic role as aiding the progress of civilization. Her scrapbook, with its theme of progress, can be seen as an object lesson reproducing this civilizing message.

The power of the notion of progress and its relationship to the domestic sphere was not lost on the exposition's advertisers and marketers, nor did it escape inclusion in Raddin's scrapbook. Images of progress include advertisements for new products and technologies such as the refrigerated railroad car, illustrated in a card from the Swift and Company meat packers' booth. The inclusion of advertising cards in the scrapbook represents a combination of their visual appeal (some have lovely golden frames or provide useful images for the scrapbook's narrative, like the "Apotheosis of Columbus" card), the relevance of certain products or industries to Raddin's life, their relationship to her identity as a consumer, and their contribution to the fair's themes.[23] The most striking example of an advertising campaign revolving around the notion of progress and reproduced in the album is for Singer sewing machines (see Figure 4.2). This campaign worked with the notion of women's domestic roles—here, sewing—as integral to civilization, as well as romantic notions of traditional and exotic cultures central to entertainment, education, souvenirs, concessions, and advertising at the fair.

Each of the eight Singer cards has the name of a country, a portrait of an individual or group dressed in native or traditional clothing, and the image of a Singer sewing machine. Captions give information about the country and its history or customs, as well as describe the role of Singer sewing machines in either preserving those traditions or promoting civilization. The campaign relied on many factors. First, as a series of collectable cards, it created a desire to complete the set, a collecting process central to advertisers' marketing schemes during this period.[24] Next, the campaign played into the thirst for information and education about the "other" that was a central theme of the exposition. Susan Stewart discusses the importance of nostalgia and the exotic in evoking desire, as well as in creating a market for souvenirs of a short-lived event such as the fair.[25] The cards also evoke nostalgia, to dissipate any negative feelings that might be associated with modernization and the mingling of cultures at the fair, by emphasizing the role the sewing machines play in preserving distinctive cultural traditions.[26] Aligning progress with the growth of civilization in non-Western countries further deflects the threatening side of modernization. It allows the domestic Singer consumer to imagine herself as part of a larger mission: civilizing men and women around the world (as shown at work on the cards). The card for India reports that "the Singer sewing machine has been a factor in helping the people of India towards a better civilization for nearly twenty years," and the one for Zululand promotes Singer's role in leading a warlike people to civilization; in contrast, the card for Japan stresses Singer's corporate presence on the island. The card for each of the eight countries—India, Zululand, Japan, Bosnia, Serbia, Sweden, Norway, and Manila—adjusted its approach to speak to a range of attitudes held by Americans toward foreign peoples. A person who bought and used the Singer sewing machine could be aligned with this tradition-preserving and civilization-promoting enterprise, and one who collected and displayed the cards could reengage and promote these ideas. Each time they returned to admire the cards, consumers presumably would be reminded of the product while they reveled in the nostalgia and exotification embodied in the imagery. However, they would be reassured, modernization and progress would not threaten the preservation of cultural difference and distinctiveness.

Like the exposition itself, the images in the scrapbook highlight contrasts between primitive and progressive (or modern), and their arrangement brings to the fore salient attitudes about progress as they relate to the role of Columbus in the history of the Americas. This theme is made most explicit in a distinctive "pan-America" collage that appears early in the album (see Figure 4.3).

On the sixth page of the scrapbook, a black-and-white picture entitled "Columbia's Proclamation" shows a female personification of the United States, with distant views of the U.S. Capitol and a bust of George Washington. Above these, Raddin pasted cutouts of a U.S. flag and a Mexican flag. Columbia, standing tall and proud,

Figure 4.3. *Columbia's Proclamation collage from Gertrude Raddin's Columbian Exposition scrapbook.* (Courtesy Northwestern University Archives)

raises one arm to present the banner announcing the Columbian Exposition; in her other hand, she holds at her side a shield bearing a U.S. flag.[27] Surrounding this centerpiece are small images of what appear to be indigenous Mexicans, weighed down with loads on their backs—one leads a burro; a peasant mother carries her child on her back. This page appears to present Columbus's legacy: the foundation of the United States (Columbia) on the backs of indigenous Americans.[28] The implications of this juxtaposition are various. Does it represent a time-condensed vision of what Columbus found on "discovering" America and the progress that led to the foundation of the United States? Or does it represent a vision of two different paths taken by the United States and Mexico since the landing of Columbus—a view of pan-America, favoring the central United States? There is a clear contrast between the personification of an established system of a specific government, complete with icons of its success and stability (particularly the arts and industry), and the representations of nonwhite individuals, depicted as isolated in time and history, without the trappings of Westernized civilization.

Representing the rest of the Americas as underdeveloped industrially and culturally flew in the face of attempts by the Latin American Department of the World's Columbian Exposition to present the Latin American countries as valuable international trading partners for the United States and Europe.[29] Rather than creating a pan-American image of the progress of all of America, the Latin American Department's goal, the images chosen and arranged by Raddin emphasize the contrasts between the United States and Mexico. Here, Raddin uses her selective experience of the fair to identify herself as a white, culturally advanced citizen of the United States.

In *On Longing*, Susan Stewart cites the scrapbook as a souvenir: it contains items that individually refer to a specific place and event, allow one to reconstruct its narrative, and evoke memory.[30] Further, the standard discussion of scrapbooks includes the idea that the scrapbook is a space for the construction of identity, much as Stewart discusses the role of the souvenir in moving history into private time and creating an autobiography and sense of personal worthiness.[31] However, in contrast to Stewart, I agree with Jessica Dallow that scrapbooks can also be discussed as "collections," where meaning is centered on the organization of the contents rather than simply in each item's metonymic value.[32] Rather than being centered on memory, the collection requires the forgetting of origins, which are subsumed in the process of organization. This aspect of the distinction depends on understanding the scrapbook as existing on the border between public and private space. While the original compiler of the scrapbook would remember the origins of the images, some historical details might be skipped over when the scrapbook is shared. Further, for the historian, many of these origins are lost and their reconstruction is slow; it is primarily the visual and textual organization that remains to be explored. This is the case with the portion of Raddin's scrapbook devoted to the theme of progress.

In analyzing a scrapbook, the focus must not be confined to single items; rather, items must be considered in relationship to one another—as a collection taken as a whole or as a collage. In the Columbia collage, each item is important visually, but for exploring the meaning of the page the individual origins of the items are designed to be less important than their relationships. Specifically, the origins of the agrarian figures are obscured (they have no labels). They have become generic agrarian figures from the Americas, identified as Mexican by inference from the Mexican flag in the collage. The labeled Columbia allegorical figure is central, circled by the agrarian figures. The contrast between the graceful, statuesque Columbia with her trappings of culture and civilization and the stooped, ragged, glazed-eyed agrarian workers is paramount. In addition, the Singer advertisements emphasize the collection nature of the scrapbook. The fact of collecting the set of cards and designating Singer as a worldwide influence carries more significance than that of any single advertising card. In both circumstances, the elements in each section must be considered first as a whole and then in relationship to the entire scrapbook.

The model for approaching meaning that takes into account the relationship between the individuality of the parts in visual relationship to the whole is collage. Organization in collage, as in scrapbooks, is characterized by juxtaposition, defined by Roger Shattuck as "the setting of one element beside another without supplying the connection." According to Marjorie Perloff, the assumptions behind the art form of collage include the notion that expository linear discourse cannot convey all desired meaning and that the transfer of words and image from an original source to a collage allows for new possibilities of meaning.[33]

Scrapbooks appear to be an early embodiment of the artistic practice of collage. Their makers recognized the ability to create meaning without an explicit narrative text, relying on the juxtaposition of images and texts to create new patterns of meaning that continually shift. Individually, the images work metonymically, presenting partial meanings; taken as a whole, they provoke rather than explicate a narrative.[34] The creator of one Columbian Exposition scrapbook surrounded a guidebook image of the New York State Building with two caricatures of tourists looking confused and added the captions "bewildered" and "didn't get his money's worth," thus implying his or her criticisms of the New York display in a creative and amusing manner.[35] Scrapbooks rely on the tensions between the image's original context and its signifying system: a guidebook representing the State of New York at the exposition; and its new meaning enacted through juxtaposition, a loaded and humorous punch at New York interpreted by a reader.

In "Collage: The Organizing Principle of Art in the Age of the Relativity of Art," Donald Kuspit discusses collage as the "exemplification of the use and dominance of relativity in modern art." Collage represents a recognition of relativity, as it is the site of a struggle between an "objective and subjective sense of worldliness," which preserves the personal state of becoming.[36] This is in line with the common approach taken with scrapbooks—considering them a space in which personal identity is fluidly constructed in relationship to the outside, public world.[37] When discussing the scrapbook as a historical document, one can also consider the relativity of history: history is based on the current information available to the historian and is always more than a mere collection of facts. A scrapbook can serve as a metaphor for history's coming into being and represents the very process of an individual's construction of history.

A scrapbook has the potential to be a cross between two historical models. One, characteristic of the Enlightenment, aims to assemble empirical data, which can themselves reveal their own ordered principles, and parallels the collage. In contrast, the Hegelian model positions facts in relationship to principles or systems with theoretical underpinnings, often producing a linear, teleological arc of history. However, once one moves beyond an empirical presentation of facts through a historical period to an attempt to position those facts in relationship to principles or systems, one inserts one's own creative interpretation (and hence one's priorities, concerns, beliefs, and identity) into the process of writing history.

The narrative of a scrapbook combines the nonlinear experience of collage— the visual juxtaposition of artifacts—with the linear experience of turning the pages and reading textual excerpts. The artifacts, extracted and collected from a preexisting, meaning-loaded system—here, for example, a guidebook or display at the exposition—have been recontextualized and rearranged to become the elements forming the scrapbook's skeletal frame. The connections within such a skeletal narrative originally existed in the memory of its maker, were representative of that individual, and would have been performed with every viewing and sharing.[38] Much of the meaning constructed at the time of assembly will not be recovered and will remain secret following the maker's death.[39] For later viewers, the gaps in the narrative must be supplied, in the case of Raddin's scrapbook, by accessing external documents about the fair. However, each reading of the scrapbook will depend on the particular historian's rigor and creativity, and the meaning will necessarily remain fluid and open.

The historical model in Raddin's case is this: first, it admits from the start to being personal and subjective—scrapbooks define the personal in terms of the cultural and vice versa; second, it uses artifacts from the period, each with its own, openable history;[40] third, these facts or artifacts are arranged in collages that provoke a plurality of meanings but remain flexible and are not explicit; fourth, each reader or viewer is allowed to come to his or her own conclusions regarding the meaning of the material assembled. This model provides a point from which to access a personality and its cultural position within history, a set of historical artifacts to examine against the historical record (and vice versa), and an open system of meaning to explore.

Effects of the Exposition

The final section of the scrapbook revolves around the exposition's closing and its lasting impact. Again, a loose article offers a succinct description of the dominant concern of both Raddin's scrapbook and this discussion. This article, "All Roads Lead to the World's Fair," begins by suggesting: "Perhaps the farthest-reaching effect of the Exposition is to be found in its distribution of influences that make for civilization."[41] The scrapbook addresses this effect in two ways: in a running commentary on the fair's Midway Plaisance throughout the album and in articles in the final section geared toward this theme.

Raddin's scrapbook prominently features images of performers from the midway exhibitions, reflecting her interest in the variety of cultures represented at the exposition, as well as her desire to process and preserve this experience and knowledge of difference. The images included of midway performers portray people without signs of Western culture, in isolation from other cultures, without a sense of historical time, and often in settings that could be imagined as foreign lands. The characters depicted in photographs and drawings perform specific roles: a Native American fishes from a canoe, a Nubian with his spear raised above his head sits on a camel, an Arab sits astride a rearing horse, and in numerous pictures Mexicans lead burros or pose in family scenes in front of small huts. There are also a series of small, exaggerated caricatures depicting midway types and a few caricatures that depict Westerners on the midway—for instance, a dressed-up little girl on a donkey and a family comically squeezed onto a camel.

These images reinforce cultural, geographical, and historical distance, and their inclusion within the scrapbook serves to appropriate that distance as nostalgia. An interesting exception to these nostalgic images is a photograph of Javanese women wearing Western clothing and holding traditional instruments in their laps. An informational booklet included in the album describes the customs, economy, and arts of Javanese society and concludes by stating Java's interest in preserving political and economic ties with the United States. This image serves as a rare representation within the scrapbook of the Western culture shared by nonwhites and their stated aim to engage politically and commercially in modern society. Significantly, it is fixed on a page above a smaller image of indigenous Latin Americans in traditional dress, again emphasizing the contrast between the two.

A series of newspaper photographs emphasizes the implications of cultural exchange as the midway performers return to their homelands. The photographs are large in scale, carefully cut out, and inserted throughout the scrapbook. Their captions are preserved to varying degrees: "This Stalwart Samoan, late of Midway Plaisance" (scrapbook, page 2); "This Bedouin Woman of Pure Arab Stock, whose face was familiar to Midway Plaisance visitors, now sits in a desert tent and tells her tribe about the Glories of the Great World's Fair" (8); "This Sad-Eyed Cingalese Woman" (41); "This Tall Algerian was a famous Midway character during the World's Fair. Now under the banner of the cross and the crescent, he tells his ebony friends about the Great Exposition" (42).[42]

While acknowledging that the exposition has had a huge impact on the performers and their necessary readjustment on returning to their homelands, the clippings also reveal romanticized expectations about the nature of their reports at home. On the one hand, these images represent similarities between the people who worked on the midway—literally, they were featured as part of the exhibitions—and visitors to the exhibitions. Both groups would have to go through the process of reevaluating their perceptions of their worlds and their cultures in light of the incredible sharing of ideas that occurred at the fair. However, their message and ultimately their presence in the scrapbook also suggest a projection by Raddin and others onto these foreign types: musing about the reactions and the stories that non-Americans would tell as part of their postexposition recovery process can be seen as a way for Americans to displace and avoid confronting their need to process their own exposure to differences at the exposition. Including these images in scrapbooks can be read as a degree of identification or camaraderie with midway employees and performers, but their prominent reproduction primarily functions to reassure that the most drastic changes will occur in the direction of progress in foreign lands. In these images the exposition's effect on U.S. citizens is less clear to Raddin and the viewer.

An image of the *Santa Maria* closes the first section of the scrapbook. The caption with the photograph of the ship reads: "Columbus, the Great Navigator, sailed from Palos, Spain, August 3d, 1492, on the good ship Santa Maria, to find a New World." Like Columbus, Raddin and other fairgoers claimed to discover a new world at the Columbian Exposition. The first section of the scrapbook is a highly selective record of Raddin's reactions to and impressions of this great new world and her attempt to process the implications of this newfound sense of worldliness, with its potential and discomforts. Following a number of blank pages, the final section of the scrapbook is explicitly about the dismantling of the exposition and addresses the cultural questions, effects, and impressions it left behind.

The first article of the final section is headlined "Caravels Are Gone / Sailed from Jackson Park Yesterday Morning," once again using Columbus imagery to characterize the themes of the exposition presented in the scrapbook. This article describes the dismantling of the fair and the midway, the auctioning of furnishings from houses and sites such as the Javanese village, and the conflict over the Ferris wheel and the right to continue to run it. The next page includes an article about "novelties in the shops" and the aesthetic lessons learned from the Japanese (favorites of the Americans) as well as statistics on attendance at the exposition.[43] The last page includes an article entitled "The Close of the Fair" and the one on the canonization of Columbus.

The article on the exposition's closing, an attempt to look at the positive side, finds relief in the opportunity for life to return to normal. It argues that the intensity of the exposition experience cannot be sustained and that Chicago must get back to work; it is best that the exposition close now, in its glory. With this article, followed by the Columbus article, Raddin ends the scrapbook. These texts sum up the two closely linked narratives running through the scrapbook: the question of the effects of Columbus—or, more important, the effects of the discovery of new cultures and new worlds—and the idea that these effects are most strongly felt after the original contact.

"The Close of the Fair" suggests that it is time to get back to work, that one can move beyond the experience and return to "normal." Like the images of "The Stalwart Samoan" and his companions, the final texts in the scrapbook try to offer a comforting and nonthreatening conclusion to the fair experience. Yet the scrapbook's mere existence reveals that a return to normalcy is not so simply achieved. The underlying story of contact leaves a looming question: the effect of "discovery" will be great, but what will be its lasting repercussions for Raddin and others? Perhaps the lessons of the Columbus story suggested to her that cultural contact must proceed on a highly moral basis and that she should become an ardent supporter of missionary work, like many Methodists of the time. Or perhaps the experience convinced her of the value of worldly knowledge and learning, as reflected in her commitment to serving in the Northwestern University Guild, a women's organization founded to promote intellectual and cultural activities and develop an art collection, starting with objects purchased from the Columbian Exposition. The one indisputable fact is that she decided to make a scrapbook of the event, learning a novel form to record her exposure to novel ideas and cultures.[44]

Making History

Gertrude Raddin's Columbian Exposition scrapbook represents the way one individual began processing and exploring the global awareness that was projected onto the adventures of explorers such as Columbus and the Vikings and rediscovered at the exposition. As cultural products, scrapbooks serve a crucial function both personally and socially. They provide an opportunity for the construction of self, which can develop within a scrapbook as a dynamic relationship between personal and cultural identity. Patricia P. Buckler and C. Kay Leeper discuss scrapbooks as forms of expressive discourse, "enabling a new personality to achieve self-determination through manipulation of the world in which self is grounded."[45]

Raddin used the scrapbook to integrate her own family's visit to the Women's Building, La Rabida, the Midway Plaisance, and other exposition sites with discussions her religious community likely held regarding Columbus's character and perhaps even the need for new missionary work in far-off lands. The scrapbook is evidence of the mixing of her various social data: a woman, the oldest daughter in a merchant-class white family, the sister of a college-educated brother and sister-in-law, a Methodist, an Evanstonian living north of Chicago, and an American. These among other frames of reference shaped her pleasure and prerogative in processing her visit, producing her own view and narrative of the experience and creating a historical record that gives insight into her existence. Hence, the scrapbook represents a self-conscious engagement with a social world as part of the distinctive character of its author.

Throughout my study of this scrapbook I have reconstructed what this reaffirmed global self-awareness might have meant for Gertrude Raddin and others who experienced the World's Columbian Exposition. But what does it accomplish to study the scrapbook of a single individual whose mark on history is unclear? At what point can one begin to generalize from the information collected, even if patterns appear when one scrapbook is studied in conjunction with others?[46]

Many studies have focused on the exposition's effect on U.S. architecture (consider the City Beautiful Movement), trade and diplomacy, and the status of Chicago as an international center. It is more difficult to quantify its effect on individuals. In fact, the exposition made history when more than 27.5 million people came to Jackson Park in Chicago to visit it. Recent Columbian Exposition studies cited here have sought to determine the ideologies espoused by the fair and its organizers. However, mechanisms for assessing the impact of these ideologies on spectators are scant. Scrapbooks provide one such mechanism.

Raddin, for one, did not accept the promotion of Columbus as a hero. The theme of progress appealed to her more, perhaps because it was conveyed in compatible gender, religious, and patriotic overtones. In her scrapbook she was able to record her experience of the exposition as a debate-filled, selective, and engaged visit. The creative process visible in Raddin's scrapbook is a reminder that the World's Columbian Exposition mattered not because it acted on people but because they acted on it, choosing in what terms to incorporate their experience into their lives.

Raddin's scrapbook presents an opportunity to see how her experience of the Columbian Exposition affected her place in and outlook on history, progress, and cultural differences and commonalities. A sustained analysis of numerous scrapbooks could provide a greater understanding of the scope of the exposition's impact on these individuals, providing testament to their engagements with history on many levels—personal, social, cultural, public, and methodological.

In the end, Raddin's scrapbook is not simply a relic of the past but also an example of history in the making. History itself may be considered a collective scrapbook, shared on a public scale. It is the product of a process of culling facts and information in a variety of forms, which are then constructed into some kind of narrative by individuals and ultimately shared with an audience.[47] In making this comparison I remain aware of the difference between a private production for a small audience of family and friends and the aspirations and obligations of a historian writing for a larger public.[48] However, there are significant overlaps in the processes and, ultimately, the purposes of both exercises. The act of culling and selecting material is subjective and dependent on the available material. The intention is to represent a larger experience—a life, a trip, an event, a period of time. Both require a level of engagement with materials and knowledge that is mentally proactive and curious.

The study of scrapbooks can lead historians to become extremely self-conscious about the process of making of history, their motivations for writing history, and the forms their history might take to allow for both the fluid presentation of facts and the assertion of their individual interpretation. Ultimately, history serves a function similar to the scrapbook: it enables a person and the culture that promotes a given history to achieve self-determination through the manipulation of the objective world in which self, or subjectivity, is grounded.

[ELLEN GRUBER GARVEY]

5

〰〰

Scrapbook, Wish Book, Prayer Book

〰〰

Trade-Card Scrapbooks and the
Missionary Work of Advertising

I N THE 1880S, U.S. CHILDREN, especially girls, participated in a wide-spread fad of making scrapbooks from colorful chromolithographed adver-tising trade cards. Most of these scrapbooks consisted solely of these cards and mingled advertising trade cards, calling cards, religious verse and motto cards, and sometimes the decorative die-cut paper known appropriately enough as scrap. Advice literature of the period discussed the training functions of making and perusing scrapbooks and considered scrapbook making a discipline of self-construction, through which the taste of the scrapbook maker would be shaped by the act of carefully choosing and arranging the materials to be used. By selecting and categorizing material, scrapbook makers would internalize categories. The scrap-book would become, in effect, not a finished product but a record of self-creation, a "true history of our inmost selves—each addition to our scrap-book a milestone on our mental journey."[1]

Among the chromolithographed items collected in the scrapbooks considered here are two categories that seem part of very different registers: commercial adver-tising and Protestant religious messages. In making their scrapbooks children forged an intimate relationship with advertising and through their own labor integrated com-mercial information with religious and social messages.

If Religion Were a Thing That Money Could Buy:
Commodities and Protestantism

Advertising trade cards, with names of manufacturers or retailers and pictures that might or might not be related to the product, predominate in these scrapbooks. Ubiquitous in the 1880s but displaced in the 1890s as an advertising medium by magazine advertising, the cards helped create recognition of brand-name products and stimulate demand for them.[2] Cards reached the hands of customers through the agent who sold the merchandise to the storekeepers, and their popularity with customers gave the retailers an incentive to stock brand-name merchandise.[3] Advertisers considered it more important for the recipients to keep the card and see the name repeatedly than that the card convey a specific message about the product. If it impressed the recipient as having cost something, one advertising advice magazine wrote, "the very method you are employing shows that you are soliciting the goodwill of the customer."[4] Nineteenth-century viewers, especially children, found the color an alluring incentive to save the cards, in part because color itself conferred value.[5]

Because advertisers often used the generic cards known as stock cards—printed with flowers or birds and overprinted or stamped with the advertiser's name—trade cards were sometimes identical in form with calling cards or name cards or with proverb and psalm cards, which were overprinted with biblical verse.[6] Scrapbook compilers compounded the sense that there was little distinction among them by mingling them on their pages.

While merchants used the cards to inspire customers to keep the store or product name always at hand, churches and Sunday schools used cards as attractive rewards for attendance or for learning biblical passages and as incentives to keep biblical sayings at hand. The parallel must have seemed a pragmatic and logical one. Both the advertising and religious materials invited recipients to make the pictures and sayings a part of their intimate lives. And yet an examination of the scrapbooks in which children saved and arranged these materials reveals the contradictions the religious institutions confronted as they attempted to use the new materials of commodity culture.

The clash between commercial and religious messages is evident in the use one scrapbook compiler made of a card issued by the Sunday School Union and entitled "The Folly of Finery." It appears to have been saved and included in the scrapbook because it attractively illustrates the vice it condemns: a girl dressing in colorful clothing. In a "pretty lady" grouping common in scrapbooks, the compiler placed it next to a card of a little girl dressed in ribboned and ruffled finery on a beach, which advertised pianos, and below a picture of a woman in an elaborate mantilla, which advertised shoe blacking. The Sunday School Union card's monitory verse warns against children's "wearing fine ribbons and caps; / But this is a very ridiculous sight, / though they do not know it, perhaps." Ribbons and caps "make [children] look vulgar and vain."[7] In one sense, the compiler herself has subverted the card's meaning through her placement of it, and yet her apparent reading of it was determined by the Sunday School Union's use of the advertising medium to condemn what it makes attractive. The advertising discourse as a whole, a discourse in which commodities star, subsumes the individual advertiser's anticommodity message and makes the card speak for the attractiveness and desirability of commodities.

Other cards display incomplete biblical verses that depend on the reader's familiarity with Scripture for their resonance. One scrapbook compiler, for example, arranged small motto cards: "Your joy no man taketh from you"; "He sent His word and healed them"; "He was wounded for our transgressions"; "Ye are my witnesses, saith the Lord"; and "He hath done all things well." These mottoes depend on an assumed religious context, or at least familiarity with the biblical context from which they come, to make them intelligible as religious messages. But this compiler placed them on the same page with scraps in similar style used for valentines and calling cards, bearing such sentiments or dedications as "To my dear," "Hope sustain thee ever," and "Ever faithful and true," suggesting that all are to be taken in the same register. A different context thereby emerges. Moreover, because this page places the religious cards alongside ornamental scrap, they become visually equivalent to a cupid holding hearts in a saucepan, a zebra, and a fairy in a bouquet of flowers elsewhere on the page.

Like scriptural sayings, advertising cards and their pictures could speak eloquently to a compiler's wishes and experiences. In scrapbook making, prayer and fantasy may not have been far apart. Saving an advertising card of a sewing machine in an idealized home expresses a compiler's wish for a home prosperous enough to afford a sewing machine and grant her a life free of tedious hand sewing; surrounding it with calling cards, as one scrapbook keeper does, suggests that the idealized home includes a particular social network.[8] Obviously, this arrangement of a large card for a Hartford sewing machine ringed by smaller calling cards and reward-of-merit cards can be interpreted in other ways: perhaps the calling cards represent fellow members of a sewing circle, owners of sewing machines, people who use the compiler's machine, or people the compiler knows in Hartford; the reward cards might have been given for good sewing. A second, similar arrangement at the end of her book, using a different model of the Hartford sewing machine but again surrounded by calling cards, a reward-of-merit card, and a biblical verse card reinforces the sense that the sewing machine has an honored place in her real or desired home. In this sense, all these scrapbooks are wish books or even prayer books. However, what was wished for may not have been the merchandise but a particular relationship to the world expressed by the cards. That relationship was, nonetheless, mediated by the advertising image.

Handwritten notes in trade-card scrapbooks are relatively rare, but one maker here referred to as Anna Skinner (the name that appears on a card on the first page) amplifies her conversation with the cards with her own notations. On page 14 of her scrapbook, for example, Lord and Taylor cards are placed at each corner of the page,

Figure 5.1. *Personal notes and references within a trade-card scrapbook.* (Joseph Downs Collection of Manuscripts and Printed Ephemera, Henry Francis DuPont Winterthur Museum and Library, Scrapbook 3365, Thelma Mendsen collection)

each different in subject and format (see Figure 5.1). One, imprinted with "A Happy Christmas, Lord & Taylor, Grand Street," shows a basket of forget-me-nots; below it, the compiler has written in quotes: "'This flower is a sign to awaken thought, in friends who are *far away*.'" She verbally articulates the wish she projects onto the card, but scrapbook compilers who pasted pictures of flowers next to pictures of groups of happy children may have intended the same meaning.

One spread of Anna Skinner's book consists of a variety of religious and other messages: two handwritten calling cards (one each for Anna Skinner and Bertie), Christmas and Easter cards, some scrap, and a card of a child wearing beads that spell out "Horsford's Acid Phosphate." A newspaper clipping contains an anecdote of two "Sabbath School pupils." One asks how God made apples, and "little Ada replied, 'Just like He make light. He said, 'Let there be apples, and there was apples.'" Anna has written in red, within quotation marks, "'This all my hope, all my plea, for *me* the Saviour died'"—a line from the beginning of a Methodist hymn. At right angles to that, with a Christmas card half pasted over it, is this handwritten verse: "'The highest duties oft are found / Laying in the lowest ground / In sudden and unnoticed ways, / In household work or [illegible] days, / What e'er is done for God alone / Thy God [illegible] will own.'"

Another page spread may reflect the popular nineteenth-century hobby of extra-illustration, in which practitioners pulled apart books to insert illustrations commenting on the text. Here, however, it is difficult to tell whether the pictures or the handwritten texts are primary. Page 8 has three Thanksgiving pictures, without commercial messages. They surround the handwritten Bible verses, carefully enclosed in quotation marks, "'Be ye thankful,'" "'In everything give thanks,'" and "'Rejoice in the Lord always; &, again I say *rejoice*.'" Facing this arrangement, three cards with floral pictures from the Grand Central Flower Emporium and four other floral cards surround the handwritten lines from another Methodist hymn: "To comfort man to whisper hope / Whene'er his faith grown dim."[9] These are followed by two lines of doggerel—"There's scarce a spot where they are *not*, /And so, I love the Flowers"—before she returns to the hymn: "For whoso careth for the flowers / Will care much more for Him."

Scrapbooks can be tantalizingly illusive and allusive. It is impossible to know precisely what even Anna Skinner, who annotated her selections, had in mind. What is most remarkable is that using such aggressively public items as advertising cards, hymns, religious verse, autograph-book inscriptions, and other unidentified texts, she created such a private world. Perhaps these public materials seemed to her so self-evidently to express her sentiments, to be so articulate—"a sign to . . . friends who are far away"— that she did not need to explain herself more fully. And perhaps their value for her was that they held and carried her thoughts without overtly revealing them to people from whom she wished to conceal them—parents or prying siblings, perhaps.

Scrapbooks, then, evidently had a variety of uses for their compilers. And yet, even in as complex a book as Anna Skinner's, in which advertising cards were pressed into service to carry personal information and illustrate hymns, the cards are still advertising cards, and so wishes and prayers are now translated into their language.

Advertising Protestantism

Yet Anna Skinner's handwritten inscriptions of prayerful religious messages among her trade cards, seemingly praying for salvation and acid phosphate at once, are less idiosyncratic than they initially seem. Practices of advertising, commodity culture, and religious institutions overlap considerably. Religious groups draw on advertising techniques in creating trade cards—the Sunday School Union's card decrying vanity or, in another scrapbook, flowered stock cards commemorating a church-sponsored children's day issued by a local pastor, who also signed another card with a temperance message. But it was advertising that more commonly borrowed and elaborated older practices for inculcating religion. The boundary between advertising and promulgation of religion can look symmetrically permeable, with each drawing from the other, but advertising references were displacing religious references in the late nineteenth and early twentieth centuries. As T. J. Jackson Lears argues, interaction with commodities took on the cohering role that religious institutions once held.[10] Nationally, advertising and commodities increasingly provided a broadly intelligible set of cultural references.

In the 1880s, however, Protestant religious beliefs and the Bible were still a widely recognizable, easily accessible source of references. Advertisers not surprisingly used them on trade cards, producing elaborately printed biblical scenes with ads for root beer and patent medicines on the back.

The grouping of religious cards and trade cards in the scrapbooks thus reflects both advertisers' interest in eroding distinctions between the discourses of commodity culture and Protestantism and the religious institutions' desire to draw on the power of advertising. Further, girls themselves echoed and reinscribed commonalities between biblical verse and advertising by grouping them together in their scrapbooks. For girls and women, eliding distinctions between the discourses of religion and consumption enlarged the range of socially approved activities and settings available to them.

Churchgoing and shopping had much in common. In an anecdote printed in the *New York Times* in 1894, an English visitor to Philadelphia complained that the city lacked spiritual sustenance. At home, she said: "'Whenever I was dull or cross, I used to run up to Westminster and go into the Abbey. A half hour spent in meditation would always make me ashamed of myself, and I would go home strong and happy.'" An American woman replied: "'Why can't you do that in Philadelphia—there's Wanamaker's!'" Elaine Abelson, quoting the passage, notes that this may have been self-conscious parody but hears in it "the ring of truth for an increasingly secular and commercial culture."[11] Religion in the late-nineteenth-century

United States was a realm closely associated with women, in which approval and legitimation elsewhere in short supply were available to them.[12] Yet both this anecdote and the scrapbooks suggest that women used the familiar and approved discourse of religion to legitimize and annex approval for shopping and for interaction with commodities and their symbols.

Some religious institutions made even more deliberate use of advertising trade-card scrapbook making. Norman Mather Waterbury and Lucy McGill Waterbury, a U.S. missionary couple in India, used advertising materials in missionary work in a manner that resolutely elided advertising and religious messages. While Protestant religious beliefs and biblical passages served advertisers as a source of references, the popularity of trade cards and scrapbooks made them as appealing to religious proselytizers as the printing of the cards had been to Sunday-school groups. And yet the apparently tidy symmetry here—advertisers use religion, religion uses advertising—conceals the issue of what is being advertised when trade cards are put to use promulgating Christianity.

Mary Waterbury of Saratoga Springs, New York, reported in an 1882 letter to *The Helping Hand*, a Baptist monthly, that before her brother and sister-in-law, Norman and Lucy Waterbury, sailed for Madras in 1881, "they suggested that some picture-books made of advertising cards might be useful in the mission work there."[13] She invited her Sunday-school class to make them. "All came, each bringing a package of bright advertising cards. . . . Soon, all were seated about tables, busily engaged in arranging and pasting their pictures. The work itself was fascinating, but the thought that they might be helping to tell 'the story of the Cross' increased the enjoyment; and, when the call to the dining-room came, none seemed in a hurry to go."[14]

Telling "the story of the Cross" evidently referred not to a narrative arrangement of the cards but rather the use to which the books were to be put. Lucy Waterbury, writing from India, thanked the class for the books: "I did not believe that a class of girls could reveal such possibilities in a heap of advertising cards," she marveled. She reported that one scrapbook had already been used as a school prize for one of the "[high] caste girls," whose jewelry she described at some length; individual cards had been given to "pariah" children, "'real heathen' you would say, if you should see them.'" The advertising cards were powerful rewards. Lucy Waterbury reported in *The Helping Hand*:

One Sunday, after teaching the children a short verse, I promised picture-cards to all who could recite the verse on the following Sabbath. To my surprise, not only those to whom I had taught the verse repeated it, but some whom I had never seen before recited it quite perfectly. They had learned it from the others in the hope of getting a card too. You see, they value these bright advertising cards enough to do real work for one of them.

A few days before Christmas, a package of cards came to us from a Sunday-school class in New York. We selected the cards without printing upon the back, and wrote upon each a text of Scripture in Telugu. On Sunday, Christmas day, we gave each member of the Sunday-school one of the cards. There were some heathen present; and we were pleased to see that, after reading the texts, they put their cards carefully away to take home with them. We have written on many more cards since then; and, whenever we have an opportunity, we give them to those whom we hope they may help. The cards that are printed on the backs, we give to those who cannot read. They are excellent rewards for attendance, good behavior, etc. If you could see the little dark faces light up at [the] sight of some card which you would throw aside as worthless, you would feel repaid for the trouble of sending it.[15]

For the Indian children, the cards were proposed as part of a substitution: interest the "heathen" in the brightly colored cards, and they will absorb the Bible along the way. They are premiums—not for buying coffee but for showing interest in Christianity. From the Waterburys' point of view, a persuasive medium could evidently be used for any end, because the qualities that made the cards good advertising for products were fungible, available to appropriation for religious propaganda use. The trade cards became items of Western largess, as well as rewards for learning: Lucy Waterbury noted in her diary that she gave a card to a woman who cleaned her house to give to her son.

What the Indian children actually thought of the cards is not known, but for the U.S. children involved in missionary scrapbook making, the cards gained spiritual as well as commercial value. Advertising cards were already firmly stitched to fantasy. Their use in missionary work enhanced their value as a commodity that was ordinary and worthless in the United States but that would make its possessor valued and powerful in another setting—a fantasy familiar from Mark Twain's 1889 *A Connecticut Yankee in King Arthur's Court* and other works.

What the cards advertise is Westernness—Western goods, clothing, houses, culture—associated with the missionaries' Christianity. For a missionary who believed that "heathenness" is a physical attribute ("'real heathen' you would say, if you should see them"), Christianity was similarly visible in pictures and idealizations of U.S. life. Lucy Waterbury's Christian mission included Westernizing Indian children, readying them for a Western, Christian order. The advertising cards touted not only the commercial product but also an idealized vision of Western life inextricably and totemically linked to the advertised products and the institution of advertising itself. Images of Westernness become the reward for Western behavior.

Reasonably, then, Lucy Waterbury seemingly made no distinction between religious verse cards and advertising cards: All were bait—attractive rewards—and represented much the same attributes. When she briefly acknowledged a slight difference between religious and advertising cards, she saw it as easily bridged by writing a religious verse on the back and leaving the commercial message on the front untouched. If the recipient could not read, the card functioned as pure reward, color and attractiveness without language. It is telling that in the United States, the term *missionary* became slang for a commercial traveler, or drummer, whose work included the distribution of trade cards to retailers.[16]

The Waterburys cast a wide net back home seeking cards. To save "heathen souls," Sunday-school classes in New York City; Hartford, Connecticut; Missouri; and Saratoga Springs, New York, collected and sent cards advertising sewing thread, stove polish, and retailers. Nor were the Waterburys the only missionaries using these materials. The Women's Missionary Union Society of America for Heathen Lands, a multidenominational organization that did not include the Waterburys' group, reported on money and goods raised for missionary work and referred to sending "the usual assortment of dolls, scrap-books, material for fancy work, etc.," in 1886 and 1887 and collecting, among other things, "five hundred sixty-five Christmas and other cards" and "a large number of cards sent by Miss Shubuck's class in Camden, N.J." for Calcutta. These materials sometimes had powerful significance for their donors, especially if they had been transfigured by their placement in scrapbooks. An inventory of gifts received for missionary work recorded an instance of sentimental value accrued to advertising ephemera, then passed along to Indian children: "Says a friend from St. Louis, consigning boxes to us for Calcutta: 'As I write these figures of valuation, I think how little they express the worth of some of the contents of the boxes. There is a doll and a scrap book, begun for this box by her own dear hands, the treasure of a darling gone to be with Jesus. She was not quite ten years old.'"[17]

A Miss Winthrop wrote from India in 1887 of the contents of the box her mission received: "There are other things to be glad of, scrap-books, pictures, etc. We hope all the bands and the individuals who have worked for us this year will reap the blessing promised to those who do their utmost for the Master."[18]

Already quasi-religious artifacts, the cards must have been ennobled in the eyes of those U.S. children who collected them for the missions or who, as they pasted down their cards, believed that they were "helping to 'tell the story of the Cross'" and doing "the utmost for the Master."

Trade-card scrapbooks, like other forms of advertising, taught the fused gospel of Americanness and commodities to U.S. immigrants as well. Giving a trade-card scrapbook initiated a new immigrant into the national culture. In Willa Cather's *My Ántonia*, also discussed by Jennifer L. Bradley in this volume, ten-year-old Jim Burden, recently arrived in Nebraska from Virginia in the 1880s, makes a picture-book for his Bohemian immigrant neighbor, Yulka Shimerda, Ántonia's younger sister. On the homemade scrapbook pages, Jim "grouped Sunday-School cards and advertising cards which I had brought from my 'old country.'"[19] The cards are linked to the project of teaching Yulka to read and speak English. Jim hears that the Shimerdas were pleased with their presents. But distributing this vision of U.S. wealth, recirculating these gifts from the world of commerce, proves problematic: when the Shimerda family subsequently visits the Burdens, Mrs. Shimerda eyes the household goods enviously and demandingly and is given a cooking pot. Ántonia tells Jim that his grandfather, who is rich, should help her family. While her statement is more directly related to the Burdens' household goods—and Mrs. Burden tells her grandson that it is seeing her children want for things that makes Mrs. Shimerda grasping—the juxtaposition of the scenes suggests that the advertising cards effectively incite desire for a life filled with more goods. Jim has imagined himself generous in giving out pictures of wealth, tokens of plenty, as a sample of his heritage, but he is offended when the Shimerdas understand them as direct representations rather than good wishes and ask his family for the goods of which they have received pictorial samples.

Although the Indian children saw trade cards with exotic pictures of material goods that might never appear in their own world, thus remaining as ethereal as the religious goods, Yulka and the Shimerdas must learn to read the language of advertising as well as English to understand that the advertisements are not promises. For those already acculturated to advertising, who understood that the cards did not promise the goods, they offered a different sort of pleasure. The cards not only existed as identical duplicates but also pointed to the still-novel mass-produced goods, each package a duplicate of the next. Collecting these duplicated cards brought into the home the novelty and glamour of the new commercial realm of mass-produced goods, in which everyone could possess the identical item. The collector could amass many of these cards, which both represented mass-produced goods and were mass-produced goods themselves.

Although chromolithographed advertising cards were plentiful, the scrapbook compilers treated them as though they were not. They saved them, they treasured them within the often-elaborate gold-stamped bindings of the scrapbooks, and they arranged them on the page to maximize their appeal.

In incorporating them into what one commentator has called a salvage art, like quilting, collectors fitted cards into a paradigm of scarcity, in which colorful printed material was valuable and worth saving.[20] Saving all scraps was a virtue advocated by housekeeping books earlier in the century. In 1835, for example, Lydia Maria Child told her readers that "the true economy of housekeeping is simply the art of gathering up all the fragments, so that nothing is lost. . . . Nothing should be thrown away so long as it is possible to make any use of it, however trifling that use may be."[21]

Displaying these virtuously saved cards lavishly on the page enhanced the sense of abundance promoted by the scrapbooks as a whole and created visual celebrations of plenty. Compilers demonstrated that goods and their surrogates—images of goods and cards given out on behalf of goods—were so plentiful that they were available for many sorts of treatment. Cards could be simply thrown together on a page or elaborately arranged, left to represent their publisher's message or required to speak for their compilers.

It was the work and play of amassing the cards, sorting them, and pasting them down that taught scrapbook makers how to read advertising, how to fantasize with its seeming promises within the social worlds of home and religious life without seeing it as overwhelming or as a repeated betrayer. Making scrapbooks from advertising cards allowed girls an area of expertise and authority even as it trained them in skills that already had acknowledged value. Now let us examine more closely the skills and habits of looking that scrapbook compilers cultivated as they pasted advertising cards into scrapbooks.

Taking Possession of the World

Scrapbook making was a popular hobby during the late nineteenth century, as indicated by the articles, memoirs, and instructions in women's housekeeping manuals and girls' books on pastimes and amusements. An 1884 housekeeping-hints book, for example, assumes that scrapbook making is a routine household activity, mentioning it casually in the course of advising the reader to keep two teakettles, so that hot water can always be ready "when the children want to make paste for scrap-books, or Lucy wants to do up her lace ruffles, or somebody wants hot lemonade for a cold."[22]

Scrapbooks could serve as cheap, colorful picture books for young children. Janet Ruutz-Rees's book of home amusements fits scrapbooks into an ages-of-childhood scheme with pictures largely confined to childhood: "The scrap book is absolutely invaluable in the nursery; from it the child gains his first ideas of pictures, of form and color; then, later on, the growing boy has his book for quaint oddities and scraps, and the budding girl preserves all sorts of sentimental poetry—shows her appreciation of an author by copious extracts copied into her scrap-book."[23] Another writer saw scrapbooks and their creators as inextricably intertwined: "We are all Scrap-books, and happy is he who has his Pages systematized, whose clippings have been culled from sources of truth and purity and who has them firmly Pasted into his Book."[24]

Strategies for Collecting

Trade-card scrapbooks primarily reflect the interest of the compilers in amassing and arranging several kinds of chromolithographed materials. In this, they are like the scrapbooks described in the manuals and amusement books, especially those to be made for toddlers to look at, in which the pictures' colorfulness is central. E. W. Gurley's 1880 manual on making scrapbooks also suggests that arranging the material is important middle-class training: under guidance, children "will soon show much skill and taste in arranging their little books, and also grow into a love for order and beauty."[25]

Middle-class Victorian Americans were passionate collectors and classifiers.[26] Collecting was praised as good training in observation and the valued skill of assigning and recognizing categories, of visually and tangibly taking possession of the world by naming and classifying it. Advertisers welcomed children's interest in the cards for two reasons: to persuade them to choose specific brands when they were sent on errands to stores and, through the children, to get the cards into the home to be seen by adult shoppers. They wanted people to notice the brand name and remember it. Some trade-card collectors evidently did: they classified cards according to product or manufacturer, regardless of the appearance of the card. One compiler made a page of cards for products sold by Ayers—sarsaparilla, hair tonic, pills, and so forth—grouping them despite the cards' different styles and formats. Similarly, another compiler followed the lead of the manufacturer E. S. Wells, whose cards themselves made unlikely connections between the company's Rough on Rats rat poison and its patent medicines such as Wells' Health Renewer, Mother Swan's Worm Syrup, and Buchupaiba kidney disease cure; he or she grouped cards for all the Wells products on one spread.[27] Advertising trade writing of the period suggests that this use suited the intentions of the advertisers, who wanted people to think of the cards in relation to the products and who liked advertising their own names, as well as the products. The practice is also akin to the sorting and categorizing of nine-teenth-century nature study—grouping acorns and oak leaves, for example.

Some compilers collected cards in series, hoping to assemble a complete set. Complete sets might tell a story or define a category—for example, the military uniforms of different countries. Collecting a series might prompt children to act as an auxiliary sales force. One child boasted that he "made advertising pay" by calling on other households and coaxing them to buy the brand of coffee for which the cards were given.[28]

Another strategy—arranging cards by generic product category, such as thread or perfumes—highlights the product and its uses. These compilers show their attention to the categories of goods, possibly comparing them or recreating the array at the dry-goods counter. Within the 1880s rationale and understanding of collecting, seeking out trade cards and amassing them were understood as sharpening the collector's eye to notice more trade cards as well as other forms of advertisement, learn their language, and learn about the world through them. Interests "naturally" sprang up in relation to them. Among stamp collectors, "no lad who studies his stamp-book can be ignorant of changes of rule and nationalities," according to one writer on collecting; similarly, no girl who collected trade cards could remain ignorant of brand-name goods, their claims, and the images and narratives associated with each.[29]

That several retailers might use the same card design allowed some collectors to group cards strictly by design. Stock cards with the same picture of flowers or ducks might be used both for various advertisers and for calling cards, so a collector could group several cards (identical except for their messages) according to retailer, manufacturer, or individuals or blank message space. Juxtaposing chromolithographed blanks and advertising cards might also call attention to the value of the blank card to the compiler and the coup of having gotten it free from the advertiser. People often knew how much the chromo card had cost its purchaser because they themselves had bought chromolithographed items such as calling cards with their own names printed on them. The same cards listed in a catalog for direct sale to consumers for decorative use were distributed free as advertising addressed to some of those same consumers. This overlap between the advertising and nonadvertising uses of stock cards probably made advertising trade cards even more desirable, while the overlap between calling cards, blanks, and trade cards gives the trade card a quasi-familiar and even quasi-familial status. In these displays the advertiser is positioned as a social caller, a friend, or an acquaintance who leaves a card on the silver tray on the hall stand.

But more often and more suggestively, scrapbook arrangements cross lines of product, manufacturer, and designer to group pictures of animals, travelers, children at the seashore, or flowers, regardless of what the cards advertise. As in the Anna Skinner scrapbook, the groupings override not only categories of products but also social categories: trade cards are pasted next to calling cards, reward-of-merit cards given as prizes in school, Sunday-school verse cards, holiday greeting cards, and decorative die-cut embossed paper scrap. Some groupings make elaborate, even quilt-like patterns, using the cards' colors, intensity, or design as compositional elements.

When compilers made patterns with the cards in their scrapbooks, they demonstrated and developed their ability to make fine distinctions in shades and combinations of color. This was a valued ability in dressmaking and home decoration, as the ever-finer division of the palette concocted by the growing dye industry brought more elaborate standards of color use to sewing. In the 1870s, according to Elaine Abelson, a feminist could complain that for women, "as much time is devoted to matching a peculiar shade of olive-green as would go to the writing of an epic upon Jerusalem," while in the 1880s and 1890s a middle-class woman might often be preoccupied with matching colors for sewing.[30]

Duplicate cards were particularly useful for making patterns, and scrapbook compilers seized on the availability of copies of identical cards for other sorts of play as well. One compiler, for example, set side by side two copies of a stock card for Niagara starch showing a toddler in a scanty shift falling off one shoulder and barely covering the thighs; then she neatly colored in one card with ink to give the child a long-sleeved, leg-covering dress. Adding the new dress allows coloring book–like play; in addition, it converts the figure into a dressed and undressed paper doll and puts the compiler in the position of kindly providing clothing to an inadequately clothed child. Keeping the unadorned card heightens what the child has accomplished and lets her hold onto the difference between the plain card and the card that she has embellished.

Telling the Story of the Family

Duplicate cards allowed other scrapbook makers to create more complex scenarios. Consider some of the choices one scrapbook maker in the 1880s made in laying out her pages. In this scrapbook containing numerous duplicate trade cards, many figures

have been cut free of their surrounding cards with meticulous care, leaving the commercial message intact.[31] Cutting out the figures permitted a different kind of manipulation of the cards. One page has a Rising Sun stove-polish card at its center with
two unrelated panels. In the first panel, an angry white housewife chases two sneaky
white salesmen who have tried to sell her an inferior product. In the other, a black
couple and child kneel, staring at their reflection in the brilliantly shining stove polished with Rising Sun. The compiler cut up another copy of the card to redistribute
its figures in new configurations and pasted them on the page surrounding it, along
with new material. The kneeling black couple now kneels to a large yellow marigold,
probably from a seed catalog. Cutout sneaky salesmen flank the card. Below, the
cutout angry housewife now points to another cutout, unrelated to the card, of a
woman holding a girl on her knee. Possessing identical copies of the same material
let this compiler move characters almost magically from their original relationships and
old frames into new narratives. They take on an independent existence that nonetheless continues to refer ·to the original advertising source.

As this compiler's rearrangement hints, the scrapbook could speak of family relationships—something like a photograph album. The same scrapbook, which begins
with a series of cards with no visible ad message, is entitled "The Day of an Infant"
and follows a toddler through a day of activities. A later full page is headed "Baby,"
with the word written in letters cut from some other printed source (see Figure 5.2).
Although the compiler could easily have handwritten the word "Baby" or "Babies,"
he or she instead stayed within her strategy of using only chromolithographed,
massproduced materials, carefully cutting out the letters.

This page explodes with cutout chromolithographed pictures of babies and
young children. At the center, the page's only intact card becomes a windowlike frame
from which the babies peer as they crowd around a giant spool of Clark's thread.
The squared form seems to cordon off this group of children from the other babies,
who carom around the page. Another copy of this card has been cut up, redistrib-
uting the children so they are both contained and dispersed, with cutout children
accompanying those still contained in cards. Two copies of a Clark's thread card of
a baby holding a spool of the thread in the form of a rattle have been cut away from
their backgrounds and arranged in a scalloped lower border.

The compiler thus uses this scrapbook as a proto–snapshot album, rearranging
advertising images to refer to the compiler's own family or his or her own desires.
She makes other deliberate choices in her arrangements. The book does not follow
earlier models of arranging studio photographs, such as slipping cabinet-sized studio photographs into frames in an album. Her work is closer to the "cutomania"

Figure 5.2. *Family configurations created using commercial materials.* (Joseph Downs Collection of
Manuscripts and Printed Ephemera, Henry Francis DuPont Winterthur Museum and Library, Scrapbook 3365,
Thelma Mendsen collection)

albums from the 1860s on, in which, as Robert Sobieszek notes, alongside likenesses of aunts, uncles, and siblings appear photographs of such varied subjects "that their rationale for inclusion at times defies analysis."[32] But she does not go as far as other scrapbook makers and photograph-album keepers who cut up the small, relatively inexpensive studio portraits known as carte-de-visite photographs to arrange pictures of their friends and family into scenes that reflected their daily activities. Some such creators drew or painted a parlor scene to group pictures of family members so that they all appear to be together in the scene. Certainly the children and babies of this trade-card scrapbook could have been formed into realistic tableaux. And a few scrapbook makers did create scrap houses, in which each page or spread is a room filled with furniture and figures, as discussed in this volume by Beverly Gordon.

The compiler could also have grouped cards into the kind of illustrations suggested in Lina and Adelia Beard's *American Girls' Handy Book* (1887).[33] Complaining that scrapbooks of "pictured advertising cards" contain nothing but monotonous "row after row of cards," the Beards direct readers to cut up advertising cards and reassemble parts to illustrate nursery rhymes and stories. Their examples show the figures cut entirely free from their trade cards, with brand names obliterated. But scrapbook makers seem not to have followed this suggestion, perhaps because it ran against the marketplace attractions the cards offered their compilers. Scrapbook makers resisted allowing the figures to be subsumed within a narrative over which adults had obvious authority and which was already considered appropriate for children.

The Beards suggest that the topic of children's play be restricted to a proper children's world. But trade-card scrapbooks offered children an area of apparent autonomy and acknowledged expertise not only in the arrangement of cards but also in the knowledge of modern products, gained independently of parents or school, in which they might stand on an equal footing with parents. The new commercial discourse appeared to offer new freedoms, some of which would have been lost in reinserting its material into already acceptable topics of play. Although trade cards were, of course, produced by adults, and the albums in which they were saved often expensive enough that their purchase was presumably bankrolled by adults, many cards saved in the scrapbooks offer views of a world of children in autonomous play, without adult supervision. That adults did not entirely control trade cards' circulation and considered them of little value seems to have made the trade-card scrapbook an area of relatively free expression and play where some cards' imagery could be read as subverting the adult world. Play with advertising was mediated by the distant and apparently nonauthoritarian hand of commerce, rather than by the close inspection of parents.

The creator of the "Baby" page, then, instead of positioning the pictures of babies within nursery-rhyme narratives, preserved their ties to advertising and even translated the common imagery of plentiful goods to her arrangement of cards. Elsewhere, whole trade cards are amassed to create and reinforce visions of plenty; here the compiler does the same thing in grouping pictures of babies in virtual cornucopias, which may refer to her own family or desires. A compiling, amassing vision pervades relationships with people as well as commodities.

Yet a compiler could choose pictures to identify with her own family and familiar surroundings. As Janet Ruutz-Rees asserts in her chapter on scrapbooks: "The children who delight in scrap-books are not usually impressed by the style of the pictures. The charm for them lies in the details, in the figure of a woman that represents mamma, or of the kitten that is the exact likeness to the little beholder of the nursery pet."[34]

The distance between late-nineteenth- and twenty-first-century ideas of visual representation and physical resemblance becomes apparent here. A 1900 scrapbook made by a recent widow to show her young grandchildren what their grandparents' farm and farmwork looked like had no original photographs but derived its pictures entirely from seed catalogs and advertising pamphlets. The grandmother's captions for the pictures asserted that these were depictions of the late grandfather or uncles at work—not that the people in the pictures resembled them or worked in a similar fashion. So beneath an advertising photograph of a sledge pulling a log she wrote, "Jim, taking a load of logs to the mill, to be carved into boards for Uncle Will to use in repairing the barn at Rock Spring Farm." A picture of an old man and a dog bearing the printed caption "Only the companionship of a dog" has the handwritten legend, "Grandpa is telling his Dog 'Jessie' how he wishes he could see his little Morris Andrews." She similarly included printed pictures of children whom she says are Morris Andrews, the six-year-old to whom the book is addressed, or "Dorothy, a little bigger."[35]

An adult compiling a book for young children might have felt more license to make claims about the pictures or felt that collapsing the distance between the grandfather and the model would help the child feel closer to his memory. The grandmother herself noted: "Most of the pictures in this book were cut from the advertising pamphlets Grandpa left in his desk at Rock Spring Farm," so their provenance is an extrarepresentational tie, too. Perhaps their ongoing life in the commercial realm adds to her sense that she is keeping him alive. But to assert that a drawing or even a photograph can be a nonspecific, generic picture—anyone talking to a dog can plausibly be Grandpa talking to a dog—is a reminder that nineteenth-century viewers did not share the contemporary standard of photographic verisimilitude. (The common late-nineteenth-century comment that a photograph is or is not a good likeness of its subject, for example, is likely to strike a present-day reader as peculiar and wrongheaded: we assume that the photograph is the correct measure of what someone looks like, although we may agree that we have never seen the person look that way.) The notion that a photograph can be nonspecific also suggests an assumed ability to disregard particulars of resemblance and identify photographs with people familiar to the viewer.

At least one advertiser deliberately played to the crossover between the intimacy of owning a photograph of someone and seeing the photograph's subject as an acquaintance. The Lydia Pinkham patent-medicine company invited collectors to see its company symbol as an intimate in one brown-on-tan chromolithograph closely resembling a sepia-tone carte-de-visite photograph of the sort that people often exchanged with one another.[36] Its instruction, "Put this in your album," leaves open whether that album was a scrapbook or family photograph album and perhaps acknowledges that the distance between the two had diminished. The same principle was at work for compilers as they learned to identify their families with characters pictured in the trade cards, fantasize about themselves within the scenarios of the advertising cards, and use the advertising images as mediums for self-expression.

Souvenirs of Desire

Scrapbook compilers may not have understood the cards as exact representations of goods or as promises of goods but sometimes at least as souvenirs of goods and stores, memory prompts for recalling the experience of plenty. Even more than mail-order catalogs, which presented an overwhelming profusion of goods in black and white, a scrapbook allowed participation from afar in the luxurious and colorful pleasure of shopping, bringing it near. Preserving the experience or imagination of it in a scrapbook would keep it fresh. As one scrapbook-making instructor put it, a scrapbook is "not a grave in which you have buried all these good and beautiful thoughts, but a living treasure always open to your hand."[37] Collecting two- and three-dimensional props as memory prompts was a late-Victorian preoccupation.[38] While the scrapbook thus memorializes memorabilia and souvenirs of shopping, it also preserves, replicates, and trains the maker in the department-store experience of inadequacy: the single commodity (or advertising card) can be only an insufficient recreation of the spectacular celebration of abundance of department-store display. An abundance of flowers on the earth ("scarce a spot where they are *not*") is, for Anna Skinner and the poet she quotes, a synecdochic figure for God's favor and generosity. But an abundance of flowered cards on a scrapbook page gestures toward the inadequacy of the collection of images: there are always more to amass and paste down. No single trade card was enough. More and more of them must be arranged on the page in a profusion of color and form.

The disparate and contradictory materials together distanced the experience from the ordinary.[39] Trade cards became both a tantalizing reminder of the visual abundance of stores and products and a take-home sample of it—luxurious color, a surplus of information, and, as well, a surplus of desire.

The cards were gifts from the world of commerce, even trophies for shopping. That the present was mass produced may have made it more desirable: not only did its duplication offer new ways to play with it, but also the collector had the pleasure of being like every other girl. As the national distribution of brand-name goods shaped a national vocabulary, trade cards contributed to a national children's culture: all over the country, children were pasting cards for Lautz's soap into their scrapbooks.

A child could compare her scrapbook with another's, could imitate another child's work or see what unique pattern he made of the same material, could send her scrapbook off to India along with others made by Sunday-school classmates to convert the heathen to Christianity or the desire for Western goods and their pictures.

Products were made in localities, in different regions of the country often sharply divided from one another by history, culture, and economics. National distribution and promotion of goods, however, made consumption a unifying bond that overrode regionalism. The advertisement reader's awareness of a national culture of advertising defined any purchase or acquisition of a card as participation in this national culture. Although scrapbooks from different regions have cards from different retailers, the scrapbook itself, like the department store, became a unifying frame. Trade-card scrapbooks from different parts of the country are identifiably trade-card scrapbooks and part of the national creation of trade-card scrapbooks, replicated in many homes. Through scrapbook making, advertising became part of a national culture duplicated home by home.

6

〜〜〜〜

Scrapbook Houses for Paper Dolls

〜〜〜〜

Creative Expression, Aesthetic Elaboration, and
Bonding in the Female World

O NE OF THE MOST DISTINCTIVE and intriguing types of scrapbook is the "paper dollhouse," popular in the United States between approximately 1875 and 1920. Such albums are known by a variety of names. In their own time, they were called homes for paper dolls, book houses, or scrapbook houses. More recently, they have also been descriptively referred to as collage albums. Such varied rubrics hint at the multiple levels of meaning of this largely forgotten genre. Each scrapbook functioned as a conceptual house, with double-page spreads containing collages of individual rooms; pasted-in pictures constituted the architectural features, furniture, and accessories. The books were a type of amusement; they were made for and sometimes by children and played a memorable role in many of their growing-up years. However, they were much more than toys. They embodied the experience and values of the turn-of-the-century female domestic domain—they were aesthetically saturated and people oriented, and they helped inculcate or reinforce those qualities for several generations of girls. At the same time, paper dollhouses were also important to adults, who were, often as not, their creators. They functioned as aesthetic outlets—as self-contained, imaginary worlds into which the women could pour their creative energy. The aesthetic power of the albums can still be felt today; opening one of these books often produces astonishment or delight. Many are startling in their detail, sophistication, and depth. The paper-dollhouse genre represents, in fact, an early but largely unknown and unrecognized form of collage. It warrants closer examination as an art form, as a part of childhood, and as a representation of women's values and domestic experience in a particular era.

This essay explores this form of scrapbook with just such a holistic approach. Through close textual analysis of the advice literature and a thorough examination of extant paper dollhouses (including the handful of commercially produced copies that appeared toward the end of the genre's popularity and reinforced its conventions), I reconstruct the history of the genre, its characteristics, and its multiple meanings.[1] I use the book houses to look at women's lives on their own terms—their assumptions and foci and the way they presented their imagined selves. I include considerable descriptive detail because that is what the makers were concerned with, and I discuss the steps they went through because to understand the genre as an art form, we must understand the creative process.

A House of Their Own

Every paper-dollhouse scrapbook was a self-contained, particularized world. The rooms were freestanding but conceptually (and sometimes physically) linked to the others surrounding them. They unfolded successively; the first page of the album would represent the porch or entryway, for example, and the next two would represent the front hall. Moving into the subsequent pages was like moving farther and farther into the reaches of the house. True to the current architectural standard and the Victorian mindset, this meant that the more personal spaces were toward the back. All the books followed the same general conceptual template, with rooms such as parlors, bedrooms, and kitchens placed in their expected spatial positions. The individual house maker could elaborate on the form as much as she wished, however, and some expanded to more than forty separate spaces, including dressing rooms, pantries, backyard gardens, and even outdoor cottages. The spaces themselves were also elaborated according to personal taste, dependent to some extent on the types of printed images of furniture and other household objects the house maker had come up with. These images were taken from magazines or commercial sources such as trade catalogs and greeting cards. They were typically arranged against backdrops of wallpaper or other specialty papers and were sometimes embellished with hand-drawn or painted vignettes. Some house makers made slits or pockets in furnishings such as staircases or beds into which they could slide freestanding paper dolls, but because most of the rooms included pasted-in images of people engaged in various domestic activities, the books were complete unto themselves even without separate "inhabitants."

The paper dollhouse appears to have become popular in the last quarter of the nineteenth century, when the printed material found in mass-market magazines, catalogs, and advertisements had begun to proliferate. The idea of making an architectural setting for paper dolls was not new at that time, although they had not previously been arranged in books. Sheets of pasteboard with printed images of furniture and people that might be cut out and arranged according to personal taste were available in Germany as early as the eighteenth century, and similar sets were sold in the United States by the Victorian era. Some, such as "The Girl's Delight," available about 1850, came complete with images of architectural details, including ceilings and floors.[2] This type of commercial set was a forerunner of the paper dollhouse, but the genre can be better understood as part of the scrapbook mania of the latter part of the century. Only when there was an abundance of easily procured printed material could individuals amass a large collection of images of their own choosing, and the idea of compiling them in a book must have arisen as a logical extension of scrapbook keeping.[3]

By 1880, when the first article about paper dollhouses appeared in the "Fun for the Fireside" column in *Godey's Lady's Book* as a "help to mother," the idea was already said to be familiar. The author, Jessie Ringwalt, gave detailed instructions for fashioning the houses, suggesting they might be made in any convenient blank book (including a ledger or schoolbook) with pages of at least eight by nine inches. Her directions outlined the style that was to stay popular for generations, including the front page of the book representing the front door. The house was presented overall as if it were "being viewed by a guest," and the general goal was to make each room into a "perfect" vignette. The model was theatrical; some rooms were even flanked on either side by a drawn curtain or portiere, rather like a stage set revealing an ongoing play (see Figure 6.1). Descriptive details in the advice literature were also highly dramatic. Ringwalt noted that a "pretty little girl-doll" in the dining room should be placed so that "she seems just ready to spring upon the table," and the doors of a pasted sideboard should remain half open so as "to suggest a meal in progress."[4] Each collage or page was in effect a miniature two-dimensional tableau that echoed the kind of three-dimensional staged vignette popular at this time. There were tableaux at public and private "parlor theatricals," for example, and tableaux-like booths at charity fairs or bazaars. Historians have discussed the rise of these amusements in the nineteenth century, arguing that they reflected a self-conscious theatricality in social relationships. These paper-dollhouse pages were one of the ways in which women expressed this idea.[5]

Aesthetic Elaboration and a Love of Detail

Ringwalt also indicated the importance of the fanciful, textural details that made these collages come alive. Curtains might be made of lace or net, she explained; gilt or silver paper could be used for door knobs and mirrors, and "gorgeous flowers" could rest on a golden table. Even a figure in the front hall would ideally appear in a "fanciful costume, well bedizened with buttons." Ringwalt's language expressed how much pleasure these houses could afford their makers and users. She spoke of the "many unconsidered trifles [scraps of paper and so forth] that constitute the treasured wealth of children" and the inventiveness involved in constructing the books.

Figure 6.1.   *The unidentified maker of this dramatically presented album (1903) conceived of it as a grand house, which she dubbed Kenilworth Inn. Here, bright red crepe paper curtains are gathered back with "cords" of metallic paper stars, and the garland and platters are hand colored.* (Joseph Downs Collection of Manuscripts and Printed Ephemera, Henry Francis DuPont Winterthur Museum and Library, folder 36 [85 x 41.3]) <JF: note from Tucker: Check in permission from Winterthur if [85 x 41.3] must be included.

She indicated too the satisfaction working with miniatures could provide, claiming the "very heart" of the house she described was its own dollhouse, pasted into the playroom. Attention to tiny and aesthetically pleasing detail is perhaps the most salient quality of the paper dollhouse and a strong part of its fascination.[6] The art historian Linda Roscoe Hartigan noted that her first encounter with pages of scrapbook houses was a "sheer thrill." She was brought under the spell of their "dizzying" array of detail and their "flirtation with scale, space, texture and pattern," described as "disarmingly picturesque."[7] The experience reverberated with her strongly.

The saturated color and exuberant minutiae of these books was an elaboration of what appeared in actual homes. On a typical double-page spread, the room might be divided into three or four horizontal bands, representing respectively the floor, walls, ceiling and other architectural features. Very much as if she were arranging a three-dimensional space, the house maker would first organize these background areas and then arrange the furniture, accouterments, and people. In many cases the floor and wall coverings seem to have been chosen for their color and texture rather than their suitability as backgrounds—different patterns are intermingled, and their large-scale designs are often overwhelming in proportion to the furnishings. Even by themselves, they create a fantastic interior that dances on the page, and, with the additional texture and pattern of the trappings, the effect can indeed seem dizzying. This very visual density, fashionable in the late nineteenth century, was characteristic of the look favored by those who associated themselves with the Aesthetic movement.[8] The scraphouse makers were thus demonstrably up-to-date and in alignment with the aesthetic of their day, although many of them took the elaborative tendency beyond the decorative norm. They pieced in mica inserts or hand-colored panes to simulate stained glass on closet doors or made parquet floors of bits of wood-grained wallpaper, for example, or fashioned picture frames from embossed gold foil or braid. To make the spaces come alive, they cut out individual fish to outfit tiny aquariums and placed tiny shoes by the side of a bed, as if waiting for the owner to wake up and put them on. They positioned paper cats as if they were chasing mice on fringed hearthside rugs. In one startling example in Rochester, New York's Margaret Woodbury Strong Museum, the artist went so far as to cut out small shapes from one patterned paper and paste them at odd angles onto another to form the background effect she desired. Some house makers hand-colored the black-and-white engraved images they had cut from magazines, making them suit their particular rooms and aesthetic preferences.

Many of the book houses play with layering, a quality that feminist theorists have associated with a particularly female aesthetic.[9] As Ringwalt had suggested, doors open to reveal something hidden—a nicely browned roast in the oven, a closet full of crepe paper dresses, even a potty chair secreted in a convertible chair. (She also indicated that, following the model of clothing a paper doll, one might hide the bare "wood" of a paper table with a tablecloth outfitted with folding tabs, but I have not seen any examples of this.) A few of the most skillfully done houses work with the effect of layered pages. Kenilworth Inn (the name is proclaimed on the first page—that is, the front door), a 1903 example now housed in the Winterthur Library, part of the Henry Francis du Pont Winterthur Museum in Wilmington, Delaware, has cut-out windows on several pages that allow the viewer to see into the next room.[10] An album in the Strong Museum carries the idea even further. Not only can one look through an artfully cutout section on many of the pages into the next vignette, but the revealed section helps create the story on the first page as well. The pièce de résistance is the ballroom, essentially made of two interactive layers: an indoor scene on the top page, and an adjacent outdoor patio behind it. Layering of another sort is also evident on the people who occupy these book houses. One enterprising individual transformed cutout fashion-magazine figures into the characters she wanted for her house by cutting them apart, adding additional details, and reconfiguring them so they worked in their new roles. For example, the arms of a maid were repositioned so as to fit neatly over a newly created apron. In addition, the pages contain a more abstract kind of layering whereby diverse realities and references are freely intermingled. Some of the vignettes juxtapose individuals in eighteenth-century dress with others dressed in contemporary styles, so that a man in a powdered wig and breeches might be seen gesturing to a woman in an Edwardian hat. Everything becomes subsumed into the story the house maker wants to tell. The collages are sophisticated, reflecting aesthetic and conceptual complexity and careful planning and execution.

That creating this kind of detailed world brought pleasure to the house makers was well recognized at the time. Imaginative elaboration and creative reconfiguration was not only encouraged by nineteenth-century advice givers but also acknowledged as the major "charm" of the scrapbook.[11] As Ringwalt's "Fun for the Fireside" column indicated, moreover, these pastimes were considered amusements and were spoken of in positive, happy terms. The word *fun* appeared in almost every article that discussed paper dollhouses, and although we cannot know exactly what the authors had in mind when they used that term, it is telling that they applied it to different aspects of the house-making experience. Carolyn Wells suggested in 1901 that openable doors would "add greatly to the fun," while Mary White spoke of the fun of "house hunting"—that is, first finding an appropriate blank book. Emily Hoffman spoke in 1904 of the huge pleasure of fashioning houses where imagination ruled; in such a world, every girl could be "her own architect." Because she was able to create a world of her own while working on a book, "ennui [was] forgotten." Reminiscences also bring out the specialness of the paper dollhouse. Marian Richards wrote of her particular attachment to one of the paper dolls she had as a child: "Block houses were not good enough for her, so I took to making houses [for her] in books."[12]

A sense of the book owners' personal involvement is also evident in extant examples. Individual style and preference clearly come through. Some house makers liked to fill the space completely, indicating a kind of *horror vacuii*; others liked more free-floating figures and minimal furniture. Some seemed to care about linear perspective much more than did others. Most liked to include human figures in the interiors, but some preferred to leave them unpopulated, allowing the furnishings to take on a life of their own and serve as the houses' sole inhabitants. A few even included commentary in their vignettes. The maker of Kenilworth Inn not only named her house but also included handwritten aphorisms, such as "Too many cooks spoil the broth" in the kitchen. A house maker from Bennington, Vermont, pasted preprinted mottoes in a number of spaces, including, in a well-appointed music room, "Let the sound of music creep into our ears." Personal connection to the houses is also demonstrated by the owners' often conceiving of rooms as belonging to particular individuals. Pages are tagged "Laura's room," "David's room," and the like, and some of the inserted paper dolls bear names to match. If, as the advice literature implies, these book houses were sometimes carried to friends' houses or taken on journeys, it would have been like taking along not only a homey companion but also a whole world of one's own creation.[13]

Cross-Generational Bonding

The advice literature spoke of making paper dollhouses as a girl's pastime, and although the age of the would-be makers was not made explicit, Mary White included a photograph in her 1905 *Child's Rainy Day Book* of three girls who are "planning a book house" and who appear to be about ten to twelve years old. Richards's memories of making book houses would put her at about the same age.[14] Some books bear sure signs of a child's hand; one at the Smithsonian Institution, for example, has pages marked with the backward letters of a young person learning to write. However, a young child was not skilled enough to have made such a book, and paper dollhouses must be taken seriously as works of art frequently, if not usually, made by adults. Documentation with many of the extant houses indicates that they were made by grown women—sometimes well-trained art students—and given to girls as gifts. Another Smithsonian example bears a childishly penciled inscription by Edith E. Washburn of Thomaston, Maine, who wrote: "Miss Scanison (my nurse) made this when I was sick in 1892. I am always going to keep it to remember her by." Other girls received books from their mothers. Harriet Green Brown of Mystic, Connecticut, made one for her children in the 1880s, and a Chicago girl received not one but two books from her family in the next decade. One is inscribed: "Painted for Anita C. Blair . . . by the Baltimore Decorative Arts Society. A gift from her mother and father, Mrs. and Mrs. Henry A. Blair." The second of her books was prepared or at least painted by Miss Jenks, a student at the Art Institute of Chicago. It was clearly made specifically for Anita, for it includes personal references—for example, a printed view of Ceylon Court, a building said to have been moved from the 1893 World's Columbian Exposition to Williams Bay, Wisconsin, by a friend of the Blairs.[15] The previously mentioned Kenilworth Inn may also have been made by an art student from the Art Institute (Kenilworth is a Chicago street name), as its fine construction implies a maker who was formally trained in composition and presentation.

Several books appear to have been made by different hands, some surer and more accomplished than others, suggesting that some girls may have received scrapbook houses as presents and then added rooms of their own. Fifteen of the rooms in Anita Blair's first book appear to have been worked by a trained person from the Decorative Arts Society, for example, while three are cruder, suggesting they might have been worked by Anita herself. Similarly, the backgrounds in Emilie Hickey's book appear to have been worked by a skilled adult, but the furnishings were clearly filled in by someone younger. In addition to these apparently collaborative efforts on the part of girls and their elders, there is evidence that friends sometimes worked on the houses together. When they were about eleven or twelve years old, Christine Ruth Grier and Martha Ross of Lebanon, Pennsylvania, collaborated on a book representing Christine's actual house. Martha was skilled at drawing and rendered the settings, but Christine helped paint them in. The illustration in White's book echoes the same cooperative effort. Clearly, the very production of a paper dollhouse at the turn of the century afforded opportunities for inter- and intragenerational female bonding.[16]

The idea of cross-generational bonding is reinforced by the possibility that girls who had worked on scrapbook houses when they were children in the 1880s and 1890s returned to the occupation when they were grown women after the turn of the century, giving the finished books to a new set of youngsters. Richards, who reminisced in *Ladies' Home Journal* in 1902 about the book house she had made as a child, wrote about making them for little girls.[17] One example in the Strong Museum that, in light of the furnishings and clothing of the pasted-in figures, appears to date from the 1880s, has tucked-in paper dolls dressed in the style of about 1913. Conceivably, more than one generation of girls had played with it. The hypothesis that the book-house idea was resurrected for a second generation is supported by the long hiatus between the first magazine features on paper dollhouses around 1880, and the next group of articles, which appeared after 1900. Whether the same individuals were involved in successive generations, the genre stayed remarkably consistent for nearly fifty years. Flora Gill Jacobs, who made a paper dollhouse for a cousin two years her junior, remarked that "such residences were as cheerfully gaudy in the 1920s as in the nineties."[18] The style of the furnishings and clothing of the cutout people was updated and the books tended to get a little larger over time, but the type of represented rooms, the layout, and the general concept of the houses remained the same.

The Satisfactions of Making a House

Anyone who made a house was afforded hours of sustained attention and intense activity. It was a long-term project. First, the maker had to collect foil, crepe paper, wallpaper samples, and other materials for the interior settings, as well as hundreds of suitable pictures for the furnishings. The advice literature seemed to presume that, as with scrapbooks of other types, the girls would amass quantities of images ahead of time, cut them out, sort them, and store them for future use. A few extant books have envelopes of just such unused cutouts tucked into them, and the case of the Kenilworth Inn gives a sense of how long the preparation period might last—it includes images from the Pan-American Exposition, held in Buffalo in 1900, three years before the book was put together. Wells captured the almost obsessive excitement the search for appropriate materials could stimulate when she commented in 1901: "If you once begin to make paper dollhouses, you will soon find yourself pouncing on pictures suitable for your use wherever you happen to run across them—and running across them everywhere." It is possible that the collecting process was especially drawn out in the earlier decades of the paper dollhouse, when printed images were less abundant than they were after the turn of the century. In 1920, when Maude Cushing Nash wrote about the "dollhouse scrapbook" in *Children's Occupations*, she alluded to the ever-greater plethora of material that simplified the "hunt" for appropriate images. She indicated that "any furniture store of a large city [would] send a catalog upon request" and that its "page after page of pictures" would adequately fill the rooms of a given book.[19]

After the materials were collected, the house had to be organized. Although the general idea of the book starting with the front public rooms and moving to the more private spaces was well established, the maker still had to decide just how extensive the house would be, what would be included, and what would follow what. (Where layered openings afforded views of sequential spaces, preplanning was particularly important.) Most houses include pages for very specific types of activities—music rooms, schoolrooms, gyms, and, in one remarkable example, a home theater. Such spaces called for targeted cutouts—pianos and harps for the music room, for example, and clocks, desks, and blackboards for the schoolroom. A house maker might have decided to include such rooms only if she already had the requisite images in hand, but as in making any collage there was always a dynamic interplay between idea, image, and construction. Actual arrangement of the room—decisions about what would be in the foreground, what would overlap what to create the right kind of three-dimensional space, and what would sit on the table or the mantel—offered many opportunities for experimentation. Emily Hoffman instructed *Harper's Bazar* readers that it was best to first make the corners of the rooms and later fill in the center, putting images down first without pasting so that they could be moved around for a more pleasing composition.[20] Some house makers followed this advice, while others chose to follow another organizational strategy.

Conceiving of and making a paper dollhouse was an important aesthetic outlet, a complex, ultimately satisfying activity; it was a way of making a world—fashioning a complete, unified living entity out of literal scraps and organizing it according to one's own fantasies and ideas. If collecting the scraps that would become the house furnishings and inhabitants could be obsessive, turning them into tableaux or vignettes was a way of taking that obsession in a creative direction. It meant making order out of disparate pieces or making something whole and new. Whatever the idiosyncratic preference of the creator, every house reflected a personal vision; as an idealized environment, it reflected a play with a sense of self. If the books were collections of stage sets that formed a minitheater, then the scrapbook house maker was the director, set designer, costumer, and stage manager. If she later actually played with the book, she was also the author and producer of ongoing or ever-changing plays. Most books show enough wear to indicate that they were indeed pored over and played with repeatedly.[21]

This kind of personal and aesthetic meaning has not been recognized in the few previous scholarly treatments of paper dollhouses. Rodris Roth, who did much of the pioneering investigation of this genre, focused on the way the houses helped socialize girls and train them to become good consumers. There is no question that making a scrapbook of this type would create familiarity with advertisements and similar trade material, and the houses certainly embodied and reinforced contemporary ideals of consumerism, the home, and women's place within it. The houses featured the most up-to-date products; Ringwalt called them "delightfully complete" homes. "There will be a telephone of course, and a phonograph, and possibly ... a typewriter," noted Hoffman in her 1904 "Homes for Paper Dolls." Even today, some of the extant houses can be dated because of their inclusion of specific brands and consumer products. The Strong Museum has a book with scenes fashioned from cutouts from Ivory soap advertisements, for example, that can be definitively dated to 1886, when the ads appeared in *Ladies' Home Journal.* Most houses were also outfitted with a battery of servants. As Hoffman put it, tongue-in-cheek: "The most delectable serving-maids are to be had for the cutting out. [They] are always irreproachably capped and aproned, and offer chocolate or steaming soup with an ingratiating smile and a small tray."[22] Many houses had governesses and gardeners in addition to servants who cooked and cleaned. Servants and spaces such as billiard rooms, conservatories, and wine cellars certainly showed children what to aspire to, and servants sometimes appear as Irish or African Americans, indicating that the prevailing culture's racist assumptions and expectations were fully embedded in the scrapbook houses.

Nevertheless, training in consumerism was not what these houses were primarily about. Consumer issues were not mentioned in any of the writings about them, and there was no rhetoric or implication that girls would learn to value household products by playing with their images. These were dream houses, and they did not necessarily represent an expectation or even a hunger for luxuries in daily life. One did not have to be well-off to create a house like this; several of the descriptive articles stressed, in fact, that all one needed to make book houses were scraps or advertising materials and flour paste or a jar of mucilage. Endless rooms did not so much represent a longing for consumer goods as they represented playing with luxury; as Hoffman wrote in *Harper's Bazar,* the paper-doll family and its pampered pets could "revel" in such splendor.[23] Additional rooms meant more opportunities for cutout tableaux and thus more opportunities for a maker to order and elaborate a world of her own creation, according to her ideas of the moment. They provided more of the sensual, aesthetic pleasure that came from handling the books and the scraps within them. Richards noted, in fact, that some children kept adding to their house books because blank pages represented additional avenues for creative expression: "If pages still remain, they may be devoted to . . . an art museum, a 'zoo,' stores . . . and railway stations [or] views of the countryside. . . . A child may play so entirely in [a] book that there is no place she can devise that has not some page devoted to it."[24]

Paper Dollhouses as Aesthetic Training

Roth concluded that scrapbook houses were also an ideal medium for introducing young girls to their future roles as homemakers; she saw this as their primary, constraining, function.[25] There is no question that the houses reproduced prevailing gender roles, and learning to fashion a proper house would certainly have reinforced the kind of skills a girl was expected to master. Once again, however, the training involved was not about housekeeping; it was largely focused on the aesthetic. The aesthetic domain was experienced as an expansive rather than a restrictive arena (see Figure 6.2). Aesthetically focused pastimes were never unpleasant or grim; on the contrary, what was aesthetically sound was pleasing and inseparable from the idea of good feeling. Articles on paper dollhouses did not discuss appropriate behavior or stress moral training; moreover, they were certainly not humorless but repeatedly mentioned the pleasure involved in making the books. The writers also stressed the artistic skills that might be fostered by this activity. For example, Richards mentioned the excellent training with perspective that making a book would afford. Nash spoke of "training the eye" toward good taste, and Hoffman similarly wrote of house making as a way of "acquiring discriminating taste."[26]

Taste was of particular concern in the late nineteenth century when these book houses first came into being, the result of the abundance of mass-produced objects and the perceived difficulties of choosing wisely among them. There was a particular concern with "household art," a phrase in use since Charles Eastlake's *Hints on Household Taste* was published in 1868. The general belief was that if good taste and beauty were brought into the home, the environment would exert a positive influence on those who lived there (as one Eastlake disciple put it, "We must have beauty around us to make us good").[27] This was especially important for children, whose character was in the process of being shaped. In the long run, a properly appointed, well-designed home would help ensure that successive generations would be brought to a higher standard and quality of life. Because women were the overseers of the home, responsible for its well-being as well as that of the children, women became the primary arbiters of taste. Contemporary commentators talked of this as a "natural" relationship: Women were the most attuned to matters of color, texture and form; they were the "sensitive ones," best able to relate to sensual stimuli and concern themselves with harmony and proportion. Every issue of the burgeoning array of women's magazines gave advice about what was tasteful, and most of the advice givers were themselves women. Many saw themselves as "missionaries of the beautiful" and acted through a variety of organizations, including women's clubs and art societies, to spread their message. Women were disproportionately represented in the Aesthetic and Arts and Crafts movements, both of which were dedicated to raising the level of popular taste, and they worked to get art training into the public schools.[28]

That some of the extant paper dollhouses were made by art students or members of decorative art societies indicates how central the aesthetic is in any consideration of this genre. Conceivably, the scrapbook houses might even have been undertaken as class projects in women's art-education classes. Scrapbook keeping was a common pedagogical tool or practice at the turn of the century and the first decades of the twentieth; students in "Related Art" classes at the University of Wisconsin, for example, were encouraged to arrange pictures of artworks, color and fabric swatches, and other such materials in bound books.[29] Students concerned with harmonious interiors, as those involved with decorative arts societies were likely to be, would have found working on such two-dimensional house models an interesting exercise. The books that feature interdependent, layered room arrangements (pages) seem like the kind of tour-de-force that might have come from sophisticated experimentation with volume, view, and perspective.

Even in the less masterfully made book houses, it is evident that there was a concern with artistic skill and aesthetic issues. In many books, hand-drawn lines are carefully rendered in one- or two-point perspective, and obvious effort is made toward effecting pleasing color harmonies. The dated houses each reflect the latest design ideas and most current styles of interior decoration; examples from the early 1880s are filled with Eastlake furniture, Japanese fans, and other accouterments of the Aesthetic style, while the 1903 Kenilworth Inn and Christine Grier's 1905 book both have a sparer look, with up-to-date Arts and Crafts–style furnishings. The introduction of new furniture styles is striking enough, in fact, that I feel confident about assigning dates to the unattributed examples on that basis. In addition, most house makers approached their material in a particularly aestheticized manner. The Ivory soap characters described earlier, for example, were removed from their advertising context and repositioned into new, imaginary settings that had nothing to do with product recognition or association and everything to do with composition, arrangement of pictorial elements, and creation of an emotionally satisfying story.

Paper Houses as Collage

It is time that we take the scrapbook house seriously as a form of art—a deliberate adult creation, a significant early form of collage. Collage is deemed one of the most important categories of twentieth-century art, and the general literature on this genre speaks of its "discovery" or "invention" in the twentieth century by male artists such as Picasso, Braque, and Joseph Cornell. However, Linda Hartigan demonstrated that Cornell himself collected and was undoubtedly influenced by scrapbook albums. She argues that the collage form was especially evident in paper dollhouses, which were characterized by many of the same qualities that Cornell is known for, including intimate scale; love of detail; contrasts and contradictions of scale, material, and idea; and the transformation of the imagery of mass production. That women and girls

Figure 6.2. *The exuberance created by the juxtaposition of differently scaled images is apparent even in this black-and-white image of an album made by Louise Hovey in the 1880s. Hovey manipulated many of the details on this page and the other twenty-three pages in the album to achieve her intended effect.* (Division of Domestic Life, National Museum of American History, Smithsonian Institution; accession no. 232.559, catalog no. 61.293, photograph no. 79-11535)

worked with collage in the nineteenth century had been acknowledged by others before Hartigan, but they discounted the women's work, categorizing it as "household art" (unlike their nineteenth-century foremothers, they used the term pejoratively) fashioned by mere "amateurs." Harriet Janis dismissed such "folk collage" as a "simple pastime" that was "no concern of serious artists."[30]

Why have these dismissals been so categorical, and only Hartigan has recognized the paper dollhouse as an art form? The form's visual density does not fit the kind of modernist aesthetic expressed by artists such as Cornell and so deeply internalized by late-twentieth-century scholars, and its very aestheticized treatment tends to strike those with contemporary sensibilities as "overdone." This unconscious reaction is so strong and subtle that I believe it affects even the most conscientious observer. Roth studied the house scrapbooks in depth and clearly appreciated them but still did not value them as collage or see them as creative aesthetic expressions. Their domestic imagery and context also kept many from seeing their artistry. Diane Waldman recognized that collage's special appeal is that it brings "the incongruous into meaningful congress with the ordinary and gives the uneventful, the commonplace, the ordinary a magic of its own," but she could not see the paper dollhouses as "real" collage; she apparently could not find magic in the commonplace imagery of the household. Despite arguing that in collage, process is as significant as end product, she dismissed the process of making a paper-doll book house as mere "busywork."[31]

Domestic imagery was not seen through this kind of negative filter at the time the book houses were made. Descriptions of interior details were considered important; they were read as reflections of something deeper, even to the point of being treated as clues to the inner life of the people who created and lived among them. Popular novelists such as Henry James and Edith Wharton used such details to show nuances of character, taste, and subtleties of interpersonal interaction. In 1897 Wharton herself co-authored an advice book on interiors that struck such a chord that the first edition sold out immediately; it remained in print for more than forty years.[32]

Paper Houses as Women's Spaces

In the paper dollhouses, domestic imagery appeared as a strength rather than a weakness; they were conceived and executed from the woman's point of view, and there was pride rather than defensiveness in their presentation. Roth was correct in looking at house making as an activity that reinforced prevailing gender roles and ideologies, but this view did not suggest a sense of limitation. The houses were documents of the female experience and were treated as a natural part of it. They were, to begin with, made only by girls or women (boys occasionally worked on other forms of scrapbooks, but this was apparently never the case with this type associated with dolls).[33] Every aspect of the houses referenced women's concerns. As indicated, the aestheticized presentation and its emphasis on good taste would have themselves been linked in the turn-of-the-century mind with women. Even further, the very materials that filled the books were often gender linked. For example, crepe paper, which came in a wide range of sensually appealing colors and textures at the turn of the century, was specifically marketed and thought of as a woman's medium. Women both gave and attended classes on craft projects that could be made with this novel material, including personal items such as hats and party costumes, and household decorations ranging from portieres to table runners. Wallpaper too was an aesthetically rich material that was marketed to and conceptually linked with women. The right wallpaper was of such concern in the turn-of-the-century period that reformers waged passionate campaigns about it, often linking it to women's moral and emotional well-being. The broad expanse and striking juxtapositions of wallpaper patterns that dominated so many paper-dollhouse pages would have been noted for their bold color and visual effect and, further, would have been associated with something essentially and almost anthropomorphically female.[34]

By compartmentalizing specific household functions into the different zones of their books, house makers not only replicated current ideas about decorating and appropriate uses of space but also reinforced the nineteenth-century conceptual schema that associated the inside (private) with the female, and the outside (public) with the male. (This explains why Nash spoke of stores and railroad stations as extra spaces, included in the back pages of an elaborate book house; those vignettes belonged beyond the back door, literally outside the boundaries of the house itself.) Even within the home, the pasted-in characters were placed in gender-specific rooms; male figures might appear in the library or music room, for example, but not in the nursery or kitchen, considered female domains. Male figures sometimes were given their own, distinctly masculine spaces. One book house has a man's dressing room, complete with all the necessary outfits for a fine gentleman (perhaps the house maker had found a tailor's catalog), but more commonly men's rooms referenced outdoor, nondomestic activities such as hunting (dens included gender-linked objects such as pistols and trophy heads) or unladylike indoor leisure pastimes such as playing pool or smoking (separate rooms were equipped with the necessary spittoons).[35] The practice of setting aside designated spaces for nonfemale activities was also common in actual homes in the late nineteenth century. It represented a tacit acceptance of the prevailing Victorian belief that the house was a woman's space. Because, as T. J. Jackson Lears put it, the interior was filled with body-related details that "embodied the iconography of female experience," many men felt the need for nondomesticated retreats where female values did not hold sway.[36] In addition to spatial separation, there are many subtle furnishing details in these books that demonstrate distinctly different expectations for men and women. Bedrooms marked with men's names, for example, are never outfitted with lacy curtains or pillowcases. Cutout cats are frequently found near women, while dogs appear near men.

The men's spaces were never very dominant in these book houses; although men were usually given a place, their concerns were overshadowed by those of the women. Not only were more pages devoted to women's activities than to men's, but also the men were heavily outnumbered—most of the collages included a disproportionate number of female figures (for example, eleven to one, even on a single page). Male figures were often positioned alone, while cutout women were frequently positioned together, sometimes, as with the Kenilworth Inn, in intense-looking tête-à-têtes. To return to the theatrical metaphor, the stage set portrayed in this book world was a feminized one; the paper dollhouse embodied a domestic drama—both a household theater, and a theater of the household. In commenting on nineteenth-century scrapbooks, Patricia P. Buckler and C. Kay Leeper remarked on the way they reflected themes of women's magazines such as *Godey's Lady's Book*. Middle-class women "were portrayed . . . as true heroines of unparalleled, unnoticed dignity and virtue," they explained, but always within the context of the domestic sphere. The paper-dollhouse scrapbooks took this general presentation to an extreme: they represented the very spaces that those heroines inhabited. In *Bazaars and Fair Ladies: The History of the American Fundraising Fair*, I have explored the ways women created similar domestic dramas in three dimensions, using the kind of tableaux mentioned earlier in this essay. Women dramatically highlighted and played with their domestic skills—sewing, cooking, and decorating—in the more formal environments of bazaars, church suppers, and thematic tea parties, which were at their peak at the turn of the century.[37] The paper dollhouse was a two-dimensional representation of the same domestic theater idea.

Paper dollhouses also reflected—and furthered—other kinds of domestic values. Kenneth Ames has made the point that a primary part of women's role in the Victorian United States was to foster and preserve a sense of interpersonal connection and intergenerational family bonding. Some material objects were made to reinforce that role, Ames maintains, and I believe that the scrapbook houses fall into this category.[38] On one level, these values were reinforced in their iconography. One example in the Strong Museum literally references the idea of nurturing and the importance of harmony: on the walls of its well-appointed nursery, pasted-in mottoes remind everyone to "Love One Another" and "Help One Another." Many other houses include collages of families gathered around comfortable chairs and sofas, cheerfully sharing one another's company, or even miniature framed pictures on parlor walls that feature happy domestic scenes. The emphasis on sharing and family connection was also evident in the idea that the books were made by one generation and lovingly presented as gifts to another. Finally, the owners themselves valued them for this same sense of connectedness. This is evident in Edith Washburn's inscription indicating that she would always keep her scrapbook as a way of remembering her nurse, and it is implied in Janet Ruutz-Rees's 1883 statement that boys turned to their scrapbooks as a place for their "quaint oddities," while girls used them to preserve sentimental items.[39] The scrapbook house clearly took the preoccupation with sentimentality to its ultimate conclusion.

Commercially Produced Paper Dollhouses

The popularity and cultural resonance that the paper dollhouse must have enjoyed is demonstrated by the fact that after the turn of the century, commercial manufacturers and publishers tried to cash in on the idea by coming out with their own versions of the handmade prototype. Sheets of commercially preprinted settings for paper dolls (some made as folding dollhouses) may have been available throughout the period under consideration, but these were not conceived as book houses.[40] It was only toward the end of the paper-dollhouse phenomenon that a handful of commercial book-type houses appeared, always following the conventions established in the handmade genre. *The House That Glue Built*, which appeared in 1905, written by Clara Andrews Williams and illustrated by her husband, George, included seven rooms of Arts and Crafts–style furniture, each of which came with a story about its inhabitants. *A Paper Home for Paper People*, published in 1909, included nine rooms of furniture and figures, but the author, Edith Root, indicated that "Mr. and Mrs. Cut Paper" needed more than the basic furnishings she had provided. "It will be found that there are not nearly enough [articles] for the house," she wrote; "the real pleasure will be found when magazines, catalogs and even the daily newspaper are searched to supply vases, pictures, books, rugs, hangings, etc. to complete the luxurious home." It is apparent from this statement that the author realized the preprinted version would not prove satisfying if it did not provide an opportunity for creative participation or working with the all-important details. A fixed house—and one fixed according to someone else's image, at that—did not hold the same fascination.[41]

There do not seem to have been many of these published book houses—I have cited the only ones that I am aware of—and it was a relatively short-lived phenomenon, lasting about a decade. Although it is impossible to know how many people saw or used them, everything about them referenced and reinforced the same values embedded in the handmade ones. The latest one I have found was published in 1921 in England, about the time paper-dollhouse making was ending in the United States. *My Dolly's Home*, written by Doris Davey, is a brightly colored book that comes with an envelope of paper dolls and a separate storybook called *Biddie's Adventure: The Story of My Dolly's Home*. The dolly's home is "just like fairyland": it is printed in glossy, bright color and includes rich metaphorical language with references to "sky scooter" clouds or a fountain where the dolls "kept their own rainbows." The book's physical layout follows the handmade prototype, with double-page spreads beginning at the front gate, progressing up to the bedrooms, down the back stairs to the kitchen, and out to a garden, an orchard, and a garage. Almost every room has some sort of openable door. The storybook also reinforces the magical quality of miniaturization. It features a girl who receives a paper doll as a present and then suddenly finds herself small enough to follow the doll into her little world. In her miniaturized state, the girl goes into the doll's house, looks in cupboards, joins a tea party in the garden, and so on. She later discovers that her visit has been a dream, but her parents give her a picture book where the same happy house is represented. *My Dolly's Home* underlines once again how much the scrapbook house's attraction—indeed, its most important function—was the aesthetic pleasure it afforded.[42]

A New Appreciation of Paper Dollhouses

There are many reasons that the paper-dollhouse genre has not been appreciated. For one thing, these scrap houses are very little known. Few remain intact. They were made of paper and filled with commercial or trade images, which were always treated as trivial and throwaway materials. They did not fit easily into any category, so that later generations did not know what to make of them. Some of those that do exist are now found in ephemera collections—a rubric that by definition implies materials that are light not only in weight but also in importance. I have argued, furthermore, that the houses' emphasis—indeed, insistence—on aesthetic detail and sensual pleasure causes many who have grown up with a modernist attitude to feel uncomfortable; these qualities were not highly valued during much of the twentieth century. There are signs that such qualities are becoming less suspect in the postmodern age, but they have certainly colored the way the houses have been seen and have added to their devaluation or invisibility.[43]

Related to this idea is the fact that paper dollhouses functioned or were at least presented as girls' toys. Amusements of all kinds are not typically taken very seriously or looked at as a meaningful part of culture. Once they are identified as children's pastimes, they are thought of as childish—as the kind of thing that serious people outgrow. Their gendered identification confounds or exacerbates the issue even further, because girls' pastimes have been taken less seriously in this culture than boys'. In fact, the paper dollhouse was not just a child's pastime but a genre that demonstrated the skill, creativity, and artistic integrity of adult women; as Hartigan has argued, it is a neglected form of collage.[44] The women's artistry has remained invisible, however, largely because the artists were women. Scholars have demonstrated that the reception of any art form is highly dependent on the way the dominant culture views the artists or makers: important works are by definition those made by important people, and, conversely, work made by those viewed as less important (women, so-called primitive people, minorities, and so forth) is automatically perceived as less significant.[45] These biases have further kept the scrapbook or paper dollhouse from being seen, much less acknowledged, as a highly creative, artistic form of expression.

Underlying this invisibility and inseparable from the makers' gender is the fact that the scrapbook houses are dominated by domestic imagery. The prevailing culture has not generally valued the domestic or the everyday, which has been equated with the ordinary rather than the extraordinary. The very "houseness" of these objects has blinded contemporary viewers to their artistry. Hartigan wrote at length about the compositional artistry of the scrapbook-house pages but treated them as freestanding compositions rather than as part of a broader, even more complex creation. She removed them from their social and cultural milieu and their function as conceptual houses and thus missed much of their meaning.

It is time to fully recognize the inexorable fascination, the pleasure, and indeed the magic of these albums and to fully acknowledge the creativity and artistic integrity of the house makers. Paper dollhouses are works of art; they represent an underacknowledged and undervalued form of collage. At the same time, we must not remove them from their domestic context. On the contrary, we should, as their makers did, recognize their intimacy and everydayness as part of their strength, understanding that the home and its activities—the domestic context—can serve as a source of creative imagery and expression. What emerges from these books is a heavily aestheticized world where domestic values prevailed and what mattered was human relationship and the detail of everyday life. All these houses demonstrate a multilayered reality that was physically as well as conceptually complex. Our assessment should be similarly layered. We should see them simultaneously as toys and as serious works of art, as vehicles of socialization and artistic training and as opportunities for the expression of a personal vision, as a genre with well-understood and structured conventions and as a form of theater, with room for individualized storytelling and aesthetic exploration.

[MELISSA A. JOHNSON]

7

〜〜〜〜

Souvenirs of Amerika

〜〜〜〜

Hannah Höch's Weimar-Era
Mass-Media Scrapbook

SOMETIME DURING 1934 THE GERMAN artist Hannah Höch (1889–1978) created a 116-page scrapbook using images she had clipped from the photographically illustrated press of the Weimar Republic (1918–33).[1] In making this scrapbook Höch created a complex, multi-layered narrative that reflects much of the social, cultural, and political tenor of this time. As such, the scrapbook provides a general collective commentary on how individuals experienced their surroundings during a time of great technological, social, and political change. At the same time it offers specific commentary on Höch's personal memories and articulates her desire to comprehend the world around her through the formulation of a new visual language of images.

The broad and diverse range of subjects that Höch included in her scrapbook becomes clear in paging through the work. Many of the images represent what we have come to call Weimar culture: the New Woman with her *Bubikopf* (pageboy) haircut, technological wonders, cabaret and revue theater, modern expressionist dance, sports, *Körperkultur* (body culture), silent films and the actresses and actors who starred in them, magazines, U.S. culture, photography (especially what was called the New Photography), and "mass ornament" images (images of people or things arranged into ornamental patterns). In addition, Höch chose to include images of foreign and exotic people and places, animals (both wild and domestic), plants, images of children and babies, shots of European and U.S. factories, and industrial landscapes and metropolitan cityscapes. The range of subjects Höch included is so broad, in fact, that it becomes impossible to assign any one interpretation to the scrapbook. This impossibility is compounded when one considers how Höch positioned the images on the pages, creating an associative montage narrative that encourages multiple readings. Elsewhere I have explored a number of these readings, examining how through her scrapbook Höch participated in and drew on contemporary photographic and filmic practices and theories, how she reflected on the experiences of modern travel, how a number of the images refer to personal memories through references to friends and colleagues, and how the scrapbook visually articulates the phenomenon of Amerikanismus, or the Americanization of German culture.[2] This last interpretation is the focus of this essay.

To appreciate how the theme of Amerikanismus coexists with these other readings, we must know what Höch's scrapbook looks like, how Höch made it, and why. The first two issues can be addressed relatively straightforwardly, but discussion about why Höch made her scrapbook is a more speculative exercise, for if Höch wrote about her scrapbook, no record exists. There are no documents in her archive in Berlin that indicate that she wished to publish or exhibit the work. It appears to have been entirely private.[3] Yet the amount of effort Höch must have put into collecting and selecting the images and constructing the work—and the evident pleasure she took in the images—signifies its importance to her. Furthermore, because scrapbooks are books into which an individual collects a variety of materials to remember something, the issues of collecting and memory are central to any interpretation of Höch's scrapbook, and both will be discussed here.

A Hunger for Images: Childhood
Pleasures and the Modernity of Vision

Höch's scrapbook has as its foundation a March 1925 and a May 1926 issue of the German women's fashion magazine *Die Dame*, published by Ullstein Verlag. Placing the two issues back to back, Höch pasted onto their pages 421 images she had clipped from Ullstein magazines such as *Die Dame, Berliner Illustrirte Zeitung, Uhu, Der Querschnitt,* and *Die Koralle*. Höch had easy access to copies of Ullstein's numerous magazines, for from 1916 to 1926 the artist worked for Ullstein as an editor on the staff of *Die Dame*. Höch also used images from magazines by other publishers, including *Die Woche; Atlantis: Länder, Völker, Reisen; Das Magazin;* and *Arbeiter Illustrierte Zeitung.*[4]

The illustrated press (*Illustrierte*) was considered by many a vehicle of modernity, and the editors of the Weimar Illustrierte sought to educate their readers to see photographically. This point was stressed to such a degree that some individuals argued there was no longer any need for the written word.[5] The desire and ability to see the news was especially strong in Germany, where after World War I the illustrated press developed at a rate greater than anywhere else in Europe.[6] The typographer Jan Tschichold acknowledged this when he wrote that the "photograph has become such a characteristic sign of the times that our lives would be unthinkable without it." He spoke of modern humankind's "hunger for images [that was] mainly satisfied by photographically illustrated newspapers and magazines."[7] To satisfy and encourage this hunger was the aim of the mass media.

Höch took great enjoyment in these magazines and their images. While living in the Netherlands from 1926 to 1929, she wrote to thank her sister, Grete, for some magazines she had sent. They were such a "great pleasure," Höch wrote. Seeing the Illustrierte allowed her to both "hear and see what [was] going on."[8] Part of this pleasure seems to have been a sense of connectedness with news and events in Germany, but Höch must have also taken great pleasure in the visual access she had to the world made possible by developments in photography and improved modes of travel. Yet Höch's montage work—both her scrapbook and photomontages—demonstrates that while she enjoyed the magazines for what they showed her of the world, she responded to this worldview with an astute and critical eye. I suggest that we see Höch as an avant-garde artist whose use of the popular mass media depended on the related issues of visual pleasure and radical critique. A brief look at Höch's montage technique will help make this clear.

In her photomontages Höch cut apart images and pieced them together to create works that, while they reveal their provenance in the Illustrierte, take on new and critical meanings through their juxtaposition with fragments of other images. Höch's monumental and dynamic Dadaist photomontage *Schnitt mit dem Küchenmesser Dada durch die letzte weimarer Bierbauchkulturepoche Deutschlands* [Cut with the Kitchen Knife Dada through the Last Beer-Belly Cultural Epoch of Germany], 1919–20, offers one example. In this work the pleasure Höch took in these images is fully evident, but her pleasure is neither passive nor contemplative. It is critical and reactive; it interrogates, reworks, and recontextualizes each of the Illustrierte images she selected to create new spaces of meaning through a critical grammar of juxtaposition of montage elements.[9]

Höch called on this same critical grammar of montage with very different results when she made her scrapbook fourteen years later. In this work Höch's montage technique does not depend on the act of cutting images into fragments and piecing them together; rather, it depends on the juxtaposition of whole images. The images in Höch's scrapbook are not intended to be read on their own but to be seen and interpreted in relationship with one another. Thus while the form of Höch's scrapbook resembles that of a traditional codex—to read or view it one turns its pages in a linear fashion from front to back—it is a nonlinear and almost entirely visual text.

Höch's scrapbook may be seen to develop out of both her avant-garde photomontage practices and her practice of creating picture scrapbooks as a child and young adult with her siblings. Yet, while Höch's Weimar scrapbook must be seen as emerging from this childhood hobby, it differs greatly from our general understanding of what constitutes a scrapbook. Scrapbooks in the nineteenth century and later were most often constructed as popular pastimes or as educational tools. Höch's childhood scrapbooks fit this model, but her Weimar scrapbook—with its selectively celebratory embrace of modernity and her experiences with Dada, photomontage, and photography—occupies a place very different from those of her childhood.

Between the 1890s, when Höch was making her childhood scrapbooks, and the 1920s, enormous and revolutionary changes took place in the mass media and photography. High-speed printing presses allowed for faster and more immediate publication of photographs. From one week to the next, readers of the mass media were assured the most up-to-date images. This emphasis on visual immediacy had an enormous impact on how people experienced and viewed their surroundings. By the late 1920s and early 1930s, the German cultural critic Siegfried Kracauer and others argued that the world had become mediated almost entirely by the visual.[10] As a result, people began searching for a way to recapture a sense of "real" or "authentic" experience. Collecting offers one means by which a person can reestablish contact with this sense of the authentic. In her scrapbook Höch appears to work through issues of knowledge and identity by observing the world around her and re-presenting it through the images of the illustrated press. Thus Höch's collecting practices come to be seen as central to her work.

Höch's Scrapbook as Collection and Souvenir

Collecting is one method by which an individual can place herself in a meaningful relationship with the rest of the world.[11] By collecting objects that speak to both similarities and differences between the self and the world, a subject-object relationship is formed that positions the individual as subject and the things collected as object. Mieke Bal notes that the activity of collecting may be an individual's response to what is a radical separation of subject and object. This separation, Bal explains, "makes for an incurable loneliness that, in turn, impels the subject to gather things, in order to surround him- or herself with a subject-domain that is not-other," thus diminishing the distance felt between subject and object and extending a sense of self. A sense of mastery over the world, no matter how false, may be perceived as a result of this appropriation. This move to diminish the distance between subject and object through collecting is also addressed by Susan Stewart. But rather than emphasizing this loneliness, Stewart emphasizes longing and breaks the activities of collecting down into two concepts: the collection and the souvenir.[12]

Stewart defines a *collection* as a group of objects that have been removed from their original context and placed into a new context according to a different scheme of classification and categorization. Thus the history and origin of these objects is no longer present, or is at least obscured, and memory is frustrated. Where Stewart does allow for memory to play a role in the act of collecting and display is in what she terms a *souvenir*. A souvenir is an object or a group of objects that stands in for or refers back to an original experience. Unlike the objects in a collection, the souvenir retains the context of original experience and allows its creator to remember. Despite the important role that memory plays in the souvenir, however, Stewart maintains that ultimately "the souvenir is destined to be forgotten."[13] With the passage of time and the passing on of the creator, the memories to be found in the souvenir may disappear. In other words, what once functioned as a souvenir might later become part of a collection. Yet, despite the fact that in the collection the original context of an object is destroyed or obscured and in the souvenir traces of the original context remain, in each case a new space of meaning is produced in the ordering and arrangement of the objects.

Considering Höch's scrapbook with Stewart's categories in mind, it becomes clear that the work may be categorized as both collection and souvenir. First, by taking the Illustrierte images out of their original context in the magazine and creating a new scheme of classification, Höch's scrapbook constitutes a collection. Rather than base this new organizational schema on the Illustrierte's function—to present the most recent images as news and the most recent news as image—the new organization is based on Höch's own schema of meaning and memories of the Weimar Republic.

Simultaneously, Höch's scrapbook functions as a souvenir. It clearly gives away the origin of its images, for, as noted, Höch used *Die Dame* as the foundation on which to build her scrapbook, and she allowed parts of the magazine to show through. Thus, while on the one hand the scrapbook rejects the context of the Illustrierte, on the other hand it retains it and functions as a souvenir of the magazines themselves, Höch's employment at Ullstein, and the experience of reading the 1920s Illustrierte. The scrapbook also functioned as a souvenir on a more personal level for Höch. Because it represents a return to an activity of her childhood and young adult years, the scrapbook may have been for Höch a souvenir of that time, as well as of the beginnings of her montage practices. In addition, Höch's scrapbook contains many personal references to herself, her friends and acquaintances, and her artistic work. This personal schema of both public and private meaning justifies positioning the work within and between Stewart's two categories.

It must be noted that the status of the scrapbook as souvenir is temporally bounded. Although the scrapbook begins as a souvenir for Höch, over time it moves closer to the status of a collection. This happens as the distance between the Weimar Republic and the present increases and once Höch is no longer present to make the connections between herself and the images. On a certain level, however, the scrapbook can remain a souvenir as long as a connection can be maintained between Höch and the book as a memory book. It seems that Höch almost anticipated this, for she put her own handwriting on two pages of her scrapbook, ensuring this connection. Under an image of the German modern dancer Gret Palucca, Höch wrote in pencil, "Palucca," and under an image of the German artist Max Liebermann's hands, she wrote, "Liebermann!" Although Höch's writing on both of these pages functions as a caption—like the captions placed with images in the Illustrierte—it also acts as a signature, laying Höch's personal claim on the work.[14] Yet what this means is that while we may recognize the book's souvenir status, we do not necessarily have access to its meanings. We can speculate as to why Höch wrote Palucca's and Liebermann's names under their images, but we cannot truly know why. For this reason I do not make a case for Höch's scrapbook to be read as an explicitly autobiographical narration of her life. However, I do suggest that the scrapbook be seen as a model for Höch's collecting activities and as a collection-souvenir constructed by Höch in an attempt to reconcile a number of issues and events that occurred in Germany and in her life during the late 1920s and early 1930s.

The last years of the Weimar Republic brought many changes for Höch. She began to exhibit more frequently and, as a result, to receive due recognition for her work in both photomontage and painting. She was less fortunate, however, in her personal life. In November 1929 Höch and her partner, the Dutch writer Til Brugman, returned to Berlin from the Netherlands, where the two women had lived since 1926. In April 1930 Höch's mother passed away, and a year later her close friend and colleague Theo van Doesburg died. By 1932 her relationship with Brugman had begun to encounter difficulties, and as many of her friends began to leave Germany to escape persecution from the Nazis, Höch's world grew smaller, more isolated, and more dangerous. In the spring of 1934 Höch became very ill with Graves' disease (an inflammation of the thyroid gland); she underwent an operation in June and convalesced through the month of October. I suggest that it was during her recuperation—when she would have had the time to reflect on the past fourteen years and her recent losses—that Höch created her scrapbook.

The models of collecting set forth by Bal and Stewart are clearly demonstrated here. From these losses and the resulting distance between subject and object emerges a loneliness or longing for reunion. Several aspects of this distance are articulated in Höch's scrapbook: time, space, and alienation. The distance in time may be seen in the time elapsed between Höch's childhood scrapbooks and her 1934 scrapbook, as well as between the beginning of the Weimar Republic and its end (the range of dates of the images Höch used in her scrapbook). The distance in space may be perceived as a geographical distance, such as that between Höch as a white, Western European woman and the many images of people from faraway and exotic places that she included in her scrapbook. And the distance expressed as alienation—and its counter, familiarity—is understood as a relationship of comfort with oneself in relation to, or mastery over, one's perceived world. Thus Höch might have felt the distance, or "otherness," alternately diminish and lengthen as she collected images around her and made her scrapbook.

With all of this in mind, we may see how in creating her scrapbook Höch simultaneously constructed an account of the collective and individual experiences of modern life during the Weimar Republic. As noted, an individual level of experience is expressed through Höch's decision to construct a scrapbook (a genre from her child-hood) by using the Illustrierte images that were the medium of her modernist and avant-garde photomontages and by using images with references to everyday experi-ences and people she knew. On a collective level, the experience of reading the illus-trated magazines and of the many facets of Weimar culture are addressed, and within these experiences is expressed the cultural phenomenon of Amerikanismus.

Amerikanismus

Performances by the popular revue and cabaret dancers were one of the predomi-nant cultural experiences during the Weimar Republic. The Tiller Girls are especially familiar, thanks to the writings of Siegfried Kracauer. Beginning in 1924 the "Girl Troupes," as they were called, performed regularly in Berlin cabaret theaters, such as the Metropol and the Wintergarten. Typically scantily dressed, the "Girls" were praised for their ability to dance quickly and with machinelike precision.[15] The Tiller Girls were founded in England in the 1880s by John Tiller, the former cotton mag-nate. Following great success in England, Tiller expanded his show, and by the 1920s there were several Tiller Girls troupes touring throughout Europe and the United States.[16] A German, Herman Haller, hired one of Tiller's troupes, the Empire Girls, away from the Ziegfeld Follies in New York City and brought them to perform in Berlin as the Haller Revue.

Despite the fact that the "Girls" were originally from England and included women of all nationalities, it was commonly thought that they were all American. In an account of the Haller Revue's first Berlin performance in 1924, the German theater critic Herbert Ihering may have begun this confusion by referring to the women as "American Girls."[17] Kracauer continued the confusion by describing the women as "products of American distraction factories" and as being "mass-produced in the USA." Similarly, Fritz Giese, a professor of "psychotechnics" at the University of Stuttgart, characterized the dancers as "the product of an American mentality."[18] This confusion as to the nationality or origin of the Tiller Girls is a direct manifes-tation of the phenomenon of Amerikanismus.[19]

The term *Amerikanismus*, as used in the 1920s, is a reference to the influx into German culture of what were perceived as U.S. values, lifestyles, and economic sys-tems beginning at the end of 1923. The writing and visual imagery through which Amerikanismus was communicated centered on how Germany would reform and transform itself as a modern nation after World War I. Amerikanismus was an impor-tant and integral element of Weimar culture. It was not about the United States per se; rather, it was a German preoccupation with what Germans imagined the United States and things American to be, and it formed a locus for the debates on modernity.

Depending on one's views, Amerikanismus was a phenomenon to be embraced or rejected. Pro-Amerikanismus sentiment was characterized by an enthusiastic embrace of U.S. culture; U.S. capitalism, methods of rationalization, and mass culture exemplified the path that Germany should follow. Anti-Amerikanismus sentiment rejected everything the phenomenon stood for as a threat to the German soul; for these individuals (mostly conservative), Amerikanismus meant the downfall of German *Kultur*.[20] As Mary Nolan writes, Amerikanismus "provided not only a model to emulate or modify but a vivid and controversial language in which one could debate modernity." Aside from communism, she claims, the language of Amerikanismus was the only language available with which to debate modernity. "Germans spoke it with different political, class, and gender accents," Nolan explains, "but they could not avoid using it to talk about a world that would be rationalized, efficient, functional, untraditional, in short, modern."[21] To most Germans during the years of the Weimar Republic, America became synonymous with modernity.

Amerikanismus was grounded in a foundation of capitalism and rationalization and thus had its most obvious references in the workplace and a new kind of worker. Henry Ford's automobile assembly line and the related concept of Taylorism, or scientific management, are two prime examples, both of which isolated the production process into its most efficient parts and forced the worker to function as a machine. However, the significance of the Amerikanismus phenomenon was also manifest outside the economic realm. While present in the performances of the Tiller Girls, Amerikanismus made its way into almost every aspect of German popular culture. In 1926 Bertolt Brecht, working as a dramatist for Max Reinhardt, wrote a script for a revue show on the theme of Amerikanismus containing the following numbers: "Record, Girl, Smiling, Advertising, Boxing Match, Revue, Tarzan, Sixday Races, Slow Motion Film, Business, [and] Radio."[22] Other forms of U.S. entertainment and products adopted by Germans as a means of imagining a new future included Hollywood films, the Charleston, skyscrapers, black jazz music, the New Woman, and chewing gum. Specific individuals or groups, such as the Tiller Girls, Josephine Baker, and Charlie Chaplin, were consistently held up as symbols of the United States.

Writers and cultural critics were quick to notice and comment on this phenomenon. In his 1925 essay "Amerikanismus," Rudolf Kayser, publisher of *Die neue Rundschau*, spoke of the phenomenon as "a new European catchword [that has] nothing or only little to do with the American, whom we, after all, know less than any other national type."[23] Like Brecht, Kayser offers a list of Americanisms—"trusts, highrises, traffic officers, film, technical wonders, jazz bands, boxing, magazines, and management"—and then asks, "Is that America?" "Perhaps," he answers, but he cannot be sure because he has never been there. He is sure, however, that Amerikanismus is a "new orientation" that indicates a "new European method . . . completely attuned to spiritual and material reality." Linking Amerikanismus directly with the discourses of modernity, Kayser exclaimed: "Americanism is a fanaticism for life, for its worldliness and its present-day forms." In the end Kayser comments that Amerikanismus is not something about which to "complain" or "rejoice over." It has vitality, he observes, and "we should not measure its manifestations against false standards." Kayser holds up the jazz band as an example of this and asks, "Why, as we listen to the pounding of its instruments, speak of classical music?"[24]

Amerikanismus proper manifests itself at two points during the Weimar Republic. The first dates from 1924, the year of the Dawes Plan, when U.S. credit, along with U.S. culture, was injected into the German economy in a successful attempt to revitalize and stabilize Germany after a period of drastic inflation.[25] As a result, Amerikanismus blossomed into a full-blown myth of great proportions, and magazines and newspapers were filled with articles and photographs depicting the United States as a land of progress and opportunity. The stock market crash in 1929 ushered in a second manifestation, and at this point the perceptions and portrayal of the United States in the German media dramatically shifted. Articles discussing the actual state of life in America began to appear in publications that earlier had been only favorable to the United States.

These two attitudes are evident in Höch's scrapbook, but it is vital to acknowledge an earlier, anticipatory phase of Amerikanismus shortly before 1920. Although it cannot be defined as Amerikanismus proper, this phase shares many of the same elements and, as such, is crucial: the Berlin Dadaists' embrace of U.S. culture as a stand against the bourgeois Wilhelmine values they were so intent on destroying.[26] Georg Ehrenfried Gross and Johann Herzfelde, for example, both Americanized their names (to George Grosz and John Heartfield), and a number of the male Dadaists adopted what they considered American dress and manners. One of the many roles at which Grosz played was "George, the businessman from Manhattan."[27] All the Dadaists incorporated into their work American slogans and imagery depicting machines and technology and American people, places, and things. For these Dadaists and for other avant-garde artists in postwar Berlin, U.S. mass culture was a means of the "radical modernization and democratization" of Germany.[28]

Höch incorporated many images of North America into her Dadaist photomontages. Her best-known work, *Schnitt mit dem Küchenmesse*, shows this clearly. Within this photomontage are evident many Americanisms: smiling girls, New York City skyscrapers, dancers, U.S. swimmers, photographers, women with pageboy haircuts, boxers, wrestlers, and machine parts.[29] Many of Höch's other photomontages also make clear her awareness and use of Americanisms. *Und wenn du denkst der Mond geht unter* [If you think the moon is setting, 1921] offers one example.[30] To construct this photomontage Höch placed the head of the U.S. millionaire John Rockefeller on top of the body of a French actress, while at the right she pieced together the torso and head of an orangutan with the body of an U.S. dancer.

Höch continued to use images depicting Americanisms in her photomontages throughout the years of the Weimar Republic. Her 1925 photomontage *Equilibre* [Balance] demonstrates this particularly well. She originally titled this work *Amerika balanciert Europa* [America Balances Europe] but changed it during World War II.[31] Although her exact reasons for this change are not known, the original title and its date may refer to the role the Dawes Plan played in balancing Germany's financial accounts. In this photomontage Höch created two composite androgynous figures that balance on a seesawlike strip of paper. Presumably the androgynous New Woman figure standing on the seesaw is the United States, while the infant with what appears to be an old man's mouth and a ballerina's leg is Europe.

Amerikanismus in Höch's Scrapbook

From its initial phase in 1924 to the eventual recognition in the late 1920s that the United States was not the ideal place presented in the mass media, the discourse of Amerikanismus emerges clearly in a reading of Höch's scrapbook. Given her Dadaist background, Höch must have watched with great interest the influx of U.S. culture into Germany at the end of 1923, and she could not have helped but be aware of, and participate herself, in imagining the United States and, in the process, imagining a new Germany.

The references by Kracauer, Giese, and Ihering to the Tiller Girls as American and the conflation of machine and the Girl Troupe's bodies represent one of the central manifestations of Amerikanismus. Höch took note of this and in her scrapbook used a number of images that refer directly to the Weimar revues. On one double-page layout (pages 26–27), for example, Höch pasted across the top two almost identical images of the revue dancer Raquel Meller.[32] The only difference between the two images is that Höch clipped the caption off the image on the left but left it intact under the image on the right. The effect of this doubling is interesting, for in marking the difference between the two images of the same revue dancer Höch contradicts Kracauer's notion of the collective body of the mass in which each member is a "fraction of the figure" and the whole dance troupe is a single collective mass of legs and smiles.[33] At the same time, this doubling performs the replication of images that became possible and prevalent in the photographically illustrated press.

On another double-page layout (pages 68–69), Höch referred directly to the performance of these revues when she used a photograph of the dancer Senta Born. As the caption indicates, this image replicates and mimics a performance by a "Girltruppe."[34] Born, who danced with the Nelson Revue, performs a "shadow dance." She posed with a number of strong lights aimed so that multiple shadows were projected on the wall behind her, an image that refers directly to the rationalization, mass production, mechanical reproduction, and uniformity so important to the debates surrounding Amerikanismus. In writing about the revue dancers, the drama critic Alfred Polgar spoke of "the submersion of the individual into the group, the concentration of bodies into a single collective 'body.'" And Kracauer observed that once the Tiller Girls began dancing, they were "no longer individual girls, but indissoluble girl clusters."[35] The image of Born articulates clearly just such a conflation of one woman into an "indissoluble girl cluster." Moreover, the way Höch juxtaposes this image of Born with the images of the synchronized swimmers seen underneath and the women who have formed a clock with their bodies on the next page serves to illustrate even more clearly the relationship of the individual to the mass.

Returning to Brecht's and Kayser's lists of Americanisms, we find other direct references to Amerikanismus in Höch's scrapbook. At the lower right corner of a double-page spread (pages 98–99), Höch included an image of four bicyclists on a racecourse. The image has no caption in the scrapbook, yet to a contemporary of Höch's, the subject would have been clear: the cyclists are racing in one of the six-day bicycle races (marathon races that took place in the Sportpalast in Berlin and that Brecht included in his Amerikanismus revue). And on another page (page 19), Höch pasted an image of the African American dancer Josephine Baker wearing her famous banana skirt.[36] If the revue dancers were a reference to the fascination with rationalization and mechanization, then in the minds of many Germans, Josephine Baker and other representations of African Americans and the jazz music that was so closely associated with them, stood for America's primitive and wild side.[37]

Another of Brecht's Americanisms is reflected in Höch's inclusion of the slow-motion, or time-lapse, clip from the popular 1925 culture film *Wege zu Kraft und Schönheit* (Paths to Strength and Beauty) (pages 34–35).[38] In a 1973 radio interview with Wolfgang Pehnt, Höch commented on her fascination with slow-motion films. She recalled seeing her first slow-motion film with her friend the Hungarian artist Laszlo Moholy-Nagy, a film in which the blooming of a chrysanthemum over a period of three weeks was condensed into the space of a minute or so. "It was *kolossal*," exclaimed Höch to Pehnt; she held her breath the entire time.[39]

Kayser's list contains an interesting Americanism that cannot be left out of a discussion of Höch's scrapbook: magazines. Given that Höch made her scrapbook out of the Weimar Illustrierte, this is important. Even more important is that one of the magazines she used extensively—*Uhu*—was conceived by Ullstein as an "American"-style magazine. Advertised as "thick as a book, clever and amusing, full of good temper and joie de vivre," *Uhu* was the most popular monthly illustrated magazine in Germany from 1924 until 1933.[40]

In his memoirs Hermann Ullstein noted that he and the magazine's editors fashioned *Uhu* as a *Magazin*, not a German *Zeitschrift*.[41] According to Ullstein, "American" magazines had uniquely U.S. "methods of propaganda," and *Uhu* was modeled specifically on a magazine entitled *The American Magazine*.[42] Yet although the editors at Ullstein believed that they had created a specifically U.S.-style magazine, what they in fact created was a magazine that offered a specifically European vision of modernity.

This modernity and thus the Amerikanismus of *Uhu* can be found in its physical format as well as in its stories and images. *Uhu* was a smallish magazine that easily fit into the pocket of a man's coat or a woman's handbag. It was designed to be read on the go by the modern man and woman during those moments when they found themselves waiting for a bus or train or sitting in the doctor's office.[43]

One way the editors Americanized *Uhu* was to use English phrases untranslated. In the October 1928 issue, Anita Daniel used the phrase "sex appeal" in the otherwise German title of an essay: "Sex Appeal. Ein neues Schlagwort für eine alte Sache" [Sex appeal. A new catch-phrase for an old subject]. And the July 1930 issue included a page with more than one hundred words and phrases that had come into use only after World War I. Ten of these were English—*Frigidaire, dirt track, sex appeal, trench coat, prohibition, orangeade, weekend, gigolo, noncooperation,* and *flapper*—and four incorporated English into the German—*Jazzoper* [jazz opera], *Dollar-Schatzanweisung* [dollar treasury bond], *Standardisieren* [standardization], and *Trainingsanzug* [track suit].[44]

Uhu was an important magazine for Höch. Between 1924 and 1933 she clipped fifty-two images to use in her scrapbook. Of course *Uhu* was not the only magazine to Americanize itself or publish images reflecting the discourses of Amerikanismus. Many others did this as well, and examples of the Amerikanismus debate may be found in all the magazines used by Höch. What sets *Uhu* apart, however, is that it is the one magazine conceived from the very beginning as an "American"-style magazine.

Amerikanismus appears in Höch's scrapbook in the images she used of people and places in the United States. These images on their own are not necessarily representative of Amerikanismus, but the captions and in some cases the juxtaposition of images Höch chose anchor the identification with the Weimar debate on modernity. Images of U.S. metropolitan, agricultural, and industrial landscapes, often shown from an aerial perspective, present a country of great size, power, and resources. In some images the caption simply refers to the place in which the photograph was taken and notes a specific aspect of the shot. For the aerial view of Manhattan that Höch used on page 15 of the scrapbook, the caption simply points out that eight million people live in the Borough of Manhattan.[45]

Likewise the caption to a shot of a fig field in California that Höch used on page 52 merely notes the great size of the field.[46] In other images, however, the captions emphasize a specific quality of the United States; the tone is sometimes admiring, sometimes damning. On pages 22–23, for example, Höch pasted a shot of a lumberyard in the United States, the caption to which notes that, with stacks of lumber twenty-five meters high, America is "the country of boundless possibilities."[47] Likewise, the caption to the aerial view on pages 110–11, which depicts abandoned "gold country" along the Yuba River in California, emphasizes the strangeness and immensity of this place; the caption writer likened the dug-up land to a "fantastical moon landscape."[48] In both images the captions stress not only the nation's largeness but also its resources and riches. Furthermore, equating the gold country with a lunar landscape distances this place from the knowable world and provides a sense of wonder at the strangeness and alien quality.

Two images chosen by Höch for pages 74–75 showcase places in the United States with which Germans made especially close associations to Amerikanismus. At

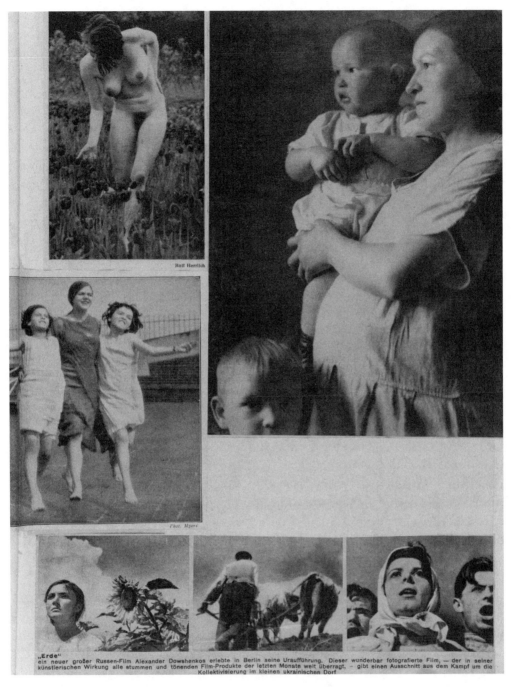

Rolf Herrlich

Phot. Myers

„Erde"
ein neuer großer Russen-Film Alexander Dowshenkos erlebte in Berlin seine Uraufführung. Dieser wunderbar fotografierte Film, — der in seiner künstlerischen Wirkung alle stummen und tönenden Film-Produkte der letzten Monate weit überragt, – gibt einen Ausschnitt aus dem Kampf um die Kollektivisierung im kleinen ukrainischen Dorf

Figure 7.1. *The image of two "street children" running across a New York City rooftop with their teacher, all three of them barefoot, is shown on the left of page 37 of Höch's scrapbook. Many of the other images on this page also refer to children.* (Hannah Höch Archive, Berlinische Galerie, Berlin)

the lower left is an aerial shot of the Hollywood Bowl, an outdoor amphitheater in Hollywood, California, which, the caption notes, is the "largest outdoor theater in the world." And at the bottom of this page Höch included an aerial view of the ice-skating rink in New York's Central Park.[49] Hollywood and New York City represented the United States for many Germans: New York was the port of entry from Europe, and Hollywood was the point of origin for the U.S. movies that had flooded the German market since the early 1920s.

Other images focus on more negative aspects of the United States. The caption writer who marveled at California's "gold country" also notes that America's resources and riches are not inexhaustible. Other images Höch chose are more explicit in their critique. An image on pages 36–37 depicting two young girls running barefoot with their teacher across a rooftop garden in New York City is from *Uhu* (see Figure 7.1).[50] The caption identifies these girls as "street children," but the term does not imply homelessness, as it does today. The article accompanying this image notes that in New York City children have only streets to play in; there is no grass or trees—some ten-year-olds have never even seen a tree. This image, despite the carefree appearance of the girls, conveys a critical tone. Like the image of the abandoned gold country, it implies that life in the United States is not as perfect or as rational as previously portrayed.

Höch made many references in her scrapbook to U.S. films and film stars, and these constitute another facet of the Amerikanismus debate. Thomas J. Saunders notes that for many Europeans, U.S. films were the main conduit of Amerikanismus.[51] While travelers' reports or photographically illustrated accounts offered ways for Germans to learn about the United States and its way of life, film was unequaled in its scope. Saunders writes that the U.S. film industry brought to Europe "'live' impressions" of America, "giving visual contours to the American dream—the moral, social, and economic foundations of beauty, success and happiness." Cinema itself, notes Saunders, "epitomized U.S. culture in its mass orientation, tempo, monumentalism, sensationalism and profit urge."[52]

Although the Illustrierte played as major a role as film in communicating the idea of the United States, it is highly significant that many of the articles and photographs in the illustrated press mediated the representation of America through film stills and photographs of movie stars. Höch used a number of stills from U.S. movies: Robert Flaherty's 1926 film *Moana* (pages 96–97), Merian C. Cooper and Ernest B. Schoedsack's 1927 jungle film *Chang* (pages 57 and 104), and the 1927 film *The Gorilla* (page 105). Even more interesting for a discussion of Amerikanismus are the publicity shots of female movie stars that Höch included. On one page layout (pages 42–43), Höch pasted shots of Katherine Hepburn, the Chinese American film star Anna May Wong, Greta Garbo, Dolores del Rio, Dita Parlo, and Valerie Boothby. In each of these images the movie stars are shown as Americanized, whether or not they are American: they are glamorous, beautiful, and desirable (see Figure 7.2).

Figure 7.2. *Höch pasted photographs of movie stars, including Katherine Hepburn and Dolores del Rio, and other unidentified beauties on a page layout of her scrapbook.* (Hannah Höch Archive, Berlinische Galerie, Berlin)

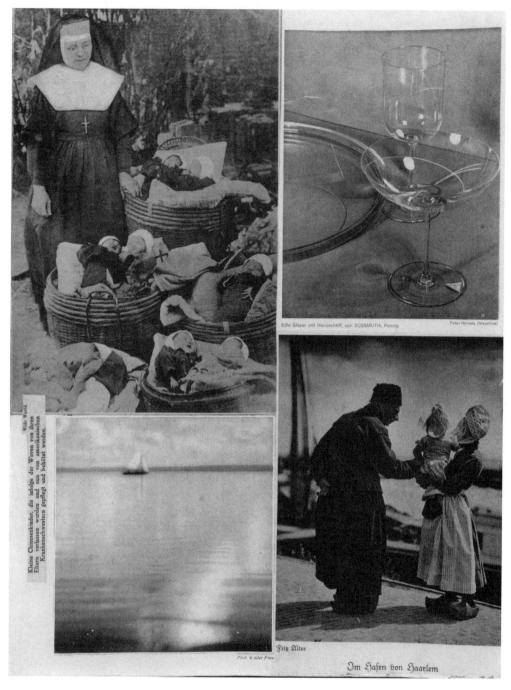

Kleine Chinesenkinder, die infolge der Wirren von ihren Eltern verlassen wurden und nun von amerikanischen Krankenschwestern gepflegt und behütet werden.

Wide World

Edle Gläser mit Handschliff, von SÜSSMUTH, Penzig

Foto: Hoinkis (Mauritius)

Phot. Walter Plew

Frih Alter

Im Hafen von Haarlem

Figure 7.3   *Höch almost always juxtaposed a wide range of images. Here she pictured a Christian nun with abandoned Chinese children; a Dutch man, woman, and child; an arrangement of glassware; and a photograph of a sailboat on the water. Opposite them but not visible here she placed several images depicting elderly people, including the illiterate U.S. woman farmer from Tennessee discussed in the essay.* (Hannah Höch Archive, Berlinische Galerie, Berlin)

In contrast to these images, Höch juxtaposed other diverse images that suggest the choice to explore visually cultural representations. For example, on page 98, she presented a Christian nun with orphaned Chinese babies, Dutch people in traditional costume, a sailboat, and the clear image of modern glassware (see Figure 7.3).

Opposite this page, she made an important reference to U.S. film when she used an image from a December 1929 issue of *Uhu* of what appears to be an old woman from Tennessee. The caption in *Uhu* places the image squarely within the discourse on Amerikanismus: "Portrait of an American female farmer as she is not portrayed in movies. This woman, from the state of Tennessee, accidentally learned that ten years earlier there had been a World War. She can neither read nor write."[53]

While it is shocking that, after ten years, this rural, illiterate woman did not know there had been a world war, the significance of this image for a discussion of Amerikanismus lies in the fact that this is the U.S. woman who has not been portrayed in films; the U.S. woman shown in U.S. films and in the images in Höch's scrapbook is exposed as a lie. Although Höch did not include the entire caption in her scrapbook, she allowed the phrase "portrait of the American female farmer as she is not portrayed in movies" to remain visible. The title of the *Uhu* article—"The Twilight of America: Enthusiastic Europe Begins to See the Wrong Side of America"—unmasks this lie further.

Although the images of U.S. movie stars in Höch's scrapbook are easily recognized as American, one does not see the Amerikanismus of these images when they are viewed on their own. Only when they are seen in relationship to images like that of the female farmer from Tennessee is the debate on Amerikanismus exposed. December 1929, the date of the *Uhu* article and only two months after the crash of the U.S. stock market, may have marked the high point for the recognition by Germans that the United States was not the prosperous place the German imagination—or U.S. films—had made it out to be.

THE THEME OF AMERIKANISMUS brings to the forefront the debate on modernity that has so clearly shaped how we view the years of the Weimar Republic. Hannah Höch was an active participant in this debate. Although she did not publish manifestoes or speak out in public as her male colleagues often did, through her montage work Höch engaged with the ideas and materials of modernity. As we have seen, Höch's scrapbook clearly embodies the theme of Amerikanismus and positions her as a consumer and critic of the debate. She brought to the construction of her scrapbook all the skills honed in her avant-garde photomontages. Yet in her choice to return to her childhood pastime of making scrapbooks, she presents us with an interesting move by an avant-garde artist of the 1920s and early 1930s that calls into question how we understand the relationship between an avant-garde artist and his or her participation in popular culture. As understood for so long, this relationship has been characterized not by an embrace of the experiences of modern life but by a negative and critical response to them.[54] To my knowledge, no other artist active at the time created a work that expressed such pleasure in the materials of mass culture or was so firmly rooted in the practices of childhood or "feminine" genres as Höch produced with her scrapbook. Certainly there are artists whose work might be compared to it, but Höch's scrapbook stands out. Höch enjoyed the mass media; she consumed it, and it shaped how she viewed herself in the world. Her montage practices show her to be an astute and critical observer, and her scrapbook demonstrates more clearly than any of her other works the degree to which this balance of visual pleasure and radical critique was integral to her entire oeuvre.

PART II

~~~~~~~

Books of the Self

8

~~~~~

The Secret Scrapbook of a "Soiled Dove"

~~~~~

FOR MANY YEARS A SMALL, tattered blue scrapbook, the former property of one of Laramie, Wyoming's soiled doves, sat on a shelf in the Toppan Rare Books Library at the University of Wyoming's American Heritage Center in Laramie.[1] Its bright blue fabric cover, embossed with a delicate design of ferns and flowers twining around the word *Scrapbook* emblazoned diagonally across the front, was now nearly separated from its spine. Its seventy-four gummed pages, with its creator's mementos carefully affixed, were scuffed and faded. The scrapbook might have remained there, neglected by researchers for many years more, if Anne Marie Lane, the Toppan Rare Books curator, had not decided to prepare an exhibit on Victorian books for her History of Books and Reading class. Brittle and worn, the scrapbook was lifted from the shelf and gently placed on a pillowed book cradle. As the cover was opened, a faded inscription written in pencil was revealed on the flyleaf: "Mrs. Monte E. Grover / Laramie Wyo. / Came to L July 16, 1881."

I had stopped by the Toppan Library on the day of the class to browse through the books on exhibit. When I saw the scrapbook's inscription, I was overcome with excitement. Monte Grover was a name I knew well. In fact, by the time I defended my master's thesis on Laramie prostitution in the summer of 1994, I had come to think of her as an intimate acquaintance. Monte Grover was a young prostitute who had worked in and later managed Laramie's notorious bordello, Grover's Institute. The scrapbook was an amazing find, providing me with the opportunity to learn more about a woman whose life story both intrigued and saddened me.

I was consumed with curiosity about how the scrapbook had come to be in the Toppan Library's collection. Information about the book's provenance before its arrival there was extremely limited, but the bits of information available indicated that the scrapbook had been acquired by the University of Wyoming Library on September 21, 1938, and added to the Hebard Library, a collection of Wyomingana established in the late 1800s by Grace Raymond Hebard, a University of Wyoming professor.[2] A stamp on the lower right corner of the front flyleaf shows that the book was withdrawn from the library's collection, but the date of withdrawal is unavailable. The scrapbook was later added to books housed with the American Heritage Center's Fitzhugh Collection and then transferred to the Toppan Rare Books Library.

Further research indicated that the scrapbook was probably acquired by the University of Wyoming as part of a donation from the Laramie Woman's Club.[3] This discovery was almost as amazing as the discovery of the scrapbook itself. I wondered if the club members had realized what the scrapbook was and to whom it had belonged. Initially, I assumed they had not, but further research caused me to revise this assumption.

When the Laramie Woman's Club was organized in 1898, its charter offered membership in the club to all women in Laramie.[4] The club's founders were firmly dedicated to this principle of inclusiveness. Even so, it came as a bit of a surprise to the community—and attracted comment in the press—when two of the founding members took the unprecedented step of visiting each of Laramie's brothels, personally inviting the prostitutes to become members of the Laramie Woman's Club.[5] Early membership rosters do not indicate that any of the prostitutes accepted the invitation, but perhaps they participated indirectly by making contributions to the club's early projects, which included the establishment of a library and a museum. Although Monte Grover was no longer living in 1898, when the Laramie Woman's Club was organized, it is possible that another prostitute had kept the scrapbook after Monte's death and later donated it to the library or museum project.

The scrapbook is primarily autobiographical in content. The arrangement of items seems to correspond, for the most part, to the chronology of documented events in Monte's life during her marriage to John Grover. However, there are inconsistencies which suggest that some items have been placed in the scrapbook randomly. For example, Monte's marriage announcement does not appear until several pages after an item that seems to commemorate her first anniversary. One item in the scrapbook, a legal notice regarding the divorce of an acquaintance, predates Monte's arrival in Laramie. It is possible that Monte started the scrapbook before coming to Wyoming and placed this item in the book herself. It is also possible that the scrapbook originally belonged to Christy Grover, a madam who employed Monte when she first arrived in Laramie. On the scrapbook's second page is a legal notice, probably published on or about December 29, 1877, informing Uriah Branch that his wife, Christy Branch (later Christy Grover), was petitioning the court for an annulment of their marriage, which had taken place on July 9, 1873, in Minneapolis.[6] In the petition Christy alleged that Uriah was a minor at the time of their wedding, that she and Uriah had separated immediately after the ceremony, and that they had not consummated their union. The text of the notice indicated that Christy was residing in Chicago in 1877. A number of other items in the scrapbook make reference to events in Chicago, but some were printed in newspapers after 1882, the year of Christy's death, and so could not have been placed in the book by her. Because of this, it seems more plausible that the scrapbook is solely Monte's creation.

The Wyoming censuses of 1870 and 1880 have no entries for Monte, and so it is likely that she was not residing in the territory at that time. It seems quite possible that Christy and Monte may have become acquainted in Chicago and that Monte's arrival in Laramie in 1881 was linked to this earlier acquaintance.

Mattress Capitalists

Laramie, Wyoming, sprang up during construction of the transcontinental railroad in 1868 as a rough, wild, end-of-tracks town. By 1880, more settled, Laramie was enjoying a period of economic prosperity, but on Front Street, just east of the Union Pacific Depot, one could venture into the Laramie tenderloin, a rough thoroughfare lined with saloons, gambling halls and brothels. Crime, poverty, and disease were staples of life in the tenderloin. Laramie Justice Court records reveal that shootings, garrotings, stabbings, robberies, and suicides occurred there with distressing frequency. Because of the revenue generated for the city from the sale of liquor and gambling licenses and the fines and fees collected from prostitutes, attempts by the city council to address problems in the tenderloin always focused on regulation rather than eradication of the district. Most restrictive ordinances imposed by the city, such as one authorizing the collection of monthly "fees" from prostitutes and another restricting the manner in which prostitutes could move about the streets, targeted only the women of the tenderloin.[7] These ordinances were intended to impose social, economic, and political controls to decrease prostitutes' visibility in the community. Although Christy and Monte, as parlor-house prostitutes, were at the top of the occupational hierarchy in the tenderloin, they would have been subjected to the same social marginalization as their lower-status colleagues.

In 1880 Christy Branch—known also by the names Puss Newport, Dollie Baillie, and Christy Finlayson—was working as a prostitute at Ida Hamilton's infamous House of Mirrors in Cheyenne, Wyoming.[8] Later that year Christy moved on to Laramie and went into business for herself. Eschewing the seamy environment on Front Street, Christy contracted with the carpenter L. W. Schroeder to build two houses on South B Street, in the middle of the Laramie business district, two blocks east of the Front Street tenderloin.[9] The larger of the two structures was a parlor house known as the Blonde's, and the structure on the adjacent lot served as Christy's private residence. A few months after the opening of her parlor house, Christy married John Grover, a Laramie grocer who immediately abandoned his grocery business to devote himself to the sporting life.[10]

Christy must have done well for herself, because her property was valued at more than $3,500 and both houses were insured, a costly undertaking in those days of wood buildings and frequent fires.[11] The furnishings of Christy's houses included a five-hundred-dollar piano, silk chairs and chaises, fancy mirrors, carpets, walnut and ebony furnishings, decorative lamps, and costly silver and china. Christy also spent substantial sums at various Laramie businesses for elegant clothing, fine lingerie, and custom-made jewelry for herself and her "girls." Her account at Trabing's Grocery store shows regular purchases of expensive liquors and delicacies such as eels to be served at the lavish dinners she provided for her patrons.

Monte arrived in Laramie during the summer of 1881 and began working for Christy as a parlor-house prostitute, using the name Monte Arlington rather than her given name, Mamie Lambert.[12] As a resident of the Blonde's, Monte enjoyed a style of living far more opulent than that of most Laramie residents. Little is known about Monte's life or about the nature of Monte's relationship with John Grover during the early months of her residence at the Blonde's. However, whether it began before or after Christy's death, Monte and Grover began a romantic relationship that would eventually bring Monte only despair, hopelessness, and an early grave.

On February 19, 1882, Christy and Grover returned to the parlor house from an excursion to the Laramie Brewery for an afternoon of billiards and drinking to discover that Mamie Hall, a young prostitute Monte had befriended, had run away during their absence, taking along Christy's sealskin cape and hat. Christy flew into a rage and accused Monte of conspiring with Mamie to steal the furs. Monte denied having any part in the episode and left the house to avoid further unpleasantness. Christy stormed off to her bedroom. Less than a half hour later, a shot rang out. Grover subsequently testified that he burst into the room and discovered Christy lying on her bed, a bullet in her brain and his pistol in her hand.[13]

A coroner's jury impaneled the following day heard testimony from Grover, along with brief statements from Monte and a laundress who had spoken to Christy just before she retired to the bedroom. Although no one could verify Grover's whereabouts at the time of the shooting, the coroner's jury accepted his testimony without comment and ruled Christy's death a suicide.[14] Whether the coroner's jury was satisfied with the witnesses' accounts of the event or whether they simply did not consider the death of a notorious prostitute worthy of further investigation will never be known.

Whether Monte had any direct role in Christy's death is a matter of conjecture. Suicide was all too common among the prostitutes of Laramie's demimonde, but so was murder. Grover, as Christy's sole heir, could have been motivated to harm Christy by the desire for financial gain, and court records show that he had a history of violent attacks on other prostitutes. Although violent encounters frequently occurred between prostitutes, Monte's court record does not indicate that she was ever charged with any acts of physical aggression. She appears in the Albany County court records only for offenses related to fornication and violation of liquor ordinances.

Grover quickly arranged to be appointed executor of Christy's sizable estate and laid Christy to rest, marking her grave with an impressive stone obelisk.[15] He took over control of the parlor house, which then became known as Grover's Institute. Christy's estate left Grover in comfortable circumstances, allowing him to dabble in real estate and purchase a saloon.[16]

In October 1883, a year and eight months after Christy's death, Grover married Monte Arlington.[17] After their marriage Monte was left in charge of the day-to-day management of the parlor house, while Grover occupied himself with his new saloon. Most of the material in Monte's scrapbook seems to date from this point in her life.

The Private Thoughts of a Public Woman

Because many nineteenth-century prostitutes were unable to read or write, they left behind few first-person accounts of their experiences. Consequently, most information about the lives of these public women must be gleaned from other primary sources, such as court records, newspaper articles, probate papers, and coroner's inquest transcripts. These records provide important bits of information about the public lives of prostitutes but reveal little about the intensely private, backstage realm of their lives or their perceptions of themselves as women, wives, daughters, sisters, and mothers. Monte Grover was a notable exception.

Monte's creation of the scrapbook and the notations she made on some of the pages indicate that she could read and write and thus was more educated and probably more cultivated than many of the women working in Laramie's vice district. The creation of the scrapbook also indicates that she had leisure time to devote to a creative activity, mirroring that of many middle-class women of her day.[18] Much in the scrapbook seems to suggest that Monte identified with women of middle-class society, despite the fact that as a prostitute she was permanently barred from any hope of acceptance as a member of the middle class.

Monte's reading habits seem to reflect middle-class tastes as well. Although the sources of most of the items in the scrapbook are unidentified, certain items indicate that Monte had access to such magazines as *Waverly Magazine, Youth's Companion,* and the *Pacific Christian Advocate,* as well as such newspapers as the *Laramie Boomerang, Cheyenne Leader, Denver News,* and *Chicago Herald.* The clippings in her scrapbook indicate that she was interested in domestic issues, current events, and political news, as well as topics concerning members of the vice community.

The scrapbook provided Monte with a medium for self-expression, commentary, and reflection through which she attempted to make sense of her environment and define her sense of identity. Through the poetry, jokes, news articles, and mementos in the scrapbook, she wove a story of her life that allows people today to know her as an individual. The scrapbook may have given Monte a sense of empowerment by allowing her to determine the way in which the events of a life characterized by chaos and disorder would be given structure and order. It also allowed her to exert ownership over her thoughts, feelings, and aspirations—ownership that she could not exert over her own body in the external reality of her world. The scrapbook tells much about who Monte perceived herself to be, as well as who she might have liked to have been.

The bits of sentimental poetry, household tips, home remedies, and announcements of graduations, weddings, and community events in Monte's scrapbook were no different from items typically found in scrapbooks created by other middle-class Victorian women of her era.[19] Yet there are other items, such as a prostitute's calling card, which provide a jarring contrast to these mementos of middle-class life and locate Monte as a denizen of the demimonde rather than a middle-class matron.

From the items Monte selected for the scrapbook, it is clear that she viewed herself as simultaneously occupying dual roles: a prostitute and a faithful, devoted wife. It is equally clear that she did not perceive these roles to be, by their very nature, mutually exclusive. Although it was not uncommon in the 1800s for prostitutes to marry, the marriages frequently ended in divorce, separation, or abandonment.[20] Monte's marriage to Grover lasted longer than that of any other known couple in Laramie's demimonde during the late 1800s, but the quality of the relationship does not appear to have been much different from that of other tenderloin marriages.

Much of the material in Monte's scrapbook presents an idealized view of matrimonial bliss and moral rectitude that could not be more at odds with the harsh realities of her life. There seems to be little logic associated with her selection of these items, given her occupation. Yet the items create a text that reflects Monte's interior struggle to construct her own worldview and identity in a world that struggled equally hard to make her invisible. Patricia P. Buckler, quoting from the work of Suzanne L. Bunkers, argues that "[the scrapbook as] a catalog of life, with its reflection of the culture and society in which that life was lived is both true and accurate if viewed through the eyes of the author. That perspective was/is shaped by the author's experience of race, ethnic origin, economic/social class—her perceptions of the world around her."[21]

The poetry in Monte's scrapbook begins with a romantic, idealized view of courtship and marriage followed later by poems that address themes of marital discord and a wife's longing for reconciliation. The poetry on the last few pages of the book deals with dark topics of despair, disillusionment with life, and death. The sequence of the poetry appears to follow the progression of verifiable events in Monte's life—her marriage to Grover; the difficulties she experienced during her life with Grover, a man known for his abusive behavior toward women; and the fear and despair that she must have felt during the final months of her life, when she began to fear that she was going to be murdered.[22]

Marriage and Morality

The first page of the scrapbook contains newspaper clippings announcing the marriage of a Kansas couple and the arrival of a new priest, who was coming to assist the Episcopal bishop in Laramie and would be bringing his wife. There are also news clippings about the litigation of a property dispute, an article on regional and community pride, an account of a professional gambler who forsook his occupation to become a missionary, and a humorous anecdote about a woman who made a nuisance of herself by borrowing eggs from her neighbors. Ironically, the overall impression given by this initial page is that the scrapbook belongs to a woman who is probably religious, has high moral standards, and is concerned with good citizenship. The following page is devoted to humorous anecdotes and a fragment of a romantic poem, which seems to have had a special significance for Monte:

> The rose that in some winter room
> So fraily grows, so palely blows
> Knows in its heart a brighter bloom
> And longs to be a summer rose—
> In sun and shower a summer rose. . . .
>
> The love that lurks in every breast,
> So kind a thing, so blind a thing,
> If with a smile or word caressed
> Would wake and rise and be a King—
> Of life and death the Lord and King.

Except for the article about the new priest, there is nothing to conclusively link Monte to Laramie until page 5 of the scrapbook. The entire page is devoted to a single item, which appears to commemorate Monte and Grover's first anniversary. The date—October 31, 1884—is written in pencil at the bottom of the page, although the date of their first wedding anniversary would have been October 2, 1884. The page contains the clipping of a poem entitled "Growing Old." The poem begins with the line "We are growing old together, John and I" and goes on to describe a lengthy committed relationship in which the married couple meets life's challenges together and are bound by an even stronger bond of love and devotion as they become elderly. The announcement of Monte's marriage to Grover does not appear until several pages later. In the announcement, Monte is listed by her given name, Mamie Lambert.

The scrapbook also contains a newspaper clipping reporting an action brought by Grover to restrain the sheriff from closing his saloon after the former sheriff absconded with the money Grover paid for his liquor license. This clipping is followed by a brief editorial describing the ex-sheriff's wife's determination to make restitution for any shortage in her husband's accounts by selling her homestead. The editorial urges the injured parties in the case to refrain from doing anything to inflict further pain on the poor woman and her children. Monte may have included this article in her scrapbook out of satisfaction at her husband's success in obtaining restitution for his loss. However, it may also indicate that she felt some sympathy or admiration for the unfortunate but honorable woman.

The poetry Monte selected for her scrapbook focuses heavily on two themes: romantic love, in which the woman is pure and chaste; and unrequited love, in which one partner, usually the woman, dies after rejection by her lover. Ironically, Monte appears to have strongly identified with the pure, chaste women in the poetry and does not appear to have regarded her occupation as an impediment to this type of self-identification. Many of the stories and articles interspersed with the poetry on these pages are allegorical, calling the reader's attention to the triumph of good over evil, the rewards of morality over immorality.

A number of items in the first half of the scrapbook indicate Monte's delight with married life and suggest that she felt a sense of true contentment. One poem, "The Wife's Kiss at the Door," stresses the importance of being a devoted, loving wife and reminds women to refrain from taking their husbands for granted:

> Be loving and sweet to your husband;
> Be just as pretty and bright
> As the girl he came a-courting
> When he comes home to-night;
> And when he goes in the morning, once more
> Run down and kiss him "good-bye" at the door.

As Monte settled into married life, the tone of the poetry she selected for her scrapbook became more lighthearted. Jokes and humorous anecdotes fill many of the pages, along with poems celebrating the change of seasons and the beauty of nature. The overall sense is one of happiness and contentment. One poem she selected for inclusion in her scrapbook was entitled "Wyoming," perhaps indicating that she viewed coming to Wyoming as a pivotal event leading to her life as a married woman:

> Grand and majestic, great land of wonders!
> Tender, yet strong, like thy Master's heart.
> Healing with thy breath the sick and feeble.
> Giving to those who seek thee a home and a start. . . .
>
> Fair land of life! Which Nature's hand hath favored.
> The star which gleams the brightest in the West,
> Where thousands yet from every land and nation
> May dwell within thy realms in peace and rest.

Life in the Social Margins

Monte seemed to accept her role as a prostitute and take an active interest in matters pertaining to the vice district. However, one item in the scrapbook, a poem entitled "Judge Not That Ye Be Not Judged," indicates that Monte may have been saddened by the alienation and rejection she undoubtedly experienced from some members of the community:

> Perchance the friend who cheered thy early years
> Has yielded to the tempter's power:
> Yet why shrink back and draw away thy skirt,
> As tho her very touch would do thee hurt?
> Wilt thou prove stronger in temptation's hour?
>
> Perchance the one thou trustedest more than life
> Has broken love's most sacred vow:
> Yet judge him not—the victor in life's strife
> Is he who beareth best the burden of life
> And leaveth to God to judge, nor questions how.
> Sing the great song of love to all, and not
> The wailing anthem of thy woes;
> So live thy life that thou mayst never feel
> Afraid to say, as at His throne you kneel,
> "Forgive me, God, as I forgive my foes."

Although she lived on the social margins of the community, Monte often attended city council meetings and worked with another prostitute, Della Briggs, to get the city to authorize repairs to the sewer system and make improvements to the cemetery.[23] The city council did not welcome Monte's and Della's suggestions and attempted to discourage their participation in civic affairs by revoking their liquor licenses during a local social purity campaign.[24] On May 26, 1887, an editorial appeared in the *Laramie Daily Boomerang* complaining about Grover's Institute and a new bordello Grover and Monte had opened near a residential district. The editorial fumed that Grover's places were fostering immorality among young people attending the University of Wyoming and were circumventing local liquor-licensing ordinances. Monte carefully preserved the article in her scrapbook. Even allowing for the writer's bias and tendency to embellish, it provides a graphic description of the world in which Monte lived.

> On the core corner of the town stands a crazy, tumble-down rookery, full from
> cellar to shingles of liquors, gambling devices and everything that can be

Figure 8.1. *A card announcing Sadie Florington's new business address is typical of those used by higher-status prostitutes to solicit patrons.* (Courtesy American Heritage Center, University of Wyoming)

used to corrupt and rob men. Ruffians and tin-horn gamblers make night and day hideous with their orgies. Half a block away on the principal residence street, under the same management is a house full of shameless women as vile if possible as the men who support them . . . the saloon . . . does occupy the most prominent corner on the main street of the city and in addition to the usual stock of liquors, contains the paraphernalia of certain games licensed by the city and, like all gambling devices, not conducted for the purpose of enriching the patrons of the place at the expense of the proprietor. One or two of these games are noisy and . . . the noise cannot help reaching the street. . . . The piano playing, which is one of the features of the establishment, is if anything a worse nuisance than the cries of "Roll the wheel once more," "Lucky diamond in the lucky red," etc. . . . In regard to the other iniquity . . . which is a stone's throw from the business streets, . . . in the past the "boarders" have been permitted to do pretty much as they pleased and they have flaunted themselves in the face of decent people until it has become at times unbearable. They parade the streets in daylight as well as in the dark and have been known to insult decent women on the chief thoroughfare of the city. Under the influence of whiskey or absinthe they ride about in their hired hacks and carriages and intrude their presence at all sorts of assemblies. Within a few days a dame who has since left town perpetrated a gross outrage by daubing the front of a house with filth. They seem to take delight in making their presence felt and making themselves obnoxious to everybody. There are exceptions, it is true, but they are in the minority.

The following page is devoted to a single card, tastefully engraved on vellum paper (see Figure 8.1). The card announces the opening of Miss Sadie Florington's new residence and requests that visitors call after 7:00 p.m. The card is that of a prostitute, presumably an acquaintance of Monte's, discreetly announcing to her customers that she is now doing business at a new address.

Despite her preoccupation with affairs in the tenderloin, Monte's scrapbook indicates that she not only kept up with local events but also was interested in history and followed world affairs as well. There are clippings announcing awards given to various local businessmen (possibly patrons of Monte's) in appreciation for their contributions to the Laramie community. Another item gives statistics on the sizes of ancient cities and famous structures such as Nineveh, Babylon, the Grecian temples, and the Egyptian pyramids. An article discussing John Wilkes Booth's motivations for killing President Abraham Lincoln shares a page with another clipping entitled "The Saddest Spot on Earth," describing the plight and suffering of Russian citizens exiled to Siberia.

Humor, Propriety, Parody, and Pathos

The last twenty pages of Monte's scrapbook are a rather manic-depressive mix of items preoccupied with death, faithless husbands, and unhappy marriages but interspersed with advertisements and humorous articles, such as an item parodying two Irish immigrant women discussing fashion and another about a woman who simply cannot cook a Christmas goose. The humorous items seem oddly out of place, appearing randomly on pages otherwise filled with dark, maudlin poetry.

One page of the scrapbook is devoted to trade cards Monte appears to have received from a cigarette vendor. Most of the cards advertise Lone Jack cigarettes and feature pictures of women in a variety of costumes (see Figure 8.2). Women pictured in advertisements such as these were often actresses or other women from the fringe of society. The scrapbook also contains a business card for a traveling liquor salesman named Moritz Sachs, along with a formal engraved invitation to a party at Library Hall in Cheyenne, hosted by Sachs and his wife to celebrate their forty-fifth wedding anniversary. Although Sachs, like other salesmen, undoubtedly did business with people in the vice community, he would not necessarily have been a part of that community himself. The invitation suggests that Monte might have been personally

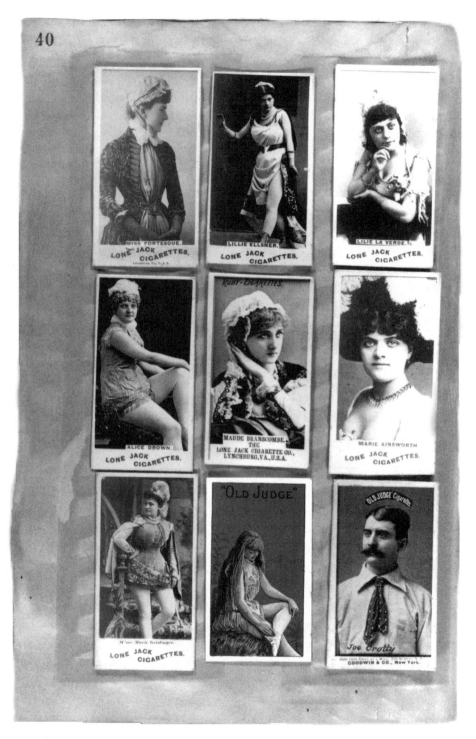

Figure 8.2. *The images of women on advertising cards, such as these collected by Monte Grover,* *depict many of the enabling and constraining roles that U.S. woman could assume in their everyday* *lives. These images of women smoking cigarettes, taboo for most women, provided role models to which* *Monte, on the fringe of society, could aspire.* (Courtesy American Heritage Center, University of Wyoming)

invited to a social event involving people outside the vice community. Perhaps that fact, rather than the party itself, is what made the invitation significant to her.

Many of the items Monte placed in the second half of the scrapbook suggest that her relationship with Grover was deteriorating. Perhaps he had found a new love, or perhaps Monte had. The poems in the scrapbook about faithful, long-suffering wives, such as the one entitled "Go Cheerily Home," may suggest that Monte was making an effort to hold her marriage together or perhaps that she wanted some recognition and appreciation for her contributions to the marriage:

> The dear little wife at home, John,
> With ever so much to do,
> Stitches to set and babies to pet,
> And so many thoughts of you;
> The beautiful household fairy,
> Filling your heart with light;
> Whatever you meet today, John,
> Go cheerily home tonight.
>
> For though you are worn and weary
> You needn't be cross or curt;
> There are words like darts to gentle hearts,
> There are looks that wound and hurt.
> With the key in the latch at home, John,
> Drop the trouble out of sight;
> To the little wife who is waiting
> Go cheerily home tonight.

Although Monte may have been unhappy, she seems to have retained a sense of self-worth. Some items in the scrapbook seem to have been chosen to affirm her sense of self-esteem, such as the poem entitled "I Will Be Worthy of It." The last two verses read:

> I may not triumph in success,
> Despite my earnest labor;
> I may not grasp results that bless
> The efforts of my neighbor.
> But though my goal I never see,
> This thought shall always dwell with me,
> I will be worthy of it.
>
> The golden glory of love's light
> May ne'er fall on my way:

My path may always lead through night,
Like some deserted by-way.
But though life's dearest joy I miss,
There lies a nameless joy in this—
I will be worthy of it.

Despite her occupation as a prostitute, there are indications that Monte tried to be a good homemaker. Two articles in the scrapbook would have been of general interest to almost all housewives of the 1880s. One article, entitled "The House-hold Physician," provides instructions for home remedies:

Turpentine, given in teaspoonful doses every eight hours in milk or coffee, is pronounced a cure for diphtheria.

The white of an egg is stated to be the best application for soothing burns and scalds. It may be poured over the wound, and forms at once a varnish which excludes the air. . . .

Oil of cinnamon, dropped on warts three or four times a day, will cause their disappearance, however hard, large or dense they may be.

The other article, "Of Interest to Women," gives numerous tips for efficient housewifery:

Whiskey will take out every kind of fruit stain. . . .

Nothing is better than turpentine for the banishment of carpet worms, buffola-moths, and insects. Oil of peppermint in water diluted even to one part in one million will kill cockroaches in an hour, they dying in convulsions.

To make paper stick to a wall that has been whitewashed, wash in vinegar or saleratus water.

Alum dissolved in water and applied to a bedstead with a feather will exterminate bed bugs.

Although she undoubtedly had many problems of her own, Monte seems to have been concerned for the welfare of others and sympathetic to the plight of the downtrodden and oppressed. One page of her scrapbook is devoted to an illustration entitled "The Boundary Post," which depicts Russian exiles under armed guard. Many of the exiles are weeping and clinging to loved ones before crossing over into Siberia. At the bottom of the illustration, the second item in the scrapbook pertaining to the plight of people exiled to Siberia, Monte has written, "They have marched away into Siberia!" This inscription seems to indicate that the Siberian exiles had a special significance for Monte—she has not written on any of the other articles except to caption the poem that appears to commemorate her first anniversary and to underline words on a few other items.

Several items in her scrapbook suggest that Monte also admired kindness and moral courage in the conduct of others. Particularly illustrative is a news article about a sheriff who received eviction papers for a poor Laramie family. Because it was raining heavily on the day of the eviction, the sheriff refused to turn the family out, stating that he did not believe it was his duty to throw unfortunate people out into the street on such a day: he would not do it because the person desiring the eviction would not benefit from it and the victims would suffer.

Monte also had some interest in politics, and the articles she selected to place in her scrapbook indicate she was probably Republican in her political affiliation. One clipping entitled "Campaign Poetry" clearly supports the election of Benjamin Harrison while disparaging his opponent, Grover Cleveland.

> Then, let us stand together, Jim, old soldiers tried and true,
> I feel as eager for the fray as when I wore the blue:
> Let Harrison ring out the charge in stirring bugle notes,
> And Cleveland, Jim, be buried in a million soldier votes!

A number of clippings are devoted to humorous anecdotes at the expense of the Irish. One tells the story of an Irish drunkard who habitually beat his wife:

Exasperated, the poor woman sought the assistance of the parish priest. The priest confronted the husband, who said that he simply could not stop drinking and control his abusive behavior. The priest, out of patience, said, "Now, see here, Pat, I'll tell you what. You'll stop this right here tonight. If you ever get drunk again, I'll turn you into a rat—d'ye mind that? If I don't see you I'll know about it just the same . . . and if you do get drunk, into a rat ye go." Pat came home drunk the following night and kicked open the door. His beleaguered wife could see that he was drunk and in fighting trim, so she dodged behind the table for protection. "Don't be afraid, darlin,'" said Pat. "I'm not going to bate you this night. I'm not goin' to lay the weight of my finger on ye. . . . Ye know his riverince was here last night, and he told me if I ever got dhrunk again he'd turn me into a rat. I'm dhrunk this minute, darlin'. The praste didn't see me, but he knows I'm dhrunk, and this night into a rat I go. I want ye to be kind to me, darlin', and watch me, and whin ye see me gittin' little, and the hair growin' out on me, an' me whiskers gittin' long, for God's sake darlin', as ye love me, kape yer eye on the cat!"

The next few pages contain a strange mix of items about characters in the vice communities of Denver and Chicago, intermingled with more advertisements, allegorical anecdotes, poetry, and bits of humor. One page holds a trade card for the Dozier-Weyl Cracker Company of St. Louis (see Figure 8.3). The card depicts a parrot gripping a dripping paintbrush in its claw. The inscription reads, "Give me a

Figure 8.3. *The only full-color item in Monte's scrapbook is this advertisement for the Dozier-Weyl Cracker Company. Its slogan would probably have struck a humorous note with members of the vice community.* (Courtesy American Heritage Center, University of Wyoming)

Royal Snowflake [cracker] or I'll paint this whole town RED."

Following the Dozier-Weyl card is a humorous anecdotal article describing the unconventional funeral of "Shang" Andrews, a picturesque character of the Levee in Chicago. Another page holds a clipping, perhaps from one of the Denver newspapers, with a drawing of an attractive, buxom woman and the caption "Miss Minnie Clifford, Queen of the Denver, Col., Demimonde." Monte also preserved a lengthy article about Ross Raymond, a Chicago swindler, to whom the article attributes the dubious distinction of being the most successful confidence man living. Possibly, Raymond, Clifford, and Andrews were all acquaintances of Monte's.

Among the clippings about swindlers and madams, saloonkeepers and sheriffs, is a carefully preserved note inscribed "Laramie City, Wyo., Nov. 3rd, 1888." Addressed to Mrs. M. Grover, the note reads:

'Tis Autumn now
And the Fall of the year.
And times have gone we've loved so dear.
But we hope for more and we trust we may
See happy times again
On your Birthday.
—With Compliments of Mary Bert

Monte appears to have treasured this birthday wish from her friend. It is the only piece of personal correspondence in her scrapbook, and that fact suggests its importance to her. Whether or not Mary Bert was a prostitute is unknown. Her thoughtful note to Monte reflects a warm bond between the two women but reveals nothing more about the nature of their relationship.

Among the final pages of the scrapbook is a clipping entitled "Letters to Country Girls." The letters, addressed to "The Girls' Club," are written by a fictitious character named Aunt Betsy, who lectures girls on good manners and stresses that "true" women exert power in the world by shunning vulgarity, conducting themselves in a virtuous manner, and setting a good example for those around them. This item provides an odd but interesting counterpoint to the articles about vice and swindlers. Perhaps Monte enjoyed imagining herself as a woman who could manifest all the qualities of the nineteenth-century "true woman"—modesty, virtue, chastity, submission, and self-sacrifice. The theme of the Victorian "true woman" is central to many of the items Monte selected for her scrapbook, and the prevalence of items of this type suggest that she was intrigued with this idealized view of woman's proper role in nineteenth-century society.

Dark Omens and Death

Many of the poems Monte selected for the last few pages of her scrapbook strongly suggest that she was experiencing feelings of despair and depression. There also seems to be an indication that she anticipated meeting an early death. One poem, entitled "A Parting," suggests Monte's unhappiness:

> Better if Death had robbed me.
> For then I could love you still:
> Your mem'ry would have nerved me
> To work with a stronger will
> Now is my dream but a sorrow,
> And my heart hath a sense of shame,
> Rememb'ring the flowers of joy
> That brought the fruition of pain,
> And the happiness that I held for an hour—
> I held it and lost it again.
> I embarked my soul's best treasure
> To drift on a boundless sea:
> I have gathered life's fairest blossom—
> There will come no fruit for me.

The final stanza of another brief poem hints that a final break with Grover or another lover may be near:

I cannot bear to see thee with the tears
of pity on thy cheek. Regret—ah, well!
Remember not! Be happy in thy love.
'Tis my misfortune, not thy blame. Farewell!

Monte has underlined the final word—*Farewell!*—twice.

Beginning on the same page as this verse, the poems begin to hint chillingly at death:

I stood at eve, when the sun went down,
By the grave where a woman lies
Who lured men's souls to the shores of sin
By the light of her flashing eyes.
Who sang the song that the siren sang
On the treacherous Larely height,
Whose face was as fair as a summer day
And whose heart was as black as night.

The final page of the scrapbook contains a poem entitled "The New Memno," which deals with the disillusionment of discovering that one has been worshiping false idols. The last two stanzas, particularly the final four lines, eerily foreshadow Monte's tragic future:

Ah! So may it be with all of me that's mortal,
If ever that tyrant, the world, should destroy
The wonderful image which stands at my portal
And sings to my spirit of hope and of joy.
When the rose flame of thought on that marble illusion
Rings music no more from its sensitive heart,
When I've waited and watched, and the faithful delusion
Sighs forth a farewell, and I feel it depart:

Ah! then in the gloom of my broken ideal,
In the concave moon shadow away from the sun,
When the horrors of earth are grown rugged and real,
By some fortunate stroke may my coil be undone.
Ah! better to pass to the sullen dumb hollows
Where sounds never jar on the ear of the dead,
Than to learn that the air which my destiny follows
By some trick of a huckster is fostered and fed.

There are no dates on the final articles in the scrapbook by which to determine the year of its completion. Therefore, it is impossible to know how long before her death Monte placed the final poem in the scrapbook.

In April 1895 Grover purchased the cemetery plot next to Christy's grave.[25] By the autumn of that year, things seemed to be going seriously amiss. Reportedly, Monte had become very despondent and had begun to refuse food, insisting that someone was attempting to poison her.[26] Despite the entreaties of the other prostitutes, Monte refused to eat, and her aversion to food intensified. Day by day she grew weaker and more wasted. In October 1895, at only thirty-seven years of age, she died of starvation.

The attending physician attributed Monte's death to "starvation caused by insanity."[27] Grover buried Monte next to Christy in the plot he had purchased a few months earlier. Christy's elaborate headstone stands in marked contrast to Monte's windswept, unmarked grave, where she lies, unidentified and long forgotten.

Although the Laramie townspeople had little use for Monte, the bizarre circumstances of her death had an effect on the town. Within days after her funeral, the members of the city council forced Grover to close Grover's Institute.[28] Soon afterward, he left Laramie for California, settling in Los Angeles, where he continued to engage in abusive relationships with women.[29] Finally, consumed with syphilis and unable to care for himself, he rigged a shotgun to the foot of his bed and took his own life.[30]

Monte's tragic death was regarded as one more example of the bad end to which a fallen woman usually comes, and she soon faded from the town's collective memory. Yet as one reads the final page of her scrapbook, the inescapable impression is that the reader has come to intimately know an intrinsically kind, compassionate, gentle woman who loved life and who aspired, in her own way, to be a good person. The secret scrapbook of this "soiled dove" tells the story of a complex woman who, in her private hours, created a record of her life that now allows others to know her as she knew—or wished to know—herself.

[JENNIFER L. BRADLEY]

9

〜〜〜

Inviting Narratives

〜〜〜

Willa Cather's Childhood Scrapbook and

My Ántonia

L OCKED IN A LARGE IRON SAFE in an old bank, which now serves as the archives at the Willa Cather Pioneer Memorial and Educational Foundation in Red Cloud, Nebraska, is Willa Cather's childhood scrapbook.[1] The book's brightly colored cover, made of woven fabric depicting circus scenes stretched and glued around the outside, instantly catches one's attention and imagination (see Figure 9.1). Willa Cather—or Willie, as she called herself in childhood—made her scrapbook by sewing together pieces of cotton cloth and binding them with her fabric-decorated cover. She filled her book with pictures cut from magazines, Sunday-school cards, and advertising cards of all kinds. In a poem that serves as a preface to the scrapbook, Cather suggests that this book, filled with different artifacts, needs to be read as a history of her life. Although she claims that the book was made while she was young and silly, Cather suggests that it is filled with both remembrances of friends and sorrows. She credits herself with having an artistic mind and a keen eye in its making, suggesting she is fashioning an object of art that reveals her insights. That is to say, Cather invites the creation of a narrative inspired by her scrapbook.

An understanding of Cather's scrapbook must begin with a brief overview of the major events of her life. Willa Cather moved with her family from Back Creek Valley, Virginia, to Red Cloud, Nebraska, in 1883, when she was nine years old, partly to reunite with other family members who had headed west earlier to take advantage of cheap land prices and partly to escape the threat of tuberculosis, which had been particularly deadly in the Shenandoah Valley.[2] At first, Cather found the change

Figure 9.1. *Cather covered her scrapbook with fabric depicting circus scenes.* (Willa Cather Pioneer Memorial and Educational Foundation, Red Cloud, Nebraska)

from lush, green valleys to flat, open plains difficult. She also found it difficult being a spirited and ambitious young girl in a small prairie town.

At the age of sixteen, Cather left Red Cloud to attend the University of Nebraska in Lincoln. Originally intending to study medicine and become a doctor, she was lured away by the humanities and studied the classics, Greek, and British literature. She wrote for and eventually became an editor of both *Hesperian*, the longest-running literary publication on campus, and *Sombrero*, her class yearbook. During her college years Cather also began writing as a drama critic for the *Nebraska State Journal*, Lincoln's daily paper.

This was the start of Cather's long career in journalism, which would include editing positions with both the *Home Monthly* and *McClure's Magazine*, which she left when her literary career became lucrative. Cather published a collection of poetry, numerous short stories, and thirteen novels during a literary career highlighted by a Pulitzer Prize in 1923.[3] Many of her best-loved stories are set in towns much like Red Cloud, the small town where "Willie" Cather created her scrapbook.

Cather was a nonconformist from an early age. When she did not like the options available to her, she would reinvent herself or the situation to create new options. This was the case when she cut her hair short, started wearing boys' clothing, and began signing her name "William Cather, Jr." or "Wm. Cather, M.D." James Woodress, Cather's biographer, explains: "For several years, until after Cather left Red Cloud to attend the University of Nebraska, she defied Victorian norms of behavior for adolescent girls. Her goal in life was to become a surgeon, but that option was not open to girls, or so she must have thought, living in a small prairie town. As a result, she refused to be a girl, adopted male values and attitudes, and continued the tomboy life she had led in her prepubescent years in Virginia and on the farm at Catherton."[4]

Not surprisingly, Cather conceived of her scrapbook as another occasion for reinvention, as she makes clear in the poem with which she introduces it. In the poem she credits her male persona, Willie, a.k.a. William Cather, M.D., with creating the book. In fact, the poem claims the scrapbook is the best thing Willie ever did. Cather gives herself a male alter ego "of an artistic mind." The young Cather was reinventing more than a scrapbook, of course; already she was working out the design of *My Ántonia*, in which she created Jim Burden as another male alter ego through whom she would write of growing up in Nebraska.[5]

Cather may have been a nonconformist in some matters, but in making a scrapbook she joined a national trend. According to Deborah A. Smith, the scrapbook was the "most accessible" collecting phenomena of the U.S. Victorian era and generally falls into one of three major categories: "albums devoted to the personal memorabilia of an individual life, albums focusing on a specific collecting interest, and albums that are compilations of many kinds of printed paper ephemera, saved for the novelty of color printing (chromolithography). The latter type of scrapbook, composed largely of advertising material, enjoyed a burst of popularity that lasted roughly only one generation, from about 1870 to 1900."[6]

Cather's scrapbook falls into this last category. Scrapbooks appealed to a wide audience, and, according to Smith, while society generally credited children with making scrapbooks, adults often created them as well, both with and without the assistance of children. Often adults would be the main compilers and would coach children through the process. Cather, on the other hand, appears to have created her scrapbook largely on her own.[7]

By examining Cather's choices about what to include and how to present her scrapbook, this essay will draw conclusions about her personal preferences and influences. It will discuss the memorabilia as artifacts that reveal cultural and social layers of history, and it will describe Cather's captions, which provide her commentary on these memorabilia. The essay will interpret ways in which each layer of history works alone and in combination with others to provide a complex and intricate look at one woman's childhood. Further, the essay will examine the ways the items in the scrapbook emerge as individual narratives and the ways Cather rewrites these narratives through her role as compiler and author of her scrapbook. Finally, the essay will examine Cather's use of her childhood scrapbook in her novel *My Ántonia* and explore the implications of its use for both the scrapbook and the novel.

Early Creativity and Childhood Influences

The collection of items gathered, arranged, and captioned by Cather in her scrapbook provides a narrative of her childhood, revealing her likes and dislikes, early talents and interests, and social influences. Each item, however—each advertising card, Sunday-school card, and cutout picture—invites its own narrative as well. As a result, the scrapbook provides narratives within narratives, resulting in layers of meaning.

Pictures cut out of magazines make up the smallest category of items in Cather's scrapbook. Although magazines were an easily accessible source of illustrations, only a limited number provided the color pictures Cather was obviously drawn to. All the objects she placed in her scrapbook are in vibrant tones. As Ellen Gruber Garvey's essay in this volume suggests, Cather was not alone; color printing held great appeal for nineteenth-century consumers. The color cutouts Cather did include are of botanicals, fruits, and women in formal attire, including a large page-size cutout of one woman in a floor-length emerald plaid dress with a silver fitted jacket. The woman dons white kid gloves, carries a walking stick, and wears an elaborate tall black hat with a large matching emerald bow. Her formal attire suggests an evening at the theater or a dinner party or any other context a young Cather might have imagined. Many of the pictures of women that Cather cut out and pasted in her scrapbook wear elaborate hats, perhaps an early sign of her own affinity for them. Although it was her prerogative to call herself "Willie" or "William" and look like a tomboy, Cather's selection of elaborately and formally attired women suggests she was attracted at least aesthetically to an upper-class lifestyle and the feminine dress her mother would have greatly preferred.

The Sunday-school cards in Cather's scrapbook, the second-largest category of items, are mostly botanicals with captions from Psalms. One with brightly colored purple flowers reads, "Satisfy us early with thy mercy. Ps. 90, 14." Another with scarlet flowers reminds, "The Lord Will Judge His People, Ps. 135, 14." The botanicals fit with Cather's attraction to color and also suggest the beginning of her interest in horticulture.[8]

Some of the Sunday-school cards celebrate religious holidays, particularly Easter and Christmas. As does the Bible, these cards tell stories. One card celebrating Easter shows a boy adrift in a turbulent ocean with an eggshell as his vessel. Perhaps a reference to the disciple Peter adrift in the water before Christ's appearance, the introduction of an eggshell as the vessel opens the image up to alternative interpretations and invites recipients to create a suitable narrative of their own. In *My Ántonia*, the title character admits she loves her son Leo the best, "maybe . . . because he came on Easter Day," making a clear connection between her son and Christ.[9] Similarly, Cather perhaps considered her Sunday-school cards reminders of special events or people. In any case, they are the only items that as a group do not contain any additional captions or names handwritten by Cather, suggesting that they held for her a certain authority or sacredness.

Advertising Cards: The Mainstay of Cather's Creation

Advertising cards, also known as trade cards, make up the largest and most varied group of items within the scrapbook. At the height of their popularity—during the 1880s and 1890s, when Cather assembled her scrapbook—the cards were either included in the packaging of a product or, more commonly, given away by local shopkeepers. Intended as advertisements, the cards became popular collectibles, and many families kept albums filled with advertising cards. As Robert Jay has noted: "No other medium could reach so many households, and no other one was saved and cherished by the consumers themselves." Designed to attract customers through their visual appeal and wittiness, advertising cards often did not display the item being advertised or disguised the item within the scene depicted. "Fascination for any color picture made it possible for advertisers to choose images not even remotely connected to the product," according to Smith.[10] If the product was prominent, it was still represented within a particular context, never alone. Instead, the advertising cards allowed the consumer to take part in a story. They helped consumers with a little imagination to travel to exotic locations, celebrate special occasions, or participate in moments of everyday life. Like Cather's invitation to narrate her history through her scrapbook, the advertising cards encouraged consumers to read and invent their own narratives.

An Early Attraction to Medicine

Patent medicines were the products most frequently featured on advertising cards. Despite a population vulnerable to many diseases, nineteenth-century medicine was wrought with therapeutic confusion, with "curative systems from homeopathy to the mind cure," and doctors were often seen as suspect.[11] As a result, housewives used home medicines in an attempt to doctor themselves and their families. Companies producing patent medicines saw their opportunity and spent up to 40 percent of their gross sales on advertising, much of it in advertising cards. One of Cather's cards boasts that its product is the "best remedy for indigestion, dyspepsia, general debility, hypochondria & C." These medicines, in fact, claimed to cure almost any and all illnesses. As primary caretakers, women were the intended audience for these advertisements, which often focused on children. According to Barbara Welter, a woman proved her value by nursing her family: "One of the most important functions of woman as comforter was her role as nurse. . . . Many homes had 'little sufferers,' those pale children who wasted away to saintly deaths. And there were enough other illnesses of youth and age, major and minor, to give the nineteenth-century American woman nursing experience. The sickroom called for the exercise of her higher qualities of patience, mercy, and gentleness as well as for her housewifely arts. She could thus fulfill her dual feminine function—beauty and usefulness."[12] Patent-medicine companies and advertisers recognized the status attached to a woman who could doctor or nurse and used it to entice women to buy their products.

Another card advertising a patent medicine in Cather's scrapbook, however, hits on one of the most popular ailments addressed: "Dr. Harter's Iron Tonic," in addition to purifying the blood and regulating the liver and kidneys, also "cures female diseases." Welter argues that the types of diseases recognized and their treatments "were partly the result of the definition of woman and of her sphere." A woman's health was tied to her fitness as a wife and mother and on a larger scale influenced the health of society as a whole. If society was faltering or not reaching its high expectations, the fault might lie with the mothers who gave birth to struggling statesmen and entrepreneurs. Welter further argues that as a whole the medical field "served as a conservative influence, supporting the traditional definition of woman's nature and role by the weight of its evidence, against attempts to enlarge or change them."[13] The image depicted on Dr. Harter's card shows an older girl, one hand on the shoulder of a younger girl, pointing with her umbrella to something out of the frame. The implication is that the older girl is educating the younger on the ways of the world—and that one of those lessons will include female complaints and the benefits of Dr. Harter's iron tonic. The card thus becomes not only an advertisement but also a narrative about the two girls and, on a larger scale, about the ways knowledge is shared among women.

Despite the large number of patent-medicine advertising cards in circulation, Cather includes in her scrapbook only a handful, evidence perhaps of the influence of Dr. McKeeby, her family doctor in Red Cloud. Cather considered McKeeby her friend and admired him, in part because he pulled her through a childhood illness. "Dr. McKeeby looked after the entire family for many years and was no doubt partly responsible for Cather's early ambition to study medicine. In pursuit of this interest she often went on calls with Dr. McKeeby."[14] Perhaps Cather limits the number of patent-medicine advertising cards out of respect for Dr. McKeeby and his profession. Or, possibly already rebelling against the confines of women's roles, she recognized the implications of the patent medicines on women's perceived medical and physical soundness.

In another connection to her interest in medicine, Cather also includes a card for Clark's spool cotton. The picture on the card has very little to do with thread—it shows a little boy who has pulled off the head of a doll, with the caption reading, "Born to be a surgeon." This card can be read as strictly humorous, but it might also offer an explanation for early childhood behavior, perhaps even offering comfort to a mother disturbed by her child's actions. Further, it suggests a larger story about destiny and callings.

Constructing Domesticity

Besides tending to the sick, a woman could prove her value to her family through other domestic duties, including sewing. Cather's collection includes a variety of cards from thread companies, including the J. and P. Coats Thread Company, Clark Thread Company, and Willimantic Thread Company. In fact, thread was the second-most-popular product on advertising cards, not surprising considering that most of the clothing worn by women and children was made in the home. The thread companies recognized that one spool of thread looked more or less like another, so they relied on name and trademark recognition, which were printed on the label at the end of the spool. Thus, spools of thread, particularly seen from the label end, were used in a variety of ingenious and creative ways.

Again, the cards focus more on the story advertisers are trying to tell than on the product they are trying to sell. One card Cather includes from the Clark Thread Company, for example, is printed in the shape of a spool of O.N.T. thread (O.N.T. was the company's acronym for Our New Thread) with a picture of a mother using a piece of thread looped under her infant's arms to help him take his first steps. The caption reads: "Nothing stronger can there be, but mother's love and O.N.T." The card invites the consumer to share this moment with the proud mother and reflect on a similar moment in her own experience. The card is designed to suggest the thread's strength, one of the product's few traits that the thread companies addressed. It also suggests much more, including the bond between mother and child, milestones in a child's development, and hopes for the future.

Another card in Cather's collection focusing on thread strength depicts Jumbo, the elephant from P. T. Barnum's circus, being captured and dragged by Willimantic Thread. The card capitalizes on the sensationalism surrounding the purchase of the largest elephant in captivity and uses thread as part of the story about his capture and transport to the United States in 1882. This card is meant to enhance Jumbo's growing popularity by helping the public visualize the efforts needed to capture such a large animal. Advice authors who promoted scrapbooks as educational tools for children encouraged creativity in the use of the cards: "Instead of pasting in those cards which have become too familiar to awaken much interest, let the young bookmakers design and form their own pictures by cutting . . . parts of figures, from different cards, and then pasting them together so as to form new combinations; . . . figures that were originally standing may be forced to sit; babies may be placed in arms, which, on the cards they were stolen from, held only cakes of soap, perhaps, or boxes of blacking."[15] As if following this advice, later in her scrapbook Cather cuts one of her Jumbo cards apart and pastes in a picture of Jumbo alone, with the thread and captors cut out. With this omission Cather demonstrates her critical reading of the trading cards. She evaluates and rejects the narrative suggested by the card, substituting her own desired outcome. In each of these cases, something incidental—thread—becomes part of a larger narrative about a boy's destiny, a mother's love, or animals in captivity.

Other household items, including polishes, cleansers, soaps, baking powder, shoes, and corsets, found on advertising cards are also included in Cather's scrapbook, as are cards for items such as farm machinery and sewing machines. The scrapbook's advertising cards for stoves and ranges were directed to both men and women. In a card suggesting female friendships, two women warm their hands over the stove. Another shows a sophisticated woman in a long pink dress walking a dog in the park, an image suggesting that those who know about the best things in life deserve a Garland stove. This sentiment is echoed in the caption: "In Garland Stoves you are sure to find / The good and beautiful combined, / Aesthetic in design and kind / To please the most fastidious mind." Stove companies tried to appeal to various types and classes of women but always reinforced the importance of a woman's ability to prepare a meal for her family. Women's magazines at this time were filled with stories of marriages jeopardized because the wife had not learned to keep house, including cooking. Domestic tranquillity depended on a woman's ability to prepare a good home-cooked meal.[16]

While advertising directed toward men also urged domestic tranquillity, the stove companies apparently believed appealing to men's stomachs would be the most effective approach. In one card a man struggles to walk against a strong wind. The caption reads, "You query why from home I go, / why bout the town I rove? / The reason why is plain, you know. / We've got no Garland Stove." In contrast, another Garland card shows a robust man wearing a checked suit, standing with his legs spread slightly, and smoking a cigar. The caption here reads: "What an appetite I now possess. Quite fat I'm sure I'm looking. And I can thank my stars and bless the 'Garlands' for good cooking." The narrative suggested by both these cards also serves as instruction for men: A wise man who wants a satisfying dinner must provide his wife with the tools she needs, including a stove. Although the overt narratives of these two cards are directed to men, they also send a clear message to women: To keep your husband happy, feed him a good meal or expect him to seek that meal, and perhaps other domestic needs, elsewhere.

Cather may have taken these advertisements to heart. She herself believed in the value of a well-prepared meal; her letters are filled with references to meals eaten during her travels and to her cook at home. In addition, several of the main characters in her novels, including Ántonia Shimerda, spend a portion of their young adulthood learning the domestic arts, especially cooking.

The Presentation of Women

Although women appear frequently in advertising cards and in a variety of contexts, their image is generally a stereotypical and narrow one. Women are invariably represented as dutiful wives and loving mothers. When she deviates from this role, a woman is portrayed as foolish or shrewish. One card in Cather's collection shows a husband and wife in bed, the man asleep with his back to his wife, who is sitting up and wringing her hands. The narrative force in the image is reinforced in the caption, "Midnight Lecture. Mr. Claude takes it all in." The implication is that a woman who worries foolishly about things she cannot control should be ignored. In another example, a woman stands over her husband and appears to be threatening him with a broom, while he sits in a chair, his hat falling off and his broken cane lying on the floor. The card advertises "Ludlow's Ladies' Fine Shoes," but the caption suggests the dark nature of the scene depicted: "Home, Sweet Home!" Here the narrative is more complex. Not only is the dominant woman represented as a shrew, but also the weak husband is scorned and gets what he deserves. When a husband and wife do not stick to their assigned roles, their relationship turns adversarial. This early exposure to the conflicting gender roles within marriage resurfaces in Cather's fiction, as her married couples struggle to find harmony and individual identity within the confines of rigid gender roles.

As a result of the narrow housewife image and the evident backlash against those who attempted to deviate from it, sex or sex appeal was rarely used to promote a product. The most explicit depiction of the female form comes in advertising cards for the most confining female product, the corset. A two-card series in Cather's collection does address the issue of sex, if only by implication. In the first card a man and woman sit close together at an open window, the woman holding a basket of apples in her lap and the man leaning slightly forward, as if the two are sharing an intimate conversation. The second card shows the same two people. The man now, however, stands behind the woman's chair and holds her wrists above her head; the basket of apples has spilled onto the floor in a scene that appears violent and sexual. Unfortunately, the information about the advertised product appears on the back of the card, which has been glued onto the scrapbook page and is thus impossible to read. Regardless of the product, the scene is a disturbing account of the relationship between men and women. The first card alone could tell the story of a man and woman courting or sharing a moment of wedded intimacy. Adding the second card, however, makes the initial intimacy ironic or manipulative. The series creates a narrative about the right of a man to exert his sexual dominance, a disturbing conscious or subliminal message for the young Cather.

Figure 9.2. *With her inscription Cather assigned her brother, Roscoe, the role of the prideful Pooh-Bah of Gilbert and Sullivan's Mikado.* (Willa Cather Pioneer Memorial and Educational Foundation, Red Cloud, Nebraska)

Social Influences

Advertisers often attempted to take advantage of the collectible nature of advertising cards by issuing cards in sets, acquisition of which might require multiple purchases.[17] Cather's collection of trade cards also reveals some of the social influences and trends of her time. Gilbert and Sullivan's *Mikado* had made an extraordinary debut in the theaters in 1885, and characters from the play appeared on advertising cards, allowing consumers to learn or retell the narrative they had heard in the play. Cather, a great fan of the theater even at a young age, had two complete sets of these cards in her collection. The play echoed Americans' fascination with Japan that had started in the 1850s, following Perry's voyage to that country, and was "reinforced by the influence that European *Japonisme* had on certain aesthetically cultivated Americans later in the century." Like the actors on stage, however, the characters shown on the cards are Japanese in costume only. "Where true Japanese culture was represented, it was as the essence of oriental exoticism and refinement,

and was thus a favorite vehicle for the marketing of perfumed soaps and other luxury articles."[18] As she did with Jumbo, Cather rewrites this narrative as well, here by inscribing the name of a friend or family member under each character's picture. She gives her brother, Roscoe, the honor of being the prideful Pooh-Bah, even adding a cartoonlike balloon coming out of his mouth that demands, "Shut up Smart Ally" (see Figure 9.2).

Unfortunately, African Americans did not receive the same favorable treatment in advertising cards, and one might assume that the racially stereotyped language used on these cards was one of Cather's few exposures to African American dialect after leaving Virginia. At best, images like that of the faithful black servant are ambiguous in meaning and paternal in nature; at worst, the images are stereotypical and degrading. Cather has several of the latter in her collection, and these are of two types: they depict either rural, unsophisticated African Americans of questionable moral character or African American urban dandies dressed in flashy clothes. An example of the first is a card showing an African American man reaching over a fence and grabbing two chickens, under which Cather has written in pencil, "how they disappeared" and "the real cat." Examples of the second are four cards depicting African American men in brightly colored jackets and trousers playing musical instruments. Often the printed caption that accompanies a black caricature is meant to represent African American dialect. On a card advertising O.N.T. thread, a black man is shown fishing, using the thread for his line; the printed caption reads: "I reckon dis yere's strong nuff suah." On an advertising card for Vacuum harness oil, an African American man with saucerlike white eyes and large protruding lips, and dressed in an orange shirt and yellow checked pants, rides a galloping black horse. The card, one of the most stereotypical depictions in the scrapbook, apparently appealed to Cather because she has written above it her childhood nickname, "Willie." The initial narrative suggested by the caption and stereotypical depiction of an African American is racist, but Cather rewrites the narrative by including her own name as a new caption and thus identifying herself as its subject.

Other cards suggest interests little acknowledged in current Cather criticism, such as politics. One card in Cather's scrapbook documents an important political event known as the Haymarket Riot but leaves the narrative open for interpretation. The card shows cameo pictures of three buildings and eight men and the date May 4, 1886; the caption states without comment or bias: "Scene of the Chicago Bomb Throwing and Vicinity together with Portraits of Persons convicted of complicity there with." In 1886 labor unions began pushing for an eight-hour workday, and on May 1 workers went on strike. Several radical and anarchist groups became involved in the campaign, and two days later, during a riot at the McCormick Harvester plant, the police intervened. Shots were fired, and one man was killed. On May 4 a protest meeting was held to denounce the police actions. The police attempted to disperse the crowd when a bomb exploded, killing eight officers. The police seized every suspected radical in the area, resulting in hundreds of arrests; thirty-one people were indicted, a number eventually reduced to eleven, and eight men were tried. Of those, only two had been at the scene of the bombing. The judge selected for the case was openly biased against the defendants, and the special bailiff appointed to the case admitted to trying to stack the jury against the defendants—in fact, one of the jurors was the brother of one of the dead policemen. All eight men were found guilty, and all but one were sentenced to death.[19] The advertising card does not openly come

Figure 9.3. *This card is part of a series Cather entitled "A Passion Flower."* (Willa Cather Pioneer Memorial and Educational Foundation, Red Cloud, Nebraska)

out on either side of the event. In fact, it notes that the men are "convicted" of, instead of "guilty" of or "responsible for," the crime. The card even omits mention of the Haymarket Riot, an allusion to uprising and protest, and describes the action as a "bomb throwing," leaving out the explosion and resulting deaths. These omissions and carefully chosen words leave room for a consumer to narrate the event from his or her own perspective, a wise advertising strategy that might have appealed to Cather.

Layering Narratives

Unlike her silence regarding the Haymarket Riot card, Cather adds narratives to her scrapbook by inscribing additional text on many other advertising cards and pictures. Most of her handwritten additions are names, as in the Mikado example. Later in the scrapbook Roscoe reappears as a baseball pitcher with Cather's caption, "Put her home boys." Captions were among her favorite additions. In one series of cards, arranged carefully on one page and entitled "A Passion Flower," Cather's captions tell the story. In the first picture a man looks over a country stone wall to see a woman taking off her shoes by the waterside. Cather's caption reads, "~~ How lovely!" Next we see the woman and the man, each standing on their own side of the wall, kissing. In pencil Cather has written, "~~ Oh" "Will I." In the next picture the man helps the woman over the stone wall, as Cather has the woman ask, "~~ I wonder if Auntie would care?" (see Figure 9.3). Finally a parson comes to the same country stone wall and sees a pile of men and women's clothing next to the lake. Cather has him remark, "Fool Female." By adding her own captions, Cather gives voice to one of the possible narratives suggested by the series. Further, she reveals enough knowledge about sexual relationships to make her captions subtle and playful, while still representing the disapproval of the parson.

Jim Burden's Picture Book

Willa Cather's childhood scrapbook can be seen as an artifact. Within its pages a reader can learn about history, social conditions, and consumer trends, as well as Cather's childhood and imagination. Further, the items contained in the scrapbook suggest and invite narratives. Cather responds to the invitation when her childhood scrapbook reappears in *My Ántonia* as the picture book Jim Burden makes for Yulka and Ántonia for their "country Christmas."

In *My Ántonia*, one of Cather's most autobiographical novels, a young orphaned boy named Jim Burden moves from his home in Virginia to live with his paternal grandparents in Nebraska, arriving on the same train as an immigrant Bohemian family, the Shimerdas. Jim quickly becomes friends with the Shimerdas' daughter, Ántonia, a few years his senior, as they both learn to live on the Nebraska plains. Jim teaches Ántonia English, and she tells him stories from her homeland. It is only after Jim leaves Black Hawk to attend college and then begins his life in New York City as an attorney for the railroad that he comes to realize the significant role Ántonia has played in his life.

Just before Jim's first Christmas in his new home, a blizzard makes a scheduled trip to town for presents impossible, so the Burdens decide to have a "country Christmas" and make all their gifts. Jim had planned to buy picture books in town for Ántonia and her younger sister, Yulka, but instead sets out to make them a book.

> Grandmother took me into the ice-cold storeroom, where she had some bolts of gingham and sheeting. She cut squares of cotton cloth and we sewed them together into a book. We bound it between pasteboards, which I covered with brilliant calico, representing scenes from a circus. For two days I sat at the dining-room table, pasting this book full of pictures for Yulka. We had files of those good old family magazines which used to publish coloured lithographs of popular paintings, and I was allowed to use some of these. I took "Napoleon Announcing the Divorce to Josephine" for my frontpiece. On the white pages I grouped Sunday-School cards and advertising cards which I had brought from my "old country."[20]

While Jim makes his picture book, the Burdens' farmhand, Otto, makes tallow candles, and Grandmother Burden bakes gingerbread men and roosters, which the three decorate with burnt sugar and cinnamon drops. By introducing the making of the book with candle making and baking, Cather places her novel—and, by association, her scrapbook—within the realm of domestic art. Unlike the picture books Jim might have purchased at the store, his homemade book is a noncommercial form of private art, domestic rather than public. At the same time, by "giving" the scrapbook to Jim and then to the reader through the publication of *My Ántonia*, Cather gives it a public life as well. The description of Jim's picture book so closely matches Cather's scrapbook that the comparison is inescapable. In essence, Cather gives Jim Burden her scrapbook and thus part of her personal history. In doing so, Cather presents the scrapbook as mediating between material and print cultures, private and public publication, domestic and commercial activity, and autobiography and fiction.

Just as Cather's scrapbook is a collection of individual narratives that together express her early creativity and childhood memories, Jim's book is full of things he had "brought from my 'old country.'" Until this point in the novel, Jim has not mentioned his deceased parents or Virginia to anyone. The only reference to them is a comment to himself as he looks over the side of the wagon on the trip from the train station to his grandparents' farm. The vast openness of Nebraska makes him believe that it is "not a country at all, but the material out of which countries are made." It has none of the familiar, comforting signs of home:

> I had never before looked up at the sky when there was not a familiar mountain ridge against it. But this was the complete dome of heaven, all there was of it. I did not believe that my dead father and mother were watching me from up there; they would still be looking for me at the sheepfold down by the creek, or along the white road that led to the mountain pastures. I had left even their spirits behind me. The wagon jolted on, carrying me I knew not whither. I don't think I was homesick. If we never arrived anywhere, it did not matter. Between that earth and sky I felt erased, blotted out. I did not say my prayers that night: here, I felt, what would be would be.[21]

Jim's reconnection to his past through his picture book is part of a larger structure going on in the text, a structure James E. Miller describes as "ultimately about time, about the inexorable movement of future into present, of present into past."[22] Each of Ántonia's narratives, however brief, have helped Jim create a larger narrative about her life. Although Jim cannot yet verbalize the events from his past, through his picture book he gives Ántonia and Yulka his story. Jim's picture book uses artifacts from his past (the Sunday-school cards and advertising cards) together with the artifacts of his present (colored pictures from saved family magazines and calico, each with an individual narrative) to create a cohesive narrative of his life.

The country Christmas Jim celebrates with his new family, including his grandparents, Otto Fuchs, and Jake Marpole, is a celebration of both past and present, as well as of narrative's power to join the two. Jake brings home a small cedar tree to decorate, and Jim remembers that it was Jake who used to help Jim's father cut

Christmas trees in Virginia. Jake remembers how much Jim loved the trees and wants to give him this special surprise. This is the first time the reader sees both Jake and Jim acknowledge their shared past, the intersection of their personal narratives.

Otto Fuchs also lets objects tell his narrative when he contributes the "brilliantly coloured paper figures" that make up the crèche his mother has sent each year from Austria to decorate the tree: "There was a bleeding heart, in tufts of paper lace; there were three kings, gorgeously appareled, and the ox and the ass and the shepherds; there was the Baby in the manger, and a group of angels, singing; there were camels and leopards, held by the black slaves of the three kings." Fuchs's addition to the tree's decorations gives the tree a religious significance. Jim, however, sees it as "the talking tree of the fairy tale," while Grandmother Burden sees it as the "Tree of Knowledge." Each character creates and narrates his or her own understanding of the image created by the tree. The tree has "legends and stories nestled like birds in its branches."[23] Thus, like Cather's scrapbook, the narrative of Jim's country Christmas is made complete by the inclusion of the individual narratives of Jim's friends and family.

Cather's Invitation to Readers

At the same time that Jim's picture book allows him to reconnect with his past and reconcile that past with the present, it also serves as an invitation to the reader. By describing in detail the process for making the book, Cather provides her readers with a guide for creating their own personal narratives. By having Jim give the items from his "old country" to Ántonia and Yulka, Cather reinforces the importance of sharing cultural and family traditions with others through narrative. This invitation is an echo of an earlier one given by Cather.

In the introduction to *My Ántonia*, Willa Cather and her fictional character Jim Burden are crossing Iowa on a train and discussing their childhood:

> We were talking about what it is like to spend one's childhood in little towns like these, buried in wheat and corn, under stimulating extremes of climate: burning summers when the world lies green and billowy beneath a brilliant sky, when one is fairly stifled in vegetation, in the colour and smell of strong weeds and heavy harvests; blustery winters with little snow, when the whole country is stripped bare and gray as sheet-iron. We agreed that no one who had not grown up in a little prairie town could know anything about it. It was a kind of freemasonry, we said.[24]

Cather suggests by this introduction that others cannot know what her life was like growing up in a small Nebraska town. But in writing *My Ántonia*, she provides her readers with a picture book filled with narratives that can be combined to help them understand. Like Ántonia and Yulka, who will use Jim's picture book to continue to learn the English language and read the narrative of Jim's life, Cather's reader can use her scrapbook to create a narrative of life in Red Cloud.

As Jim and Cather talk, they keep returning to thoughts of Ántonia: "More than any other person we remembered, this girl seemed to mean to us the country, the conditions, the whole adventure of our childhood." Here Cather begins to layer history on Ántonia herself; she becomes what Miller calls a "personal and poignant symbol" for all the events of both Jim's and Cather's childhood. As a result of their discussion, Cather makes an agreement with Jim: "I would set down on paper all that I remembered of Ántonia, if he would do the same." Only Jim fulfills their agreement. Several months later he brings his story to her in New York. As he tells the character Cather: "'I didn't take time to arrange it; I simply wrote down pretty much all that her name recalls to me. I suppose it hasn't any form. It hasn't any title, either.' He went into the next room, sat down at my desk and wrote across the face of the portfolio the word 'Ántonia.' He frowned at this a moment, then prefixed another word, making it 'My Ántonia.' That seemed to satisfy him."[25]

In *Birthing a Nation*, Susan Rosowski suggests that in *My Ántonia* Cather rewrites authorship and reimagines creativity: "This is a manuscript conceived not by a distinction between creator and created, author and subject; instead, it is conceived by the mutuality of long friendship. 'We grew up together in the same Nebraska town,' 'we had much to say to each other,' 'we were talking,' and 'we agreed' (p. ix)—the exchange of conversation establishes that this text is a collaboration that grew out of continuities of life into art, of past into present, of childhood retrieved by adults, of female author and male narrator in agreement."[26] When Jim arrives at Cather's home carrying "a bulging legal portfolio" containing his story, Cather's narrator gives verbal storytelling the physical form of a scrapbook. The very term *portfolio*, like *scrapbook*, suggests a compilation of items. Jim's story, Cather's *My Ántonia*, is a compilation of narratives.

In Jim's comment that "it hasn't any form," Cather foresees the comments of critics and tries to offer a counterinterpretation right from the start. She sees her novel as intentionally episodic, as snapshots of her childhood in narrative form. As a result, the novel is filled with inspiring and revealing moments loosely connected by narration. Woodress explains that this structure was ideal for Cather's design: "Once she had decided on her narrative voice and the first-person method, she further planned to avoid any formal structuring of the novel. Jim Burden's memories, which, of course, were her memories, would shape the narrative. She would avoid the opportunities for melodrama that the materials certainly contained and dwell lightly on the incidents that most novelists would ordinarily emphasize. The story would be made up of little, everyday happenings for the most part, for such events made up the bulk of most people's lives."[27]

Thus *My Ántonia* emerges as a collection of separate yet intertwined narratives. Otto Fuchs tells of his trip to the United States, during which a woman he's been asked to look after gives birth to triplets. The Russian, Pavel, tells of the horror of being chased in his sleigh by wolves as he and others ride home from a wedding and of throwing the bride and groom to their pursuers. Ántonia tells of Old Hatta, the old woman who told stories to the children when Ántonia was young. Widow Steavens tells of helping Ántonia prepare for her ill-fated trip to Denver to marry Larry Donovan. Cather structures her narrative so that various characters emerge to tell their own stories in much the same way that the memorabilia in a scrapbook tell their stories.

When Jim asks Cather to read what he has written as soon as possible, he reminds her not to "let it influence your own story." Rosowski suggests that the introduction "resembles a contract, filled with stipulations about how the story was written and how it should be read, in both cases as the creation of an imagination, true to experience that is individual, unique, and ongoing." In other words, by reminding us that the text is Jim's and not her own, Cather "has renounced the authority of the text"; instead, she is asserting that "meaning in an epistemological sense is an individual creation" and thereby granting authority to each reader.[28] By urging Cather not to let his story influence her own, Jim actually invites Cather to tell her own story, and Cather in turn invites us to tell ours. Thus the novel becomes both an individual narrative and a community narrative, an "individual creation" and a group collaboration.

In *Women, America, and Movement*, Susan Roberson suggests that because Americans' lives are shaped by movement and relocation, we are attracted to narratives by women who write of their experiences with relocation and who imagine relocation for their characters, because they help us reconnect with our own migrations and movements. A reader must become an active participant in exploring and discovering the narratives of women in movement:

> To some extent they tell stories similar to those by men, of new lands, of hardship, promise, and adjustment. But to examine women's narratives of movement is to discover more than the 'M-factor' of the American character—
> "movement, migration, mobility"—with a slightly feminine angle. It is to discover the traumas, the costs, and the rewards of movement, migration, and displacement that accrue to women and the texts they write because of their gender and their gendered situation in life. It is also to consider the intersections between movement and the feminine, for as Frances Bartkowski observes, "The critique of femininity, itself a contested cultural space, has taught us to recognize the mobility, plasticity, and mimicry involved in becoming a woman." To read the text of a mobile or displaced woman often requires us to probe behind and between the lines of texts, to listen to her silences and to decode subverted, subversive messages, to be ourselves explorers, uncovering and discovering the story of her migrations and dislocations and of the self shaped and revealed in the venturing forth.[29]

Throughout her novel, Cather calls on her readers to uncover Ántonia's narrative using just this strategy.

The novel's title might suggest this is Ántonia's story, but that little possessive—*my*—that Jim affixes to her name identifies this as Jim's narrative, his memories of the girl he believes has been one of the greatest influences of his life. Terence Martin sees Jim, not Ántonia, as the novel's structural and thematic center; Martin believes it is a novel of memory, of "how [Jim] has come to see Ántonia as the epitome of all he has valued." When Jim returns from studying at the university in Lincoln, he tells Ántonia just how much she has meant to him: "Do you know, Ántonia, since I've been away, I think of you more often than of anyone else in this part of the world. I'd have liked to have you for a sweetheart, or a wife, or my mother or my sister—anything that a woman can be to a man. The idea of you is a part of my mind; you influence my likes and dislikes, all my tastes, hundreds of times when I don't realize it. You really are a part of me."[30]

As with the advertising cards' images that offer the opportunity for multiple interpretations, Jim offers Ántonia several possible roles. Jim's "idea" of Ántonia, however, is based on events narrated to him by other characters—in other words, this is Jim's version of the community narrative. Cather lets Jim decide which narratives to retell to the reader and thus serve as filter for the community experience. This selection is part of a process of forgetting, which Kate McCullough argues is crucial in the creation of a national identity. McCullough argues that "the imperative both to remember and to forget produces the consequent imperative to narrate," and that published fiction, among other texts, "attempt[s] to reconcile numerous conflicting narratives of class, race, gender, region, religion, and transnational political and economic relations, all grounded in an ideology of imperial capitalist expansion."[31] While she has become a symbol of "the country, the conditions, the whole adventure of our childhood," Ántonia has yet to narrate her own story; the reader can attempt to construct Ántonia's narrative only on the basis of others' narratives and what goes unsaid.

Cather reinforces the notion that Ántonia has her own narrative to tell when Jim returns to Black Hawk after many years to find her married with a large happy family. After a day filled touring the family orchard and introducing her children, Ántonia takes Jim into her parlor and takes out "a big box of photographs: she and Anton in their wedding clothes, holding hands; her brother Ambrosch and his very fat wife, who had a farm of her own, and who bossed her husband, I was delighted to hear; the three Bohemian Marys and their large families." All of Ántonia's children gather around her and gaze at the photographs, their comments and questions suggesting that Ántonia has filled them with the stories of her childhood. She has even named several of her children after the prominent people in her stories: Yulka, Ambrosch, Charley, and Nina. When shown a picture of Frances Harling, the girls comment on how fine she looks, and Jim notes that "one could see that Frances had come down as a heroine in the family legend."[32] Harling is not a heroine in Jim's story, but she is in Ántonia's.

Just as Jim's picture book was an early draft of his later narrative, Ántonia has begun drafting her narrative through the pictures and stories she shares with her children.

Ántonia has begun the process of creating her narrative by compiling her artifacts, but her photographs are still in a box and her stories remain within the family. They have not been arranged into a scrapbook, a picture book, or a narrative. Cather leaves the reader wanting to hear Ántonia's story, perhaps a suggestion that many stories have as yet gone untold. But it is not too late. Ántonia has the makings of a book, of whatever kind she chooses; in her pictures, her stories, and her children's interest, she finds a receptive audience. In fact, as Rosowski points out, "the younger children, Anna, Jan, and Nina, the older son, Rudolph, and the parents, Cuzak and Ántonia herself—all have a voice in the family's ongoing story."[33] Like Jim's, Ántonia's narrative is both individual and communal.

Willa Cather uses her scrapbook and *My Ántonia* for instructing her reader in the process of storytelling itself: storytelling is not only telling but also gathering materials and publishing—all are ways to record the individual and communal histories of our lives. Cather gives Ántonia and her readers the directions and guidance they need to begin. She shows the way narrative builds on narrative to create a chorus that becomes a unified whole. In the end, Willa Cather offers us an invitation and gives us the authority to begin writing.

[MEREDITH ELIASSEN]

IO

~~~~~~

In the Hands of Children

~~~~~~

*A Photographic Essay of Images from
Children's Scrapbooks*

Having once acquired the art of cutting, the fascination never ceases even to all ages." So begins the chapter "The Scrapbook" in which the early-twentieth-century advice writer Maude Cushing Nash presented information on the handmade construction of albums and their completion with printed colored pictures. Her suggestions for cutting and clipping place the scrapbook as central to any modern child's life. The making of such albums would bring literacy, artistic sensibility, and even modesty and good manners. Nash carried on the "waste not, want not" precept advocated forcefully during the nineteenth century by thinkers such as Lydia Maria Child and Catharine Beecher.[1]

Beginning in the mid–nineteenth century, more and more children were raised within a culture defined by printed material. As one scholar noted about the twentieth century: "From the first cautionary advice of Dr. Spock, read by an anxious mother holding in her hand an anguished infant, to the giddy goose rhymes or *Pat-the-Bunnies* read at bedtime, to the cereal boxes of champions on the breakfast table, to the scout manuals memorized, the fugitive diaries, the Peanuts cartoons, and to those first chapter books, a child is raised by the arms of print."[2] The collection of materials for a scrapbook allowed the manipulation of this culture of print by those who might lack access to other means of dealing with memory, learning, or desires.

Children made joyful and useful creations from printed materials, just as the advice writer predicted. Primarily, they were reacting to a color revolution, collecting bright artifacts that were products, as we have seen in the Introduction, of technological advances in color printing, or chromolithography.

The printing process itself offers a story of modern discovery. Lithography (often called the first different printing technology since the invention of relief in the fifteenth century) and chromolithography are based on the chemical repellence of oil and water. Chromolithography involves several lithographic stones, with each stone representing a separate color. A German printer, Alois Senefelder, tried to use this process as early as 1810, but chromolithography was not invented until 1816, when Godefroy Engelmann and Charles-Philbert de Lasteyrie began to print two-color lithographs in Paris. Around the year 1832, another printer, this time in Germany, managed to use as many as fifteen stones. And in 1837, Engelmann patented his "litho-colour press or colour lithography imitating painting." His system, though expensive, became quite popular in France and quickly spread to Germany, England, and the United States.[3] By the last quarter of the 1800s, the steam-driven printing press and inexpensive paper made chromolithography much more affordable and thus popular.

From 1840 to 1900, Europe and North America increasingly experienced what has been called "chromo civilization"—an era when original paintings were reproduced lithographically in color and sold by the millions. These copies, or chromolithographs, "waved unchallenged as the flag of popular culture."[4] For the first time, average members of the public, not just the very rich, might have colored images on their walls and among the printed matter they used to present themselves and also to save.

Printers and entrepreneurs quickly saw how chromolithography could be adapted for other purposes. Children were central to this process. An often-told story is that of children who in the early 1800s found paper treasures on the floors of German bakers' shops. These were the leftover bits of colored paper—literally, scraps—used to decorate cakes. Printers noticed this collecting interest and began to produce small chromolithographed images in envelopes or in sheets. Sometimes the sheets were coated with a gelatin-and-gum layer, which gave them a glossy surface; embossing added another benefit, for the scraps then had a three-dimensional look.[5]

Many of the first images were small, rectangular in shape, and similar to wood-blocked, engraved reliefs of an earlier time that held images of religious figures.[6] The new images also came in sets—comic scenes, royal families, great monuments of history, animals, and so forth. Children lucky enough to have the pennies to buy them might gather then inside a scrapbook or album, or what one collector of ephemera has called "the drawing room archive."[7]

Louis Prang introduced what he called "album cards" as an advertising tool for the 1873 Vienna International Exposition. A German who had come to the United States in 1850, Prang was an exuberant professional who described himself as "Stonegrinder, Draftsman, Bookkeeper and Financial man all in one."[8] Prang had taken the United States by storm, selling thousands, perhaps millions, of lithographs and chromolithographs of fine-art reproductions, animals, flowers, leaves, and battle scenes. At the Vienna fair, he distributed floral business cards, which "pleased so well" that he began marketing designs with blank spaces for merchants. Advertisers quickly discovered this new medium and issued cards in promotional sets. Prang saw the appeal of these advertising cards for the younger set, noting that "the mania among children for collections of these . . . helped to exhaust the supply."[9]

These trade cards dominated advertising for a brief period in the 1880s and 1890s, and children were avid collectors of images that bore brand names. Trade-card scrapbooks are described in this volume by Ellen Gruber Garvey, but the illustrations that follow show how a number of manufacturers advertised their products by giving away paper dolls and other printed items (see Figures 10.1 and 10.2)

Prang's use of technology and artistry led to his becoming known as the "Father of the American Christmas Card."[10] Prompted by the suggestion of an Englishwoman that he could dress up the card for sale at holidays, Prang introduced Christmas greeting cards to the British in 1873. Shortly thereafter, these and other holiday cards crossed the Atlantic to become popular in the United States.[11] Children, of course, were avid collectors of these cards, and those introduced earlier, as well.

Children filled album after album with lushly hued trading cards, sentimental greeting cards, and postcards—all of which made their first appearances in the 1870s and became widely available by the 1890s. As Ellis Davidson noted in *The Happy Nursery*, "There are so many beautiful works of art now issued that scrapbooks can soon be filled, for the exquisite Valentines, Christmas and New Years cards are all by far too good to be wasted, and, besides, children should be taught to value them as tokens of affection, since most of them are sent by those who love them, and it is in the nursery that all the best and warmest feelings of the heart ought to be cultivated."[12]

Figure 10.1.   *This paper-doll set (ca. 1910) was distributed as an advertisement for Wheeler and Wilson sewing machines.*
(Courtesy Marguerite Archer Collection of Historic Children's Materials, J. Paul Leonard Library, San Francisco State University)

Figure 10.2: *An embossed advertising card (ca. 1880) distributed by Lion Coffee depicts a typical floral and nature theme.* (Courtesy Marguerite Archer Collection of Historic Children's Materials, J. Paul Leonard Library, San Francisco State University)

Postcards and greeting cards were often arranged in scrapbooks and collected for their images, as well as for their personal messages (see Figure 10.3). By saving and displaying their cards, children were taught to remember and value the affections of others. The greeting card industry and the trend of sending postcards reached a new peak in the early 1900s, with estimated worldwide sales of more than $200 million.[13]

Victorian social etiquette also created a demand for more elaborate calling cards, one of the most popular being "Hidden Name Cards." These cards were printed with the donor's name hidden under a flap designed to resemble a hand. The name under the hand was revealed only when the flap was lifted (see Figure 10.4). Sometimes these cards contained hidden messages of love and friendship.[14]

By the turn of the twentieth century, the Raphael Tuck Company, established in 1866, was producing forty thousand different pictorial postcards, as well as shape and linen books, paper dolls, and collectible cutouts for children.[15] Tuck catered directly to children in Europe and North America by offering books and embossed cutouts. His company became the most well-known supplier of art supplies and scrapbooks. "Oilette" was the trademarked process used by Tuck to produce advertising, seasonal greeting cards, souvenirs, and photograph cards in vivid colors and intricate detail (see Figures 10.5 and 10.6).[16]

Other prominent makers of scraps and embossed paper products for children included the London children's book publisher Ernest Nister (ca. 1889–1933), the New York firm of McLoughlin Brothers (ca. 1855–1910), and smaller firms like Julius Bion and Company (ca. 1880–1890). Known in the 1890s for their innovative movable and pop-up books, Nister and Company Ltd. produced books and albums to encourage scrapbook making, such as *Little Pinafore's Scrap Book* and *General Jack* (see Figure 10.7).[17] Beginning in the late 1850s, McLoughlin Brothers

No. 18. The Roosevelt Bears Put Out a Fire.
" They climbed up ladders in clouds of smoke,
And lifted hose and windows broke."

This picture is one-quarter size of one of the 16 full-page color illustrations in
" MORE ABOUT THE ROOSEVELT BEARS "—the jolliest book of the year
for boys and girls. Price $1.10, postpaid
For sale in Philadelphia by STRAWBRIDGE & CLOTHIER
" The Merry Christmas Store."

Figure 10.3. *Postcards were favorites of children collectors, and by the early 1900s publishers understood well to market such items with children in mind. From left, clockwise: Postcard, "Roosevelt Bears Put out a Fire" (ca. 1906–8); postcard, "The New Picture Book," printed in Germany and postmarked 1909; cutout of a fan from a postcard inscribed with a verso message dated October 4, 1911.* (Courtesy Marguerite Archer Collection of Historic Children's Materials, J. Paul Leonard Library, San Francisco State University)

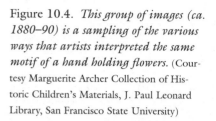

Figure 10.4. *This group of images (ca. 1880–90) is a sampling of the various ways that artists interpreted the same motif of a hand holding flowers.* (Courtesy Marguerite Archer Collection of Historic Children's Materials, J. Paul Leonard Library, San Francisco State University)

became successful because they produced affordable paper dolls, postcards, and scraps, alongside popular literature, puzzles, and board games. Their paper dolls first appeared in 1857 and were sold in sheets, booklets, and boxes. McLoughlin Brothers similarly produced products that appeared in magazines or were packaged with children's books and products so that young readers could use the paper dolls to act out their favorite stories. These were sold in sheets, booklets, and boxes, and they portrayed religious life, school life, homelife, nature, geography, patriotism, and many other facets of life—all the while advertising new consumer products.

From their stashes, children created stories and games to fit the figures and themes, but many children did not have the luxury of purchasing

their scraps. Most had to scrounge around the house for materials. Luckily the printing revolution provided families with common household items packaged in vibrant colors; pieces of colored paper salvaged off tea and other food containers, as well as pictures from newssheets and magazines. Children also knew to ask merchants and door-to-door salesmen for remnant materials that were found inside product packages.

While some "scraps" were available in sheets so that children could cut them out, others were sold or given separately, to be adhered to cards or other paper-work projects. Nineteenth-century educators promoted scrapbooks as a means of teaching cognitive skills and moral principles to students. They were used for special projects in studying natural history, geography, spelling, reading, and object lessons at the primary level.

Dr. James C. Jackson, for one, advised parents of the importance of educating through "everyday" object lessons that would develop a child's sense of familiar things: "What such children, boys or girls, need to know, are those and only those things which can be taught through the exercise of the senses; hence their lessons from day to day should be through the observation and understanding of objects which are brought to their knowledge."[18]

Another moral principle taught by scrapbook making was usefulness. As early as the 1840s, authors of child-rearing-advice books encouraged parents to teach children about reusing household fragments so that precious resources would not

"LET THE STARS AND STRIPES BE WAVING O'ER THEIR GENEROUS SACRIFICE."

Figure 10.5. *The work of the Raphael Tuck Company was a favorite of children and had many imitators. Postcard (ca. 1905) produced as no. 158 of Raphael Tuck and Sons' Decoration Day Series of Postcards. The caption reads, "Let the Stars and Stripes Be Waving o'er Their Generous Sacrifice."* (Courtesy Marguerite Archer Collection of Historic Children's Materials, J. Paul Leonard Library, San Francisco State University)

be lost or wasted. Lydia Maria Child in *The Little Girl's Own Book* included a number of "things to make and do" and advised parents:

> In this land of precarious fortunes, every girl should know how to be useful; amid the universal dissemination of knowledge, every mind should seek to improve itself; and in this land of equality, as much time should be devoted to elegant accomplishments, refined taste and gracefulness of manner. . . . In this country it is particularly necessary that daughters should be so educated as to enable them to fulfill the duties of a humble station, to dignify and adorn the highest. This is the reason why I have mingled a little of every thing in *The Girl's Own Book*.[19]

Nineteenth-century educators also promoted scrapbooks as a means of teaching art skills. By arranging images, colors, and text in tidy little blank books, young children could learn beauty, relational perspective, and composition.

Figure 10.6. *This scrap (ca. 1890), an embossed cutout of a trotting race, was possibly produced by Raphael Tuck and Sons. Scraps like this that were once affixed in a scrapbook are referred to by collectors as fugitive scraps.* (Courtesy Marguerite Archer Collection of Historic Children's Materials, J. Paul Leonard Library, San Francisco State University)

Although albums could be expensively bound and embellished, they could also be (and often were) a simply recycled magazine, ledger, or unwanted book. For example, a child might compose a scrapbook of illustrations, poetry, humor, and anecdotes, pasted over the printed pages of a catalog (see Figure 10.8). Children thus became avid collage makers and Grangerizers, creating scrapbooks within the bindings of existing books by adding illustrations.

Praise for such work often came in the form of more printed matter, or "rewards of merit," printed cards and certificates that teachers gave to students to acknowledge good scholarship and exemplary behavior (see Figure 10.9). In addition, albums and scrapbooks were often given in recognition of achievements and as gifts to children.[20]

Birthdays, graduations, holidays, and school successes could be celebrated with the presentation of a book in which a child might gather paper items that recorded or illustrated his or her own memories. While the word *memento* might be printed or embossed on the book cover, sometimes the child might be given a blank book with an inscription suggesting a specific purpose for the volume.

Figure 10.7. *General Jack (ca. 1890), printed in Germany but published in London and New York, was a gift book that encouraged the collection of military miniatures.*
(London: Ernest Nister, ca. 1890)

Such scrapbooks—filled with personal writing, cards and other endearments, and ephemera saved from various outings and achievements—became extensions of both their individual creators and the communities in which they lived. While scrapbooks compiled by a single person might express individual creativity, scrapbooks that contained materials gathered by a group expressed shared experiences, interests, or outlooks. An individual's scrapbook reveals to historians today much about private internal spheres, whereas group scrapbooks reveal public external spheres. Again, as noted in Ellen Garvey's essay in this volume, Sunday schools often made such collective scrapbooks, a fact not lost on printers and publishers of religious materials (see Figure 10.10).

Fugitive scraps—those cut, those that fell from scrapbooks, or those that do not have any known provenance—today suggest how children once interacted with materials found in their home and school environments. The Marguerite Archer Collection of Historic Children's Materials, at San Francisco State University Library, houses hundreds of such materials and several intact scrapbooks produced by children and adolescents. The illustrations here— all from this California collection—attest to the diversity of visual compositions, the wide field of desires and visions created by U.S. children in their scrapbooks between 1852 and 1945.[21]

Figure 10.8. *This scrapbook (ca. 1900) is composed on pages from a medical supply catalog for the E. A. Yarnall Surgical Company of Philadelphia. Adhered to the pages are newspaper clippings of poetry, humor, anecdotes from S. W. Gillilan, and "Reflections of a Spinster—Ancient Ann." Only one item is dated (November 28, 1903), and the last page has a cutout image of a bride.*
(Courtesy Marguerite Archer Collection of Historic Children's Materials, J. Paul Leonard Library, San Francisco State University)

AMPUTATING AND TRIENTS

NO.   PRICE.

228. Aseptic General Operating Case, and Str
Amputating Knife, 1 Medium Ca; 1 T
Metacarpal Saw, 1 Hey's Saw, 1 Strai
tating Tenaculum, 1 Straight Bg Fo
Tenotome, 2 Scalpels, 1 Aneur Exp
Knife, 1 pair Retractors, 1 Bone h
1 Pin-cutting Forceps, 6 Pear h
Needle Holder, 1 Volsellum Form
Scissors, 1 Curved Scissors, 1 V es
Tourniquet, 1 Trephine, 1 Brus.
1 Bullet Probe, 2 Probes; inst
in a brass-bound, rosewoo
Needles, Silk, Catgut, and

366. Dr. C. M.
Bistoury,
Artery
1 Stra
hav

es, in
morocco case, 8 oo
truments illustrated.

29

Figure 10.9. *This lithographed reward of merit gift card (ca. 1880), produced by Julius Bion and Company, Lithographers, is typical of the printed matter that could be given as prizes. Albums to hold such prizes were often especially valued.* (Courtesy Marguerite Archer Collection of Historic Children's Materials, J. Paul Leonard Library, San Francisco State University)

One final example is telling in its representation of the expectations U.S. adults and children brought to scrapbook making. This is an album called *Out of the Desert,* collectively made by a group of Japanese American students during World War II, and surely one of the most poignant of scrapbooks (see Figure 10.11). Conceived by an English teacher and a Red Cross director working in the Poston, Arizona, internment camp, the project called for the creation and distribution of scrapbooks via the Red Cross to its junior chapters all over the United States. The goals were to give interned students a voice, to boost their morale, and to aid them in developing pen-pal relations; their peers in the outside world would gain, in turn, an understanding of life in internment camps. Each scrapbook contained essays, poetry, wood- or linoleum-block engraved prints, and other artwork describing experiences at Poston. Bound with painted-cloth covers and construction-paper leaves in a traditional Japanese style, these collective accounts expressed the innocence and the profound optimism of Nisei teenagers during their incarceration. Yet, the original vision of intercultural communication never occurred: the scrapbooks are thought now to have never been seen outside the camps during the 1940s.[22]

Scrapbooks served their child creators—and serve scholars today—as ambiguous documents; in their choices of images, children both accepted and rejected the society in which they lived. Yet in all cases, children collecting scraps reshaped memory. They were probably conscious of this manipulation, and of other factors, as well—the limits of artifacts and text in presenting memory, the lack of opportunity and means of even trying to do so, and the wisdom of concealing some hopes and desires. Children, like adults, created, instead, semi-public, and always coded, documents. As they did so, they exercised cognitive processes by filling spaces and sorting images, skills

Figure 10.10. *Religious printed materials included this cutout, left, dated March 1896, from Little Bible Lesson Pictures, a quarterly series of Bible cards published by United Brethren Publishing House, Dayton, Ohio, and an embossed scrap cutout (1909), right, published by Hebrew Publishing Company.* (Courtesy Marguerite Archer Collection of Historic Children's Materials, J. Paul Leonard Library, San Francisco State University)

Figure 10.11.   *"Out of the Desert" (ca. 1944) was one of five known scrapbooks created by Japanese American teenagers in an internment camp in Poston, Arizona, during World War II.* (Courtesy Marguerite Archer Collection of Historic Children's Materials, J. Paul Leonard Library, San Francisco State University)

later needed with life changes. They learned to read the world and to preserve those parts of it important to them.[23]

With scraps, they learned to move among "material, aesthetic and ideological planes," paths Cathy Davidson has noticed in the reading of adults.[24] Today we observe in children's scraps—in our own reading that takes into account all the ways print was saved by children—the complexity of lives perhaps even anticipated by the advice writer with whom we began this essay, and certainly known by the parents for whom such advice givers wrote.

[SARAH McNAIR VOSMEIER]

II

~~~~~

Picturing Love and Friendship

~~~~~

Photograph Albums and Networks
of Affection in the 1860s

A MERICANS WERE MAKING PHOTOGRAPHS as early as 1839, beginning only days or even hours after the printed material describing Daguerre's process was unloaded from the ship that brought it from France. Almost no one made photograph albums, however, until commercial photographers began offering them in 1860. Once they were introduced to the consumer market, they quickly became popular, and young people were among the first to buy them. The albums young men and women compiled reveal much about nineteenth-century youth culture. In particular, they are concrete representations of networks of affection that were both heterosocial and homosocial. In the albums I have studied, close homosocial relationships—same-sex friendships such as those described by Carroll Smith-Rosenberg, E. Anthony Rotundo, and others—developed within a larger, less intimate circle of friends that included both young men and young women. Photographs and photograph albums also reveal the way young people negotiated matchmaking and courtship within this heterosocial youth culture.

The Development of Photograph Albums

Photograph albums developed much later than photography itself because early photographs, like paintings, were treated as unique items, not as images to be reproduced and shared. People thought of daguerreotypes and other early photographic forms in the same way as the painted miniatures that they resembled: they were mounted in gilded frames and cherished as individual items. There was no large-scale production of photographic prints until the 1850s, when commercial photographers in Europe developed a print-and-negative system, mounting standardized prints on cardboard cut to about the size of a calling card; thus, cartes de visite were named after the calling cards they resembled. At first only wealthy and aristocratic Europeans purchased them, but by 1859 significant numbers of bourgeois Europeans were buying them, and in 1860 commercial photographers in New York offered them to U.S. customers.

The success of the new photographic system depended on a new relationship with photography. With cartes de visite, people became collectors of photographs. Before then, a middle-class family might own a photograph or two, just as a wealthier family might own a painting or two. Cartes, however, were usually priced by the dozen. That meant that anyone who arranged for a sitting had plenty of extra prints to share with friends and relatives. The negative-and-print system also allowed entrepreneurial photographers to turn a profit by selling celebrity photographs. As a family collected cartes of friends, family members, and celebrities, they might easily collect dozens or hundreds of different photographs. With that many loose photographs, many people wanted a place to store and display them.

The photograph album seemed the logical solution—so logical that it developed almost as a matter of course rather than through one inventor's genius. As the editor of a journal for professional photographers put it, the idea of a photograph album was "reasonable and there is little doubt that it will become a permanent institution." To understand what made the album a reasonable solution to the problem of storing and displaying photographs, consider other solutions that were not adopted. In the nineteenth century as today, many people must have thrown loose photographs into drawers or boxes, and a filing drawer storage system might have developed from this tendency. Something similar to a modern Rolodex might also have been used— at least one stereocard viewer was built with such a system—but there was no similar format for family portraits. Instead, consumers and entrepreneurs casting about for the appropriate storage system for a new media thought of albums.[1]

Through the mid–nineteenth century, the word *album* connoted something closer to what is now understood as an *autograph album*. The 1847 edition of *Webster's American Dictionary* defines *album* as "a book, originally blank, in which foreigners or strangers insert autographs of celebrated persons, or in which friends insert pieces as memorials for each other." These albums could contain many kinds of collected "memorials," including quotations, signatures, locks of hair, and pressed flowers. Whatever the content, the "memorial" function of albums was important. This was especially true for albums of hair or other personal items. It was not so much the texture or color of the hair itself that was interesting; rather, the hair was valued because of its association with a person the compiler wanted to remember and hold dear. Even for albums of less personal items such as quotations or pressed flowers, the person or place associated with the item was often more significant than the item itself.[2]

Photographs, like autographs and locks of hair, are also strongly linked to the person they represent. Thus, putting collections of photographs into albums seemed appropriate. Nineteenth-century photographs did present logistical problems not associated with other memorial items, however. Nineteenth-century albums of autographs and other items were often handmade, but handmade books were unsatisfactory as photograph albums. The sturdy mounts of cartes de visite made them so heavy that the paper pages of a typical handmade album would sag under their weight. The photographs' stiffness would also make turning the pages of a handmade album awkward.

Entrepreneurs began designing commercial albums that would overcome the difficulties of handmade ones almost as soon as photographers began selling cartes de visite. They solved the problem of getting the bulky cartes into book form by making album pages out of pasteboard as thick and heavy as the cartes. Whereas pressed flowers and scrap items had been glued on top of the paper pages of handmade albums, cartes were actually embedded in and flush with the thicker leaves of commercial photograph albums. Each album page had a core of pasteboard with cutouts designed to hold the uniformly sized cartes. After purchasing an empty album, the consumer simply slid his or her cartes into the slots provided. The album binding worked like a hinge, much like modern toddlers' board books. These technical innovations allowed people to collect photographs in albums just as they had previously collected autographs. The innovations also meant that photograph albums would be store-bought items; thus, they would be inextricably linked to entrepreneurial capitalism and the developing consumer culture.

The idea of the photograph album was quickly and widely accepted. The speed with which the public adopted the photograph album impressed contemporaries. Early in 1861 a photography journal was already advising photographers to stock up on albums for their customers, predicting that they would be good sellers. By Christmas of 1862, an Easterner thought "the most noticeable thing in connection with the holidays this year is the great display of photographic albums." My own sample suggests that members of the middle class were the primary purchasers of albums, but contemporary writers were impressed by what seemed to them their nearly universal appeal. Oliver Wendell Holmes argued that "pauperism itself need hardly shrink from the outlay required for a family portrait-gallery." A Midwestern newspaper editor agreed that there were "few houses so poor as not to show beside the Family Bible the little book of home portraits."[3]

The image of the Bible and the album together on the same shelf reflects the central place albums quickly assumed in the middle-class household. A New Englander describing the development of the new medium used much the same language as the Midwesterner: "the photograph album appeared on the centre-table of the mansion and shelf of the cot, often dearer than the Bible itself." Entrepreneurs understood the connection as well. Publishers who sold elaborately bound Bibles often sold photograph albums as well. The National Publishing Company even published an elaborate "Family Bible" that included a photograph album bound into the text. Their advertising included testimonials like the one from N. Harris, of Larissa, Texas: "I sold fifty-one copies of your Bible last week. It is the book to make money on." In sum, the album, like the Bible, was part of the setting of a middle-class parlor. That the album was displayed in the parlor illustrates its significance as a marker of gentility and as a prop for social interaction.[4]

Albums for the Young

Young people from the middle class seem to have been among the most avid consumers of the new photograph albums. In my sample of albums from the 1860s, about half were compiled by people in their teens and twenties. A New York wit recognized the importance of albums in contemporary youth culture when he proposed punishments for disloyal Southern women. The appropriately severe penalty for a Southern woman between sixteen and twenty years of age who was "vituperative in the first degree" was to be "deprived of her Photograph Album," he suggested.[5]

The transitional stage of young adulthood was both longer and less clearly demarcated in the nineteenth century than it is now. Biologically, nineteenth-century young people matured more slowly than do their counterparts today. A twenty-six-year-old "young woman" of the nineteenth century was—like a twenty-two-year-old at the turn of the twenty-first—about ten years past puberty. Social maturation was also slow. In her study of Oneida County, New York, Mary P. Ryan found that middle-class men might be economically dependent on their parents for as long as twenty years. Entering the labor force in their late teens, they might then board away from home for a few years, but they commonly returned to their parents' home. They typically delayed marriage and a complete break from their parents' household until their thirties. Young women followed a similar pattern, staying at home with their parents for several years between the end of their formal education and their marriage. Mrs. L. C. Tuthill wrote an advice book for young women in this circumstance, telling them that "sheltered beneath the paternal roof, guarded from outward evil by the vigilance of love, the perplexing cares and overwhelming anxieties of life are not yet yours. You now enjoy the best possible opportunity to gain a knowledge of yourself."[6]

Young people may have found albums particularly attractive for two reasons. First, the carte-de-visite system of collecting and exchanging photographs fit conveniently into the existing culture of courtship and matchmaking. Young people exchanged photographs in this context, and purchasing an album for the photographs may have seemed a natural step. Further, the physical context of the photograph album (displayed in the parlor) made it a natural part of social calls between young people. Second, a photograph album gives tangible form to an intangible network of affection. It often depicts a circle of friends and relatives who may not be assembled in such a way again. Youth is a time of transition. In the 1860s young people often left home for boarding school or jobs in other cities, or they left a circle of friends at a boarding school to return home. Moving away from a particular network of affection must have made preserving it in an album especially appealing. Similarly, newlyweds used albums as a way of integrating two separate circles of friends and relatives into a single volume.

The first decade of the photograph album overlapped the Civil War, and the war shaped the culture of album making. Soldiers were not notable as album makers, however. An 1862 stationer's store advertisement mentioned photograph albums as appealing Christmas gifts but listed pens, portfolios, and diaries as more appropriate for soldiers. The album's association with the parlor might be one reason soldiers did not try to carry them into camp. More to the point, albums were usually large enough to be awkward to carry and might easily be damaged in camp life. Soldiers did carry photographs but usually loose in their pockets or in their luggage. Photographers certainly catered to the soldiers' market. The Star Gallery in Indianapolis, for example, promoted the fact that its photographer was a former soldier; as a result, he was "daily crowded with military," because "soldiers are not slow in finding out where they get the most polite attention and moderate prices, combined with the best style of work." A soldier who posed for a photograph could distribute the prints among his friends and relatives, any one of whom might put it in an album. Similarly, the photograph a soldier carried in his pocket was only one of a dozen prints, and the remainder might find their way into others' albums. Further, many soldiers compiled albums after the war, using photographs taken during the war itself. If the war did not drive the increasing popularity of photograph albums, it did contribute to it indirectly.[7]

Just as a soldier might collect photographs during the war but not compile them into an album until leaving the army, other young people followed a similar pattern, collecting photographs for some time before organizing an album during a time of particularly dramatic change. Annie Collins, who grew up in Lexington, Kentucky, and collected photographs as a girl, did not compile an album until she moved away from home to attend the Oxford Female College in Ohio. She had been collecting photographs for some time, but compiling an album made her want new ones. In a letter to her father she described her plans for the album: "I wanted yours and Mother's [photographs] to be side by side. I have saved a place for yours by Mother's, and a place for little Brothers by Brother's. Mine and Sister's are together, and Sue's and Val's. Collins gave me his. I put it opposite Lizzie Stroufe's. I should like to have Cousin La Collins' photograph to go opposite Cousin Alice's." Writing in haste, she added a postscript for her father: "Have you had your photographs taken?" Making an album must have been appealing to a young woman who was adjusting to living on her own. Filling an album with photographs of her parents and other friends from home was a way to reproduce the family circle she had left behind.[8]

Other young people made albums at the end of their education, faced with leaving a close circle of school friends to begin careers or return to their families. In 1860 "Duprey," a senior at Cumberland University in Tennessee, collected photographs of his friends and fraternity brothers to display in an album. His friends' signatures suggest that they expected the album to commemorate their "bonds of Betaism" and to help maintain friendships once they were physically parted. Thomas L. Harrison, a cadet at the U.S. Naval Academy in Annapolis, compiled a similar album the same year. Evidently Harrison's friendships with fellow cadets were important to him, because his school record includes the recurring offense of "visiting during study." Both Duprey and Harrison continued to expand their albums after leaving school, adding photographs and extra notations as their friends' circumstances changed in the years that followed.[9]

Homosocial and Heterosocial Friendships

Duprey and Harrison were living in all-male schools, and their albums reflect the homosocial friendships they formed there. Young people living at home had more opportunity for heterosocial friendship and acquaintance with members of the opposite sex—at church, for example, or at neighborhood gatherings. Such interactions might be entirely platonic or might include serious flirtations. Photograph albums give a glimpse of these casual nineteenth-century friendships because they include all those whom the compilers cared enough about to collect and keep their photographs. Most albums include photographs of both men and women.

In 1866 sixteen-year-old Addie Fuller of Lynn, Massachusetts, compiled a photograph album. Her sister, Mary, made one too, using duplicates of many of the images in her sister's album. Addie used more duplicates and new photographs in a second album, which was probably also compiled about this time. Together the albums include photographs of more than sixty individuals, most in their teens, and represent a youth culture centering in the girls' hometown. Many of the people appearing in the albums must have been the girls' schoolmates, but their network of friends extended beyond school to include students from schools in Boston and other nearby towns. Significantly, the Fuller sisters included both young men and young women in the network of affection their albums reproduce. Taking all three albums together, the sisters included fifty portraits of young men and ninety-six portraits of young women (they included more than one photograph of some of their friends).[10]

A nineteenth-century young person's widest circle of friends might include both men and women. Within this wide circle of casual friendship, however, many young people formed more intense same-sex friendships. This type of friendship is visible in the Fuller albums as well, especially in the few group shots. Most nineteenth-century albums are made up of individual portraits, but the Fuller girls included some images of two or three people posing together. Of these, twenty-one show two or more girls together. (In contrast, only two photographs show young men and women together, and only two show all-male groupings.) Most of the group shots represent various combinations among a group of about seven young women, including the Fuller girls themselves. The girls from the group shots are also shown in individual photographs on other pages of the albums. Thus, the Fuller girls used their albums to represent themselves as belonging to an inner circle of close female friends and a larger group of more casual friends, male and female.

Sometimes album makers included in their albums cliques to which they did not belong. Virginia Larwill Miller, a young woman from Mount Vernon, Ohio, was, like the Fuller sisters, presenting herself as part of a close circle of female friends. At the same time, her album also represents a close-knit, all-male circle within a larger heterosocial circle of young people in Knox County, Ohio. Among the few group portraits is one from the late 1860s of young men, probably all students at nearby Kenyon College. That they made special arrangements to be photographed together suggests their intention to commemorate a friendship and strengthen their group identity. That Miller had a copy of the resulting prints suggests that at least one of them considered her to be a friend, if a friend on a different level from those with whom he posed.[11]

The albums compiled by Mollie Arnold, of Mooresville, Indiana, provide yet another view of the intersecting networks of affection. The heterosocial circle represented in her albums consisted of more men than women. In the one she compiled before her 1867 marriage, thirty-four photographs are of male friends and relatives, and thirteen are of women. The nature of the relationships between Mollie and the young men she included in her album is unclear, but it seems unlikely that she was romantically involved with all of them. Of particular interest are five consecutive portraits of young men living near her home, all of whom joined Company E of the Twelfth Indiana in August 1862, as did Mollie's brother. She seems to have maintained a long-term friendship with at least one of the five, Benjamin Dakin, the only person who appears both in the album she compiled before her marriage and in the one she compiled afterward (see Figure 11.1). When her father died in 1874, almost a decade after she compiled her first album, she and her family published a notice of thanks in the local paper for those who "kindly volunteered aid and sympathy." Among those described as "especially entitled to our thanks" was Benjamin Dakin. In contrast, her albums give no concrete evidence of special female friends.[12]

Group portraits can reveal special friendships but were rare in the nineteenth century. Occasionally, close relationships can be identified even among people who appear in individual portraits. This seems to be the case for the five neighbors whom Mollie Arnold displayed together in her first album. At the least, they apparently patronized the same photographer, perhaps visiting the studio as a group. Careful examination of the young men's photographs shows that three of them are wearing the same hat, coat, vest, and tie, while the two other young men wear hats and

Figure 11.1. *The photograph of Benjamin Dakin from Mollie Arnold's album, compiled in 1866. This is the first of five photographs of local young men who joined Company E, Twelfth Indiana Regiment, and who made up a special circle of homosocial friends within a larger heterosocial circle that included Mollie.* (Courtesy Indiana Historical Society)

vests of a similar style; three have matching moustaches and goatees. Mooresville, where they all lived, does not seem to have had a photographer before the war. Thus, when the young men decided to pose for photographs, doing so probably required a special trip to Indianapolis (about fifteen miles away). Photographers often provided clothing their sitters could borrow, and perhaps three of the young men chose to borrow the same garments. Another possibility is that they traded garments among themselves. Benjamin Dakin belonged to one of the most prosperous families in Mooresville and thus could afford to dress well; possibly he offered to share his good clothes with his less prosperous friends. One way or another, three of the men seem to have had their photographs taken at the same time. They probably spent their leisure time together on other occasions as well. At the least, they were close enough friends that they shared tastes in personal appearance and grooming.[13]

Romance and Courtship

Romance usually developed within the larger heterosocial circle of nineteenth-century friendship, and photography and albums were used in connection with romantic relationships. A young man who came calling on a young woman was often received in the parlor, and looking through a photograph album together provided young people with a reason to sit next to each other and hold private conversations. A serialized novel appearing in *Overland Monthly* in 1884, "Annetta," gives a glimpse of how albums were used in parlors. In the story, Mrs. Shaw, a young newlywed, writes a letter to her unmarried friend, Annetta. She describes a call she received from Mr. Trenton, a business friend of her husband's. Casting about for a conversational gambit, Mrs. Shaw reports that "a photograph album was my first thought. I seized it. Our misanthrope [Mr. Trenton] is nevertheless courteous. He sat with the book on his knee, turning the leaves. But evidently he cared nothing for counterfeit presentments." Here the album does not serve as a prop for flirtation—in fact, it seems barely adequate as a means of smoothing conversation—but it was useful for matchmaking. When Mr. Trenton showed interest in a particular photograph, Mrs. Shaw took careful note, describing her thoughts to her friend: "Would I be questioned? Yes. He asked, 'For whom is that young lady in mourning?'" and thus revealed an interest in her. Since the woman in question was Annetta herself, Mrs. Shaw rushed to her writing desk to tell her all about it "barely five minutes" after Mr. Trenton had left her house. (The story ends happily with Annetta and Mr. Trenton married.)[14]

Like Mrs. Shaw, many young people actively encouraged their friends' romances and helped evaluate potential suitors. By the 1860s most parents did little to guide their children's marital choices or chaperone them extensively. Alexis de Tocqueville observed this parental restraint as early as the 1830s: "Long before an American girl arrives at the marriageable age, her emancipation from maternal control begins." Instead, young people turned to one another for advice on matters of romance. With parents mostly out of the picture, young people found mates largely in the context of a youth culture—they were introduced by friends, siblings, or cousins their own age. In 1860 another Frenchman, Auguste Carlier, published *Marriage in the United States*, an analysis reaffirming Tocqueville's initial impression that American girls were remarkably independent. With some astonishment and disapproval, he observed what he called "reunions," parties in which young men and women mixed without older, married chaperones. The middle-aged Carlier found the conversation at these parties insipid: "What one mostly hears is a certain small talk that aims less at wit than mere sound. . . . It is as it were a tilt of desultory remarks without apparent signification, but whose intended aim is always marriage. . . . Interest will be found more or less at the bottom of every one's thoughts."[15]

The life cycle of a typical courtship can be divided into three phases, all of which might include the use of photographs. The first, which we might unromantically call the mate-selection stage, was often discernible only in retrospect. Leisure activities that brought young men and women together might include some matchmaking and flirtation. Once two people settled on each other, the next phase was falling in love. Love at first sight was relatively rare in the nineteenth century. When nineteenth-century lovers wrote about falling in love, they usually described their attachment as weak at first, then gaining strength as the courtship progressed and the two people got to know each other well. Characteristically, a crisis or obstacle tested the couple's love during this middle phase of courtship. Choosing a life partner was stressful for both men and women, but the woman had more to lose. Women embarking on a life of economic dependency needed to be very sure that their husbands would always be devoted and supportive; thus, they were often the ones who precipitated the crisis. If a woman's lover continued to be ardent and devoted in the face of serious rejection or if he found ways to surmount difficult obstacles, she could be more confident in their future together. If the couple survived the testing period, they entered what we might call the engagement phase. Not every couple became formally engaged however; their intentions might be wholly private or poorly articulated. One way or another, though, they began to think of themselves as a committed twosome and to prepare themselves for marriage, both emotionally and economically.[16]

Matchmaking was common among young people in the nineteenth century, and photography was easily integrated into an existing culture in which young people guided one another in their mate selection. Frank Ingersoll's correspondence with his sisters, Mary and Matt, illustrates photography's place in matchmaking. When Frank left home to serve in the Union army, Matt and Mary wrote to him about their female friends and discussed him with them. Their correspondence continued after he left the army and settled in Indianapolis, some distance from the family home. The sisters might have managed this matchmaking through correspondence alone, without the aid of photographs, but photography fit easily into an already established pattern. Once Frank sat for a photograph, they requested copies of it and asked for new ones when he posed again. They showed his photograph to their friends, gave some copies away, and made so many requests for photographs that he wrote with some exasperation in June 1863: "As soon as I get some more taken I will send you a dozen but I would like to know what you want of them." As it was, he complained, he would have to have some "rising artist to emmigrate down to 'them parts' and set up shop for my especial benefit" if he were to keep up with their requests. Frank exchanged news with his sisters about young women in whom he might be interested. "Who is 'Jane' that says she thinks a great deal of me?" Frank asked Mary in 1861, adding, "tell her I am much Obliged." Significantly, Frank never discussed such things with his widower father, concentrating instead on news of military activities and his father's business associates.[17]

The correspondence between Walter Rogers of New Orleans and Elizabeth Goelet of Demopolis, Alabama, shows a similar pattern of young people depending on others their age for help in matchmaking and advice. Walter, who was serving in the Confederate army, met Elizabeth in April 1864 at a train stopover in Demopolis, en route to his assignment at a military court. He fell in love fairly quickly, calling her his "beloved, adored Bettie" by July 1864. She was more hesitant. After his visits she discussed him and his behavior with her friends—and then relayed their opinions to him in her letters. So far as can be deduced from extant letters, Elizabeth's widowed mother and her father figures—her oldest brother and an uncle—had little to say about the developing relationship. Instead, the brothers who were closest to Elizabeth in age, Edward and Frank, were the ones who took the most active interest in her love life. She seems to have shown Walter's photograph to

Edward, presumably discussing with him Walter's suitability while she did so, and she turned to Frank during a crisis in her relationship with Walter.[18]

Once two people established a romantic relationship, they entered the next phase of courtship. Photography was part of this too, although these photographs were probably not kept in an album; rather, a photograph served as a love token, something that could be carried on one's person. Photographs also served as a focus for verbal expression—discussing photographs gave lovers an opportunity to put their feelings into words. A New Hampshire man reassured his sweetheart that her photograph had not faded, although "*you would fade* if you had had the kissing that your picture has." This comment neatly conveyed to her the passion he felt for her, a point he drove home: if they were together, "I would make you think I have not done all my busing on your picture." In Fanny Fern's *Ruth Hall*, published in 1855, a henpecked husband tries to use a photograph as a means of expressing his fidelity. On his return from a business trip, having carried a photograph of his virago wife in his luggage where she packed it for him, he assures her that he "looked at it twenty times a day, and kissed it as many more." Unfortunately, he falls into her trap. Triumphantly grabbing up the photograph, she proves him the fool by showing him that it was actually only an empty frame—he had not noticed because he had never even glanced at the photograph.[19]

Photographs (and talking or writing about them) were also part of the crises that most nineteenth-century courtships endured. Walter Rogers and Elizabeth Goelet typically passed through an uncomfortable period when the relationship seemed about to end. Elizabeth was doubtful about her love for Walter, and Walter was frustrated by her lack of ardor. Offering to break off the relationship, he assured her that, whether they were together or apart, "I shall never cease to love you" and "I cannot, cannot help worshipping you." Elizabeth's brother served as a go-between during the crisis, and when he arrived to collect the parting letter, Walter added a final line: "I have just handed Frank your picture." Walter felt bound to return her photograph if the relationship was over. Still, he asked her to send him a copy, which would provide a focus for his melancholy and a means for expressing that melancholy: "Let me have at least the image of yourself. I can press that to my heart and cover it with my fondest caresses. That may be a comfort." Telling Elizabeth how he planned to use her photograph was also a way of telling her that they should continue the relationship—and thus make the comfort of the photograph unnecessary.[20]

Walter and Elizabeth negotiated the crisis successfully, and by the end of the year they were discussing wedding dates. Then in April 1865, as the Confederacy was falling apart, Elizabeth broke off the engagement again. This time the problem seems to have been less emotional than pragmatic or even patriotic. Apparently fearful of the possible chaos to come and the treatment they might receive from victorious Northerners, Elizabeth asked Walter to burn all her letters, and she determined that they should remain single. Imagining his own future as a prisoner of war and "so nervous that I can hardly hold my pen," Walter wrote, "I appreciate your feelings and honor the high, pure spirit that controls them." Although it was "very hard to have to give you up," he believed "that you have done what you think best. For your good and happiness, I am willing to yield every thing." He could not bear to meet her again if they could not marry. Instead, as he had in the crisis of the previous summer, he asked for a photograph to remember her by: "Don't fail to send me your likeness at the first opportunity."[21] Walter's and Elizabeth's fears about life after the war were unfounded. They soon began discussing wedding dates again and were married in the summer of 1867.

Once a couple had definite plans to marry or once they did marry, a photograph album was often the means of helping integrate two sets of family and friends. After Mollie Arnold married Origen Mitchell, they put together her second photograph album. The album is marked "Capt. A. O. Mitchell & Lady." Although the "& Lady" might suggest that Mollie was an afterthought, she was probably the dominant partner in creating the second album, because most of the captions refer to her relationships. For example, "Aunt Peninah Trueblood" refers to her father's sister rather than to a relation of her husband's. In any case, the album is a blending of his and her relationships—at least seven photographs are of her relatives, and at least eleven are of Origen's.[22]

Like the Mitchells, Elizabeth and Walter Rogers compiled a photograph album at about the time of their marriage. In this case, Walter was probably the driving force behind the album they both worked on. Of the photographs whose photographers can be identified, fifteen came from New Orleans. Because Walter lived in New Orleans both before and after the war, he likely purchased some or all of those photographs himself. Eleven photographs came from Mobile and probably originally belonged to Elizabeth. She had an uncle and a brother living in Mobile to whom she made extended visits. The photograph taken by an Edenton, North Carolina, photographer must have also been hers, acquired during a visit to another brother, who lived near there (Walter had no known connections to North Carolina).[23]

For Walter, at least, making connections with his fiancée's extended family was important. Returning from a visit with Elizabeth a few months before their wedding, he wrote her to say that he had forgotten to borrow a copy of her brother's picture. He asked her to mail him one so that he could have his own copy made. "I must have it," he insisted. He instructed her to get a recent photograph or else send him a specific shot he had seen when they were together. Photography also helped cement Walter's relationship with Elizabeth's brother Edward. Like Walter, Edward had served in the Confederate army and was sometimes headquartered near where Walter worked in military courts. Walter had made a special effort to meet Edward and maintain a friendship with him. In September 1864, Walter was pleased to report to Elizabeth that his first meeting with Edward had gone well: "I was very kindly received and entertained by him. . . . I like your brother very much and found him a very intelligent and perfect gentleman." Later, "3 days after the surrender 1865," Walter and Edward had their photograph taken, thus choosing to mark the end of the war by making a permanent record of their relationship. With the Confederacy in ruins, they did not know when, if ever, they would see each other again, especially if Walter and Elizabeth canceled their wedding. The photograph gave physical form to a connection that would remain tenuous unless and until Walter and Elizabeth finally married. Once they did marry, they placed the photograph in an album that served the same purpose, integrating two networks of affection on a larger scale.[24]

Among the photographs the Rogerses included in the album they compiled is one of Alex Delgado. It represents both the youth culture within which romances developed in the 1860s and the way lovers and newlyweds worked to integrate previously separate networks of affection. Delgado served with Walter in the war and posed for the photograph in a New Orleans studio. Primarily Walter's friend, he was also a link between Walter's network of affection and Elizabeth's. As Walter made more and more visits to Demopolis to visit Elizabeth, he was drawn into her social circle. Eventually he came to know many of her friends well enough to follow gossip about them and to express opinions on their character and behavior. Delgado accompanied Walter on at least one of these visits. Walter could tell Elizabeth: "I write this in Mr. Delgado's tent," where they had been talking "nearly all this morning" about their visit to Demopolis. Delgado had spoken especially about "Miss Weise." Walter confided: "The latter young lady . . . holds considerable dominion over that little fluttering organization, which lies in the bosom of my friend Delgado. He is a clever young man and Miss W. must act generously with him." Throughout their long engagement Walter and Elizabeth continued to play matchmaker for their friends—in fact, matchmaking seems to have been a way of strengthening the links between their separate networks of affection.[25]

S INGLE PEOPLE UNDER thirty years of age embraced photography and photograph albums with enthusiasm in the 1860s. Often their appeal came from their connection with family. Annie Collins may not have seen her parents and siblings much while she was in boarding school, but she could look at their photographs in her album; arranging her album to reproduce familial relationships was satisfying for her. Nineteenth-century photograph albums were not simply family albums, however. Young people used theirs to record friendships as well, and in doing so they have left a physical representation of their youth culture. The friendships they documented in their albums ranged from casual to intense. In particular, album compilers depicted intense homosocial relationships within a more casual heterosocial circle. The Fuller sisters used their albums that way, including more than sixty relatively casual friends but also featuring seven of their closest female friends. Couples who were about to be married or who had just been married found albums appealing. For them, compiling a photograph album together was a way of integrating two sets of family and friends. In all these cases, young people who were in transition between households, relationships, and identities used photograph albums to give abstract networks of affection concrete form.

12

Telling Particular Stories

Two African American Memory Books

IN THE PHOTOGRAPH ALBUM of the noted musician Fletcher Henderson, someone has scratched out the faces of two members of a group of Atlanta University students posing in a photograph from the decade 1910–20. In the 1920s scrapbook of memorabilia kept by Juanita Page Johnson of her years at a Chicago high school, a brightly dressed African American flapper dances between other pages where more staidly dressed Caucasian women predominate.

These small insertions suggest a good starting place for any study of African American scrapbooks. Revision is at the core of all collecting—whether centered in libraries and archives, photograph albums, blank books, scrapbooks, shoe boxes, or any other number of repositories. Overt revisions, after all, immediately tell us to look beyond the surface of creation and consider questions about rejecting one image in favor of another.[1]

These two marks of revisions also invite an intimate study of the details of memory books and the multiplicity of forces that influenced memory keeping among African Americans. Most important to memory gathering, scrapbooks with such changes invite consideration of the creation of selves rooted in various cultures and, over a lifetime, in changing cultures and identities.

Both Henderson's album and Johnson's scrapbook are now housed at the Amistad Research Center at Tulane University.[2] Both were mass produced and held memories firmly set within traditions of mainstream culture. Yet they also recast these traditions to manifest the distinctive memories of individuals within divergent communities.

Physically, both books are unsurprising examples of conventional U.S. memory keeping: images and words set on pages.[3] The Henderson album measures 7.25 inches high and 9.5 inches wide, has a brown cloth binding, and contains eighty-six pages. The word *Photographs* is printed on the cover. There is no indication of publisher, printer, binder, or, indeed, compiler. The album was donated to the Amistad by Henderson's niece, but no information about who made the book is known. The black pages are currently unbound but stacked within the original binding. At least thirteen items have been removed completely, although it is impossible to know who might have done this or what these items were. The inside cover contains a printed photograph of the 1924 Atlanta University football team, as well as the snapshot with the scratched-out faces. In total, there are 127 other snapshots, fifty studio or professionally made photographs, and two photographs from printed sources.

The contrast among the types of photographs—snapshots, studio prints, printed photographs—creates a subtle visual tension reflective of two communities within Henderson's life: that of a conservative family and that of a more liberal, leisurely life with friends. Viewed alongside additional biographical information, movement between the formal and informal photographs suggests the self Henderson was creating in his college years.

Such tensions are especially evident in the pages on which images of crisply dressed, proper, and unsmiling individuals posing in photographers' studios appear adjacent to snapshots of young adults playing tennis or boating. Here is the conformity and respectability of the African American middle class cast alongside the emerging youthful world of the 1920s. At the same time, because African Americans were rarely pictured in the national press, the memory book gives an alternative view of the way white Americans usually visualize the past.

The Johnson scrapbook measures 9 inches high and 4 inches wide. Its 189 pages, with their numerous inclusions, now measure three inches in thickness. Entitled *The Girl Graduate: Her Own Book*, the scrapbook was designed and illustrated by Louise Perret and Sarah K. Smith, was published by the Reilly and Lee Company, and included frames for placing specific types of memories. Although no copyright date is given, the book can be found in numerous editions of *Cumulative Book Index* and the *United States Catalog* for the years between 1906 and 1917. The 1912 entry reveals that the book had gone through fourteen editions. Other similar books, printed as late as 1930, could be found in various bindings and covers—for example, boxed with a special cover or a simple red or blue cloth, among other choices. Johnson's cover is of crushed Moroccan leather, the most expensive version of the prefabricated memory books.[4] Such books often were given as gifts.[5]

Johnson's edition shows printed images of an era when high school girls and college women wore long hair and long skirts and perhaps had an interest in completing entries related to the baccalaureate sermon or fifteen other categories. The table of contents directs the compiler or reader to points of memories in academic life, shaped around "flower, class yell, motto, class photographs, class autographs, class officers, the teachers, class prophecy, her invitations, the programs, social events, press notices, her gowns, the presents, jokes and frolics," and other topics.[6] The illustrators provide pastel, flowery, art-nouveau-style borders. Throughout the book a white schoolgirl, the budding New Woman, is drawn in the style of popular artists such as Charles Dana Gibson and Howard Chandler Christy. This white girl has the abundant, upswept hair so popular in the early 1900s; she has the posture and poses reflective of what Martha Banta has called "signs of both physical energy and regal good manners."[7] Thus one can guess that the book might well be the 1917 or earlier edition.

Juanita Page Johnson followed only those headings that fit her own community or fancy. The images of brightly clothed African American women with bobbed hair indicate that Johnson obviously saw the printed images as outdated and not reflective of her own life. Representations of physical energy and manners had changed by 1923, and Johnson's added images are both modern and African American. Her role models might have well been the socialites pictured in *Half-Century Magazine*, the *Chicago Defender*, the *Pittsburgh Courier*, and other African American periodicals. Or she might have been thinking of beauty contests—such as those staged by the *Chicago Defender*, Chicago State Street Carnival, and Chicago Club Dreamland—which featured socially prominent African American women, high school students, teachers, and others.[8] Even if she were but a casual observer of the press, she would have seen many public endorsements of African American beauty, and she seems to have copied these. Today, the juxtaposition of images prescribed by a narrowly defined and dated white culture next to those chosen by Johnson presents an overt collection of a self centered in both dominant and minority cultures.

Fletcher Henderson's Story and His Album

Although cited as the "Fletcher Henderson Jr. Album" in the records of the Amistad Research Center, there is no written information within this memory book that tells who Fletcher Henderson was. Nor do we really know whether the album was created by Henderson or for him. For the former information, we can turn to other biographical information; for the latter, we must look closely at the photographs, their placements, and their subjects.

Fletcher Henderson Jr. was born in Georgia in 1897, the oldest son in a family of distinguished teachers. He achieved fame as a bandleader, pianist, and arranger and is now considered to have been a founder of the swing era and its Big Bands. Through his jazz arrangements he brought popular dance music to its zenith in the early twentieth century. With few exceptions, today's Big Bands follow the pattern of reed, brass, and rhythm sections that Henderson developed in the 1920s. During his tenure at New York's Roseland Ballroom, he brought together musicians such as Louis Armstrong, Joe Smith, Benny Carter, and John Kirby.[9]

Before this stardom, Henderson led a different sort of life as a member of a well-known family and as a student. His father, Fletcher Sr., attended both the University of South Carolina and Atlanta University—the first, a university that only briefly in the nineteenth century enrolled any African American students; the second, a historically African American university, where such luminaries as W.E.B. DuBois taught. Both Fletcher Sr. and his wife, Ozie, were teachers, and the three Henderson children—Fletcher Jr., Horace, and Irma—were all college graduates, not the norm for white or African Americans in the United States at this time.[10]

By making comparisons with the Atlanta University yearbook, one can identify many of the album's photographs as those of young Fletcher, his family, and his schoolmates.[11] Photographs of him at all ages are interspersed throughout the majority of pages; his Atlanta classmates surround the earlier photos, and, as noted, the front endpaper contains a photograph of the Atlanta University football team. Approximately thirty young children, Fletcher's parents, siblings, and other adults also appear in the book. Thus visual clues here clearly disregard time, creating a memory book that both reveals—and masks—much of Fletcher Jr.'s life until leaving Georgia in 1920.

Yet overall the album shows the collegiality of school life for African Americans. Henderson's photographs are not unlike those of college students throughout the United States and, like these others, are clearly marked by segregation.[12] Called a "creole from Georgia" by at least one biographer, Henderson, like his family, lived in a world favored with education, leisure, and formal clothes yet bounded by the rigid discrimination of the white world.[13] Cuthbert, Georgia, where the family lived, had a population that was two-thirds African American, among whom teachers like the Hendersons held positions of prestige.[14] At the same time, biographical information notes that the Hendersons were both underpaid by all standards and had to mortgage their home to buy a piano. Like other African Americans, they were outside the circle of opportunities afforded whites.[15]

The impact of this discrimination is largely invisible within the album. Here young Henderson and his friends exhibit the elegant, dashing, sometimes sporty look characteristic of college students of the period. The young men usually wear suits, even on picnics (see Figure 12.1). When not in suits, they sport vests or wear the uniform of the Student Army Training Corps. Snapshots show both men and women carrying tennis rackets, baseball bats, and books.

Dress and other details visible in the studio prints suggest that the album was compiled without reference to chronology, showing vividly the nonlinear time evident in so many memory books. Flapper outfits appear alongside plain, long dresses. Male students in World War I training uniforms appear next to women who bobbed their hair. Studio backdrops suggest heavy Victorian interiors or balustrades of the late nineteenth century; yet a few show aspects of leisure more suited to the 1920s—for example, one young woman, dressed in a short dress, is posed on a swing.

The placement of photographs contributes to a sense of nonlinear time where precedence is given to people, rather than to the sequence of events. These details

Figure 12.1. *In this small photograph someone has scratched out two faces and labeled one of the young men "Judas Iscariot."* (Fletcher Henderson Collection, Amistad Research Center, New Orleans)

add to other unknowns, those that have to do with our twenty-first-century viewing of the album and our questions about boundaries of ownership and creation: Who made the book? Why did he or she make it? Were some images removed and, if so, why? As mentioned, space within the album is similarly appropriated, with large numbers of snapshots balanced by larger-size studio prints with no apparent regard for type of photograph. The studio prints show a self graced with kinship and closeness to people of all ages. These prints, especially in their depiction of so many different ages of people within young Henderson's community, suggest a time before he left home. On the other hand, the snapshots reflect an evolving self, away from family and intent on leisure. The most significant markers of leisure—sailboats, people lounging in gardens, and the objects mentioned earlier (rackets, bats, books)— are revealed in many of the snapshots.

Aged by light, the snapshots have a hazy quality. Their smaller size suggests the privacy and intimacy of remembering friends by perusing albums. Of course, these photographs and their details would have been more easily read by those who knew something of the story behind each particular outing and subject. Yet today their thinning paper gives the collection an ambiance of obscurity and lightness, contrasting with the clarity of the faces, the heavy paper, the standardized backdrops, and the darker tones of the more lasting studio portraits. The snapshots of leisure interrupt the staid respectability of the studio prints in a way not unlike the way the youth culture of the 1920s changed the United States.

A different dimension, symbolic of an earnest passion for community, emerges in still other snapshots showing groups of teachers. Unlike the scenes of leisure, these photographs show little clowning. These faces, like those in the studio prints, are serious; often they are not looking directly toward the camera. But here the solid-colored clothing appears sometimes rumpled, quite unlike the starched clothes seen in the studio prints. Men appear without jackets; ladies wear plain dresses with little embellishment or white blouses with dark skirts. These photographs most likely were taken on the grounds of Atlanta University or Howard Normal School, a private Congregational Church school where Fletcher Henderson Sr. and his wife taught.[16] All hues of skin color appear, reminders of the troubled legacies of black existence under white domination.

These photographs of teachers also speak to the presence of whites within Congregational Church schools, of the ways that these schools defied segregation in the South by creating a place where whites and blacks worked together.[17] Here W.E.B. DuBois's thesis on duality—that an African American was at once both "an American, a Negro"—is reinforced.[18] The solemnity and traditional poses of both these latter snapshots and the studio prints remind us that within such schools African Americans and Caucasian Americans together took on the classics of U.S. and European literature, history, and art even as they celebrated the African American heritage.[19]

Henderson came of age with these three types of photographs—formally posed studio prints, snapshots of leisure, and snapshots of teachers and parents—intact in one book. What is missing is any notice about the music for which he became so famous, an omission that might be explained by the fact that Fletcher Sr. had another career in mind for his son—chemistry. In the fall of 1911 Fletcher Jr. had been sent to Atlanta, first for high school at Atlanta University's College Preparatory School and later for college.[20] During this schooling, the family felt proud of his athletic accomplishments, notably letters in football and baseball, and something of this pride is seen in the photographs in the album, but music is not represented in any way. There are no images of bands, instruments, or musical programs, although these could have been removed earlier.

Classical music was important in the home. "It is legend in the family that his pianistic ability was inherited—a half hour before he was born, his mother excused herself from the piano where she had been playing," wrote one biographer. "The three children were taught the fundamentals of the piano by their father and mother, who were both accomplished pianists in the classical manner."[21]

In addition, Atlanta University's first yearbook notes that young Henderson wrote about music for the school newspaper, played the organ all four years, and served as bandmaster for the Georgia Student Army Training Corps unit. The yearbook also notes that he played the piano for five summers at a resort in Woods Hole, Massachusetts. His favorite quote—from William Congreve—underscores his passion for music: "Music hath charm to soothe the savage beast / To soften rocks, or bend a knotted oak."[22]

The summer after his graduation, Henderson traveled to New York City, where he remade the images of the memory book, the privilege and respectability so carefully shaped and controlled within his African American community of Georgia. Although his father wished him to enroll in Columbia University, young Henderson found a job as a pianist, quickly moved into work as a song demonstrator with Pace and Handy Music Company, and a short while later became an accompanist and recording manager for Black Swan.[23] Ethel Waters recalled her first visit to Black Swan in the early 1920s and remembered Henderson "sitting behind a desk and looking very prissy and important."[24]

This additional biographical information shows how the photograph album casts the family as central and suggests the tension young Henderson might have experienced in becoming a noted figure of the Big Band era. His father, it is said, never allowed any jazz to be played in the home even after Fletcher and his younger brother, Horace, had both become active in music across the United States.[25] The photograph album memorialized the formal and proper world preferred by Fletcher's parents. But unlike this world, the memory book also created a place for stepping outside the boundaries given by others. The images of garden picnics, tennis games, and baseball present evidence of a youth culture that would welcome new ideas, including jazz itself.[26]

The question of who created this memory book, however, remains. If Fletcher's mother or father made the album for him, it reveals something of what they thought their son should remember of his childhood and adolescence. If images of music were removed by publicists, biographers, or later readers, then this act too shows something of what was expected of Henderson—a giving self, one that preserved the private self but gave away more public images.[27]

The extant and contrasting images of the old self of the studio prints and campus scholars and the new self of the 1920s youth culture show that for Henderson the two worlds came together often enough. The images suggest that his journey to adulthood was marked by continued associations with his family rather than the separation often deemed necessary for so many adolescents. Although Linda Rugg has suggested that photographs "display many views and variant versions of the same person [and] supply a visual metaphor for the divided and multiple ("decentered") self," Henderson's memory book seems to show the chance for a centered self made up of various strands.[28] The images show a multiplicity of selves and visually suggest the maturation process of adolescents from minority cultures as described by Françoise Lionnet: finding genuine ways of perceiving difference while emphasizing similarities to others.[29] Henderson's album, then, hints at other dualities. The world of family and school hid the outside world—the segregated, white-dominated world as well as the world of jazz, the world of exuberant sounds but also of numbers runners, prostitution, and crime.[30]

Juanita Page Johnson's Story and Her Scrapbook

The Juanita Page Johnson scrapbook's problems of identity, ownership, and provenance differ from those posed by Fletcher Henderson's. No published biographical information is available for Johnson, and she is eclipsed by her husband's name in all other records. Although no guessing is required to name her as the owner and creator of this memory book—the inscription "Juanita Page" is quite clear from page 1, and the book also contains many letters, notes, and wishes addressed to her—she is noted in the Amistad Center's records under her married name, and her book is described as consisting of "photographs and collected printed items mostly about the schooling of a Chicago dentist and his wife."[31] It is noteworthy here that her husband, Lester Freeman Johnson, is mentioned in only six places in the 189-page scrapbook. Also, unlike the Henderson album, which is one part of a larger collection, Johnson's scrapbook stands alone with only marital information. The Amistad Center has no other record of her, and archivists there have heard only that the book was donated by one of the children of her husband's second wife. That Juanita Page was the child of a mother and father who migrated from Mississippi to Chicago can be guessed from census records for someone who appears to be her brother. Thus far, even census records about her remain elusive.[32]

Still, her scrapbook documents extensively her high school career, graduation, friendships, life after graduation, and honeymoon in 1928. Thus, we can learn something about her life from the memory book itself, perhaps just as she imagined someone later would.

Juanita Page came of age at roughly the same time as Fletcher Henderson Jr. Born probably around 1905, she was educated in public schools and in 1923 graduated from Wendell Phillips High School in Chicago. She also completed a two-year course at a business college and in 1928 married a Phillips classmate, Lester Freeman Johnson. He obtained a degree in dentistry from the University of Illinois School of Dentistry, which firmly placed him within the upper middle class of African American society. Their wedding and many of Juanita Page's social activities were reported in the *Chicago Defender*, clippings that she added to her scrapbook.

Johnson's scrapbook, a record of her social years and her early adulthood, reflects a more straightforward, chronological presentation of her life than does Fletcher Henderson's. At the same time, in both her conformity to and rejection of the publisher's printed headings, Johnson shows in her scrapbook DuBois's idea of duality. She is at once participating in mainstream America even as all her scrapbook's memorabilia concern a segregated African American life. The printed headings—obeyed or ignored in their requests for class photographs, autographs, mottoes, and flowers—reveal her picking and choosing from the categories of a publisher who presented all girl students as white.

Indeed, in her book she repeated many of the patterns of scrapbook making that white students used. Her first pages are devoted to images of her school, Wendell Phillips High School. Like white scrapbook makers, too, she then pasted in photographs and notes from teachers and fellow students.[33] Also like white scrapbook makers, Johnson devoted many pages to social activities, relaying some sense not only of her personality but also of high-school social life. The inclusions in the memory book show that she attended functions at the University of Chicago, the Wabash

Avenue YMCA, and other private clubs. She was invited by the Fisk University Women to a tea honoring all graduates of 1923. She was a member of the "well known gang," as one engraved invitation notes, and once attended a party that lasted from 10 P.M. to 3 A.M. She enjoyed the movies and theater. In short, like many other scrapbook makers, she wished to fix within her pages those activities that represented a busy, socially prominent life.

On the other hand, Johnson's world, shown in print and image, is wider geographically than that of most white high school scrapbook makers and that of Henderson in his album. She can and does choose to clip from at least two newspapers: the *Chicago Defender*, the black press, and her school paper. Her network of friends extends across the United States. She includes a printed invitation from Greenville, Mississippi, for the "Young Men's Social Club's Christmas Entertainment with Prince and Robinson's Syncopated Orchestra, in the new Colored High School Auditorium." One friend marries and moves to Texas, as a wedding announcement indicates, and another has family in New Orleans, noted in a clipping about visiting relatives. Migrations by other classmates from all over the South are noted, their place within her book a reminder of the many thousands of African Americans who, by moving away from the South and its harsh segregation, sought the chance for a better life. Chicago beckoned, especially the chance to attend a well-established public high school, something not possible in almost all southern cities.[34]

In her treatment of the city, Johnson might also be seen today as a documentarian of African American Chicago life. In page after page of more that sixty items of ephemera, the world of her neighborhood becomes visible in the scrapbook. Commencement programs, news of academic clubs, and notices of good grades are interspersed with photographs of athletic teams and programs for musical performances of works not only by European composers but also by Noble Sissle, Henry Creamer, and Turner Layton *(America's Greatest Colored Song Writers in America's Greatest Musical Show)*. Printed invitations to more than twenty-five parties—for example, a sheik and sheba party ("If you are a Skeik, bring a Sheba") and a party given by the Four Percolators ("Come Percolate") —give a glimpse into the Chicago social scene for middle-class African Americans.

Yet Johnson's scrapbook, like Henderson's album, places her world close to that of her parents and other adults. Her classmates' biographies often mention their parents, and printed material about Johnson always names her mother. She is invited by the parents of others on outings and is included by the alumnae of other schools in their teas and other events. One of her fellow students admonishes her: "Remember your only friends are those who have guided you all the way, your father and mother." Although we do not know if Johnson included all notes or even if inclusion of this one was intended as humor, the presence of adults in her scrapbook is significant. In my studies of the albums of some eighty white students from the same time period, only three noted parents at all. I believe, then, that her maturation as part of a community is more similar to that of Henderson than is first apparent.[35] The covenant between parent and child, rather than their separation, is emphasized.

Certainly Johnson's parents, like Henderson's, seem to have provided her with some affluence and the time for leisure. She does not seem to have paying work, as do at least two of her classmates.

Yet problems caused by racial inequities would have been familiar, at least somewhat, to Johnson. She was in her early teens when the Chicago race riot of 1919 occurred. She lived in a part of town touched by it, and Wendell Phillips High School itself changed after the riot. The 1920 Commission to Investigate the Riot brought to light vivid details about the poverty and discrimination suffered particularly by recent migrants from the South, as well as information on student life at integrated Wendell Phillips. The commission found that many African American students at Phillips worked after school, that many had to drop out of school for periods of time to earn money, and that school authorities approved segregation of white and black students and at times refused black students membership in clubs and other activities.[36] An earlier 1915 report noted that whites and blacks joined segregated clubs at the school. In 1920, 5 percent of Wendell Phillips was African American, yet African Americans belonged to no official clubs and made up only half of the basketball team. Further, only one teacher was African American.[37]

By the time Johnson began her scrapbook in 1921 or 1922, some of the same conditions were still evident, but some changes had occurred. Clippings and photographs show that at least five teachers were African American, Johnson herself was a member of numerous clubs that seem to have included both black and white students, and African Americans made up 100 percent of the football team.[38]

Johnson's ephemera reveals that Phillips itself by the 1920s offered a course on "the history of the colored people," and her basketball photographs and clippings show even more about the growth of African American leadership at the high school. For example, her interest in sports predates the fact that the school excelled in basketball (five of the original Harlem Globetrotters first played at Phillips). Her record of teachers underscores the fact that by her time there the school employed a number of well-known African Americans. One of these was Ida Taylor James, who wishes Juanita well and calls her "dignified." James, a graduate of the University of Chicago, was a founding member of a black sorority there and a leader in the African American community.[39] In her photograph and in her note, James balances modernity: she has long hair, in contrast with the students' bobs, and writes a brief, reserved wish.[40]

What is certainly depicted in Johnson's book is a changing although still segregated world, one of deep attachments. Similar to Henderson's album, Johnson's scrapbook provides a place where the group snapshot predominates in depicting the cohesion of African American youth. The compilation can be seen not only as marking the solidity of her group, something that Philip Stokes notes in group shots across cultures, but also as reinforcing the interactive process required of scrapbook making among her fellow students.[41] Thirty-one pages contain letters her friends wrote directly into the scrapbook. In this way her scrapbook resembles the friendship albums of the mid–nineteenth century, most of which are studied today from collections of white New England girls and women.[42] My own research suggests that, more than did white student scrapbook makers of the 1920s, Johnson treated her memory book as a communal project.

The generation crossing and collective effort apparent in Johnson's scrapbook perhaps mirrors a strength that would have been needed as African American students entered the segregated workforce or continued further studies. The class mottoes, "Know thy work and do it" and "No victory without labor," suggest that the students were told and retold of an enduring belief in U.S. capitalism but recognized the hard task ahead of them.

This would have been the message of mainstream white America, but Johnson rephrased it to her own liking. She may have recognized how the outside world would not be entirely hospitable to the school's mottoes of "work," "labor," and "victory." The out-

Figure 12.2.   *Here someone has drawn a Josephine Baker–like dancer onto the pages of a scrapbook. In contrast, the publisher's printed images show staid, early-twentieth-century Caucasian women.* (Juanita Page Johnson Scrapbook, Amistad Research Center, New Orleans)

side world printed—and preferred—images of Caucasian women, and this might have been reminder enough of the exclusion of African Americans. But Johnson had an answer to this injustice, at least within her memory book; she entered her own images and those of her friends over the images of whites. She edited the printed images.

Johnson did this most vividly through hand-drawn and hand-painted images in the scrapbook. In these, someone named Georgie Washington provided six depictions of young African American women. With their bobbed hair, slinky clothes, and lively movement of arms and legs, these young women (see Figure 12.2) dance among the subtly colored, demure images of white women supplied by the publisher.

The name Georgie Washington and the date 1923, written with some flourish beneath each drawing, add both specificity and complexity. Because 1923 was Johnson's graduation year, it seems evident that this is a classmate. But nothing is said of Georgie Washington or her Josephine Baker–like subjects in the clippings or handwritten notes.

In this way Johnson intervenes with considerable style in the script of the published memory book and balances the white images with an overwhelming amount of printed and visual material from African American culture. What is revealed are the places she was welcomed and the places she and her friends created or recreated. One of these latter places was the scrapbook itself— the manipulation of photographs, clippings, good wishes, and drawings especially presented to tell her own story.

The Tradition of African American Memory Keeping

Probably neither Henderson nor Johnson was conscious of being part of larger traditions of record keeping or autobiographical effort. Yet their roles in these traditions are what make his album and her scrapbook so important today. Their memory books allow readers today to consider the diversity of life not shown in mainstream print culture, the choices of images not readily available, and other ways of using a memory book to tell a distinctive story. Their memory books suggest the means by which dominant and minority representations of culture are incorporated, rejected, or hidden in the lives of individuals.

Earlier traditions of manipulating printed and visual matter allowed for significant revelations of the many truths about African American life. The compiling of clippings from the press, for example, was critical to the antislavery movement. The most famous of such compilations was, in reality, a scrapbook, later published in 1839 as *American Slavery as It Is: A Testimony of a Thousand Witnesses* by the white abolitionist Theodore Weld.[43] This appropriation of the words of "thousands upon thousands of southern newspapers" straightforwardly disclosed facts about the cruelty of slavery. Proslavery publishers themselves wrote about the punishment of slaves; slaveholders themselves wrote the ads posted for runaways. Thus, Southerners could not denounce the compilation as false.[44]

Another reader of the press who could not relinquish articles on African Americans was Joseph W. H. Cathcart. Like Weld, Cathcart began his collection of ephemera around an 1856 notice of a reward offered for a runaway slave. Cathcart, "a great reader of newspapers," wanted to "to preserve the good things and some bad things he read about black people in newspapers." By 1882 he had compiled one hundred huge volumes: "Each volume of four inches or more in width had the subject stamped in gold on the back . . . followed by the letters 'G. S. B. M., meaning 'Great Scrap-Book Maker.'"[45]

Other Philadelphia collectors included William C. Bolivar, Robert M. Adger, and the prolific William Dorsey.[46] During the years 1870 to 1923, Dorsey compiled some 338 scrapbooks and 914 biographical files, more than half of which were devoted to people of color and 140 devoted wholly to African Americans. Dorsey's work became a communal effort, added to by contributions from others and used by the African American community at large to know its history.[47] Dorsey and others had a zeal for their memory books, which held within them evidence of a historical past unsurpassed among other minority or ethnic groups in the Americas. Indeed, Tony Martin called a number of early African American collectors "unsung heroes," noting how they combined a preoccupation with "items of history as an inherent part of their activism." Dorsey and others "would counter the pseudo-scientific racism that was so prevalent during the nineteenth and early twentieth centuries, . . . would provide a body of information for posterity, . . . [and] would correct the record of American history, rescuing missing pages of history, and restoring, perhaps even initiating an African consciousness."[48] In his preface to *The Philadelphia Negro*, W.E.B. DuBois thanked Dorsey for the use of his scrapbook collection.[49]

DuBois, himself a great compiler of albums, was especially well known for a collection of photographs he sent to the 1900 Paris Exposition.[50] DuBois most certainly would have been known to all in the Henderson family through their joint associations with Atlanta University. Whether the maker of the Henderson album consciously was influenced by DuBois's choice of photographs for Paris to represent African Americans will never be known. But today the image of a young Henderson in a sailor suit (see Figure 12.3), adjacent to three photographs of his contemporaries at Atlanta University (the small child next to three young women) and the many other studio portraits—these are reminiscent of the albums of DuBois and, as noted earlier, his belief in the duality of consciousness, at once "an American, a Negro."[51]

DuBois's overall album project was aided by Thomas Calloway and representatives of the historically black colleges. Together they gathered portraits, snapshots, statistics, and other materials about Georgian African Americans, many of whom would also have been known to the Hendersons. DuBois wished to show African Americans as not different from whites with respect to religion, politics, language, and daily life but different only in their membership in another "vast historic race."[52] As Shawn Michelle Smith has argued, the Georgia portraits transformed his argument into visual form and urged consideration of the fact that "Americans and Negroes" were combined. The exhibit did "not lift *the Veil* that distorts images of African Americans" but rather made visible evidence that "cultural logics and privileged practices" reproduced racism.[53]

Henderson's and Johnson's memory books demonstrate youthful understanding of such logics and practices. Although there are significant and large differences between their collections of images and words and the earlier ground-breaking and still well-known African American compilations of print and visual culture, a strong argument can be made for similarities. Not only did all these traditions exist in a world where people of color usually lacked healthy images of themselves in published works, but all these individuals acted to correct this lack. Henderson's and Johnson's communal life of home and school and the actions of earlier scrapbook makers to document identities can be seen as real traces of how print and visual cultures were reshaped by people outside the dominant culture.

By removing, recreating, or making new images, Henderson and Johnson shaped their own identities. They collected, arranged, and rearranged cultural codes, placed and absented the self in the milieu of their times, and therefore showed how individuals of their generation pushed back prejudicial renderings—DuBois's "veil"—of African American life. All the while, they maintained strong ties to their communities of origin. These two memory books thus incorporate visible interpretations of the multiple communities and even expand

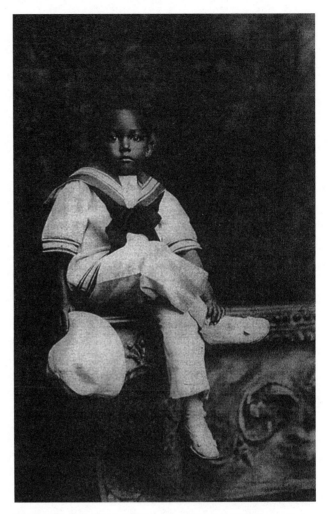

Figure 12.3.   *This studio print of Fletcher Henderson Jr. as a child is positioned opposite two photographs of his college classmates, thus vividly displaying the lack of chronology within the album even as it provides a detailed view of African American upper-middle-class life.* (Fletcher Henderson Collection, Amistad Research Center, New Orleans)

DuBois's thesis of duality by showing the print, visual, African American, Caucasian American, familial, and scholarly cultures in which their makers lived. Such rearrangements, such revisions, required what Marianne Hirsch has described as an agency to make and read images and, in so doing, a "political" intervention.[54]

Today the two memory books manifest not merely the records of a specific time and individual lives but also a constantly evolving collection of historical identity. The scholar bell hooks has written of the huge display of her grandmother's photographs, of their symbolic presence as part of the "ongoing loss marking the psychohistory of African Americans."[55] Using images, Henderson and Johnson made known the world in which they were included, hinted at the world they were remaking, and hid the world from which they were excluded. Their memory books tell distinctive stories that join others in providing clarity about the past.

[JAMES KELLEY]

13

〜〜〜

Maternal Records and Male
Modernist Identities

〜〜〜

The Family Albums of Ernest Hemingway and
Christopher Isherwood

INFLUENTIAL ACCOUNTS OF LITERARY modernism from the mid-1980s and early 1990s, such as those by Michael Levenson and Dennis Brown, have constructed all-male genealogies of authorship and literary production. Levenson's model of literary filiation moves from Joseph Conrad, T. E. Hulme, and Ford Madox Ford to Ezra Pound and T. S. Eliot.[1] Similarly, Brown offers an analysis of a male modernist foundational group marked by intense comradeship and rivalry; he understands these "men of 1914"—Pound, Eliot, Wyndham Lewis, and James Joyce—to be the literary heirs of the great nineteenth-century sages Carlyle, Ruskin, Dickens, and Morris.[2] In *Children of the Sun: A Narrative of "Decadence" in England after 1918*, an earlier and influential study of British "men of sensibility born between 1900 and 1910," Martin Green goes even further in this construction of all-male genealogies, noting: "There are comparatively few literary portraits of powerful mothers or powerful female presences. It was only the women who felt their mothers as powerful; for instance, Virginia Woolf, Vita Sackville-West, and Nancy Cunard." Of male authors, by contrast, he writes: "Their mothers were figures of affection and reassurance to nearly all of these people; however they may have undermined their children's confidence in their bolder gestures, they offered no significant challenge or inspiration. Beside the father, they counted for nothing."[3] Given this critical tendency to produce all-male accounts of literary and psychological influences, it is hardly surprising that when the scrapbooks, photograph albums, and other family records of male modernist writers are considered—all relics of the popular and material culture against which high

modernism often defined itself—the critical focus tends again to privilege male pred-
ecessors and male lines.

Thus, for example, the newspaper scrapbooks of Ezra Pound's paternal grandfather, Thaddeus Coleman Pound, are valued by critics for their use as source material for the *Cantos* as well as for their importance to the development and expression of Pound's social and political agendas.[4] In Pound's case, such approaches are
clearly authorized. In his *Draft of XXX Cantos*, published in 1930, Pound incorporates aspects of his grandfather's life, particularly in Canto XXI and the beginning
of Canto XXII, and throughout his later years he makes statements reaffirming the
importance to him of his father and grandfather.[5]

What nonetheless remain to be explored are approaches to male literary modernism that resist the general tendency to privilege paternal lineages and that reeval-
uate the importance of mothers' photograph albums and other maternal records to
male modernist writings and identities. Albums compiled by the mothers of two male
modernist authors—Ernest Hemingway and Christopher Isherwood—come under
examination here. These volumes of photographs and other media are considered
with respect to their creative formats as well as their constructive influence on the
works of the two adult male writers.

In his influential essay "The Cult of Unity and Cultivated Difference," Pierre
Bourdieu writes that photography serves the *"family function* . . . of reinforcing
the integration of the family group by reasserting the sense that it has both of itself
and its unity." The wedding photograph and the child photograph in particular,
Bourdieu continues, serve to capture and record "those climactic moments of social
life in which the group solemnly reaffirms its unity."[6] Bourdieu is one of several critics to have addressed these integrating functions and operating ideologies of family
photography. Susan Sontag makes similar, although less generously phrased, observations; she groups the family unit with the police, the military, and the press—all
"important institutions of control"—regarding their common use of photography
to "record, diagnose, inform."[7] Even more critical are the British feminist photographer Jo Spence and the other members of the Polysnappers group, who in writing about their 1981 exhibition assert that the Western nuclear family "is seen as a
universal state, outside of history, outside of power relations. . . . Visual representation privileges this dominant grouping of people, naturalizing, romanticizing and
idealizing family relationships above all others."[8]

The following examination of maternal records and male modernist identities
applies and extends this notion of photography's "family function" and its uses in
legitimizing and reinforcing nuclear and heterosexual family structures. This inquiry
confirms parts of Bourdieu's analysis—particularly his evaluation of the central role
played by mothers in the compilation and interpretation of family albums—even as
it challenges or revises other aspects of his argument.[9] The same maternal records
and practices that consolidate and transmit traditional family unity and identity can
be used, as the following sections will reveal, to redefine the notion of family itself.

Spaces are thereby opened up for unmarried, homosexual, or otherwise queer members who are excluded from—or, at the very least, marginalized within—conventional formulations of the family.

Ernest and Grace

Taking family photographs and the corollary tasks of assembling and assigning meaning to these photographs are often maternal duties, writes Bourdieu: "The sexual division of labour gives the wife the responsibility of maintaining relations with the members of the group who live a long way away, and first and foremost with her own family." Wives and mothers are therefore most frequently the ones who assemble photograph albums and who serve as curators of the information relating to the images preserved within these albums' covers. "The reading of old marriage photographs," Bourdieu explains, "often takes the form of a course in genealogical science, in which the mother, a specialist in the subject, teaches the child about the connections which bind him or her to each of the people shown."[10] The scrapbooks of Grace Hall-Hemingway, mother of the author Ernest Hemingway, illustrate and confirm this aspect of Bourdieu's analysis. Housed at the John F. Kennedy Library in Boston, these albums comprise five volumes chronicling Hemingway's development up to the age of eighteen and his entry into young adulthood.[11]

The first of these five volumes covers Hemingway's life from birth to nearly two years of age. Its opening pages present a photograph of Hemingway as an infant alongside a narrative account of his earliest moments. A hand-drawn banner containing the child's name stretches above this account, and just beneath the banner are two clipped newspaper announcements of Hemingway's birth, the first in German and the second in English, indirect records of the father's and mother's respective ethnic backgrounds. This and Hall-Hemingway's subsequent volumes of photographs, handwritten narrative passages, pasted-in letters, and newspaper clippings serve as more than records of heterosexual couples and the products of their couplings. These documents literally construct and reaffirm both the family's and the individual's history and identity—in Bourdieu's words, "the sense that it has both of itself and its unity."[12]

These documents are themselves fabrications that were created some time after the events they record. The opening pages of Hall-Hemingway's first volume, for instance, present the narrative account of the child's first day in the simple past, and the photograph accompanying this handwritten passage is of a five-month-old infant, as the caption reveals, not a newborn. The newspaper clippings, furthermore, were pasted in after the account had been written; the English-language announcement of the birth covers the tips of some of the taller handwritten characters. All the same, these retrospective fabrications have implications for the subject's future. Of particular interest here are the ways in which Hall-Hemingway uses the album format to record—and thereby shape—the identities of her two oldest children, Ernest and his sister Marcelline, who was one year older. As will be detailed in this section, patterns of identification strikingly similar to those presented in the mother's albums are taken up in Hemingway's writings as an adult.

The next two volumes of the mother's albums trace not only the physical but also the gendered development of her son. The second volume covers Hemingway's life from the age of roughly two to five-and-one-half years and contains a series of photographs depicting Marcelline and Ernest as twins. In one set of photographs, the two children are shown outdoors, on the trimmed lawn to one side of a house. Marcelline and Ernest are dressed identically and posed on opposite sides of a tree stump as if they were mirror images of one another. The children are the only subjects in the first photograph; their white dresses and bonnets stand out sharply against the dark hues and shadows of the background. A second photograph of the set includes, in addition to the paired children, an older girl centered behind them and a female doll in the foreground. This cluster of subjects calls attention to the importance of both biological and cultural forces in the creation of gender identity. On the page in the album opposite this pair of twinned photographs is pasted an envelope containing clippings of hair from both children, the "blond hair of Ernest Miller Hem." and the "dark curl of Marcelline Hemingway." Even as the emphasis on the contrasting hair colors and the lines drawn across the envelope in Hall-Hemingway's hand, separating one child's name from the other's, set the two children apart as distinct from one another, their hair clippings commingle in the envelope and thus gesture toward the same lack of distinction between the two children and their differing sexes that is recorded in the accompanying set of photographs.

The third of Hall-Hemingway's albums, covering the boy's life from the age of roughly five-and-one-half to nine-and-one-half years, contains images that contrast sharply with those preceding it. Here, for example, one finds photographs of the author as a young boy, dressed in hat, shirt, and pants and positioned in what looks like the untamed wild, particularly when compared to the clipped lawn and straight trees of the previous set of photographs. In these wild settings of tall grasses and twisted or fallen trunks and limbs—settings that anticipate the safaris and war zones of his adult works—the young Hemingway stands alone and holds a boy-sized rifle or a fishing rod in his hands, allowing it to project outward or downward from the hip (see Figure 13.1). Hall-Hemingway's handwritten comments on this second set of photographs—"Can cock my own gun" and "His father's own boy"—affirm the visual connections made in the photographs between the boy's developing independence and masculine gender identity.

The representational shift suggested in these contrasting images from the second and third volumes—a shift from pairing to individuality and from gender malleability to fixity—was a gradual one and took place over a couple of years, as recorded in the mother's albums. In an increasing number of photographs Ernest Hemingway's development as a young boy is signaled. The third, fourth, and fifth albums offer no parallels to the earlier twinned photographs and other markers of malleable and shared

Figure 13.1. *Ernest Hemingway as a young boy.* (Courtesy John F. Kennedy Library, scrapbook II, page 54; photograph EH 10178D)

gender identity. They are, however, rich in examples of the young Hemingway's masculinization and developing interests in war, hunting, and boxing. Examples of the latter include a drawing of soldiers on parade, a shot-up Winchester championship target attesting to Hemingway's early skill with a rifle, and a sketch of a boxer watching his knocked-down opponent attempt to get back to his feet.

By recording what was "important and unique" to their lives, Marilyn F. Motz writes in an essay on turn-of-the-century photograph albums, "women were able to construct identities for themselves—examine their pasts, place themselves in the setting of their families, friends, and environments, and even comment on the choices they made."[13] In compiling albums and scrapbooks such as these by Hall-Hemingway, mothers could similarly position their children in relation to their pasts, their families, their friends, and their environments. The photographs and accompanying text in these albums do more than simply record significant or representative moments in a child's progression toward adulthood; these materials also develop the narrative of progression itself and position the child within multiple settings and environments. In shifting the discussion of Hall-Hemingway's albums from one of simple representation and historical record to one of positioning and identity construction, it becomes possible to argue for a close and even perhaps a causal relationship between the early, ambiguously gendered depictions of Hemingway in these albums and the mature author's fascination with—and, at least equally, anxiety about—fluid sexual and gender identity.

My purpose in comparing Hemingway's baby books with his adult works is not to be purely diagnostic, as is Kenneth S. Lynn, one of the few biographers to discuss at any length these representations in Hall-Hemingway's scrapbooks of the young Ernest and Marcelline.[14] Lynn argues in his 1987 biography of the author that Hemingway's conflicted adult interest in androgyny reflects a deep-seated complex dating back to childhood: Hemingway found himself "caught between his mother's wish to conceal his masculinity and her eagerness to encourage it" and consequently grew up to be "anxious and insecure" about his gender identity. In short, Lynn argues that Hemingway's childhood experiences effectively came to determine his adult literary production, providing him with "a full set of old fixations in which to pack new images."[15] I too wish to suggest connections, but ones more tentative and less pathologizing, between Hall-Hemingway's scrapbooks and the recurring themes of twinning and fluid sexual identity in the author's mature writings.

As Lynn makes clear in various places in his biography, there are numerous occurrences of these themes in Hemingway's works.[16] In Hemingway's 1940 novel *For Whom the Bell Tolls*, for example, a woman observes that the central pair of lovers, Robert and Maria, "could be brother and sister by the look." Later in the novel Robert proposes dreamily that the two of them have their hair cut the same, at least for a while. Maria embraces this plan, saying the haircut would make her look more like him, and adds: "Then I never would want to change it." Lynn does not, however, go on to discuss the man's response in this and related instances of twinning in Hemingway's works. In *For Whom the Bell Tolls*, Robert quickly counters with a move to reassert rather than to erase the sexual difference between Maria and him. Her already roughly cropped hair, he says, "will grow all the time," and having her hair cut short like his "will only be to keep it neat at the start while it is growing long," down to her shoulders.[17]

This interest in male-female twinning and the possibility of reshaping or even exchanging sexual and gender identities between male and female partners becomes all the more apparent in Hemingway's posthumously published works, as Lynn has also briefly noted in his study.[18] In Hemingway's story "The Last Good Country," written in the 1950s but first published in 1972 in the posthumous collection *The Nick Adams Stories*, the young protagonist, Nick, breaks one or more game laws and consequently must flee his mother's house and enter the wilderness, an unsettled section of northern Michigan and "the last good country" of the story's title.[19] Nick's favorite and younger sister, Littless, insists that she be allowed to accompany him and succeeds in convincing him to let her do so only after meeting his objections that a girl and a boy traveling together would arouse suspicion. Nick returns to their camp in the wilderness one morning to find that Littless has cut her hair. He is initially resistant to her symbolic switch in gender, first asking, "What did you do, you monkey?" and then making his opposition clearer: "I don't want to trade you for a brother." But he soon admits, "I like it. . . . The hell with everything. I like it very much."[20] The siblings entwine their bodies, joke about marrying one another, and end up sleeping together amid blankets and a gun[21]—a cluster of images that recalls a related scene in a second posthumous work, *Islands in the Stream*. In that work, Thomas Hudson dreams that he—much like Nick—is in bed with his wife and his gun. He is the passive partner in this dream, and his wife—like Littless—initiates the game of collapsing or trading identities. She begins:

> "Should I be you or you be me?"
> "You have the first choice."
> "I'll be you."
> "I can't be you. But I can try."[22]

These fantasies of twinning and of gender transpositions are treated most famously in *The Garden of Eden*, published in 1986, a work Hemingway had begun in 1946, returned to irregularly during the 1950s, and abandoned by the end of 1958. In the posthumously edited and published version of *The Garden of Eden*, the married couple Catherine and David Bourne are first presented to the reader dressed in matching outfits, their skin tanned and their hair lightened by the sun: "Most people thought they were brother and sister until they said they were married." As in the case of Littless in "The Last Good Country," there is foreshadowing in Catherine's cryptic remark to David that she is "going to be changed," and Catherine returns from a brief trip with her hair "cropped as short as a boy's."[23] When the two go together to the hairdresser, it is again the woman who voices the desire to collapse or undo sexual difference, the man who seeks to retain it. Catherine instructs the hairdresser and presses to have her way:

> "Please make it the same as mine," Catherine said.
> "But shorter," David said.
> "No. Please just the same."[24]

After his hair has been cut, it is bleached to match hers even more perfectly. Here again, Catherine's insistence overcomes David's reluctance, and he soon admits to himself that he likes it.[25] The sense of solidarity between the two of them—"We're us against all the others"[26]—is both strengthened and challenged by these experimentations and clearly echoes the sentiment behind the pairings in the other Hemingway works mentioned earlier.

Critics generally have not commented on the pattern of insistence and resistance that thus emerges. In these works, the female characters are generally the ones who insist on the collapse or even erasure of sexual difference, perhaps because they hope to gain some aspect of masculine power in this process of twinning. The male characters, by contrast, generally seek at least for a time to resist this collapsing of sexual difference, again perhaps because they stand to lose power, status, or, at the very least, a stable point of reference against which their own masculinity is defined. As Susan Beegel has pointed out in response to my earlier discussion of this pattern, this same set of dynamics—insistence and resistance—structures not only female-male relations in Hemingway's fiction; in the short story "Fathers and Sons," sexual sameness is the point of departure.[27] In an episode in this story, Nick is forced to wear "a suit of his father's underwear that had gotten too small for his father." Nick objects from the start, feeling "sick," just as Harold feels at his mother's forced intimacy in "Soldier's Home," Hemingway's short story published in 1925, and resists by hiding the underwear and then claiming to have lost it.[28]

It is possible to extend the loosely Freudian argument developed by Lynn and to see Hemingway's mother resurfacing in these fictional authority figures, insisting that her son adopt the identity first of a little girl, then of a little boy. The transgressions and collapses of conventional sexual distinctions pervading Hemingway's literary works, however, might be read as more than merely the resurfacing of sexual roles "imposed" by the mother or poorly modeled by the father, to draw on the language and subtext in Lynn's biography;[29] Lynn writes, for instance, that the mother "tamper[ed]" with Hemingway's apparently preexisting masculine identity and "assert[ed] her authority over even the sexuality of her son."[30] The experimentations in Hemingway's adult works might be read more productively as acts of affiliation with the mother, as variations on and modifications of the roles that she developed for her son at various stages in his infancy and youth. This reading, moreover, might be redescribed so that it does not necessarily privilege some

innate masculinity (or even maleness) in the author as a little boy and instead rec-
ognizes the subject's gender and sexual identity as always shaped through parental
intervention. What I suggest is that through the pictures and text of Hall-Hemingway's albums, as well as through the lived experience that these albums both
record and memorialize, the mother provides the son-author with the language,
tools, and images for his later thinking, writing, and experimentation with sexual
identity. This argument provides a new perspective for reading "Soldier's Home."
This story is not discussed in any detail by Lynn but is rich in associations with
the previously mentioned works by Hemingway.[31] Although published much earlier in his career, this story makes explicit connections between sibling pairing and
a powerful maternal presence.

The photographs described without comment in the short opening paragraphs
of "Soldier's Home" invite comparison of the story with the mother's albums. The
two photographs are presented as follows:

> There is a picture which shows him among his fraternity brothers, all of them
> wearing exactly the same height and style collars. . . .
>   There is a picture which shows him on the Rhine with two German girls
> and another corporal. Krebs and the corporal look too big for their uniforms.[32]

Much like the images in the mother's second and third albums, these photographs
demonstrate the difference that a couple of years can make in a young man's development. Similarly, they contrast group identity and sexual uniformity with individual growth and sexual differentiation, a contrast parallel to that mentioned in the
earlier discussion of the photographs in Hall-Hemingway's albums.

As a number of critics have noted, "Soldier's Home" is the fictionalized account
of the conflict between Ernest and Grace Hall-Hemingway and depicts the son's
desire to escape from, if not kill, his powerful mother. The names of the people and
places have been changed—Hemingway's home of Oak Park, Illinois, for example,
becomes a "home town in Oklahoma" in the story[33]—but, as Ann Douglas observes
in *Terrible Honesty*, the narrative is closely modeled on the Hemingways' familial
struggles.[34] In this story the young male protagonist Harold Krebs returns from
Europe and World War I and comes to live at home with his parents and siblings.
"Now back home in the small Midwestern town of his origin," Douglas explains,
"Harold is fighting to keep alive whatever autonomy the war gave him; his mother
is fighting to extinguish it."[35]

What Douglas does not go on to note in her analysis of the story is that Harold's
response to his mother's veiled demands and interventions is to ally himself with his
sister in a way that collapses the customary boundaries between the two siblings and
thereby uncannily echoes the childhood twinned photographs in Hall-Hemingway's
early albums. Called his "best sister" in Hemingway's story, Helen is the only one
in the family with whom Harold feels any connections.[36] While their mother is in

another room preparing breakfast, Helen jokes with Harold about being romantically involved with him. "I can pitch better than lots of the boys. I tell them all you taught me," she begins:

> "I tell them all you're my beau. Aren't you my beau, Hare?"
> "You bet."
> "Couldn't your brother really be your beau just because he's your brother?"
> "I don't know."
> "Sure you know."[37]

Helen continues with this line of inquiry, and it is her playful insistence that leads Harold to agree noncommittally to the next few things she proposes:

> "Couldn't you be my beau, Hare, if I was old enough and if you wanted to?"
> "Sure. You're my girl now."
> "Am I really your girl?"
> "Sure."
> "Do you love me?"
> "Uh, huh."
> "Will you love me always?"
> "Sure."
> "Will you come over and watch me play indoor?"
> "Maybe."
> "Aw, Hare, you don't love me. If you loved me, you'd want to come over and watch me play indoor."[38]

On the simplest level of the narrative, Helen toys here with her brother, first getting him to answer affirmatively to a number of questions—"sure," "uh, huh," "sure"—and then attempting to extract from him a promise to watch her pitch in the coming game. Harold never makes that promise; he says only "maybe." But his closing thought in the story—almost an afterthought and, indeed, his final resolution to act "before he g[ets] away" from his mother by moving to Kansas City and finding a job—is to "go over to the schoolyard and watch Helen play indoor baseball."[39] Harold will thus play the role of spectator, a mostly passive role like that of Nick's in the game of gender transgressions in "The Last Good Country," of Thomas Hudson's in *Islands in the Stream* (1970), and of David Bourne's in *The Garden of Eden* (1986).[40] All these instances of merged or collapsed gender and sexual identities are structured around the woman's insistence and the man's resistance. In each case, the man concedes in the end.

"Soldier's Home" thus serves as one of the earliest instances of the author's enduring fascination with male-female twinning; Harold and Helen are twins by name, if not by age. Their bisyllabic names echo and oppose one another, as they are pronounced nearly identically before the forking of the liquid "r" or "l"—an opposition that marks the point of difference and individuation and signals a reliance on opposition itself for any sense of meaning. More important, "Soldier's Home" also reveals the connections in Hemingway's literary imagination between this sibling intimacy and maternal dominance. In the story Harold responds to the pressures and demands from his mother that he go on dates with the neighborhood girls (for the end purpose of marrying and settling down with one) by aligning himself with his sister. Sexual differentiation is countered by a move toward androgyny and hints that would lead to marriage by intimations of incest. This alliance between Harold and Helen, of course, is at once enabled and circumscribed by the present and powerful mother. On whatever level of conscious or unconscious thought, Hemingway appears to have drawn the images from his mother's albums and from the experiences these albums memorialize for his adult literary explorations and experimentations in sexual and gender identity.

Christopher and Kathleen

As suggested by Hemingway's works, the material of a mother's family albums can be adapted to serve new purposes that deviate from socially prescribed heterosexual identity formation, pairing, and child rearing. In his brief treatment of alternative uses of photography, however, Bourdieu writes only that "deviants"—a term by which he designates bachelors, childless families, and younger people, and in short, all those who share "the lowest level of integration" within the family—are seen to treat photography as an aesthetic activity rather than a social function.[41] Rather than adhere to the cult of unity, Bourdieu argues, the deviant photographer is one who seeks instead to cultivate difference. Christopher Isherwood, a gay writer and contemporary of Hemingway, was unmarried and without children—and thus a "deviant" in more senses than one—yet he uses the materials and metaphors of family albums in ways that are not limited to the purely aesthetic. He uses family photography and family albums for the purpose of reintegrating himself into the family that threatens to exclude him or, more precisely, for the purpose of re-visioning family ties so as to make possible a stronger sense of both belonging and identification.[42]

A scene in Isherwood's first published novel, *All the Conspirators* (1928), attests to the author's early interest in the integrating "family function" of the photograph album and other maternal records. In this scene the character Victor Page comes to dinner at another family's home as a step in his courtship of Joan Lindsay. As part of this courting process, the mother and other members of the Lindsay family share with Victor their family album: "After dinner, Victor was shown an album of snapshots taken of the family at all ages. Joan had been a serious podgy child. She pointed out particularly hideous pictures of herself in gym-costume or old-fashioned bathing-dresses. It was like a confession to him of the whole of their past lives." Victor's immediate response is to feel "jealous of all those days" and to wish "that he had been there."[43] But he has also been drawn further into their confidence; the photograph album is used in this scene, in short, to help bring the young man more fully into the family's sphere of identity and belonging. Isherwood's first novel as a whole, however, is critical of this assimilation to and containment within the traditional family structure. As Claude J. Summers perceptively writes in his book-length study of Isherwood's novels: "*All the Conspirators* devastatingly indicts the corrosive influence of the family and the inability of the young to escape the domination of the old."[44] It is not until his second novel, *The Memorial: Portrait of a Family*, that Isherwood explores alternative formulations of the family that allow both for continued identification with past and present members and for individual development and deviance.[45] A full discussion of the re-visioning of Isherwood's family histories in his early and later writings—particularly, *The Memorial* (1946) and *Kathleen and Frank* (1971)—is beyond the scope of this essay; the focus in this section will remain on the photograph albums compiled both by Isherwood's mother, Kathleen Bradshaw-Isherwood, and by Isherwood himself.[46]

Bradshaw-Isherwood's travel diary, housed in McFarlin Library at the University of Tulsa along with many of Christopher Isherwood's early diaries and albums, contains daily entries for the trip she took with her husband, Frank, from October 4 to November 4, 1909.[47] These entries are measured to fit within the confines of the bound volume; of the one hundred or so pages in the bound notebook, only the last seven are blank. The opening pages to the travel diary present a pasted-in panorama of Florence, Italy—their destination city—and the details of the first day of the trip with her husband from their home in England. Later entries in the volume are similarly illustrated by postcards and other memorabilia.

This first entry in her volume opens with an assertion of conjugal identity—"Frank and I"—and family unity and identity, in keeping with Bourdieu's thesis, remain a central concern of the diary. An only son at the time, the young Christopher did not accompany his parents on the trip, but he figures prominently at several points in the account. In the first two weeks of entries, Bradshaw-Isherwood records her concerns about the health of her son, who was slightly ill when she and Frank left on the trip, and she inserts midpoint in the volume a telegraph from their home estate of Marple Hall reassuring her that "Christopher [is] quite well." The closing sentence of the final entry begins, "Dear C. very bright + happy + skipping about in the hall to welcome us."

Bradshaw-Isherwood's travel diary does more than write Christopher into the family narrative even when he is absent. It also tells of the hopes and concerns she has for her son extending far beyond his recent illness. The November 2 entry of her travel diary, describing the Palazzo Durazzo, focuses on a set of busts of the Durazzo-Pallavione family in the building's entrance hall, but her selective use of description and detail suggests a meaning beyond the surface one. She writes: "In the center are a Mother + her son, the present occupiers." The mother appears as "a handsome young woman, + he a good looking boy of 7 or 8 years old—They are now, she over 80, + he a man of sixty with no son to succeed him + separated from his wife who the butler told us lives in Florence . . ." The repeated use of the addition sign in place of the conjunction "and" in the mother's prose descriptions suggests a desire to combine the female and male pairs of the "Mother + her son," "she" and "he," and "his wife" and "him" in ways that resist separation and distance. The detail in this passage, the focus on the two central busts and the omission of the others, and the ellipses with which the passage ends further suggest an unspoken statement about Bradshaw-Isherwood's own hopes and concerns for her son's future, hopes that her son would marry and go on to produce children of his own yet remain all the while close to her physically and emotionally.

Christopher Isherwood's boyhood album "Jottings from a Holiday Diary" of 1917–18 opens, much like his mother's travel diary, with a pasted-in postcard, a descriptive narrative passage, and a unifying "we," referring to his mother and others with whom he undertook the journey. As Isherwood explains in an endnote he added when expanding the album a year later, the first half of the completed "Jottings" was exhibited in his school's Holiday Competition in the summer of 1917 and earned him a prize. The exhibited section covers thirty-two pages; subsequent entries, an index, and notes added to the album in 1918 contribute another thirty-two pages to the final document. The "we" of this expanded account is clearly identified as "my Grandmother, my mother, a friend + I." The young Isherwood is perhaps even mimicking here his mother's use of the addition sign just as he borrows from the format of her earlier travel album.[48]

Indeed, the format of his travel album is nearly identical to that of his mother's. As in Bradshaw-Isherwood's travel album, the first entry of the young Isherwood's "Jottings" makes reference to a guidebook, and his travel account's subsequent entries—like hers—borrow from this or related guidebooks, although the sources are no longer mentioned. More important, his "Jottings" reflects his mother's interest in familial unity and continuity. Pasted-in postcards of one estate—particularly the postcard entitled "Haddon Hall, Dorothy Vernon's Door"—are accompanied by his handwritten tales of elopement and marriage. These tales of heterosexual unions are brought closer to home with the mention of a brass memorial plaque to Bernard Wells, "whose daughter married Henry Bradshaw of Wybersley + Marple Hall," one of Christopher Isherwood's ancestors on his father's side.

Bourdieu's opposition between the cult of unity and the cultivation of difference seems to be upheld when one moves from these earlier "Jottings from a Holiday Diary" to Isherwood's photograph album dated March 1934, a bound volume labeled with the German word *Fotos* and carefully composed so as to make use of all of its sixty-four pages. By 1934 Isherwood had made gestures of independence from his family; these included moving on his own to Berlin and remaining and working there until the rise of fascism, dropping his middle names William and Bradshaw,

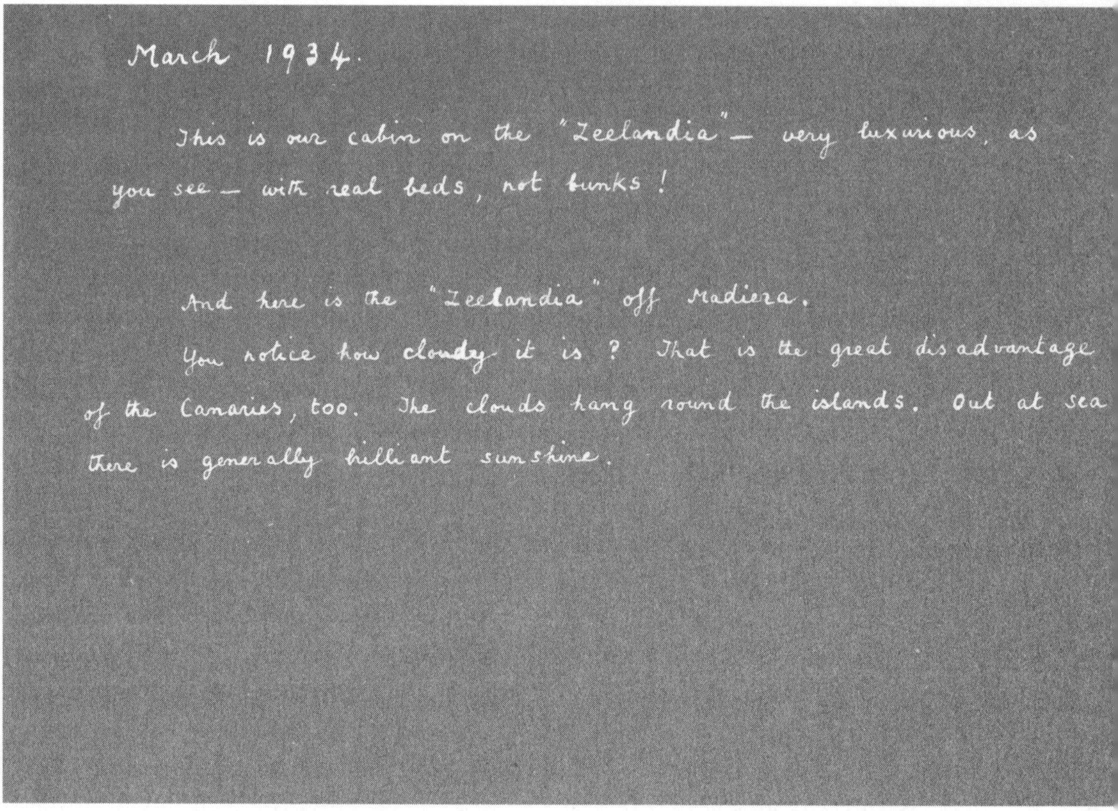

Figure 13.2. *The opening of Christopher Isherwood's 1934 album.* (Special Collections Department, McFarlin Library, University of Tulsa, box 10, folder 5)

and taking male lovers and introducing them *as* lovers to his mother and other family members. This later photograph album has a more aesthetic layout, as Bourdieu's brief analysis of the deviant photographer would lead us to expect.[49] The writing is in white ink against a black background, and the small photographs and their correspondingly brief captions are subordinated to large amounts of blank space (see Figure 13.2).[50]

Yet closer consideration reveals that through this album the son is not discarding but rather inverting traditional formulas of the heterosexual family and the records that sustain it, just as the album itself inverts the customary use of black text on white paper. Isherwood's 1934 album opens, as his mother's travel diary opened, with an affirmation of his romantic relationship. "This is our cabin on the 'Zeelandia,'" the white text reads: "And here is the 'Zeelandis' off Madeira." The text thus introduces the topic of a boat trip to the Canaries that Isherwood took with his German lover, Heinz, and recorded in the first half of the album. The two men

are depicted in the album's opening pages in separate but paired photographs: Isherwood is photographed close up, sitting on a bed in their shared cabin, whereas Heinz is shown from far off, standing on the deck of the ship, the water and a mountain range filling out the background. Captions to subsequent photographs offer additional assertions and affirmations of their relationship. One entry speaks of "our bedroom" in a represented hotel, another explains of a depicted lighthouse, "At one time, we thought of living there." Isherwood's albums, much like Hemingway's fictional family portraits, demonstrate an indebtedness to maternal records even as they seek to develop new models for living that draw from but do not wholly replicate conventional familial patterns.

THE PHOTOGRAPH ALBUM, as Motz writes, is "a private familial genre" and thus a traditionally acceptable outlet for female artistic creativity;[51] but to limit an analysis of the album and other maternal records to this narrow sphere of influence is to overlook the broader impact such documents may well have. The materials of the Hall-Hemingway and Bradshaw-Isherwood family albums seem frequently to aim for a larger, at least semiprivate audience, and the handwritten text that accompanies and explains the photographs and other illustrations is perhaps intended—and necessary—to inform viewers who have not participated in the scenes represented in the photographs as much as to refresh the memory of those who have.

Whether this material is measured to fit within the confines of a single bound volume, as in the case of Kathleen Bradshaw-Isherwood's travel diary, or worked into almost infinitely expandable formats, as in Grace Hall-Hemingway's multiple albums, the images and text are used in creative conjunctions and serve both personal and broader social purposes. In many ways, the compilation of scrapbooks and photograph albums stands as a metaphor for the construction of legitimizing lineages and enabling identities: closer critical attention to these unique and crumbling documents left by the mothers of significant male modernist writers will provide a broader understanding of their influence on the individual authors and the literary movement as a whole. Equally, and no less important, closer attention to such albums and novelists' figurative use of photograph collections will allow readers to test and revise influential critical analyses of familial records, such as those by Pierre Bourdieu. This line of inquiry reveals that "family" and "deviance," while contradictory, are not always mutually exclusive terms.

[ELIZABETH E. SIEGEL]

14

~~~~~~~

"Miss Domestic" and
"Miss Enterprise"

~~~~~~~

Or, How to Keep a Photograph Album

I N AN 1872 ISSUE OF THE BALTIMORE trade publication the *Photographer's Friend*, an impassioned writer named Nod Patterson, weary of looking at hackneyed family photographs again and again, addressed his photographer-readers thus:

> Reader, did you ever visit any house of respectability, without discovering the inevitable photographic album upon the centre table? Did you ever notice in what a peculiar manner the gentle sex turn the album leaves over, dropping here and there a comment on the picture of some acquaintance. It seems strange that every one that we are pleased to visit, should seem to consider we ought to feel a great interest in the pictures in the album, when in fact they are *anything* but interesting to parties not *interested*.[1]

To remedy this sorry state of affairs, in no little part caused (he argued) by shoddy workmanship on the part of studio photographers, Patterson urged his readers to fill up albums with higher-quality celebrity portraits and views. He sketched out two classes of album pictures, those of "Miss Domestic" and those of "Miss Enterprise." Miss Domestic, sad to say, forces on the visitor Uncle Adolphus in yellowed prints, Aunt Jane in an ungainly pose against a dark and cloudy background, and the likenesses of Rev. Smoothtalk (the minister), Mr. Calico (the dry-goods merchant), and more "family beauties." Patterson painted an unpleasant scene of the album and the album keeper's accompanying narration, which, in its exaggerated and exasperated tone, is worth quoting at some length:

> First, we visit Miss Domestic; this lady's album is always found on the centre table conspicuously in sight, and no matter how often you visit her, as soon as there is the least *lag* in the conversation, she gives you her album to admire the pictures. . . . The first picture we are gravely informed—"that's grand-pa, papa's father." Grand-pa is copied from an old Daguerreotype, poorly copied too. He is seated *a la statue* by a table, which dwarfs his appearance. "That picture is papa, when he was a young man," this is also a copy, and "papa" is seen standing by a tall column (not all shown) holding with a tight grasp a large straw hat in one hand, while the other is spread like an American eagle under full sail, over the front of his waist coat. "That picture opposite is *mama*, when she was a young lady; ("mama's" hair is combed smoothly down, way down over her forehead, while her waist looks too long to be continued, and her collar is considerably the most prominent feature in the picture).[2]

He continued for some duration in this vein, pointing to the many technical defects in the posing and execution of the pictures as well as the physiognomic defects of relatives and small-town figures who held no interest for the outside viewer. He ultimately lamented that there existed neither a decent photograph nor a celebrated person in this assemblage.

By contrast, Miss Enterprise has on display in her parlor an edifying collection of national notables and views, beginning with the U.S. Capitol and including both Grant and Lee (with autographs), European royalty, Victor Hugo, P. T. Barnum, Niagara Falls, and so on. Moreover, she does not limit her collection of faces to only those most admirable of characters but displays a variety of important figures representative of the period. A model of exemplary photography behavior, she sensibly keeps her album of family and friends tucked safely away in the sitting room. By this example, Patterson delivered a plea to his fellow photographers, arguing that the tiresome conventions and family eyesores that filled albums and were imposed on hapless viewers lowered photography in the eyes of consumers; photographers should instead encourage the collection of pictures such as those in Miss Enterprise's album. "Who would, after examining an album similar to that of Miss Domestic," he asked, "think of going to become a like subject?"[3]

This fear of industry contamination by inferior products and lowered prices was typical fare in the photography press. But what is most noteworthy about this short editorial is the presumption that intimate practices of assembling and displaying albums within the home could have such a direct effect on commerce and that commerce should in turn dictate how individuals—particularly women—kept their family albums. Moreover, by delineating two kinds of album pictures, Patterson really portrayed two kinds of album owners and album-keeping practices, contrasting not only the contents of the collection but also the sites of display and even the verbal tour of the images conducted for viewers. The seemingly private spaces of the home take on varying degrees of publicness here, as even the subtle differences between albums—the family album in the sitting room for relatives, the celebrity and view album in the parlor for visitors—recategorize what might be considered solely a personal collection and display. The photograph album, in this view, blurs the boundaries between private and public spheres, individual selection and the directions of industry, the images of family and the portraits of a nation and world.

Nod Patterson was not alone in dictating to the women of households across the United States the proper ways to maintain and display a family photograph album. By 1872 (when Patterson's article was published), the photograph album had been an established fixture in the home, with entrenched associated practices, for a little more than a decade.[4] Articles and advice on this new development—its symbolism and worth, its proper place and contents—spilled into the pages of the popular and photography press. As national figures such as Abraham Lincoln rubbed shoulders with family members on these cardboard pages and publishers likened the purchase of an album to patriotic support of the country's photographers, buying, keeping, and displaying albums took on implications beyond the individual family cell. At stake here was not only the expansion of the photography industry but also the definition and visual representation of family and home at a moment, in the midst of a civil war and incipient signs of modernity, when those institutions were changing. The conventions of filling, ordering, and exhibiting photograph albums—practices that continue to shape our own collections of family pictures today—were tied up in these definitions of family and were established and modified in the album's early years.[5]

This essay will explore the public expectations of family albums in the press and the realities of their compilation and exhibition in the nineteenth-century U.S. home. It will examine how the popular and photography press marketed photograph albums as an essential part of the family unit by playing on sentiments from nostalgia to patriotism and will look closely at what was at stake for those dispensing advice on how to collect and display album photographs within the home. The surviving albums, however, reveal that not all advice translated into convention, and the second part of this essay explores the practices of ordering photographs in albums and ways in which album keepers, especially women, personalized albums standardized by industry. Here, albums will be treated as elements of feminine visual culture, their assemblers participating in a kind of domestic craft production. Such confusion between public prescriptions and private practices shaped the standards of the family photograph album, which in turn helped shape definitions of family itself.

A Fixture of the Parlor

When carte-de-visite photographs were introduced in the United States in the late 1850s, they provoked as manic a craze as they had a few years earlier in Europe. These full-length studio portraits, 4 by 2 1/2 inches in size, differed from the earlier daguerreotypes and portrait miniatures most notably in that they were reproducible and exchangeable in large numbers and required a means of organization and display.[6] For the first time ever, images of national notables as well as family members were available, affordable, and plentiful. As early as 1861, photography journals urged their readership, which consisted of photographers as well as some consumers, to participate in the new and worthwhile trend of collecting their multiplying images in albums produced especially for this purpose. The family album, born of clever marketing, rapidly joined the family Bible on the center table, becoming an indispensable fixture of the household parlor.

Before the snapshot (the Kodak was introduced in 1888), albums were composed of slots designed to fit certain standardized print sizes, allowing photographers to sell more pictures—arguably the primary function of the album. Albums held anywhere from a dozen to five hundred cartes, and the range of prices attests to the range of purchasers: by the early 1870s photograph albums cost from fifty cents (for a small pocket album) to fifty dollars (for an elaborate, extrafine Turkey morocco, multiple-card album).[7] Covered in velvet or leather, embossed with gold lettering, and hinged with ornate clasps, early albums connoted preciousness and importance. Yet carte collecting and album making were activities for the middle class. By the 1860s a card photograph could be purchased for as little as ten cents, but maintaining an album was more expensive: the cost of the album plus sufficient cartes to exchange with friends and family could, in extravagant cases, exceed seventy dollars.

Albums were seen as the perfect genteel accompaniment to the lady's table, provoking conversation or providing edification about the great figures of the day. (And, perhaps more important, they did not place undue stress on the visitor to invent some witticism on the spot, as the earlier keepsake album or commonplace book, according to some quoted in *Godey's Lady's Book*, apparently did.)[8] They were marketed as gifts for the holidays and played St. Valentine for young lovers in courtship rituals.[9] They were viewed as the current vogue (several fashion plates in women's journals portray women holding small albums), the latest development in the technology of photography that promised continually renewing gifts.

Immediately the invention was also framed as a lasting development, one integral to the fabric of the family and of the nation. The *American Journal of Photography* called the display of photograph albums "a sign and proof of the best feature in our civilization," claiming: "It tells of the universality and strength of the domestic affections."[10] Even acknowledging the cozy relationship among photographers, supply houses, and the photography press, it is still striking to note this early enthusiasm and faith in the card album's importance to family—and to Western civilization as a whole. Women's magazines such as *Godey's* echoed the populist claims made for albums, declaring: "And thus *photograph albums* have become not only a luxury for the rich, but a necessity for the people. The American family would be poor indeed who could not afford a photograph album."[11] For the first time, a collection of family likenesses was available to all but the least financially fortunate; the transformation from luxury to necessity catapulted the album from a craze to a symbol of both family unity and middle-class status. The family and often guests assembled in the central parlor, and it was here that the album was displayed and family history shown to relatives and friends. Next to the album usually stood the family Bible, and together the two transformed any house into a home. A pioneer-turned-memoirist recalled that in 1864 his family called their new dirt-floored, log-cabin home when the Bible and album took their rightful place on the center table.[12] This symbol of family could be carried across the country (or ocean), paradoxically allowing families to divide, migrate, and settle elsewhere while at the same time bringing them closer together. The family photograph album became more than a passing fad: it became an object and a set of practices that practically defined the family as such.

Marketing Memories

It is important to learn how family albums were marketed and, once acquired, how purchasers were instructed to use them. With albums produced and sold by stationers, photographers, and photography distribution houses and constantly updated and improved—between 1861 and 1873 twenty patents were taken out for albums and related devices[13]—sellers needed to market individual albums and, simultaneously, the idea of the album itself. The pitches in photography journals (largely to operators) and popular magazines (largely to consumers) played mostly on the family heartstrings. They varied in angle but all had the same message: purchasing a photograph album will make a family even more of a family.

One tactic was to play on sentiments of nostalgia and loss, absence through distance or death; photograph collections, in the sentimental paeans that dot the magazine pages of the era, seem almost literally to replace the departed. "Scarcely any lodging now so poor but in it may be found the picture of some cherished one," John Cussans wrote in *Humphrey's Journal.* "The lessening influence of time may in a great measure efface from our mental vision the form and features of those who are absent, though their memory may still be warm in our hearts, but with these faithful remembrances before us—shadows less fleeting than the realities—the absent ones seem to return once more to our embrace, and remain with us just as they appeared in life."[14] If memory failed to reproduce the dead or distant, photographs succeeded beyond expectations in bringing them back to life or hearth. Other writings on the topic expressed the value of the well-filled album to the emigrant or wanderer, locating loss not only in death but also in the uprooting that accompanied modernity. "Should a time come," one essay in *Anthony's* expounded, "when we have to change our place of abode, or, sadder still, when, as we advance in years, our friends depart from us one by one, then we often love, if somewhat regretfully, to turn to the familiar faces, and, pondering over their features, we try to console ourselves for the times that have gone."[15] The album seemed to provide a kind of rootedness both spatial and temporal, and the very act of reviewing its contents returned a person to an earlier moment. By 1876, the date of this article, the photograph album was already seen to encompass the past as well as—or more than—the present.

Another string to pull was that of national sentiment or patriotism, especially in the trying times of nation rebuilding in the wake of the Civil War. In 1866, in an attempt to invigorate a stagnating photography industry, photographers in the United States introduced the larger cabinet-card photograph (5 1/2 by 4 inches), along with albums specifically designed to house the new size. Carte-de-visite sales were flagging—"All the albums are full of them, and everybody has exchanged with everybody," complained editors at the *Philadelphia Photographer*.[16] The cabinet card represented a refreshing change with more artistic potential because of its larger size, and empty albums in the new format guaranteed photography sales. Some of the first albums produced exclusively for the cabinet card were by William Flint of Philadelphia. One of Flint's earliest albums, copyrighted in 1866 (an example of which is now filled mostly with actors and singers, in the collection of the Eastman House), opened with a short preface addressed directly to the owner. In it Flint played on the purchaser's patriotism, arguing that by buying the album, and thus by implication the photographs to fill it, the reader was supporting U.S. photographers: "The artists of this country have for years been unappreciated," he wrote, "and their skill being second to none in the world, they need encouragement, and by giving them the support they justly merit in this small specimen, there is no doubt, that ere long America will far surpass the old world."[17] Once at home in the parlor, the album served as a reminder of a family's duty to the photography artists and industry of the country. Again, as in Nod Patterson's admonition to photographers and album keepers, there existed the assumption that something as intimate and personal as having one's family photographed and displayed in the parlor would support not only an entire industry but also an entire nation. Flint also played on the very definition of family, ending his preface with this conclusion: "The size is admirable, and the receptacle here offered is that which no family could be complete without." The potential purchaser, thumbing through the album at the counter of Appleton's or Anthony's, was confronted with the completeness (or lack thereof) of his or her family. The U.S. family's integrity was seen, at least in the eyes of those peddling albums, to be predicated on the presence of a family album; even more than that, however, it was based on a new, bigger, and better album.

Having made the purchase, the owner of an album was entreated to fill it up. Although maintainers of albums were usually women or adolescents, occasionally the industry would appeal to a father in his role as head of the family.[18] An 1865 article in *Humphrey's Journal* noted that in the family in which a child has died there is an "eternal infant." But, it went on, with photography one could have an eternal infant "without the intrusion of death." The article urged men to have their families photographed often to chart the faces and figures of childhood: "By having his family photographed once a year, Paterfamilias may, for a trifle, preserve all the looks they ever wore—Jack's progress from the juvenile pinafore to the shooting coat and the turned-down collar of manhood—Miss Mary's growth through all its charming stages."[19] The article charts the potential future of a family album as it should look, predicting children's maturation into bourgeois adults of proper appearance and status (Miss Mary enslaves the heart of a stockbroker and now graces his home). The card picture's distinct advantage over the daguerreotype lay in its multiplicity and affordability; the ability to obtain annual photographs and arrange them in a narrative progression marked a striking break from the past and went hand in hand with this new mode of picturing the family.

Once the album was filled with pictures of family members, dear friends, and the eminent figures of the day, it was a collection to be preserved and protected. In a display of class distinction generally not associated with the photograph's democratic properties, an editorial titled "Keep Your Albums Locked" exhorted owners of albums to save their contents from the grubby hands of domestic servants and the nimble fingers of carte thieves.[20] The photograph album, in this case, represented more than a collection of prized portraits; it was also a display piece to be handled gently. The article provides a glimpse of the care that might have been taken in assembling such an album:

> You yourself have been very careful with that album, for it contains selections, from previous books, of your best friends, probably, and your best photographs. You leave it on the table, as it is a handsome book, and a present from a friend, but you never let the children have it without you are by to see it is properly taken care of. And yet, as we have said, with all your precautions the leaves become soiled, and the portraits thumbed and marked.[21]

This album, unlike the singular family collection many households possessed, has been selected and assembled from the prize pictures of previous albums; this article at once identifies the album as something precious and suggests a different kind of consumption and display that would entail the purchase of more photographs and more albums. The editorial imagined the scene that might take place in the album owner's absence, as the house servants page through the portraits, violating the sanctity of the family unit inside. In a cheaper imitation of the oral retelling of family history that accompanied the family album, the domestics point to the pictures and tell their

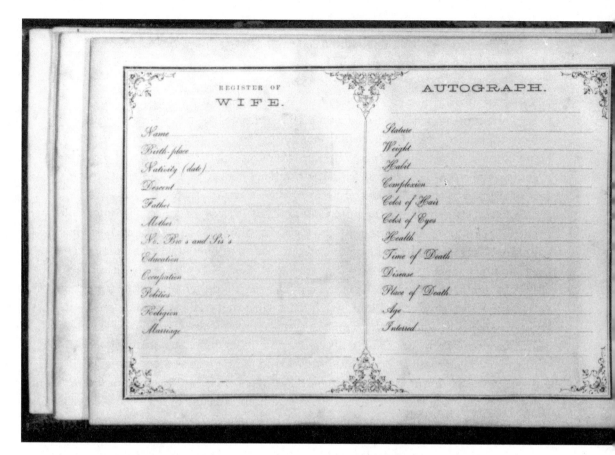

Figure 14.1. *"The Photograph Family Record" (1865), published by A. H. Platt.* (Courtesy George Eastman House)

own version of the story: "'This is missis, in that new yellow gown of hers; and this is missis again when she was a young 'un.—This is a picture of that gent, what comes here very often, wearing a red tie, and a short pipe; you know, him as gave me a half-a-crown one Sunday, that I bought a parasol with.—Oh! ain't I grand? Here's master in his long ulster, smoking a cigar.'"[22] The idea of the servants acting out the family history while pulling out and reinserting photographs seems intended to disturb the reader, who was positioned as the album's owner and family matriarch or patriarch; the narrative of the album seems as sacred as the photographs within.

"The Photograph Family Record"

The most striking prescription on how to fill a photograph album I have encountered is found not in the press but inside the pages of an album itself. Published by a Dr. A. H. Platt in 1864 and revised in 1865, this genealogical album came with

slots for cartes de visite, ample room for physical and personal data, and explicit instructions for use (see Figure 14.1).[23] Its full title, as written on the opening page, reveals the scope of Platt's project:

The Photograph Family Record,
OF
HUSBAND, WIFE, AND CHILDREN;
ADAPTED TO
RECORDING IN A PLAIN, BRIEF AND INTELLIGENT MANNER,

The Name, Birth-place, Date of Nativity, Descent, Names of Parents, Number of Brothers and Sisters, Education, Occupation, Politics, Religion, Marriage, Stature, Weight, Habit, Complexion, Color of Eyes and Hair, Health, Time and Place of Death, Disease, Age and Place of Interment of Each Member of Any Family,

With Album Leaves for the Insertion of Photographs of the Same.

The album has separate pages for the father, mother, and up to eleven children. On the right side of each page spread is room for two cartes, presumably to record loved ones' appearances at different stages in life; on the left is the designation of the family member ("Register of Wife," "Register of Second Child," etc.), space for his or her authenticating autograph, and lines for the various characteristics (cited on the title page) to be filled in.[24]

In the wake of the Civil War (as we learn from the extended preface to the album), Dr. Platt worried that the widows and orphans of those who gave their lives in the war would be unable to prove their relationship to the deceased and would lose the lands and pensions due them by the government. He viewed this photograph album as part family history, part legal document, and argued that "a family record, such as this is intended to be, would set the matter forever at rest." To accomplish this goal, the album had to function as a certificate of authenticity, with the text and images corroborating one another. A concern with proof and legitimacy pervades the album's text, not only in the exquisite specificity of the physical details but also in Platt's instructions to the album keeper. The family head was urged to date the photographs and provide the age of the person at the time the picture was taken, and on the matter of the family member's signature Platt was equally cautious: "When, by reason of death or absence the autograph of an individual cannot be personally affixed to the register," he advised, "it may be obtained from a letter or other document, and neatly pasted on the leaf, in the place assigned to it." The authenticity of the signature mattered more than the means by which it was obtained or its actual inscription in the album. Furthermore, two marriage certificates were to be included (although not found in the extant albums), one for the magistrate uniting the parties and the other for the married couple to preserve. The album takes on the function of legal witness as much as family remembrance, its autographs and photographs securing present property and past lineage.

Besides playing on the fear of losing land and patrimony, this album also invokes loss and absence, calling to mind the sentimental memories of deceased friends and family. The foreword opens with these lines to grab the reader: "Few things in life are so dearly and universally cherished, as the fond recollection of departed friends. Gifts and keepsakes, of comparatively trivial value while we enjoy the society of the donors, are treasured like jewels, when death or distance deprives us of their company." The photographs placed carefully in the slotted pages would recall the features of dear ones, returning them to life for the viewer. (Or, at least, that would be one of the functions of an album in general. This album is particularized to the family—the "departed friends" Platt cited would have to reside elsewhere.) At the end of the book, blank pages are supplied for recording memories, with two different purposes suggested. They could, Platt wrote in an undisguised appeal to maternal emotion, serve the memory of a mother who had lost a child in infancy and wanted to record the events of the baby's brief life. Or the pages might hold a record of military service, thus linking a family history (and, in many cases, a family death) with a national event. The overall sentiment here is sentimentality: again and again, the album's owner is reminded of loss, and the album—even as it perpetuates that loss—is set forth as its antidote.

Perhaps of even greater importance than the album's legal potential or memorial function was its ability to reconstruct families' genealogies, to serve at once as a monument to the past and a legacy for the future. Platt sensed a deficiency throughout the families of the country, one in which heritages and histories stood to perish entirely; with this book he intended to provide a useful system for the many families who were desirous of records of their past. What individual would not rejoice, he argued, to obtain an accurate genealogical history of his father's family and of his father before him? The problem was that, up to now (read: before the publication of this album), there had never been a proper vehicle for its recording:

> There is now no work especially adapted to recording either the leading physical peculiarities of the individual, or the simplest events in the history of the family; and with the single exception of occasionally a meagre memorandum in a family bible, there is nothing that can claim to be a substitute for it, and rarely do we find a family that possesses any correct information as to its own private history or genealogical descent. . . [and] we can account for the fact in no other way than that there has been no convenient means for collecting and preserving such information.

There is little of the traditional genealogy here: no heraldry, no mention of titled origin or Old World connection, no *Mayflower* ancestor. What Platt was interested in—and what he believed everyday Americans to be interested in as well—was a limited record of a few generations back (more, if possible) that supplied some details about what these people were like. In this kind of genealogy, physical peculiarities take center stage; at a moment when outward appearance was linked so closely with inner character, it was important to learn not only the deeds and social standing of one's ancestors (a textual or oral history) but also the way they looked. The photograph was uniquely capable of providing this information and was the most appropriate vehicle—in its affordability and availability—to furnish a large number of families with the kind of genealogy all families, not just the most prestigious, possessed. "The Photograph Family Record" represents a break with previous notions of lineage and descent, allowing even the most humble of households to obtain and maintain a past.

Having established the preservation of personal histories as a desirable thing, having played on the sentimental memories of deceased friends and family and the very real fear of losing lands and patrimony, Dr. Platt suggested a few reasons why the reader should purchase more than one of these albums. First, genealogies of other branches of the family could be obtained by sending additional copies of the album to relatives all over the world, to be filled up and returned. (Presumably, every family would do this, sparking a proliferation of albums, some circulating, some remaining at home.) Furthermore, not only the head of each family but each child therein could have his or her own record of the whole family, which could be handed down to future generations. Information that would otherwise be forever lost could now be preserved, and, Platt maintained, "the general collection of such knowledge, by a whole nation, like the American people, will aid materially in the important study of Hereditary Descent." This album, then, had scientific as well as social merit. Finally, "The Photograph Family Record" was available in different styles "to suit the varied tastes of the multitude." Platt closed his passionate treatise on the recording of genealogy with his own personal plug for a business-minded person to sell the album exclusively by subscription throughout every county of the United States. The modern reader senses his anxiety about a disappearing past but also cannot help noting the underlying commercial concerns.

Once purchased (for whatever of these reasons), the album dictated its own assembly. The owner was urged to date the photographs (either on the back of the picture or below it if placed permanently in the book), sign in the appropriate space for autographs, and fill in the blank pages with certain prescribed remembrances. On the subject of second or third marriages, Platt was understanding but adamant, stating that the album recognized only one husband and one wife and their offspring per book; each additional marriage would require a separate family record. The wife was even told exactly how to write her name so that her maiden name would always be clear to future readers searching for genealogical facts. Although the album has less to say about the use and display of the accompanying photographs, on the written text it states its rules clearly: "The writing should be legible and the wording specific."

At stake in these elaborate instructions was more than producing an authentic legal document, more even than recalling the features of departed loved ones. Platt envisioned the collection of this material as a national project—an infinite number of private genealogies adding up to a nation's history, a permanent record of a country's past. In its circulation and repetition through children and extended family, the album expanded its scope beyond the cell of the household; each individual family, in its purchase and filling up of the record, acted as a link in this chain. Furthermore, these genealogies were maintained through a means of archiving only now accessible to more than just the higher levels of society. "It is obvious, therefore," Platt wrote, "that before an accurate lineal record can become general among us, some appropriate work, especially adapted to the purpose, must be placed within the reach of all classes." The only way to achieve this visually was through photography. The carte de visite, in particular, was well suited for this purpose as it was comparatively inexpensive, reproducible (usually sold by the dozen), and easily inserted in books alongside text. There seemed to be a strong sense, even this early in the game, that personal memories would from this point on be constructed through photographs and, furthermore, that individual histories would intersect more with national ones, which were also beginning to take shape in photographs. The form of this genealogical album marks a new kind of record keeping and a new kind of knowledge, one in which images and text justify each other and one that would influence the shape of family histories in years to come.

Given the specificity of the album's instructions and the imminent danger of losing the past, it is all the more surprising that the family who owned this album chose to disregard Platt's directions entirely.[25] Not one of the pages is filled in with accurate measurements of height and weight, details of complexion and build, or facts of education and political leanings. The page for the wife's record, for example, has been claimed by cartes representing specimens of both genders, and that of the second child has suffered a similar fate, showing a bearded young man and a woman with careful curls on her forehead. It seems as if the family that owned this album simply found it a convenient and readily available home for their photographs and probably placed them in the book as they were acquired. The careful urgings of the album's producer fell on deaf ears.

Personalizing the Mass-Produced Album

It is unclear to what extent some album owners resisted the conventions imposed by the commercial apparatus of photography. The prescriptions of the press and of album manufacturers to photographers (who in turn passed ideas on to their sitters) and directly to consumers constituted only one aspect of the way conventions were shaped in a commercial market. Mass-produced backgrounds, photographer's chairs, and props such as balustrades, curtains, and even falsely hanging swings littered photographs across the country, lending a sameness to pictures and leveling status and individuality in a way that did not escape notice. Unimaginative or less well-equipped photographers might even shoot members of entire families posed in the same stiff position, next to the same chair or column. Handbooks and manuals offered suggestions to patrons on what colors to wear, how to pose, and what time of day to visit the photographer. The sizes of the cartes de visite and later cabinet card were standardized and albums produced for them expressly to accommodate their size; in the eyes of the photography industry, albums were an equation in which empty slots added up to increased picture sales. Most photographs and most albums looked pretty much the same.

Within the album, photographs were often arranged according to certain prescribed patterns of placement, usually beginning with the family's patriarch and matriarch and continuing through the rest of the relatives, according them the status in the album that they held within the family circle. One commentator in a photography journal remarked on this pattern: "The contents of albums (inseparable adjuncts to the ornaments . . . of all parlors and drawing-rooms) bear a most distressing similarity. First come the old folks, then the immediate members of the family, afterwards a collection of friends and acquaintances, and finally, if these are not sufficient to fill up the pages, there will be likenesses of theatrical or other public characters."[26] This formula is a combination of family hierarchy and random collection practices; the album is seen to be filled as much by staging a family tree as it is by acquisitive desire.

This was not always the case, however. Although Nod Patterson advocated keeping two kinds of album pictures, family and celebrities, and A. H. Platt implored his readers to maintain a singular family history, there were almost as many practices of ordering photographs as there were album keepers.[27] Some albums separate relatives from the relatively famous, but others allow them to mingle within the book's cardboard pages. Beginning with Queen Victoria and Prince Albert, some albums go on to track European royalty and actresses; some collections contain exclusively Civil War generals. In other cases, Abraham Lincoln or Tom Thumb gazes out from a carte on the same page as elderly aunts and squirming babies (see Figure 14.2). A young woman might keep her own personal collection of photographs of her beaux and school chums in an album whose contents would mirror those of her close friends. Albums do sometimes begin with the patriarch and matriarch and then fan out from the immediate to the extended family, but they also sometimes have seemingly no apparent order or hierarchy. Some album keepers probably held on to a sufficient number of cartes before entering them in the book or later replaced them in the proper sequence, while others most likely simply slid them into slots in the order in which they were obtained. The family to whom Platt's "Photograph Family Record" belonged may have been acting like many others when they just went ahead and filled up their photograph album as they pleased.

Against the exhortations of the press and the mass production of photography and albums, maintainers of albums within the domestic parlor could individualize their families' collections through skills learned in the home. Women, who were most often the purchasers and keepers of albums, occasionally drew around, cut and pasted, or otherwise manipulated the images within. (This can be seen most extravagantly in the albums of British upper-class women, in which photographs painstakingly cut out take their place in fantastic watercolor scenery; in these, portraits become the faces atop frog bodies on lily pads or slats in a delicate ladies' fan, or find themselves in conversation in dreamlike domestic interiors. U.S. women's photograph albums tend toward comparative drabness.) Such behavior may be read as an attempt to rally against the conformity imposed on family albums by the necessities of mass production; a different kind of production could take place in the home.

In the middle of the sameness of repeated poses and props, one album keeper visually inserted herself into the album. In a carte-de-visite album from the Baltimore area, around the early to mid-1860s, a series of photographs that look almost identical is punctuated by one that looks very different. This collage seems to be a small memorial to a child who has died young, and it was probably constructed by his mother. A hand-tinted photograph of a boy of about eight, head resting on his hand, has been cut out and stitched to a light blue valentine with a lace-mesh interior. A colored flower surrounds his torso, and scattered leaves frame his head. At the top of the image, above the boy's head, is a golden cutout circle, a halo that

Figure 14.2. *Carte-de-visite album, early 1860s.* (Courtesy George Eastman House)

marks his place in a better world. Although postmortem photographs, especially of children, were not uncommon, this image seems special: its difference among the photographs seems intended to call out to the viewer and revive the memory of a lost child in a way that surpasses these same functions in an untouched postmortem image. Carefully cut out and lovingly assembled, this memorial collage is an artistic creation inspired by mourning and remembrance. The family album has been transformed from a common receptacle for photographs to a place where fantasy and invention can play, albeit within a limited range; the album's arranger has become its artist-creator.

As many of the essays in this volume attest, scrapbooks and albums in their myriad forms served as sites of creative self-expression for their producers. Like other kinds of compilations, such as autograph and postcard collections, commonplace books and "women's albums" filled with verses and drawings, photography albums can also be seen as part of feminine visual culture. In the second half of the nineteenth century, this gendered image production was changing from a domestic to a consumer orientation; in albums, for example, watercolors and invented or transcribed lines of poetry gave way to photographs and fashion plates from a new feminine press. Women's journals such as *Godey's Lady's Book* extolled the virtues of the home and family and the woman's central place within it. Women were also becoming targeted as consumers through pages such as these, and albums and mass-produced cartes were among the items they were entreated to purchase.

In her article "Secluded Vision: Images of Feminine Experience in Nineteenth-Century Europe," Anne Higonnet has suggested that women's albums were a means of female self-expression, representing not women's lives but women's self-definition as seen through specific gender conventions. The images drawn and painted in albums, often by serious amateurs, portrayed a variety of female social experiences, from visual travelogues and landscapes to scenes of appropriate domestic occupations, often among groups of friends or family. As painters of pictures or assemblers of ready-made elements, women compiled a whole that was greater than the sum of its parts: "Women presented in their albums and amateur paintings their version of what bourgeois femininity should be. Album imagery is highly selective and coherent. Each individual picture works toward the meaning of the album as whole. Each album adds its part to an overarching pictorial structure." The collective image that emerges from the singular ones (which, Higonnet argues, cannot properly be read separately) reveals women's gendered roles—daughter, sister, wife, mother—in a distinctly feminine, if relatively public, world. Through albums, women were able to project selected aspects of their gender identity and hide others, as much consciously playing a role as being reflected by the images they created. "Women were performing in their images; the images themselves were their performance."[28]

If Higonnet's idea of the author or maker of albums and album images is extended to the selective consumption and ordering of photographs, then family photograph albums can also be seen as sites of usually female expression. Even acknowledging the differences between the serious amateur and the mere collector of images and between painting and ready-made photographs, we can still approach photograph albums as a limited case of Higonnet's argument. Like other women's albums, photograph collections reveal only the most social of domestic spaces, as the parlor is repeated over and over again in the photographer's studio. Each image acts as an individual piece within the assembled puzzle of the whole, be it the family or a representation of one's social circle; if there is a performance here, it is that of a collective. Expression—in its limited capacity given the formulaic dictates of the carte album, with framing, page decorations, and position already established—takes the form of consumption and selection, assemblage and collage. The joint creation of the final product that we know as a family album can be seen as taking place at once in the manufacturer's factory, the photographer's studio, and the album keeper's home.

Somewhere in between the advice of the press and album manufacturers and the collecting and display practices of consumers lay the idea, if not the reality, of the nineteenth-century photograph album. Album producers, suppliers, and even the popular press projected ideals of family predicated on the presence of a family album. Behind every set of prescriptions on how to keep a personal album, every intervention into the private parlor, was a larger, more public issue, from supporting an industry to recording a nation's past. Albums blurred boundaries of public and private spheres, homogenization and individuation, when commercially mass-produced but uniquely arranged albums—all alike but singular to each family—took a central place in the U.S. household.

Just as family albums reflected the conventions of self-presentation and family order, they also shaped, through the repetition and reenactment of these conventions, an understanding of family. The album defined who was included or excluded, preserved family histories, and marked one's position within a social circle of family or friends. Nod Patterson chose Miss Enterprise as his ideal, for women like her who kept albums encouraged the improvement and expansion of the photography industry. But it was Miss Domestic whose album withstood the test of time; collections like hers, pictures of purely personal value, would become the family-album norm. The world of enterprise shaped the rise and proliferation of photograph albums, but their meaning was produced within the realm of the domestic.

15

〰〰〰

Horizons

〰〰〰

*The Scrapbooks of a Small-Town,
Depression-Era Preteen*

LUCIE THRELKELD JENKINS was born in 1927 just thirty-five miles south of Louisville in Elizabethtown, a small Kentucky town centered in the midst of old crossroads, historic landmarks, and natural beauty. To the northwest is the Ohio River. South of Elizabethtown's cedar-covered hills is Mammoth Cave, the world's longest cave system, which became a national park in a property transfer that Lucie's grandfather helped broker. Prehistoric Indian artifacts are plentiful in fertile farm fields, and familiar are the wilderness tales handed down through generations of families who settled the Kentucky frontier in the late eighteenth century, as Lucie's family did. Abraham Lincoln was born in a cabin in Hodgenville, twelve miles southeast of Elizabethtown, where his father, Thomas Lincoln, had earlier built a double log house on a farm that came to be owned by Lucie's father. Fine Federal architecture attests to the early prosperity of Elizabethtown, as well as nearby Bardstown, where Stephen Foster penned "My Old Kentucky Home." John James Audubon, before pursuing his great work as an ornithologist and illustrator, was a merchant in Elizabethtown. The Louisville and Nashville (L&N) Railroad ran through the town. The Dixie Highway and the Western Kentucky, Bluegrass, and Cumberland Parkways all go through or around "E'town," as it is known regionally. The nation's gold is stored just north of town, in Fort Knox, reinforcing the notion of all who live there just how rich Elizabethtown is in its own pride of time and place.

This small town provided a secure setting for Lucie's childhood during the Great Depression. Between 1938 and 1940, between the ages of eleven and thirteen, she made seven scrapbooks. Despite her proud connection to her home, these scrapbooks reveal the lure of a wider world. Lucie set her sights on distant horizons, using her scrapbooks to collect what she saw, what she learned, who she hoped to become. The scrapbooks relate to her known world, sometimes endorsing the importance of things familiar. Yet they also capture things new and glamorous; they define emerging tastes, interests, and aspirations. Essentially, they reveal a young girl who wanted to learn something, to go somewhere.

Lucie's first scrapbook (see Figure 15.1) was a birthday gift from her younger brother, Willard, which she filled entirely with images in three categories: the Dionne quintuplets, "Children," and "Women." She dated that book carefully, noting that it was begun in July 1938 and finished in August 1939.

The first scrapbook is filled with direct visual representation: the birth and growth of the Dionnes is shown through news clippings and images from commercial product endorsements (see Figure 15.2). The section entitled "Children" shows boys and girls in contemporary dress, seemingly unaffected by the economic hardships of the Depression. Reflecting an innocent and reassuring understanding of life, the children are playing, eating, being bathed, relating to family, and celebrating special occasions. The images in the "Women" section are humorously introduced

Figure 15.1. *For her eleventh birthday in 1938, Lucie Jenkins received a blank scrapbook from her younger brother, Willard, who purchased the gift at the local dime store for thirty-nine cents.*

Figure 15.2. *Born on May 28, 1934, the Dionne quintuplets—Marie, Cecile, Emilie, Annette, and Yvonne—were dubbed "the World's Darlings." Lucie's sixth-grade teacher traveled to Ontario, Canada, to see them in their clinical nursery. The quintuplets were used to advertise everything from Colgate toothpaste to Ivory soap.*

Figure 15.3. *The school-assigned project to create a notebook on the topic "Appreciation of Music" led to three additional scrapbooks devoted to opera stars, composers, and the history of music.*

with a wickedly satirical portrayal of a woman getting a permanent in a beauty shop, and the following pages document the style, accessories, and glamour of the times. When asked, decades later, to explain the selection of these categories to her daughter, Lucie showed how scrapbooks can be reread.

Lucie explained that she, along with the rest of the world, was fascinated by the Dionne quintuplets but also concerned about their situation. She was intrigued that their care was supervised by a doctor in a full-time nursery, not their home. As for the "Children" section, Lucie was at the age when she began to take care of children and notice how other families treated their own. The fashions she selected for the "Women" section were inspired by the styles worn by two important role models—her glamorous aunt Glad, who shopped in distant Louisville, and her aunt Nel, a single career woman and an officer at the bank in town.

Lucie's second scrapbook (see Figure 15.3) was actually a notebook created for a seventh-grade school project, titled and dated "Appreciation of Music, September 1939," for which she was graded "A + = Fine Work." Inspired, perhaps, by her good mark, Lucie compiled, on her own over the next two years, three more scrapbooks related to music: one a celebrity scrapbook of stars of the Metropolitan Opera Company and two other reference books on composers, conductors, instruments, and music in general.

In May and June 1939, Lucie carefully clipped the papers to follow the daily progress of King George VI and Queen Elizabeth's "triumphant" tour of Canada and the United States. This "royal" scrapbook was completed with retrospectively collected clippings and images of George's 1937 coronation and contemporary information about Princess Elizabeth and the Duke and Duchess of Windsor. The final and greatest undertaking was an enormous, beautifully illustrated scrapbook entitled "Art" (primarily painting).

By the time she was fourteen and fifteen, Lucie was out of middle school and working at her first job in the Elizabethtown post office. She no longer had time for scrapbooks, although later in life she continued to tuck articles, obituaries, and entire magazines into all of the early volumes. Lucie's scrapbook making was educational, entertaining, and a creative, aesthetic exercise—all healthy and economic endeavors during the Depression.

Lucie's first scrapbook, made at age eleven, is entirely visual and artistic in presentation. The fine cutting, careful pasting, balanced placement, and neat presentation of her images indicate a craftlike approach to assembling her books. She loved to cut profiles, trim along the border of a geometric design, or shadow the graceful flow of calligraphy in a headline.

This collage-like art of selection, cutting, and symmetrical composition falls within the earlier Victorian tradition of creating beautiful scrapbooks from the colorful advertising and holiday ephemera that proliferated after the advent of chromolithographic printing in the nineteenth century. It was also in the Victorian tradition that primarily women and children pursued such a pastime. Lucie's detailed cutting and careful placement are evident and continue in the other volumes, notably in the celebrity volumes on opera stars and royalty, as well as the final "Art" volume, in which the content is very image oriented.

Applied Learning: Collecting Images and Information

Lucie's first scrapbook was dutifully completed, but beginning with the school project "Appreciation of Music," her scrapbooks became more substantial information sources, combining articles, news, and publications with appealing images. This educational function harkens back to the eighteenth-century commonplace book, a precursor to the scrapbook. Relying less on collected, published, or printed ephemera ("scraps") and more on hand-copied snippets of personal records, quotations, and miscellaneous facts, the commonplace book was a repository for information. Having a book in which to put the information implied ownership of it; the education process, so self-directed, was in the discovery and collecting effort.

Lucie's school assignment—to fill a notebook on the topic of music appreciation—perfectly matched her personal passion for the music she heard on the radio twice a week: broadcasts of the Saturday matinee at the Metropolitan Opera House in New York City and the Ford Sunday Evening Hour, a concert series emanating from Detroit that was broadcast coast-to-coast on CBS. The school notebook includes handwritten essays on music; profiles of "great musicians" (singers, composers, conductors, and musicians such as Lily Pons, Victor Herbert, Berlioz, Yehudi Menuhin [see Figure 15.4], and Mozart); lists (of musical dates, terms, Verdi operas in order of composition, and national anthems); lyrics; and summaries of operas, including plots, characters, composers, and nationalities. Margaret Edith Harding, the art- and music-appreciation teacher for Elizabethtown's sixth, seventh, and eighth grades, was shrewd in her assignment of the essays and topics covered in the notebook. In addition to names like "Rimski-Korsakov," she included those with Kentucky connections, such as Stephen Foster and Jenny Lind, the "Swedish Nightingale," who, as all good Kentuckians know, was a friend of Henry Clay. In addition to the lyrics copied for Robert Burns's "Comin' thro' the Rye" are Foster's "Old Folks at Home" and a spoof of *Aïda*. Supplementing opera synopses for Wagner's entire *Ring Cycle* is an essay on folk music, a vernacular with strong Kentucky representation in regional ballads.

A relatively small number of clipped images and articles illustrate the autograph essays comprising most of the notebook, but a final few pages of celebrity images from the "stupendous" marriage of Jeanette MacDonald and Gene Raymond signal the beginning of the star watching soon to be gathered in the next volume.

Lucie's school project also provided a solid foundation for the more sophisticated intellectual exercises of organizing and arranging the contents of her next three scrapbooks on music appreciation. She set up a basement work space where nobody bothered her: she had a large worktable in front of some ground-level windows, and nearby hung some shelves. She kept boxes on the shelves to sort and collect clippings. When she had enough, she arranged her pages and worked on several scrapbooks at once.

The stylish stars of the Metropolitan Opera Company in New York City dominate the first scrapbook (see Figure 15.5); they were evidently as popular as screen stars in the fashion, home, and news magazines of the day. But this volume also includes articles about the radio programs and the power of that medium to popularize music. A 1935 article that Lucie clipped from the *Literary Digest* describes radio as the "long arms of the air, which reaches out to gather in and distribute to listening millions the struggles, accomplishments, thoughts, feats and talents of man." In addition to bringing "the horrors of the battlefield, the masterpieces of drama, and events in the lives of man . . . just so can the great compositions of the masters of music be made available to all for the simple turning of a radio dial. That exactly is what the WHAS-CBS Sunday Evening Hour does for all those who love good music."

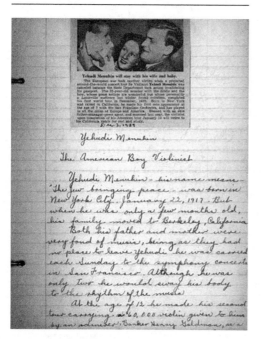

Figure 15.4. *Illustrated with a news clipping dated December 3, 1939, Lucie's composition on Yehudi Menuhin noted that the name of the famous "American boy violinist" meant "the Jew bringing Peace."*

Topics in Lucie's second music scrapbook encompass composers, conductors, instruments, and musical genres such as folk, band, and spirituals, with additional articles on history. An extensive source for

Figure 15.5. *Carefully arranged, this page presents a constellation of opera stars and concert musicians.*

biographical material was a serialized feature on classical composers carried by the *Louisville Courier-Journal.* Contemporary artists in this volume include John Jacob Niles, "the Bard of Boot Hill" (Lexington, Kentucky); the Canadian bandleader Guy Lombardo; the recently immigrated Trapp Family Singers; the "Negro" singers Marian Anderson and Dorothy Maynor (see Figure 15.6); and the pianist Ignace Jan Paderewski. The third volume in the music series includes finely printed portrait plates of composers, with additional newspaper profiles and articles, and images of instruments.

King George VI and Queen Elizabeth's 1939 tour of Canada and the United States inspired Lucie's "royal" scrapbook. She carefully followed the daily press and

Figure 15.6. *Lucie's scrapbooks included several clippings about Marian Anderson and another "distinguished Negro singer" of the day, Dorothy Maynor, as well as information about spirituals and "jump-up" songs.*

clipped reports of "lusty cheers" from Canadians and a visit with "the darling Dionnes" in Toronto; articles about oppressive heat and highly sought invitations to the garden party at the British Embassy in Washington, D.C.; and stories of the Roosevelts' Hyde Park picnic for the king, which included a menu of hot dogs (see Figure 15.7). At the end of this section, she satisfied her newly acquired interest in the royal family by combing old magazines for biographical profiles and creating a section from earlier collected clippings about the 1937 coronation.

Lucie's categorization of information continued with her final and most ambitious scrapbook, the "Art" scrapbook, which consisted primarily of paintings by European and American masters but also included some Asian art and classical sculpture. As with her other projects, the content was largely driven by biographical profiles, although contemporary cultural highlights and magazine serializations of several artistic themes or genres provided other topical arrangements. One section was created from a *Louisville Courier-Journal* rotogravure supplement featuring European paintings exhibited at the Masterpieces of Art Museum at the 1939 World's Fair in New York City. Andrew Mellon's gift of his priceless art collection (see Figure 15.8) to the National Gallery of Art in Washington, D.C., inspired additional information about other galleries and museums, from the Boston Museum of Fine Arts, to Cranbrook Institute in Detroit, to the Huntington in California.

Unwittingly documenting a major works project of the Depression, Lucie saved articles on muralists commissioned by the WPA Federal Art Project (see Figure 15.9), many of whom painted works in post offices around the country. Lucie, the daughter of Elizabethtown's postmaster, instinctively appreciated these public art projects. She

Figure 15.7. *To the delight of the U.S. press who covered the 1939 royal tour, President Franklin Roosevelt and his wife, Eleanor, treated the king and queen of England to a hot-dog picnic at their home in Hyde Park.*

followed additional Americana, such as the *Life* magazine series "Historical American Scenes" and anything related to Audubon, who had once lived in her hometown.

There's a Story in the Sources Too

Lucie's scrapbook-making provided economic, wholesome entertainment in the final years of the Depression. Asked if any of her friends had kept scrapbooks too, Lucie replied: "Oh, sure, but they mostly followed the film stars. I didn't have a dime to

Mellon Art to Capital Gallery

President Roosevelt has announced the offer of Andrew W. Mellon to give his famed $50,000,000 art collection to the Nation.

Mr. Mellon, shown above, has offered to build a gallery for the paintings in Washington, D. C., at a cost of $8,000,000. His offer has been accepted pending approval of Congress.

Raphael's famous "Madonna of the House of Alba" (left), which cost Mr. Mellon $1,166,000, is also included in the gift.

Included in the gift is the famed "Annunciation," by Jan Van Eyck, which cost Mr. Mellon, former Secretary of the Treasury, $500,000 when he bought it from the Soviet Government.

Figure 15.8. *Congressional approval was still pending when this clipping reported Andrew Mellon's offer to build an $8-million gallery to house the gift of his art collection to the nation.*

spend every Saturday at the movies. You see, Father had not only a family of four at home to support, but also the eight in the [tenant] family on the farm." Economics aside, the family's Baptist affiliation may have been another influence: "Oh, probably. I guess," she laughed. The Jenkins lived in a modest Craftsman-style bungalow on West Dixie Avenue. Their morals would have held movie going as an extravagance not to be indulged over responsibilities to provide a comfortable home and meet expenses for the Jenkins farm, just outside town.

Education, especially self-improvement, was fundamental to the Jenkins family's values. The family could afford home subscriptions to a few magazines, Lucie's grandparents provided access to several more as well as major newspapers, and she also received copies of other magazines from family friends when they were finished with them. Recycling these sources, Lucie read current events and learned. She

Figure 15.9. *Of the 1,125 government murals described in this article, 95 percent were located in post offices, a fact of personal interest to Lucie, whose father was a postmaster.*

remembers three regular magazines at home: the *Delphian Quarterly, Ladies' Home Companion*, and *Life*. The family subscribed to the *Elizabethtown News* but received only the Sunday issue of the *Louisville Courier-Journal*; however, Lucie was able to read all the weekly issues of the *Courier-Journal* during Sunday-afternoon visits at her grandparents' house while the "old folks" talked. Her grandfather, Harvey Lewis Igleheart, was a farmer, auctioneer, and bank trustee, so she occasionally found items in his *Wall Street Journal*. The constant and most varied source for her, however, was her grandmother, Lucie Rush Igleheart.

Lucie Igleheart was a teacher before she married. She loved books and learning and managed to travel to Europe several times in the 1920s after rearing six children. She gave her namesake free reign of all old issues of magazines in her house: *Delineator, Etude, Collier's, Country Life, Literary Digest, Saturday Evening Post*, and

Figure 15.10. *Decades after making her scrapbooks, Lucie sat down—at her daughter Rebecca's request—to talk about them. The section entitled "Women" in her first album closed with this picture of a girl, probably about Lucie's age, watching a young woman, probably her sister, packing a trunk. Lucie explained the image: "And this is packing to go away to college. And I could hardly wait to get away." Rebecca responded, "So you were eleven years old and you already knew you wanted to go to college?" With remembered enthusiasm Lucie replied, "Oh absolutely, absolutely. And that's the way you packed."*

Woman's Home Companion. "Grandmother Lucie" or other family friends also supplied random issues of *Better Homes and Gardens, Good Housekeeping, House and Garden, McCall's, Pictorial Review,* and *Time.*

The source material for Lucie's scrapbooks and the scraps she selected reflect a not-unusual affinity between women and the arts. Her grandmother and mother provided a number of beautiful prints from brochures and publications they obtained in pursuit of their own interests. Mary Lee Igleheart Jenkins, Lucie's mother, joined the Delphian Society and organized a home-study group in Elizabethtown that was affiliated with this national "sorority" dedicated to the advancement of culture. For the music scrapbook, she gave her daughter the portrait plates of great composers and musical instruments from the Effa Ellis Perfield Picture Edition (Chicago Art Museum) that had accompanied a Delphian lesson. For Christmas 1939, Mary Lee Jenkins gave her daughter *Beautiful Masterpieces and Their Stories: Stories Arranged by Bertha H. Lewis,* filled with rich color prints, for her "Art" scrapbook.

Lucie seemed to absorb the message and consciously included articles that advocated women's role in the arts. From a 1924 *Better Homes and Gardens,* she cut an article titled "Musical Inheritance of America," deemed "a suitable program for April for Women's Clubs" by the national music chair of the General Federation of Women's Clubs. She included several articles by the critic Marcia Davenport, who was also the musical commentator for the Saturday-matinee radio broadcasts from the Metropolitan Opera House. Davenport called for women to take the lead in gathering municipal support for musical performances, citing the popularity of San Francisco's opera season and the success of Richmond, Virginia, in raising money by subscription for a city symphony. A 1936 article by the aging opera star Ernestine Schumann Heink called for women, "patrons of culture and civility," to resist the threat of yet another international war.

This role of women as cultural leaders, the government sponsorship of murals on public buildings, the radio as a medium, the lionization of opera stars, the pre-war popularity of England's royal family, the newsworthiness and commercial promotion of the Dionne quintuplets, advertising and fashion of the day—all are historical notes found in the scrapbooks. From images and articles that were selected and assembled by an impressionable but intelligent young preteen, the scrapbooks capture information available beyond the town limits of Elizabethtown. Lucie was as attracted as any other young girl to celebrities and followed tales of romance, marriage, astronomical earnings during the Depression, and fabulous wardrobes, but she focused on opera stars or royalty, more suitable subjects, considering her Baptist upbringing. She couched any idolization of opera stars in a broader appreciation of their musical talents and cultural heritage. Women, children, music, and the arts were safe grounds from which to view distant horizons, acceptable points of departure for this Kentucky preteen.

Lucie Jenkins later left Elizabethtown to attend two years at Averett College in Danville, Virginia, a Baptist junior college for women (see Figure 15.10). She obtained her BA from Wake Forest College in Wake Forest, North Carolina, before obtaining a master's degree in social work from Tulane University. The young girl who worried so much about the Dionnes and how they were growing up became a social worker in family services. Her own daughter, who grew up in the family tradition of collecting and keeping old things, became an archivist.

Notes

〰〰〰

AN INTRODUCTION TO THE HISTORY OF
SCRAPBOOKS

1. Scholars have looked at isolated albums and offered some generalizations about how to put scrapbooks in context, but there is no sustained analysis of scrapbooks. See, for example, Patricia P. Buckler, "A Silent Woman Speaks: The Poetry in a Woman's Scrapbook of the 1840s," *Prospects* 16 (1991): 149–69; Ellen Gruber Garvey, *The Adman in the Parlor: Magazines and the Gendering of Consumer Culture, 1880s to 1910s* (New York: Oxford University Press, 1996); Todd Steven Gernes, "Recasting the Culture of Ephemera: Young Women's Literary Culture in Nineteenth-Century America" (PhD diss., Brown University, 1992).

2. For more on self-representations of identity, see John Shotter and Kenneth Gergen, eds., *Texts of Identity* (London: Sage, 1989); Katherine Hoffman, *Concepts of Identity: Historical and Contemporary Images and Portraits of Self and Family* (New York: HarperCollins, 1996).

3. Langstroth's 120 scrapbooks are in the collections of the Cincinnati Public Library. John Fleischman, "The Labyrinthine World of the Scrapbook King," *Smithsonian Magazine* 22 (February 1992): 79–87.

4. "A Portfolio of Personalities," *Coronet* (January 1939): 156–57.

5. For more on this aspect related to gender, see Susan Griffin, *The Historical Eye: The Texture of the Visual in Late James* (Boston: Northeastern University Press, 1991).

6. Much more could be said about the performative elements of scrapbooks—that is, of their creation in placing objects on pages on the basis of one's idea of acting a role in society. This introduction is intended to be suggestive rather than exhaustive. Of particular relevance to the performative aspect of making scrapbooks are Erving Goffman, *The Presentation of the Self in Everyday Life* (New York: Doubleday, 1959); and Victor Turner, *The Anthropology of Performance* (New York: PAJ, 1987).

7. For more on resolving the conflicting claims of the real and of the imaginary or remembered, see Hayden White, "The Value of Narrativity in the Representation of Reality," *Critical Inquiry* 7 (1980): 5–27.

8. For a discussion of Derrida and Freud on the idea of supplements to identity, see Edward Sampson, "The Deconstruction of the Self," in *Texts of Identity,* ed. John Shotter and Kenneth Gergen (Newbury Park, Calif.: Sage Publications, 1989), 1–19. For more on the complexity of analyzing subjectivity, see Lawrence Watson and Maria-Barbara Watson-Franke, *Interpreting Life Histories: An Anthropological Inquiry* (New Brunswick, N.J.: Rutgers University Press, 1985).

9. For more on reading culture in this way, see Miles Orvell, *The Real Thing: Imitation and Authenticity in American Culture, 1880–1940* (Chapel Hill: University of North Carolina Press, 1989), especially chap. 2, "The Hieroglyphic World."

10. For archivists, scrapbooks often seem not to be manuscript, record, or book but some hybrid form, usually with a conservation problem. Some archivists are particularly averse to clippings scrapbooks because this information, at least in theory, is available elsewhere. See, for example, some of the problems described in Book and Paper Group and Photographic Materials Group, ed., *Conservation of Scrapbooks and Albums* (Washington, D.C.: American Institute for Conservation of Historic and Artistic Works, 2000); Barbara Zucker, "Preservation Basics: Preservation of Scrapbooks and Albums," National Cooperative Information Project, leaflet no. 1 (Washington, D.C.: Library of Congress, 1991); Merrily Smith, "Scrapbooks in the Library of Congress," in *Preserving America's Performing Arts* (New York: Theater Library Association, 1985).

11. Topoi—as places or topics—are traced from the time of Aristotle through the Renaissance in Ann Moss, *Printed Common Place Books and the Structuring of Renaissance Thought* (Oxford: Clarendon Press, 1996); and Sister Joan Marie Lechner, *Renaissance Concepts of the Commonplaces* (Westport, Conn.: Greenwood Press, 1962). See also Jonathan Spence, *The Memory Palace of Matteo Ricci* (New York: Viking Books, 1984).

12. Moss, *Printed Common Place Books,* 24–50. For a beautiful facsimile of an illuminated manuscript with flora and fauna that seem to inhabit the pages, see Lee Hendrix and Thea Vignau-Wilberg, *Mira Calligraphiae Monumenta* (Malibu, Calif.: J. Paul Getty Museum, 1992).

13. See William W. Robinson, "This Passion for Prints," foreword to *Printmaking in the Age of Rembrandt,* ed. Clifford Ackley (Boston: Museum of Fine Arts, 1981), xxvii–xxxi.

14. Robert DeCandido, "Out of the Question," *Conservation Administration News* 53 (April 1993): 2.

15. Robinson, "This Passion for Prints," xxvii.

16. For more on the history of cabinets of curiosity, see Oliver Impey and Arthur MacGregor, eds., *The Origins of Museums* (Oxford: Clarendon Press, 1985); Arthur K. Wheelock, *A Collector's Cabinet* (Washington, D.C.: National Gallery of Art, 1998); Rosamond Purcell and Stephen Jay Gould, *Finders, Keepers* (New York: W. W. Norton, 1992).

17. The *Oxford English Dictionary* dates the first written use of the term *commonplace book* from 1578.

18. Thomas Fuller, quoted in Peter Beal, "Notions in Garrison: The Seventeenth-Century Commonplace Book," in *New Ways of Looking at Old Texts,* ed. W. Speed Hill (Binghamton, N.Y.: Medieval and Renaissance Texts and Studies, 1993), 131.

19. John Locke, *The Posthumous Works of Mr. John Locke* (London: A. J. Churchill, 1706), 318–19. Among the Locke collection of manuscripts in the Bodleian Library is a written explanation of his categories for commonplace books. See Moss, *Printed Common Place Books,* 278.

20. Kenneth Lockbridge, *On the Sources of Patriarchal Rage: The Commonplace Books of William Byrd and Thomas Jefferson and the Gendering of Power in the Eighteenth Century* (New York: New York University Press, 1992).

21. Among those publishing such literary notebooks over the years were Robert Southey, Robert Burns, Samuel Butler, Thomas Hardy, E. M. Forster, and H. P. Lovecraft.

22. Maurice Rickards, *The Encyclopedia of Ephemera: A Guide to the Fragmentary Documents of Everyday Life for the Collector, Curator, and Historian* (New York: Routledge, 2000), 103. Rickards here notes that commonplace books often became inherited books, filled by successive generations of families.

23. James Granger, *A Biographical History of England* (London: T. Davies, 1775). For more on Grangerized books, see Marcia Pointon, *Hanging the Head: Portraiture and Social Formation in Eighteenth-Century England* (New Haven, Conn.: Yale University Press, 1993), 53–78; Daniel Tredwell, *A Monograph on Privately Illustrated Books: A Plea for Bibliomania* (New York: DeVinne Press, 1892).

24. Rickards, *The Encyclopedia of Ephemera*, 283–85; Alistair Allen and Joan Hoverstadt, *The History of Printed Scraps* (London: New Cavendish Books, 1983).

25. Gernes, "Recasting the Culture of Ephemera," 57–109; Starr Ockenga, *On Women and Friendship: A Collection of Victorian Keepsakes and Traditions* (New York: Stewart, Tabori, and Chang, 1993), 20–31.

26. For more on this, see Leigh Schmidt, *Consumer Rites: The Buying and Selling of American Holidays* (Princeton, N.J.: Princeton University Press, 1995). See also Deborah Smith, "Consuming Passions: Scrapbooks and American Play," *Ephemera Journal* 6 (1993): 63–76; and Garvey, *The Adman in the Parlor*, 8.

27. Samuel L. Clemens, June 24, 1873, patent no. 140245.

28. Bernard Devoto, ed., *Mark Twain in Eruption* (1922; repr., New York: Grosset and Dunlap, 1940), 160.

29. See, for example, the patents of Bernard Beck, March 28, 1876 (no. 175328); Robert Sneider, September 9, 1879 (no. 219370); George Shepard, November 14, 1882 (no. 267604); and Edward Anderson, April 26, 1898 (no. 602817).

30. Norman Brosterman, *Inventing Kindergarten* (New York: Abrams, 1997), 22, 124. See also Grace Storm, *The Social Studies in the Primary Grades* (Chicago: Lyons and Carnahan, 1931), 267.

31. Katherine McClinton, *The Chromolithographs of Louis Prang* (New York: Clarkson Potter, 1973); Larry Freeman, *Louis Prang: Color Lithographer, Giant of a Man* (Watkins Glen, N.Y.: 1971), xx.

32. See, for example, Dorothy Canfield, *What Shall We Do Now? Five Hundred Games and Pastimes: A Book of Suggestions for Children's Games and Employments* (New York: Frederick A. Stokes, 1907), 276; Bertha Johnston, *Home Occupations for Boys and Girls* (Philadelphia: George Jacobs, 1908), 111; Janet Ruutz-Rees, *Home Occupations* (New York: D. Appleton, 1883), 97–101. For a discussion of the popularity of the middle-class ideal of domesticity as a means of achieving authentic experience, see T. J. Jackson Lears, *No Place of Grace: Anti-Modernism and the Transformation of American Culture, 1880–1920* (New York: Pantheon, 1981), 247–51.

33. E. W. Gurley, *Scrap-Books and How to Make Them* (New York: Authors' Publishing, 1880), 10–11, 51, 13.

34. For more on how visual literacy functions, see Paul Messaris, *Visual Literacy: Image, Mind, and Reality* (Boulder, Colo.: Westview Press, 1994). See also David Morgan, *Protestants and Pictures: Religion, Visual Culture, and the Age of American Mass Production* (New York: Oxford University Press, 1999). For a step-by-step guide to scrapbook-page design, see Lina Beard and Adelia Beard, *The American Girls Handy Book: How to Amuse Yourself and Others* (New York: Charles Scribner's Sons, 1898), 395–402.

35. Gernes, "Recasting the Culture of Ephemera," 12, 56; Tamar Katriel and Thomas Farrell, "Scrapbooks as Cultural Texts: An American Art of Memory," *Text and Performance Quarterly* 11 (1991): 1–17.

36. See also Russell W. Belk and Melanie Wallendorf, "Of Mice and Men: Gender Identity in Collecting," in *Interpreting Objects and Collections,* ed. Susan M. Pearce (New York: Routledge, 1994), 240–53; Jaap Boerdam and Warna Martinius, "Family Photographs: A Sociological Approach," *Netherlands Journal of Sociology* 16 (1980): 95–120; Sandra Gardner, "Exploring the Family Album: Social Class Differences in Images of Family Life," *Sociological Inquiry* 1 (1991): 242–51; Pierre Bourdieu, "The Cult of Unity and Cultivated Difference," in *Photography: A Middle-Brow Art,* ed. Pierre Bourdieu, trans. Shaun Whiteside (1965; repr., Stanford, Calif.: Stanford University Press, 1990).

37. Deborah Smith found evidence that an equal number of girls and boys probably engaged in album making. Smith, "Consuming Passions: Scrapbooks and American Play," *Ephemera Journal* 6 (1993): 66–67.

38. See, for example, Nina Archabal, "MHS Collections in Memoriam: Cameron Booth, 1892–1980: A Chronicle from His Scrapbooks," *Minnesota History* 47 (1980): 100–110.

39. For more on middle-class identity formation, see Pierre Bourdieu, *Distinction: A Social Critique of the Judgment of Taste,* trans. Richard Nice (Cambridge: Harvard University Press, 1984); Norbert Elias, *The Civilizing Process* (Oxford: Blackwell, 1994); Richard Bushman, *The Refinement of America: Persons, Houses, Cities* (New York: Vintage, 1993).

40. For more on how scrapbooks supported consumers, see D. Smith, "Consuming Passions," 63–76; Garvey, *The Adman in the Parlor,* 16–50.

41. For a discussion of nineteenth-century gift books, see Isabelle Lehuu, *Carnival on the Page: Popular Print Media in Antebellum America* (Chapel Hill: University of North Carolina Press, 2000).

42. A discussion of blank books used as scrapbooks and their titles, marketed to female students, is found in Susan Tucker, "Reading and Re-Reading: The Scrapbooks of Girls Growing into Women," in *Defining Print Culture for Youth,* ed. Anne Lundin and Wayne Wigand (Westport, Conn.: Libraries Unlimited, 2003), 1–26. Blank books marketed to different groups of potential scrapbook makers included, among many others, Maud Humphrey and Paul de Longpre, *The Bride's Book: A Souvenir of the Wedding* (New York: Frederick Stoke, 1900); James O. Smith, *My Fraternity* (Chicago: Reilly and Britton, n.d.); Elizabeth Colborne, *Stunt Book* (Chicago: Reilly and Britton, 1914).

43. Richard Horton, "Historical Photo Albums and Their Structures," in *Conservation of Scrapbooks and Albums: Postprints of the Book and Paper Group/Photographic Materials* (Washington, D.C.: American Institute for Conservation of Historic and Artistic Works, 2000), 13; Elizabeth E. Siegel, "Galleries of Friendship and Fame: The History of Nineteenth-Century American Family Albums" (PhD diss., University of Chicago, 2003); Sarah McNair Vosmeier, "The Family Album: Photography and Family Life, 1860–1930" (PhD diss., Indiana University, 2003).

44. James Reilly, *Care and Identification of Nineteenth-Century Photographic Prints* (Rochester, N.Y.: Eastman Kodak, 1986), 4; Beaumont Newhall, *The History of Photography, from 1839 to the Present Day* (New York: Museum of Modern Art, 1964), 40–41.

45. Barbara McCandless, "The Portrait Studio and the Celebrity," in *Photography in Nineteenth-Century America,* ed. Martha Sandweiss (New York: Abrams, 1991), 48–74; Alan Trachtenberg, *Reading American Photographs: Images as History, Mathew Brady to Walker Evans* (New York: Hill and Wang, 1989); Mary Panzer, *Mathew Brady and the Image of History* (Washington, D.C.: Smithsonian Institution Press, 1997).

46. Horton, "Historical Photo Albums," 14; Jane Rutherston, "Victorian Album Structures" (Master's thesis, Victoria and Albert Museum, London, 1996).

47. International Center of Photography, *Encyclopedia of Photography* (New York: ICP, 1984), 99; Elizabeth McCauley, *A.A.E. Disderi and the Carte de Visite Portrait Photograph* (New Haven, Conn.: Yale University Press, 1985), 1–4, 204–17.

48. "Photography and Its Album," *Godey's Lady's Book* 68 (March 1864): 304. Because of this use of photograph albums, the volume editors have chosen to include here essays on a few books called albums, rather than scrapbooks. For more on this, see Graham King, *"Say Cheese!" Looking at Snapshots in a New Way* (New York: Dodd, Mead, 1984); Richard Chalfen, *Snapshot Versions of Life* (Bowling Green, Ohio: Bowling Green State University Popular Press, 1987).

49. International Center of Photography, *Encyclopedia of Photography* 222, 284, 437.

50. Roger Chartier has written about the ways in which a text's form influences the meanings it produces in *Forms and Meanings: Texts, Performances, and Audiences from the Codex to Computer* (Philadelphia: University of Pennsylvania Press, 1995), 83–97.

51. Walter Benjamin, "The Work of Art in the Age of Mechanical Reproduction," in *Illumina-tions: Essays and Reflections,* ed. Hannah Arendt, trans. Harry Zone (New York: Schocken Books, 1969), 219–53.

52. For a rich discussion of how the artist's book functions, see Keith Smith, *Structure of the Visual Book,* book 95 (Rochester, N.Y.: Visual Studies Workshop Press, International Center of Photography, 1984).

53. Ibid., 45.

54. Elaine Hedges, "The Nineteenth-Century Diarist and Her Quilts," *Feminist Studies* 8 (1982): 293–308; Schnuppe von Gwinner, *The History of the Patchwork Quilt: Origins, Traditions, and Symbols of a Textile Art* (West Chester, Pa.: Schiffer, 1988).

55. See, for example, Florence Temko, *Chinese Papercuts: Their Story and How to Make Them* (San Francisco: China Books, 1982).

56. See William Brown, "Joe Louis Scrapbooks, 1935–1944," *Journal of American History* 74 (March 1988): 1401–2.

57. Scrapbook Guild, *The Simple Art of Scrapbooking* (New York: Dell, 1998).

58. The largest collections of scrapbooks in the public domain include the more than six thou-sand volumes at the Library of Congress, Washington, D.C., and the significant collections at the Historical Society of Pennsylvania, Philadelphia; the Library Company, Philadelphia; the Winterthur Museum, Winterthur, Delaware; and the National Museum of American History, Smithsonian Institution, Washington, D.C. However, virtually every special collec-tions unit has scrapbooks.

59. Catherine Johnson, "Interpreting Performance through a Scrapbook's Eye View," paper pre-sented at the Society of American Archivists Annual Meeting, Washington, D.C., 1995; tran-script in possession of Susan Tucker.

60. See, for example, Caroline Jones and Peter Galison, eds., *Picturing Science, Producing Art* (New York: Routledge, 1998); Barbara Maria Stafford, *Good Looking: Essays on the Virtue of Images* (Cambridge: MIT Press, 1997); Gill Saunders, *Picturing Plants: An Analytical His-tory of Botanical Illustration* (Berkeley: University of California Press, 1995); Harry Robin, *The Scientific Image from Cave to Computer* (New York: Freeman, 1992).

61. Susan Pearce, *Museums, Objects, and Collections: A Cultural Study* (Washington, D.C.: Smith-sonian Institution Press, 1993), 69–88. See also Werner Muensterberger, *Collecting, an Unruly Passion: Psychological Perspectives* (Princeton, N.J.: Princeton University Press, 1994).

62. For more on shifts in perception of time and space, see Stephen Kern, *The Culture of Time and Space* (Cambridge: Harvard University Press, 1983).

63. For more on world's fair sites as ruptures, see Patricia Morton, *Hybrid Modernity: Architec-ture and Representation at the 1931 Colonial Exposition, Paris* (Cambridge: MIT Press, 2000); Robert Rydell, *All the World's a Fair: Visions of Empire at American International Exposi-tions, 1876–1916* (Chicago: University of Chicago Press, 1984); Christopher Vaughn, "Ogling Igorots: The Politics and Commerce of Exhibiting Cultural Otherness, 1898–1913," in *Freakery: Cultural Spectacles of the Extraordinary Body,* ed. Rosemarie Garland Thomson (New York: New York University Press, 1996), 219–33.

64. Nor should one overlook the imposition of one's will inherent in both assembling a collec-tion and creating a display. For what was happening in the development of museums, see Steven Conn, *Museums and American Intellectual Life, 1876–1926* (Chicago: University of Chicago Press, 1998). See also John Elsner and Roger Cardinal, eds., *The Cultures of Col-lecting* (Cambridge: Harvard University Press, 1994); Brenda Danet and Tamar Katriel, "No Two Alike: Play and Aesthetics in Collecting," *Play and Culture* 2 (1989): 253–77.

65. For a discussion of this appropriation of public materials as it shaped Duchamp's visual sense, see Molly Nesbit, "Ready-Made Originals: The Duchamp Model," *October* 37 (Summer, 1986): 53–63.

66. See, for example, Katherine Hoffman, ed., *Collage: Critical Views* (Ann Arbor: University of Michigan Press, 1989), xxi, 1–37.

67. Diane Waldman, *Collage, Assemblage, and the Found Object* (New York: Abrams, 1992), 11.

68. For a concept similar to the hidden rhyme of scrapbook collage, see Nicholas Humphrey, *Consciousness Regained* (New York: Oxford University Press, 1984), 121–37, which describes rhyming elements in relation to stamp collecting.

69. Matthew Teitelbaum, *Montage and Modern Life, 1919–1942* (Cambridge: MIT Press, 1992), 7.

70. For some background on montage, see Dawn Ades, *Photomontage* (London: Thames and Hudson, 1986); Robert Sobieszek, "Composite Imagery and the Origins of Photomontage, Pt. 1: The Naturalistic Strain," *Artforum* (September 1978): 58–65; Sobieszek, "Composite Imagery and the Origins of Photomontage, Pt. 2: The Formalist Strain," *Artforum* (October 1978): 40–45; Cynthia Wayne, *Dreams, Lies, and Exaggerations: Photomontage in America* (College Park: University of Maryland Press, 1991); Dziga Vertov, *Kino-Eye: The Writings of Dziga Vertov*, ed. Annette Michelson, trans. Kevin O'Brien (Berkeley: University of California Press, 1984).

71. For a discussion of advertising and consumption, see Roland Marchand, *Advertising the American Dream* (Berkeley: University of California Press, 1985); Gary Cross, *An All-Consuming Century: Why Commercialism Won in Modern America* (New York: Columbia University Press, 2000); Grant McCracken, *Culture and Consumption* (Bloomington: Indiana University Press, 1988); Jackson Lears, *Fables of Abundance: A Cultural History of Advertising* (New York: Basic Books, 1994); William Leach, *Land of Desire: Merchants, Power, and the Rise of a New American Culture* (New York: Pantheon, 1993); Pamela Laird, *Advertising the American Dream: American Business and the Rise of Consumer Marketing* (Baltimore: Johns Hopkins University Press, 1998).

72. For instructions on collecting and displaying trade cards, see Beard and Beard, *The American Girls Handy Book*, 396–97.

73. For more on the conversion of objects from the alienable into inalienable through social relationships, see Daniel Miller, *Material Culture and Mass Consumption* (London: Basil Blackwell, 1987); Marcel Mauss, *The Gift: Forms and Functions of Exchange in Archaic Societies*, trans. Ian Cunnison (Glencoe, Ill.: Free Press, 1954); Mary Douglas, *The World of Goods: Towards an Anthropology of Consumption* (London: Routledge, 1996).

74. For a fuller discussion of the nature and definition of ephemera, see Chris Makepeace, *Ephemera: A Book on Its Collection, Conservation, and Use* (Brookfield, Vt.: Gower, 1985); Rickards, *Encyclopedia of Ephemera*; Rickards, *Collected Printed Ephemera* (New York: Abbeville, 1988).

75. Richard Berner, "On Ephemera: Their Collection and Use," *Library Resources and Technical Services* 7 (1963): 335–39; Richard Berner and M. Gary Battle, "Disposition of Nonmanuscript Items Found among Manuscripts," *American Archivist* 33 (1970): 275–81. The problems with ephemera and scrapbook reformatting, whether by microform or digitization, continue to be heatedly discussed by archivists.

76. Some of the basic texts on ephemera include Allen and Hoverstadt, *The History of Printed Scraps*; Jefferson Burdick, *The American Card Catalog* (Franklin Square, N.Y.: Nostalgia Press, 1967); Diane DeBlois, *Cameo Cards and Bella C. Landauer* (Schoharie, N.Y.: Ephemera Society of America, 1992); Gernes, "Recasting the Culture of Ephemera," 12–56; G. Hudson, "Printed Ephemera and the Industrial Historian," *Industrial Archeology* 12, 4 (1978): 357–68; Robert Jay, *The Trade Card in Nineteenth-Century America* (Columbia: University of Missouri Press, 1987); John Lewis, *Collecting Printed Ephemera* (London: Studio Vista, 1976) and *Printed Ephemera: The Changing Use of Type and Letter Forms in English and American Printing* (London: Faber and Faber, 1969); Makepeace, *Ephemera*; Lou W. McCulloch, *Paper Americana: A Collector's Guide* (San Diego: A. S. Barnes, 1980); Rickards, *Encyclopedia of Ephemera* and *This Is Ephemera: Collecting Printed Throwaways* (London: Newton Abbot, David and Charles, 1977); Dale Roylance, *Graphic Americana: The Art and Technique of Printed Ephemera from Abecedaires to Zoetropes* (Princeton, N.J.: Princeton University Press, 1992); Leslie Shepard, *The History of Street Literature* (London:

Newton Abbot, David and Charles, 1973); David Winslow, "Trade Cards, Catalogs, and Invoice Heads," *Pennsylvania Folklife* 19 (1970): 16–23.

77. "Editor's Corner," *AB Bookman's Weekly* (March 7, 1994): 1015; Rickards, quoted in Makepeace, *Ephemera*, 2.

78. Allen and Hoverstadt, *The History of Printed Scraps*; Jefferson Burdick, *The American Card Catalog* (Franklin Square, N.Y.: Nostalgia Press, 1967); Rickards, *This Is Ephemera*, 66–67.

79. Some of the professional issues related to the importance of studying scrapbooks are discussed in Katherine Ott, "It's a Scrapbook Life: Using Ephemera to Reconstruct the Everyday of Medical Practice," *The Watermark* 20 (1996): 1–7.

80. Therese Lawrence, "Are Resource Treasures Hidden from Scholars in Our Libraries?" *Special Libraries* 64 (1973): 285–90.

81. For a discussion of Dickinson's practices, see Jeanne Holland, "Scraps, Stamps, and Cutouts: Emily Dickinson's Domestic Technologies of Publication," in *Cultural Artifacts and the Production of Meaning: The Page, the Image, the Body,* ed. Margaret Ezell and Katherine O'Keeffe (Ann Arbor: University of Michigan Press, 1994), 139–81.

82. Lydia Maria Child, *The Frugal Housewife* (London: Thomas Tegg, 1832), 3.

83. For more on ephemera's circulation in the market, see Mary-Elise Haug, "The Life Cycle of Printed Ephemera: A Case Study of the Maxine Waldron and Thelma Mendsen Collections," *Winterthur Portfolio* 30 (1995): 59–72; Igor Kopytoff, "The Cultural Biography of Things: Commoditization as Process," in *The Social Life of Things: Commodities in Cultural Perspective,* ed. Arjun Appadurai (Cambridge: Cambridge University Press, 1986), 64–91.

84. Michael Thompson has written about both the transience and durability of the value of objects in terms of rubbish in *Rubbish Theory: The Creation and Destruction of Value* (Oxford: Oxford University Press, 1979). See also Susan Strasser, *Waste and Want: A Social History of Trash* (New York: Metropolitan Books, 1999).

85. Michel de Certeau, *The Practice of Everyday Life,* trans. Steven Randall (Berkeley: University of California Press, 1984).

86. Ibid., xviii.

87. Guy Debord, *The Society of the Spectacle,* trans. Donald Nicholson-Smith (New York: Zone Books, 1994), 25–46.

88. David Lowenthal, *The Past Is a Foreign Country* (Cambridge: Cambridge University Press, 1985), 238–59.

89. Roy Rosenzweig and David Thelen, *The Presence of the Past: Popular Uses of History in American Life* (New York: Columbia University Press, 1998), 177–207.

90. Ibid., 89–104. See also Michael Kammen, *Mystic Chords of Memory* (New York: Alfred A. Knopf, 1991); Susan Stewart, *On Longing: Narratives of the Miniature, the Gigantic, the Souvenir, the Collection* (Durham, N.C.: Duke University Press, 1993); James McConkey, ed., *The Anatomy of Memory: An Anthology* (New York: Oxford University Press, 1996); David Thelen, ed., *Memory and American History* (Bloomington: Indiana University Press, 1989).

91. Typical titles found in bookstores include Scrapbook Guild, *The Simple Art of Scrapbooking* (1998); Rebecca Carter, *Scrapbooking for the First Time* (1999); Wendy Smedley, *The Complete Idiot's Guide to Scrapbooking* (1999); Michele Gerbrandt and Deborah Cannarella, *Family Scrapbooks: Yesterday, Today, and Tomorrow* (2001); Emily Hitchingham and others, *All-Girl Scrapbook Pages* (2004). A recent visit to a large bookstore uncovered eighteen books and six magazines on scrapbook making, figures all the more surprising when one considers that in the late 1980s and early 1990s one could not easily buy a scrapbook or any published advice on scrapbook making.

92. Dan Shaw, "Domestic Bliss; Memory Mania," *House and Garden* (May 2000): 37–39.

93. Mihaly Csikszentmihaly, "Why We Need Things," in *History from Things: Essays on Material Culture,* ed. Steven Lubar and David Kingery (Washington, D.C.: Smithsonian Institution Press, 1993), 20–28.

94. "Mania for Scrapbooks: Homespun Hobby Is Pricey Labor of Love," *Wall Street Journal,* July 16, 1997.

95. Nadya Labi, "Only the Best Scraps Go into These Books," *Time* (June 2, 2000): 66–67.
96. For a discussion of one particular set of home movies, see Grace Elizabeth Hale and Beth Loffreda, "Clocks for Seeing: Technologies of Memory, Popular Aesthetics, and the Home Movie," *Radical History Review* 66 (Fall 1996): 163–71.
97. Amy Silverman, "How to Win at Life," *New York Times*, October 31, 1999.
98. Rodris Roth, "Scrapbook Houses: A Late Nineteenth-Century Children's View of the American Home," in *The American Home: Material Culture, Domestic Space, and Family Life*, ed. Eleanor Thompson (Winterthur, Del.: Henry Francis DuPont Winterthur Museum, 1998).

CHAPTER 1: BETWEEN PERSON AND PROFESSION

1. For a discussion of performance, see Victor Turner, *The Anthropology of Performance* (New York: PAJ, 1986); John J. MacAloon, ed., *Rite, Drama, Festival, Spectacle: Rehearsals toward a Theory of Cultural Performance* (Philadelphia: Institute for the Study of Human Issues, 1984).
2. For more on commonplace books, see the introductory essay in this volume.
3. For a discussion of visual style and literacy in this period, see, for example, Jonathan Crary, *Techniques of the Observer: On Vision and Modernity in the Nineteenth Century* (Cambridge: MIT Press, 1990); Isabelle Lehuu, *Carnival on the Page: Popular Print Media in Antebellum America* (Chapel Hill: University of North Carolina Press, 2000); Shawn Michelle Smith, *American Archives: Gender, Race, and Class in Visual Culture* (Princeton, N.J.: Princeton University Press, 1999). Physicians were also subject to the cultural pressures on their role and behavior as men, about which there is a vast literature. A good place to start is Gail Bederman, *Manliness and Civilization: A Cultural History of Gender and Race in the United States, 1880–1917* (Chicago: University of Chicago Press, 1995).
4. The "relapsing fever" image can be found in William Osler, *Principles and Practice of Medicine* (New York: Appleton, 1895), 49. For a critical analysis of scientific illustrations, see Harry Rodin, *The Scientific Image from Cave to Computer* (New York: W. H. Freeman, 1993); Barbara Maria Stafford, *Artful Science: Enlightenment, Entertainment, and the Eclipse of Visual Perception* (Cambridge: MIT Press, 1994); Brian Ford, *Images of Science: A History of Scientific Illustration* (New York: Oxford University Press, 1993); Caroline Jones and Peter Galison, eds., *Picturing Science, Producing Art* (New York: Routledge, 1998); and the works of Edward Tufte, such as *Visual Explanations: Images and Quantities, Evidence and Narrative* (Cheshire, Conn.: Graphics Press, 1997).
5. Medical education today continues to rely heavily on graphic knowledge, although digital and CD-ROM images have taken pride of place, in both instruction and diagnostics.
6. For some background on late-nineteenth- and twentieth-century medical education, see William Rothstein, *American Medical Schools and the Practice of Medicine* (New York: Oxford, 1987); Kenneth M. Ludmerer, *Learning to Heal: The Development of American Medical Education* (New York: Basic Books, 1985); Horace Davenport, *Doctor Dock: Teaching and Learning Medicine at the Turn of the Century* (New Brunswick, N.J.: Rutgers University Press, 1987).
7. Norris's scrapbook is in the collections of the College of Physicians of Philadelphia, Z10/37.
8. For biographical information on Joseph Carson, see *The National Encyclopedia of American Biography* (New York: James T. White, 1922), 18:175–76.
9. Carson's scrapbook is in the College of Physicians of Philadelphia, ZZ10c/4.
10. For biographical information, see David Cowen, "Joseph Carson," in *American National Biography* (New York: Oxford University Press, 1999), 4:472–73.
11. For a discussion of styles of recording sequential events, see Hayden White, "The Value of Narrativity in the Representation of Reality," *Critical Inquiry* 7 (1980): 5–27.
12. Susan Stewart, in *On Longing: Narratives of the Miniature, the Gigantic, the Souvenir, the Collection* (Durham, N.C.: Duke University Press, 1993), analyzes how within exchange economies such as the contemporary U.S. one, ordinary objects come to realize and concretize the experiences of memory, time, and space. Stewart notes, although not in relation

to the composition of scrapbooks, that among the strategies individuals use to construct personal narrative from ordinary objects are the souvenir, which authenticates the past and discredits the present, and the collection, which replaces history with classification and order, making all time simultaneous and synchronous.

13. For the record, the Victorians also gave us Jell-o.

14. Not much has been written about mug books. They were equal parts booster book, vanity press, and senior yearbook. See Oscar Lewis, "Mug Books: A Dissertation Concerning the Origins of a Certain Familiar Division of Americana," *The Colophon* 17 (n. p., 1934).

15. For some background on Gould, of whom no book-length biography has been written, see Sam Alewitz, "George Milbry Gould," in *American National Biography*, 9:341; H. Edwin Lewis, "George Milbry Gould—A Great Physician," *Journal of the American Editors Association* 5 (1925): 19–31; Bayard Holmes, "George Milbry Gould," *Medical Life* 29 (1922): 591–603.

16. George Milbry Gould, *Anomalies and Curiosities of Medicine* (Philadelphia: W. B. Saunders, 1896).

17. Medical College of Pennsylvania, Philadelphia, Acc. 135.

18. The Woman's Medical College of Pennsylvania was an important training institution in the nineteenth century. Founded in Philadelphia in 1850 as the Female Medical College of Pennsylvania, it was the first school devoted to the education of women as physicians. For more on the graduates, see Steven J. Peitzman, *A New and Untried Course: Woman's Medical College and Medical College of Pennsylvania, 1850–1998* (New Brunswick, N.J.: Rutgers University Press, 2000).

19. Lane's papers are in the Wellcome Institute, London, GC 127, file A3.887.907. I am grateful to Shirley Dixon for bringing the Lane scrapbooks to my attention.

20. William Tanner, *Sir W. Arbuthnot Lane: His Life and Work* (London: Bailliere, Tindall and Cox, 1946), 34.

21. Sir William Arbuthnot Lane Papers, Wellcome Institute, London. Scrapbooks compiled by nurses seem to represent a contrast to the mass of ego gathered into physicians' medical scrapbooks. The few nurses' scrapbooks I have examined at the Center for the History of Nursing at the University of Pennsylvania focus on buildings, teachers, and friendships rather than on individuals and their glory.

22. National Library of Medicine, National Institutes of Health, Bethesda, Md., MS 8B 127.

23. It is unclear exactly who made Keefer's scrapbook, although the obvious replication of military orders in the posting of the documents strongly implicates Keefer. It may also be the case that the Armed Forces Medical Library, on receiving Keefer's papers, compiled them into book form. Some of the pages were trimmed down to fit the dimensions of the album. However, the identity of the compiler remains a mystery.

24. William Dinwiddie, "Hospitals of Manila," *Harper's Weekly* (August 4, 1900): 21–26. This article features a photograph of Keefer.

25. See Allen Millett's entry on Bullard in *American National Biography*, 3:901–2. Millett also wrote a biography of Bullard, *The General: Robert L. Bullard and Officership in the U.S. Army, 1881–1925* (Westport, Conn.: Greenwood Press, 1975).

26. Bullard went on to serve along the Mexican border during the Mexican Revolution but is best known as the World War I commander of the American Expeditionary Force's Second Brigade, First Division, second in command to General John J. Pershing.

27. National Library of Medicine, MSC 206.

28. For biographical information on Middleton, see *National Cyclopedia of American Biography* (Clifton, N.J.: James T. White, 1979), 58:261–62.

29. Medical College of Pennsylvania, Philadelphia, Acc. 126, 1892–1949.

30. College of Physicians of Philadelphia, A10/164, 1908.

31. For an overview of Philadelphia ophthalmologists, see Daniel Albert and H. G. Schie, *A History of Ophthalmology at the University of Pennsylvania* (Springfield, Ill.: Charles C. Thomas, 1965).

32. College of Physicians of Philadelphia, 10c/147, 1876.
33. Twain received a patent for an album in 1873. Examples of the Twain type of album, distinguished by pregummed lined pages, can be found in nearly every archive with more than a dozen scrapbooks.
34. No explanation exists as to why the doll was named Nicodemus, but most likely it was a pun on a biblical reference. In John 3:1–7, Christ tells Nicodemus, one of the Pharisees, that he must be born again to enter the kingdom of God. The doll baby was born and reborn many times each semester.
35. Medical College of Pennsylvania, Acc. 124, 1904.
36. For an account of another medical missionary, see Edward Bliss Jr., *Beyond the Stone Arches: An American Missionary Doctor in China, 1892–1932* (New York: John Wiley, 2001). For more context, see Patricia R. Hill, *The World Their Household: The American Woman's Foreign Mission Movement and Cultural Transformation, 1870–1920* (Ann Arbor: University of Michigan Press, 1985); Margaret Jones, "Infant and Maternal Health Services in Ceylon, 1900–1948: Imperialism or Welfare?" *Social History of Medicine* 15 (2002): 263–89; David Arnold, ed., *Imperial Medicine in Indigenous Societies* (Manchester, Eng.: Manchester University Press).
37. Peitzman, *A New and Untried Course*, 65–67.

CHAPTER 2: DAILY LIFE ON A SOUTH CAROLINA PLANTATION

1. Drew Gilpin Faust, *Mothers of Invention* (Chapel Hill: University of North Carolina Press, 1996), 23; Anne Firor Scott, *The Southern Lady from Pedestal to Politics, 1830–1930* (Chicago: University of Chicago Press, 1970), xi, 8 (quoting Longstreet), 17.
2. Anne Sinkler Whaley LeClercq, *An Antebellum Plantation Household, Including the South Carolina Low Country Receipts and Remedies of Emily Wharton Sinkler* (Columbia: University of South Carolina Press, 1996).
3. The only one of these African American women whose last name is documented was Cat, whose full name was Catherine Beaty.
4. See Anne Sinkler Fishburne, *Belvidere: A Plantation Memory* (Columbia: University of South Carolina Press, 1949), and Emily Fishburne Whaley, *Mrs. Whaley and Her Charleston Garden* (Chapel Hill, N.C.: Algonquin Press, 1996).

CHAPTER 3: LETTERS, SCRAPBOOKS, AND HISTORY BOOKS

1. Jean V. Matthews, "'Woman's Place' and the Search for Identity in Ante-Bellum America," *Canadian Review of American Studies* 10 (Winter 1979): 291; Carl Degler, "The Two Cultures and the Civil War," in *The Development of an American Culture*, ed. Stanley Cohen and Lormar Ratner (Englewood Cliffs, N.J.: Prentice-Hall, 1970), 103; E. McClung Fleming, "Early American Decorative Arts as Social Documents," *Mississippi Valley Historical Review* 45 (September 1958): 280.
2. David Thelen, Introduction to *Memory and American History*, ed. David Thelen (Bloomington: Indiana University Press, 1990), xvii, viii.
3. Ibid., viii.
4. William B. Hesseltine, "The Challenge of the Artifact," 100; John A. Kouwenhoven, "American Studies: Words or Things?" 81; Wilcomb E. Washburn, "Manuscripts and Manufacts," 102, 104, 105, all in *Material Culture Studies in America*, ed. Thomas J. Schlereth (Nashville: American Association for State and Local History, 1982).
5. Thomas A. Schlereth, "Material Culture Studies in America, 1876–1976," in ibid., 3.
6. Jerome Bruner, "Life as Narrative," *Social Research* 54 (Spring 1987): 15.
7. James Kinneavy, *A Theory of Discourse: The Aims of Discourse* (New York: W. W. Norton, 1980), 404. Kinneavy provides a full explanation of expressive discourse.

8. Simon Bronner, "Visible Proofs: Material Culture Study in American Folkloristics," in *Material Culture: A Research Guide,* ed. Thomas J. Schlereth (Lawrence: University Press of Kansas, 1985), 130.

9. Estelle C. Jelinek, *The Tradition of Women's Autobiography from Antiquity to the Present* (Boston: Twayne, 1986), 69.

10. For the full argument that women's scrapbooks can be read as autobiographical documents, see Patricia P. Buckler and C. Kay Leeper, "An Antebellum Woman's Scrapbook as Autobiographical Composition," *Journal of American Culture* 14, 1 (1991): 1–8.

11. Joanne E. Cooper, "Shaping Meaning: Women's Diaries, Journals, and Letters—The Old and the New," *Women's Studies International Forum* 10, 1 (1987): 95, 96.

12. Christopher Keep, Tim McLaughlin, and Robin Parmar, "Intertextuality," *Electronic Labyrinth,* www.iath.viginia.edu/elab/hfl0278.html (accessed February 10, 2004).

13. Julia Kristeva, quoted in "Kristeva, Intertextuality, Hypertext," english.ttu.edu/kairos/1.2/features/eyman/julia.html (accessed February 10, 2004).

14. Julia Kristeva, "'Nous Deux' or a (Hi)Story of Intertextuality," *Romanic Review* 93, 2 (January–March 2002): 12 (7–14).

15. Buckler Family Papers, MS. 2786, Manuscripts Department, Maryland Historical Society Library, Baltimore. All subsequent letters quoted in this essay, unless otherwise noted, are from this repository.

16. "Historic Points of Interest," www.governorsisland.gsa.gov/GI/broch05.html (accessed April 1, 2001); "Highlights in the History of Governors Island" http://www.governorsisland.gsa.gov/GI/timelin2.html (accessed April 1, 2001).

17. John S. D. Eisenhower, *Agent of Destiny: The Life and Times of General Winfield Scott* (New York: Free Press, 1997), 237.

18. Robert W. Johannsen, *To the Halls of the Montezumas: The Mexican War in the American Imagination* (New York: Oxford University Press, 1985), 170.

19. Justin H. Smith, *The War with Mexico* (1919; repr., Gloucester, Mass.: Peter Smith, 1963), 2:219; D. E. Livingston-Little, "U.S. Military Forces in California" in *The Mexican War: Changing Interpretations,* ed. Odie B. Faulk and Joseph A. Stout Jr. (Chicago: Swallow Press, 1973), 156–62.

20. "Bankhead, James," *Twentieth Century Biographical Dictionary of Notable Americans,* vol. 1 (Boston: The Biographical Society, 1904); "Francis S. Drake," *Dictionary of American Biography* (Boston: James R. Osgood, 1872); Francis B. Heitman, "Bankhead, James," *Historical Register and Dictionary of the United States Army,* vol. 1 (Washington, D.C.: Government Printing Office, 1903).

21. Alfred Hoyt Bill, *Rehearsal for Conflict: The War with Mexico, 1846–1848* (New York: Cooper Square, 1969), 218.

22. Eisenhower, *Agent of Destiny,* 239.

23. Smith, *War with Mexico,* 335n10, 222–23.

24. "Bankhead, James," *Twentieth Century Biographical Dictionary.*

25. Eisenhower, *Agent of Destiny,* 241–42.

26. Charles L. Dufour, *The Mexican War: A Compact History, 1846–1848* (New York: Hawthorn Books, 1968), 208.

27. N. C. Brooks, *A Complete History of the Mexican War: Its Causes, Conduct, and Consequences* (1849; repr., Chicago: Rio Grande Press, 1965), 306.

28. The Historical Society of Pennsylvania (hereafter HSP), Philadelphia. Clippings on Mexican War, vol. 3 of Mexican War Scrapbook, TK699, "Letter from J. H. Aulick, Captain to Com. M. C. Perry, commanding Home Squadron off Sacrificios," n.p., headline "Official Bombardment of Vera Cruz."

29. Johanssen, *Halls of the Montezumas,* 16, 4.

30. Ibid., 16, 52.

31. Paul H. Bergeron, *The Presidency of James K. Polk* (Lawrence: University Press of Kansas, 1987), 90.

32. *Complete History of the Late Mexican War by an Eye-Witness* (New York: F. J. Dow and Company, 1850), 95.

33. "John Bankhead Magruder," *Dictionary of American Biography* (Boston: James R. Osgood, 1872).

34. Aztec Club Web site, www.walika.com/aztec/bios/magruder.html. The Magruder photograph is also available on the Web site.

35. Ibid.

36. "John Bankhead Magruder," *Handbook of Texas Online*, Texas State Historical Association, www.tsha.utexas.edu/handbook/online (accessed April 2, 2001).

37. Fayette Robinson, *An Account of the Army of the United States with Biographies of Distinguished Officers of All Grades* (Philadelphia: Butler, 1848), 2:47.

38. Charles J. Peterson, *The Military Heroes of the War with Mexico with a Narrative of the War* (1852; repr., Philadelphia: Smith, 1859), 42.

39. HSP, Clippings on Mexican War, vol. 2, TK699, "Correspondent of the North American," n.p., headline "The Battle on the Rio Grande."

40. Fayette Robinson, *Mexico and Her Military Chieftains from the Revolution of Hidalgo to the Present Time* (Philadelphia: Butler, 1847), 318–20.

41. Ibid., 252.

42. John S. D. Eisenhower, *So Far from God: The U.S. War with Mexico, 1846–1848* (New York: Random House, 1989), 113, 115–16.

43. Thomas Ewing Cotner, *Military and Political Career of José Joaquín de Herrera, 1792–1854* (Austin: University of Texas Press, 1949), 301–11.

44. Brainerd Dyer, *Zachary Taylor* (Baton Rouge: Louisiana State University Press, 1946), 178–79.

45. Ibid., 179.

46. Matthews, "'Woman's Place,'" 291.

47. Ibid., 291.

CHAPTER 4: HISTORY IN THE MAKING

1. Select histories of the 1893 World's Columbian Exposition, or Chicago World's Fair, in a variety of disciplines include Neil Harris, ed., *Grand Illusions* (Chicago: Historical Society, 1993); Neil Harris, *Cultural Excursions* (Chicago: University of Chicago Press, 1990); Curtis Hinsley, "The World as Marketplace: Commodification of the Exotic at the World's Columbian Exposition, Chicago, 1893," in *Exhibiting Cultures: The Poetics and Politics of Museum Display*, ed. Ivan Karp and Steven D. Lavine (Washington, D.C.: Smithsonian Institution Press, 1991); Margaretta M. Lovell, "'A City for a Single Summer': Paintings of the World's Columbian Exhibition," *Art Bulletin* 78 (March 1996): 40–55; Karal Ann Marling, "Writing History with Artifacts," *Public Historian* 14 (Fall 1992): 13–30; Judy Sund, "Columbus and Columbia in Chicago, 1893: Man of Genius Meets Generic Woman," *Art Bulletin* 75 (September 1993): 443–66. For studies of the world's fair, or international exposition, phenomenon, see Paul Greenhalgh, *Ephemeral Vistas: The Expositions Universelles, Great Exhibitions, and World's Fairs, 1851–1939* (Manchester, Eng.: Manchester University Press, 1988), and Robert Rydell, *All the World's a Fair: Visions of Empire at American International Expositions, 1876–1916* (Chicago: University of Chicago Press, 1984). Studies of Chicago that cover the Columbian Exposition include William Cronan, *Nature's Metropolis: Chicago and the Great West* (New York: W. W. Norton, 1991), and Donald Miller, *City of the Century: The Epic of Chicago and the Making of America* (New York: Simon and Schuster, 1996).

2. According to Susan Stewart: "Within the development of culture under an exchange economy, the search for authentic experience and, correlatively, the search for the authentic object, becomes critical." See Stewart, *On Longing: Narratives of the Miniature, the Gigantic, the Souvenir, the Collection* (Baltimore: Johns Hopkins University Press, 1984), 133.

3. As part of material culture studies, Thomas Schlereth discusses the idea that "human activities—particularly the tasks of making and doing—can afford the researcher something like an 'encounter of the third kind,'" providing information missed by traditional history. He also discusses the value of the visual and tactile element of history. See Schlereth, *Material Culture: A Research Guide* (Lawrence: University Press of Kansas, 1985), 10, 12.

4. The public aspect includes the fact that an industry existed for producing blank scrapbooks and material designed for inclusion in scrapbooks. See Deborah Smith, "Consuming Passions: Scrapbooks and American Play," *Ephemera Journal* 6 (1993): 63–76, and Alistair Allen and Joan Hoverstadt, *The History of Printed Scraps* (London: New Cavendish Books, 1983). Further, at the Columbian Exposition, guidebooks, pamphlets, and publications exhibit elements of a scrapbook aesthetic, printing prefabricated images that imitate collages (see Gunther Collection Scrapbook, Chicago Historical Society). The private aspect relates to the fact that scrapbooks are often discussed as spaces for construction and formation of personal identity and memory. See Patricia P. Buckler and C. Kay Leeper, "Antebellum Woman's Scrapbook as Autobiographical Composition," *Journal of American Culture* 14, 1 (Spring 1991): 1–8; Patricia P. Buckler, "Poetry in a Woman's Scrapbook," *Prospects* 16 (1991): 149–69; Anne Higonnet, "Secluded Vision: Images of Feminine Experience in Nineteenth-Century Europe," *Radical History Review* 38 (1987): 16–36; Jessica Dallow, "Treasures of the Mind: Individuality and Authenticity in Late Nineteenth Century Scrapbooks" (master's thesis, University of North Carolina, 1995); Tamar Katriel and Thomas Farrell, "Scrapbooks as Cultural Texts: An American Art of Memory," *Text and Performance Quarterly* 11 (January 1991): 1–3; Smith, "Consuming Passions," 68.

5. The information on Raddin's life comes from the 1880 Census Records and her obituary in 1939. See "Raddin, Gertrude," Cook County, Ill., 297, Chicago E.D. 218, *Federal Population Schedule IL* (1880): Federal Census Index IL201168681; "Miss Gertrude Raddin," *Evanston Review*, August 17, 1939, 136–37.

6. Belle and Charles Raddin have a third, earlier scrapbook in the Northwestern University Archives, this one containing college material.

7. Dallow enhances Miles Orvell's characterization of Victorian aesthetics in scrapbooks by discussing the order that underlies this eclecticism. See Orvell, *The Real Thing: Imitation and Authenticity in American Culture, 1889–1940* (Chapel Hill: University of North Carolina Press, 1989), 48; cited and discussed in Dallow, "Treasures of the Mind," 36–37.

8. Smith cites various scrapbook instructional texts designed for children (Smith, "Consuming Passions," 68). Higonnet focuses on scrapbooks as expressions of femininity representative of the leisure-time amateur artistic activities of upper- and middle-class European women (Higonnet, "Secluded Vision," 18–19, 20). Raddin's scrapbook does not reflect such aesthetic training.

9. For a discussion of Columbian imagery and spectacle at the exposition, see Marling, "Writing History with Artifacts," 17–18. Judy Sund discusses representations of a heroic Columbus (Sund, "Columbus and Columbia in Chicago," 443–44, 452, 465).

10. Marling documents the popularity of the ship images in "Writing History with Artifacts," 17–18. The scrapbook presented to the Chicago Historical Society by Charles Harpel contains images of the boats and references to their landing, and the Gunther Collection scrapbook (also at the Chicago Historical Society) follows the arrival of the fleet that accompanied the Caravels. La Rabida is also included in Belle and Charles Raddin's scrapbook, Northwestern University Archives.

11. Marling, "Writing History with Artifacts," 17–18. William De Wit, "Building an Illusion: The Design of the World's Columbian Exposition," in Harris, *Grand Illusions*, 63–64, discusses the range of watercraft present and the emphasis on contrast between the primitive and modern to promote the theme of progress discussed later in this essay.

12. The most spectacular pageant was the local Chicago production *America*, which ran throughout the summer of 1893. Seven vignettes from this production were restaged at an invitation-only, high-society event held at the Women's Building and written up in local papers. These seven

scenes, as well as more contemporary, local historical scenes, were made into floats and paraded through the exposition at night (Marling, "Writing History with Artifacts," 28–29). Originally, Steele MacKaye was to produce *The World Finder*, expected to be the most spectacular pageant the United States had seen to date, but ran out of funds before completing the auditorium (ibid., 26–28). Statues of Columbus included *Columbian Fountain*, by Frederick MacMonnies; *Columbus Quadriga*, by Daniel Chester French and Edward C. Potter; and *Columbus*, by Mary T. Lawrence (a student of Saint-Gauden), which stood in front of the Administration Building and was a favorite of the crowds. Marling cites at least three monumental works by unnamed artists: a statue produced in silver by the Gorham Manufacturing Company, a bronze statue from France, and an iron one from a German manufacturing company (ibid., 21). Lovell, in "'City for a Single Summer,'" 40–55, discusses history as spectacle in relationship to paintings of the exposition; see also Marling, "Writing History with Artifacts," 29.

13. Guy Debord, *The Society of the Spectacle*, trans. Donald Nicholson-Smith (New York: Zone Books, 1994), 136–37.

14. For Debord, the quest for unity guides cultural production and drives the society of the spectacle (ibid., 130); on spectacle as preserving the status quo, see ibid., 132.

15. The practice of selling products using the exposition's themes was quite common, and the connection between the product and the illustration on the card was often ambiguous (Smith, "Consuming Passions," 65–66). Interestingly, Raddin does not include tickets in her scrapbook, although tickets were one of the most common elements of the other scrapbooks I studied. See the Gunther Collection Scrapbook, Chicago Historical Society; Mulligan Scrapbook, Chicago Historical Society; W. E. Longley Scrapbook, Chicago Historical Society; Belle Raddin Scrapbook I, Northwestern University Archives.

16. Stewart, *On Longing*, 133.

17. As Katriel and Farrell discuss, scrapbooks are social in that, although they are made by a private individual, they are generally intended to be shared and performed as a social practice (Katriel and Farrell, "Scrapbooks as Cultural Texts," 11–14).

18. Sund, "Columbus and Columbia in Chicago," 443. The Charles Harpel Scrapbook also contains poetic commentary on Columbus's standing (Chicago Historical Society). See Sund for a discussion of some critiques of Columbus's status at the time of the exposition (ibid.).

19. The final article, which shares a page with an article on adjusting to the exposition's conclusion, follows several blank pages, suggesting that this arrangement reflects an intentional and literal framing. It is as if Raddin determined from the start that the album would begin and end with these debates on Columbus, regardless of how much other material was available to fill the album.

20. Act of Congress, April 25, 1890; reprinted in *The Official Directory* (Chicago: W. B. Conkey, 1893), 64.

21. See, for example, Rydell, who argues that the exposition was structured and designed entirely around the theme of progress (Rydell, *All the World's a Fair*, 38–71); Alan Trachtenberg, who discusses the theme of progress as it relates to the exposition's layout and goals in Trachtenberg, *The Incorporation of America: Culture and Society in the Gilded Age* (New York: Hill and Wang, 1992), 208–20; and De Wit, who discusses the theme of progress in relation to history, representation, architecture, and design. He also specifically discusses Columbus in relationship to this theme (De Wit, "Building an Illusion," 61–62).

22. Miller cites the late-nineteenth-century notion that women were the "housewives of the city" of Chicago (Miller, *City of the Century*, 423, 425).

23. On the advertising cards' visual appeal, see Smith, "Consuming Passions," 66; Dallow, "Treasures of the Mind," 5. Smith also discusses advertising cards in scrapbooks as consumer education tools ("Consuming Passions," 70, 73).

24. Smith, "Consuming Passions," 66.

25. Stewart, *On Longing*, 146–48, 135.

26. Neil Harris argues that one U.S. reaction to cultural mingling between Japan and the United States was concern about the dangers of Japan's modernization, which reflected the anxiety

felt by Americans at the thought of a culture like Japan's losing its distinctiveness; see Harris, "All the World a Melting Pot? Japan at the American Fairs, 1876–1904," in Harris, *Cultural Excursions,* 29–55. Dallow discusses the way scraps played a role in soothing anxieties about a rapidly changing world ("Treasures of the Mind," 41).

27. See Sund for a discussion of images of Columbia and the ideal of purity and virginity she represented (Sund, "Columbus and Columbia in Chicago," 443–44).

28. Of course, Columbus never landed in what is now known as the United States of America or in Mexico; hence, this page represents drastic historical inaccuracy. The national identities of the people in the photographs are not specified, thus emphasizing their generic quality in comparison to the central image, replete with U.S. iconography. Given the presence of the Mexican flag and the images' similarity to later images displayed under the heading "Mexico," I will assume they are intended to represent Mexicans.

29. See Frank A. Cassell, "The Columbian Exposition of 1893 and United States Diplomacy in Latin America," *Mid-America* 67, 3 (1985): 13–30.

30. Stewart, *On Longing,* 152, 134–36, 150, 157.

31. Ibid., 138–39; on scrapbooks as spaces for constructing identity, see Higonnet, "Secluded Vision"; Katriel and Farrell, "Scrapbooks as Cultural Texts"; Buckler and Leeper, "Antebellum Woman's Scrapbook"; and Buckler, "Poetry in a Woman's Scrapbook."

32. Dallow, "Treasures of the Mind," 8–19.

33. Roger Shattuck, introduction to "Art of Assemblage: A Symposium (1961)," in *Essays on Assemblage,* ed. John Elder Field, *Studies in Modern Art* 2 (New York: Museum of Modern Art, 1992); Marjorie Perloff, "Poetics of Collage," in *Collage,* ed. Jeanine Parisier Plottel (New York: New York Literary Forum, 1983), 10. Katriel and Farrell discuss the importance of the collage both in Perloff's terms (ff. note 46) and in terms of the aesthetic pleasure derived from the process and the final product (Katriel and Farrell, "Scrapbooks as Cultural Texts," 10–11).

34. Dallow, "Treasures of the Mind," 35. Dallow also points to the collage heritage of scrapbooks (Dallow, "Treasures of the Mind," 26), citing Harriet Janis and Rudi Blesh, *Collage: Personality, Concepts, Technique* (Philadelphia: Chilton, 1962), 4.

35. W. E. Longley, Oak Park, Chicago Historical Society.

36. Donald Kuspit, "Collage: The Organizing Principle of Art in the Age of the Relativity of Art," in *Collage: Critical Views,* ed. Katherine Hoffman (Ann Arbor: UMI Research Press, 1989), 47.

37. See this approach to scrapbooks as space for constructing personal identity vis-à-vis the outside world in Buckler and Leeper, "Antebellum Woman's Scrapbook"; and Higonnet, "Secluded Vision."

38. Katriel and Farrell, "Scrapbooks as Cultural Texts," 8–9.

39. Dallow discusses secrecy as the power of scrapbooks (Dallow, "Treasures of the Mind," 18, 35).

40. The notion that history contains openable moments is discussed in Joel Fineman, "The History of the Anecdote," in *The New Historicism,* ed. H. Abam Veeser (New York: Routledge, 1989).

41. The scrap was clipped from the *Chicago Record,* but the date is not visible. The article goes on to discuss the exposure gained at the exposition as an opportunity to find solutions for problems plaguing societies—in this case, the United States' "great question," the future of African Americans. The author describes the successful emergence of the nation of Liberia and describes Liberia's interest in recruiting skilled African Americans for settlement there. Liberia is seen as offering better opportunities for African Americans and as a solution for racial unrest in the United States, clearly evident at the time of the exposition.

42. A copy of the image of the Senagalese woman is found loose in the album and includes the rest of the text: "This Sad-Eyed Cingalese Woman (late of Midway Plaisance) sighed for her children in the Spicy Isle. Now she is with them and Delights them all with Wonderous Stories of the Great World's Fair."

43. On the popularity of the Japanese, see Harris, "All the World a Melting Pot?" 29. Attendance statistics appeared in many of the scrapbooks I examined, including the Belle Raddin Scrapbook I and the Charles Harpel Scrapbook.

44. Dallow suggests that the scrapbook was particularly suited for the rapidly changing late nineteenth century in that it allowed people to process their "dis-ease" by organizing and domesticating symbols of the changing times (Dallow, "Treasures of the Mind," 36–37, 48).

45. Buckler and Leeper, "Antebellum Woman's Scrapbook," 1.

46. As a result of my study of eight scrapbooks, I have made the following observations. The items that appeared in virtually all the scrapbooks are tickets from Chicago Day (one of many theme days, this one dedicated to celebrating the host city) and photographic portraits of Bertha Palmer (often with a "signature" printed underneath). Other common items included images or articles on the Women's Building and select buildings from the Court of Honor, statistics listing the exposition's attendance records on theme days, images of the *Statue of the Republic*, and programs, photographs, or articles from the opening ceremonies.

47. The terms that Katriel and Farrell use to discuss scrapbooks include *saving, selecting, organizing*, and *sharing* (Katriel and Farrell, "Scrapbooks as Cultural Texts," 4–14).

48. Higonnet addresses a related issue when she makes an important distinction between the amateur production in women's albums and traditional high art, or "between contextual private objects and autonomous public ones" (Higonnet, "Secluded Vision," 33). She notes that scrapbooks and albums refer to the specific feminine, domestic culture and reflective sentiments of their makers for meaning, while paintings are meant, ideally, to be intellectually self-sufficient and autonomous. She points out that feminine imagery inevitably loses when measured against high-art standards. I would suggest, in contrast, that high art—history, in my argument—should stand up to the standards set by reading scrapbooks as history.

CHAPTER 5: SCRAPBOOK, WISH BOOK, PRAYER BOOK

Acknowledgment: Chapter 5 is a revised and expanded version of "Readers Read Advertising into Their Lives: The Trade Card Scrapbook," in Ellen Gruber Garvey, *The Adman in the Parlor: Magazines and the Gendering of Consumer Culture, 1880s to 1910s* (New York: Oxford University Press, 1996), 16–50.

1. Janet E. Ruutz-Rees, *Home Occupations* (New York: D. Appleton, 1883), 98.

2. See Ellen Gruber Garvey, *The Adman in the Parlor: Magazines and the Gendering of Consumer Culture, 1880s–1910s* (New York: Oxford University Press, 1996), for a discussion of the use of trade cards, advertising contests, and other methods of directing consumers' attention to advertising.

3. See Susan Strasser, *Satisfaction Guaranteed: The Making of the American Mass Market* (New York: Pantheon, 1989), for more on the switch to brand names and sale of brand-name staples. On trade cards as incentives to shopkeepers, see Robert Jay, *The Trade Card in Nineteenth-Century America* (Columbia: University of Missouri Press, 1987), 39–40.

4. "Novelties as Mediums," *Profitable Advertising and Art in Advertising* (September 1899): 248.

5. As Neil Harris notes in his perceptive analysis of color and media, the addition of color to a work "testif[ies] to the greater wealth, ambition, or taste of its subjects or purchasers." See Harris, "Color and Media: Some Comparisons and Speculations," in *Cultural Excursions: Marketing Appetites and Cultural Tastes in Modern America* (Chicago: University of Chicago Press, 1990), 320.

6. Trade catalog of A. F. Hunt and Company (n.d.), Rare Book Collection, Henry Francis du Pont Winterthur Museum Libraries, Wilmington, Del. The company, described in the catalog as "Fashionable Card Printers" of Newburyport, Mass., offers "Assorted packs of Proverbs and Psalms, 25 for 16c, 100 for 40c" (8).

7. Scrapbook (70x1.39), Collection 669, Thelma Mendsen Collection, Winterthur Museum.

8. Scrapbook (3365 70x1.14), Collection 669, Thelma Mendsen Collection, Winterthur Museum.

9. A hymn found in Methodist hymnals, now known as "Beautiful Flowers," with words by Mary Howitt and music by P. P. Bliss.

10. See T. J. Jackson Lears, *No Place of Grace: Antimodernism and the Transformation of American Culture, 1880–1920* (New York: Pantheon, 1981), and T. J. Jackson Lears, "From Salvation to Self-Realization: Advertising and the Therapeutic Roots of the Consumer Culture, 1880–1930," in *The Culture of Consumption: Critical Essays in American History, 1880–1980*, ed. Richard Wrightman Fox and T. J. Jackson Lears (New York: Pantheon, 1983).

11. "Shopping in Various Places Has Different Phases in Different Localities," *New York Times*, September 9, 1894; quoted in Elaine Abelson, *When Ladies Go A-Thieving: Middle-Class Shoplifters in the Victorian Department Store* (New York: Oxford University Press, 1989), 29.

12. See, for example, Ann Douglas, *The Feminization of American Culture* (New York: Knopf, 1977).

13. The work of Lucy Waterbury, later Lucy Waterbury Peabody, is documented in Louise Armstrong Cattan, *Lamps Are for Lighting: The Story of Helen Barrett Montgomery and Lucy Waterbury Peabody* (Grand Rapids, Mich.: Eerdmans, 1972).

14. The letter from Waterbury in *The Helping Hand* was first published by the Women's Baptist Foreign Missionary Society, 1882; the letters have also been reprinted in *Ephemera News* 9, 3 (Spring 1991): 10. The clipping has been preserved in a diary kept jointly by Norman and Lucy Waterbury, now in the Barbara Rusch Collection of Nineteenth Century Advertising and Manuscript Ephemera, Thornhill, Ontario; I am indebted to Barbara Rusch for supplying me with information about and photocopies of the diary.

15. Letter from Lucy Waterbury, ibid.

16. George J. Manson uses the term *missionary* to mean "drummer" in his "Ready for Business; or Choosing an Occupation: A Series of Practical Papers for Boys: A Commercial Traveler," in *St. Nicholas* (March 1887): 357, speculating that drummers are so called "because they come . . . from afar."

17. Women's Missionary Union Society of America for Heathen Lands, *Annual Report*, Wilmington, Del., 1886, auxiliary report, 26, 43, 19.

18. Ibid., 1887, 23.

19. Willa Cather, *My Ántonia* (1918; repr., New York: Signet, 1994), 88–89.

20. The term *salvage art* is Elaine Hedges's, from her article "The Nineteenth-Century Diarist and Her Quilts," in *American Quilts: A Handmade Legacy*, ed. L. Thomas Frye (Oakland, Calif.: Oakland Museum, 1981), 58. Hedges notes the similarity of quilt making and scrapbook compiling. In a more derogatory spirit, Janet Ruutz-Rees similarly compares scrapbooks and quilts: "The scrap-book proper is like a piece of patchwork, made up of odds and ends" (Ruutz-Rees, *Home Occupations*, 98).

21. Lydia Maria Child, *The American Frugal Housewife*, 16th ed. (1835), 3; quoted in Lynn Turner Oshins, *Quilt Collections: A Directory for the United States and Canada* (Washington, D.C.: Acropolis Books, 1987).

22. Mrs. S. D. Power, *Anna Maria's Housekeeping* (Boston: D. Lothrop, 1884).

23. Ruutz-Rees, *Home Occupations*, 96. For a discussion of clipping scrapbooks and their uses, see Ellen Gruber Garvey, "Scissorizing and Scrapbooks: Nineteenth-Century Reading, Remaking, and Recirculating," *New Media: 1740–1915*, ed. Lisa Gitelman and Geoff Pingree (Cambridge: MIT Press, 2003).

24. E. W. Gurley, *Scrap-books and How to Make Them: Containing Full Instructions for Making a Complete and Systematic Set of Useful Books* (New York: Authors' Publishing, 1880), 5–6.

25. Ibid., 52.

26. On Victorians as collectors and classifiers, see Simon J. Bronner, "Object Lessons: The Work of Ethnological Museums and Collections," in *Consuming Visions: Accumulation and Display of Goods in America, 1880–1920*, ed. Simon J. Bronner (New York and Winterthur, Del.: W. W. Norton and Winterthur Museum, 1989). On the development of museum displays of artifacts, see Jay Mechling, "The Collecting Self and American Youth Movements," in the same volume, for a discussion of the place of collecting in late-nineteenth-century U.S.

culture. Both Bronner and William Leach, "Strategists of Display and the Production of Desire," in the same volume, touch on the similar display strategies used by museums and department stores of the period.

27. Scrapbook (70x1.35), Collection 669, Thelma Mendsen collection, Winterthur Museum.

28. Chalmers Lowell Pancoast, *Trail Blazers of Advertising: Stories of the Romance and Adventure of the Old-Time Advertising Game* (New York: Frederick Hitchcock, Grafton Press, 1926), 53.

29. Ruutz-Rees, *Home Occupations*, 89. For more on the gendered differences in the importance accorded trade-card scrapbook making versus stamp collecting, see Steven M. Gelber, "Free Market Metaphor: The Historical Dynamics of Stamp Collecting," *Comparative Studies in Society and History* 43, 4 (October 1992): 742–69.

30. Abba Goold Woolson, *Women in American Society* (Boston: Roberts Brothers, 1873), 235; quoted in Abelson, *When Ladies Go A-Thieving,* 36.

31. Scrapbook (3365 70x1.6), Collection 669, Thelma Mendsen Collection, Winterthur Museum. Many of the cards in this book are from upstate New York.

32. Robert Sobieszek, "Composite Imagery and the Origins of Photomontage, Part I, The Naturalistic Strain," *Artforum* (October 1978): 58–65. See also Estera Milman, "Photomontage, the Event, and Historism," in *"Event" Art and Art Events*, ed. Stephen Foster (Ann Arbor: UMI Research Press, 1988).

33. Lina B. Beard and Adelia B. Beard, *The American Girls' Handy Book: How to Amuse Yourself and Others* (New York: Scribner's, 1887, 1898), 400–401, 395.

34. Ruutz-Rees, *Home Occupations,* 99.

35. Scrapbook in the collection of Jennifer Brody and Erness Brody, West Hartford, Conn. The book is dated April 22, 1900, four months after the death of "Grandpa."

36. Scrapbook (3365 70x1.11), Collection 669, Thelma Mendsen Collection, Winterthur Museum.

37. Gurley, *Scrap-books,* 56.

38. For a development of the idea of props as memory prompts, see Kimberly Rich, "A Victorian Woman's Material World: The Life and Legacy of Mary Cowgill Corbit Warner" (master's thesis, University of Delaware, 1989).

39. Rosalind Williams, *Dream Worlds: Mass Consumption in Late Nineteenth-Century France* (Berkeley: University of California Press, 1982), 71.

CHAPTER 6: SCRAPBOOK HOUSES
FOR PAPER DOLLS

1. I have examined seventeen intact examples of handmade houses, along with miscellaneous loose pages. In addition, I have looked at published images of about ten unrelated house pages and have examined seven examples of commercially produced "houses" for paper dolls, including three published copies of the handmade books. As the genre becomes better known, perhaps more examples will come to light and further insights may be forthcoming.

2. Flora Gill Jacobs, *A History of Doll Houses: Four Centuries of the Domestic World in Miniature* (New York: Charles Scribner's Sons, 1953), 220–24.

3. Rodris Roth, in "Scrapbook Houses: A Late Nineteenth Century Children's View of the American Home," paper presented at the Henry Francis du Pont Winterthur Museum conference on collecting, Wilmington, Del., October 31, 1992, stated that the scrapbook house seems to have been particularly prevalent in the eastern and mid-Atlantic states. I suspect that this may reflect the sample in the archives she visited rather than a true geographic distribution. Instructions appear in national magazines, and at least some examples are known from the Midwest. I believe this was a national phenomenon, much like the more general scrapbook craze.

4. Jessie E. Ringwalt, "Fun for the Fireside: A Help to Mothers—The Paper-doll's House," *Godey's Lady's Book* 20 (August 1880): 160–62. Regarding the earliest paper dollhouses, I have seen one with figures dressed in fashions of the 1860s; however, I believe these were

cut out of an already out-of-date magazine or catalog, because other furnishings suggest a slightly later date. A few extant books appear to have been made in the late 1870s, a date I base on the furnishing and fashions in the cutout images.

5. Karen Halttunen's *Confidence Men and Painted Women: A Study of Middle-Class Culture in America, 1830–1870* (New Haven, Conn.: Yale University Press, 1982), is one of the classic studies of this theatricality. Another study that focuses more specifically on the turn-of-the-century period is Jack W. McCullough, *Living Pictures on the New York Stage* (Ann Arbor: UMI Research Press, 1981). I have also addressed this subject at length in my book *Bazaars and Fair Ladies: The History of the American Fundraising Fair* (Knoxville: University of Tennessee Press, 1998), esp. 72–76, 164–165.

6. Ringwalt, "Fun for the Fireside," 160–62. I have also discussed the impact and significance of miniaturization in *Bazaars and Fair Ladies,* esp. 142.

7. Lynda Roscoe Hartigan, "The House That Collage Built," *American Art* 88 (Summer 1993): 88–91.

8. For a discussion of this visually dense aesthetic, see Clay Lancaster, *The Japanese Influence in America* (New York: Walton H. Rawls, 1963).

9. See Lucy Lippard, "What Is Female Imagery?" in *From the Center: Feminist Essays on Women's Art,* ed. Lucy Lippard et al. (New York: E. P. Dutton, 1976), 81–86.

10. Ringwalt, "Fun for the Fireside," 161. The layering effect in the Kenilworth Inn is designed to work in both directions; it is equally effective if one is moving through the book from back to front.

11. Lina Beard and Adelia Beard, *The American Girl's Handy Book: How to Amuse Yourself and Others* (New York: Charles Scribner's Sons, 1893), 396–97; Janet Ruutz-Rees, *Home Occupations* (New York: Appleton, 1883), 99.

12. Ringwalt, "Fun for the Fireside," 162; Carolyn Wells, "A Paper Doll's House," *The Puritan* 9, 5 (February 1901): 273–75, reprinted in her book *Pleasant Day Diversions* (New York: Moffat, Yard, 1909), 63–73; Mary White, *The Child's Rainy Day Book* (New York: Doubleday, Page, 1905), 11; Emily Hoffman, "Homes for Paper Dolls," *Harper's Bazar* 38, 1 (January 1904): 84–87; Marian Dudley Richards, "Fun with Paper Dolls," *Ladies' Home Journal* 19, 10 (September 1902): 41.

13. The Bennington maker wrote her name in the book, but it is unfortunately illegible; the book is in the Strong Museum collection. On taking books to friends' houses, see Maude Cushing Nash, *Children's Occupations* (Boston: Houghton Mifflin, 1920), 127.

14. White, *The Child's Rainy Day Book*, 13; Richards, "Fun with Paper Dolls," 41.

15. Harriet Brown's album, like Edith Washburn's, is in the Domestic Life Division, Smithsonian Institution, Washington, D.C.; it was donated by her granddaughter. Anita Blair's books are in the Chicago Historical Society; they are discussed in Barbara Chaney Ferguson, *The Paper Doll: A Collector's Guide with Prices* (Des Moines, Iowa: Wallace-Homestead, 1982), 54–55.

16. Both Hickey's and Grier's books are in the Strong Museum. The latter too was donated by her granddaughter, Katherine C. Grier, who provided the information about the relationship with Ross (personal correspondence, November 1998).

17. Richards, "Fun with Paper Dolls," 41.

18. Jacobs, *A History of Doll Houses,* 29.

19. Wells, "A Paper Doll's House," 273. Deborah A. Smith, in "Consuming Passions: Scrapbooks and American Play," *Ephemera Journal* 6 (1993): 70, says that a scrapbook was a "collector's ultimate achievement"; I believe that this was even more true for the scrapbook houses. (The Smith article was also published as Proceedings of the Ephemera Symposium III, "The American Play Ethic: Ephemera and Recreation," held by the American Antiquarian Society in Worcester, Mass., October 22–23, 1993.) Nash, *Children's Occupations,* 127.

20. Hoffman, "Homes for Paper Dolls," 84–85.

21. I noted wear on the examples I examined, and Rodris Roth included a similar observation in her "Scrapbook Houses" talk.

22. Ringwalt, "Fun for the Fireside," 162; Hoffman, "Homes for Paper Dolls," 85. Deborah Smith of the Strong Museum was responsible for dating the Ivory soap advertisement.

23. Hoffman, "Homes for Paper Dolls," 84, 86.

24. Richards, "Fun with Paper Dolls," 41. Tellingly, the house that belonged to Christine Grier had no commercial material at all; it was made completely of hand-drawn and hand-painted furniture and represented views of her actual home. Grier and Ross followed the model of the scrapbook house, but theirs was an even greater exercise in personal creation. Further supporting the idea that consumer training was not the focus of these books is the fact that Smith ("Consuming Passions," 70) also found few period writers who linked scrapbooks of any kind with this concern.

25. Roth's conclusion is taken from the abstract she wrote for the Winterthur conference.

26. Richards, "Fun with Paper Dolls," 41; Nash, *Children's Occupations,* 122; Hoffman, "Homes for Paper Dolls," 85.

27. Martha Craybill McClaugherty, "Household Art: Creating the Artistic Home, 1868–1893," *Winterthur Portfolio* 18, 1 (Spring 1983): 1–26; Charles Eastlake, *Hints on Household Taste in Furniture, Upholstery, and Other Details* (London: Longmans, Green, 1868; repr. Boston: J. R. Osgood, 1872). The Eastlake disciple was Mrs. M. E. Sherwood, cited in Russell Lynes, *The Tastemakers* (New York: Harper, 1954), 105.

28. Sources that discuss the role of women, taste, and aesthetic education include Lynes, *The Tastemakers;* Lancaster, *The Japanese Influence in America;* Claire Richter Sherman and Adele M. Holcomb, eds., *Women as Interpreters of the Visual Arts, 1820–1979* (Westport, Conn.: Greenwood Press, 1981); Kathleen D. McCarthy, *Women's Culture: American Philanthropy and Art, 1830–1930* (Chicago: University of Chicago Press, 1991); Frances Sawyer Sherman, "The Homely Significance of Aesthetics," program, General Federation of Women's Clubs Biennial Conference, Milwaukee, 1900; Simon J. Bronner, "Manner Books and Suburban Houses: The Structure of Tradition and Aesthetics," *Winterthur Portfolio* 8, 1 (Spring 1983): 61–68; Anthea Callen, *Women Artists of the Arts and Crafts Movement, 1870–1914* (New York: Pantheon, 1979); Eileen Boris, *Art and Labor: Ruskin, Morris, and the Craftsman Ideal in America* (Philadelphia: Temple University Press, 1986); Roger Stein et al., *In Pursuit of Beauty: Americans and the Aesthetic Movement* (New York: Metropolitan Museum of Art and Rizzoli, 1986).

29. Undated books of this sort have been found in the School of Human Ecology (formerly, School of Home Economics) at the University of Wisconsin–Madison.

30. Diane Waldman, *Collage, Assemblage, and the Found Object* (New York: Abrams, 1992), 10; Hartigan, "The House That Collage Built," 88–91; Harriet Janis, *Collage: Personalities, Concepts, Techniques* (Philadelphia: Chilton, 1967), 3.

31. Waldman, *Collage,* 17.

32. Edith Wharton with Ogden Codman Jr., *The Decoration of Houses* (New York: Scribner's, 1897); Alphonse Joseph Fritz, "The Use of the Arts of Decoration in Edith Wharton's Fiction: A Study of Her Interests in Architecture, Interior Decoration, and Gardening and the Language in Which She Exploited Them" (PhD diss., University of Wisconsin, 1956). Note that Wharton was concerned more with the house's interior shell—its architectural features—than with the kind of personal accouterments and artifactual details highlighted in the paper dollhouses. I see this as another argument for the primacy of aesthetic meaning in the scrapbook-house genre.

33. Smith, "Consuming Passions," 66–67.

34. Regarding the link between crepe paper and women, see Beverly Gordon, "'One of the Most Valuable Fabrics': The Seemingly Limitless Promise of Crepe Paper, 1890–1935," *Ars Textrina* 31 (1999): 107–44. Regarding the perceived relationship between women and wallpaper, see Jan Jennings, "Controlling Passion: The Turn-of-the Century Wallpaper Dilemma," *Winterthur Portfolio* 31, 4 (Winter 1996): 243–64. As Jennings points out, Charlotte Perkins Gilman made wallpaper a metaphor for female madness in her popular 1892 story "The Yellow Wall Paper," often reprinted.

35. Dens and smoking rooms were specifically mentioned in *Harper's Bazar* as masculine spaces; see Hoffman, "Homes for Paper Dolls," 85.

36. T. J. Jackson Lears, "Beyond Veblen: Rethinking Consumer Culture," in *Consuming Visions: Accumulation and Display of Goods in America, 1880–1920,* ed. Simon J. Bronner (New York: W. W. Norton, Winterthur Museum, 1989), 87–88. For further discussion of the house as women's space, see Gordon, *Bazaars and Fair Ladies,* 4–5, and Beverly Gordon, "Woman's Domestic Body: The Conceptual Conflation of Women and Interiors in the Industrial Age," *Winterthur Portfolio* 31, 4 (Winter 1996): 281–302.

37. Patricia P. Buckler and C. Kay Leeper, "An Antebellum Woman's Scrapbook as Autobiographical Composition," *Journal of American Culture* 14, 1 (Spring 1991): 4, quoting Dominic Ricciotti, "Popular Art in *Godey's Lady's Book*: An Image of the American Woman, 1830–1880," *Historical New Hampshire* 27 (Spring 1972); Gordon, *Bazaars and Fair Ladies,* esp. 5–6, 72–76.

38. Kenneth L. Ames, "When the Music Stops," in *Death in the Dining Room and Other Tales of Victorian Culture* (Philadelphia: Temple University Press, 1992), 150–84.

39. Ruutz-Rees, *Home Occupations,* 97.

40. The McLoughlin Brothers of New York patented a lithographed folding dollhouse in 1894, and Raphael Tuck, the famous manufacturer of colorful paper dolls, advertised a "Home Sweet Home for Dainty Dollies" in 1910. This was a sheet with twenty-two pieces of furniture that formed two rooms when properly set up. One of the McLoughlin houses is in the Strong Museum, 79.1340. Jacobs discusses a number of the preprinted houses (*A History of Doll Houses,* 225). They are also covered in Barbara Whitton Jendrick, *Paper Dollhouses and Paper Dollhouse Furniture* (Author, 1975); for example, Jendricks discusses Clara Andrews Williams, *The House That Glue Built* (New York: Frederick Stokes, 1905), 8. Related printed material for freestanding paper doll settings included one published in the *Boston Sunday Globe* supplement on April 26, 1896. Copyrighted by Armstrong and Company, it was entitled "At School" and included rows of children at desks, a blackboard, and a prominent globe. The same company had published an unnamed supplement with parlor furniture in the *Globe* on September 29, 1895. Three-dimensional folding vignettes seem to have been particularly popular in the 1930s. At that time newspapers sometimes included art supplements with paper furniture that would have been too large for the typical paper-dollhouse scrapbook.

41. Williams, *The House That Glue Built*; Edith A. Root, *A Paper Home for Paper People* (Akron, Ohio: Saalfield, 1909), 10–11. Other examples of the printed-book genre include Jane Eayre Fryer, *The Mary Frances Housekeeper: Adventures among the Doll People* (Philadelphia: John C. Winston, 1914), and Clara Andrews Williams, *Children's Store* (New York: Frederick Stokes, 1910). I have seen one book that folded into three-dimensional forms: *Dolly Blossom's Bungalow* (Chicago: Reilly and Britton, 1917). Root's comment implies that individuals who received other prepublished houses may also have personalized them by adding their own tiny accessories. (It is worth noting that Root populated her house with an idealized family consisting of a mother and a father, a boy and a girl, and a cat and a dog, served by a maid and a "mammy" figure, presumably the cook.)

42. Doris Davey "after Helen White," *My Dolly's Home* (London: Simpkin, Marshall, Hamilton, Kent and Company for the Arts and General Publishers, 1921), in the collection of the Strong Museum. I do not know what the phrase "after Helen White" implies, but it is possible that White made a scrapbook house that inspired Davey to publish the book. Although I have found no other English examples of scrapbook houses, I was not expressly looking for them and therefore cannot come to any conclusions about the prevalence of such houses in England.

43. I explore the subject of modernist attitudes toward aesthetic detail and sensual pleasure at length in my book *The Saturated World: Aesthetic Meaning, Intimate Objects, Women's Lives, 1890–1940* (Knoxville: University of Tennessee Press, 2006). I have also discussed it at several scholarly presentations, including "Aesthetic Excitement and Domesticated Amusements: Presenting a New Framework for Examining Everyday Activities," at the American Studies Association meeting in Montreal, October 1999.

44. One commentator likened the paper-dollhouse phenomenon to that of the model railroad. Ostensibly presented as a child's toy, these train sets are usually actually made by adult men, who use skills with engineering, electricity, and artistic presentation in their creation. The image of the grown man "playing" with the train set he ostensibly made for his son is so much a trope that it appears repeatedly in cartoons and other expressions of popular culture.

45. Among the authors who have built these arguments are Germaine Greer, *The Obstacle Race: The Fortunes of Women Painters and Their Work* (New York: Farrar, Strauss and Giroux, 1979), and Roszika Parker and Griselda Pollock, *Old Mistresses: Women, Art, and Ideology* (New York: Pantheon Books, 1981). I dealt with the subject at length in relation to ethnic art in Beverly Gordon, *American Indian Art: The Collecting Experience* (Madison, Wis.: Elvehjem Museum of Art, 1988).

CHAPTER 7: SOUVENIRS OF AMERIKA

1. The scrapbook is located in the Hannah Höch Archive in the Berlinische Galerie, Berlin [BG HHC G322/79]. A facsimile edition has been published by the Berlinsche Galerie in conjunction with the Hatje Cantz Verlag; see *Hannah Höch: Album,* ed. Gunda Luyken (Ostfildern-Ruit: Hatje Cantz, 2004). The pages in this facsimile are unnumbered. Parenthetical page numbers given in this essay refer to page numbers from a photocopy of photographs taken of the scrapbook by the Berlinsche Galerie and sent to me in 1994. Other page references are to reproductions in Maud Lavin, *Cut with the Kitchen Knife: The Weimar Photomontages of Hannah Höch* (New Haven, Conn.: Yale University Press, 1993).

2. Melissa A. Johnson, "'On the Strength of My Imagination': Visions of Weimar Culture in the Scrapbook of Hannah Höch" (PhD diss., Bryn Mawr College, 2001; Ann Arbor: UMI Press, 2001).

3. That the scrapbook was intended to be private is Lavin's assessment, and the archivists at the Berlinische Galerie and the editors of *Hannah Höch, Eine Lebenscollage*, part 2, concur. Ralf Burmeister and Eckhard Fürlus describe Höch's scrapbook as a "private archive book" ("privates Archivbuch"). See Lavin, *Cut with the Kitchen Knife,* 73; *Hannah Höch: Eine Lebenscollage*, vol. 2: 1921–45 (2 parts), ed. Ralf Burmeister and Eckhard Fürlus (Berlin: Berlinische Galerie, 1995), 506 (item no. 33.34). Yet for Höch to have published the scrapbook would not have been out of the ordinary. Many picture books were published in the 1920s and early 1930s on a wide variety of themes and subjects.

4. After 1915, Höch clipped images from these same magazines to use in her photomontages. After her death, overflowing files of images dating from the Weimar Republic to the 1970s were found in her studio (see Lavin, *Cut with the Kitchen Knife,* 221n11), only half of which were images from the magazines mentioned. Because some of the captions are in Dutch, English, or French, Höch must have also used magazines from the Netherlands, Great Britain or the United States, and France.

5. Johannes Molzahn, "Nicht mehr lesen! Sehen!" [No more reading! Seeing!], *Das Kunstblatt*, vol. 12 (Weimar: G. Kiepenheuer, 1928), 79–81; El Lissitzky, "Our Book," in *El Lissitzky: Life, Letters, Texts*, ed. Sophie Lissitzky-Küppers (Greenwich, Conn.: New York Graphic Society, 1968), 356–59.

6. Pierre Albert and Gilles Feyel, "Photography and the Media. Changes in the Illustrated Press," in *A New History of Photography*, ed. Michel Frizot (Köln: Könemann, 1998), 599.

7. Jan Tschichold, "Photography and Typography," in *Photography in the Modern Era: European Documents and Critical Writings, 1913–1940,* ed. Christopher Phillips (New York: Metropolitan Museum of Art, Aperture, 1989), 122.

8. Hannah Höch to Grete König, January 27, 1928, correspondence in the collection of Grete König, Murnau, Germany, transcribed and cited by Lavin, *Cut with the Kitchen Knife,* 94.

9. I discuss this grammar of juxtaposition of montage elements at length in "'Strength of My Imagination'"). Briefly, it is a grammar of montage that functions as a descriptive and meth-

odological tool and takes into account the nonlinear and associative narrative aspects of Höch's scrapbook. This grammar helps illustrate four formal, thematic, and conceptual strategies of space, hybridization, scale, and exposure. For an illustration of Höch's *Schnitt mit dem Küchenmesser*, see Peter Boswell and Maria Makela, *The Photomontages of Hannah Höch* (Minneapolis: Walker Art Center, 1996), 25, pl. 1.

10. Siegfried Kracauer, "Travel and Dance" and "The Little Shopgirls Go to the Movies," in *The Mass Ornament: Weimar Essays*, ed. Thomas Levin (Cambridge: Harvard University Press, 1995), 65–73 and 291–304.

11. Susan Pearce, *Museums, Objects, and Collections: A Cultural Study* (Washington, D.C.: Smithsonian Institution Press, 1993), 37.

12. Mieke Bal, "Telling Objects: A Narrative Perspective on Collecting," in *The Cultures of Collecting*, ed. John Elsner and Roger Cardinal (Cambridge: Harvard University Press, 1994), 104–5; Susan Stewart, *On Longing: Narratives of the Miniature, the Gigantic, the Souvenir, the Collection* (Durham, N.C.: Duke University Press, 1993). See especially chap. 5, "Objects of Desire," Part 1, "The Souvenir," and Part 2, "The Collection, Paradise of Consumption," 132–69.

13. Stewart, *On Longing*, 151.

14. I do not wish to claim that my work on the scrapbook is a means of maintaining a connection between Höch and the scrapbook and thus maintaining the scrapbook as souvenir. Any interpretation that I assign to the scrapbook moves the scrapbook to the status of collection.

15. Siegfried Kracauer, "The Mass Ornament," in Levin, *The Mass Ornament*, 75–86, and "Girls and Crisis," in *The Weimar Republic Sourcebook*, ed. Anton Kaes, Martin Jay, and Edward Dimendberg (Berkeley: University of California Press, 1994), 565–66. For a history of the Tiller Girls, see Peter Jelavich, *Berlin Cabaret* (Cambridge: Harvard University Press, 1993), 175–86. See Kracauer, "Girls and Crisis," 565, for one characteristic description of the revue dancers.

16. Jelavich, *Berlin Cabaret*, 175.

17. Ibid., 176

18. Kracauer, "The Mass Ornament," 75, and "Girls and Crisis," 565–66; Fritz Giese, *Girlkultur: Vergleich zwischen amerikanischen und europäischen Rhythmus und Lebensgefühl* [Girl culture: A comparison between American and European rhythm and feeling for life] (1925), quoted in Detlev Peukert, *The Weimar Republic: The Crisis of Classical Modernity*, trans. Richard Deveson (New York: Hill and Wang, 1992), 179.

19. For a full account of the phenomenon of Amerikanismus, see Mary Nolan, "Imagining America, Modernizing Germany," and Beeke Sell Tower, "'Ultramodern and Ultraprimitive': Shifting Meanings in the Imagery of Americanism in the Art of Weimar Germany," in *Dancing on the Volcano: Essays on the Culture of the Weimar Republic*, ed. Thomas W. Kniesche and Stephen Brockmann (Columbia, S.C.: Camden House, 1994), 71–84 and 85–104; Mary Nolan, *Visions of Modernity: American Business and the Modernization of Germany* (New York: Oxford University Press, 1994); Jeffrey Herf, *Reactionary Modernism: Technology, Culture, and Politics in Weimar and the Third Reich* (Cambridge: Cambridge University Press, 1984); Peukert, *The Weimar Republic*, esp. chap. 9, "Americanism versus *Kulturkritik*," 178–80.

20. Herf, *Reactionary Modernism*, 42.

21. Nolan, "Imagining America, Modernizing Germany," 74.

22. This list is cited by Anton Kaes in "Brecht und der Amerikanismus im Theater der 20er Jahre: Unliterarische Tradition und Publikumsbezug" [Brecht and amerikanismus in 1920s theater: Nonliterary tradition and public reception], *Sprache im technische Zeitalter* 56 (October–December 1975), 371. Kaes cites it from the Bertolt Brecht Archives, Stiftung der Akademie der Künste Berlin-Brandenburg, Berlin, BBA 450/50, 51.

23. Rudolf Kayser, "Americanism," first published as "Amerikanismus," *Vossische Zeitung* 458 (September 27, 1925); reprinted in Kaes, Jay, and Dimendberg, *The Weimar Republic Sourcebook*, 395.

24. Ibid., 395, 396, 397.
25. Peukert, *The Weimar Republic,* 60–61.
26. Anton Kaes refers to the German avant-garde's use of U.S. mass culture as a means to sub-vert traditional conceptions of culture. He speaks specifically of the Berlin avant-garde's use of U.S. mass culture as a "substitute revolution" after the failure of the German revolution of 1919. See Kaes, "Mass Culture and Modernity: Notes toward a Social History of Early American and German Cinema," *America and the Germans: An Assessment of a Three-Hun-dred Year History,* vol. 2, *The Relationship in the Twentieth Century* (Philadelphia: Univer-sity of Pennsylvania Press, 1985), 317–31, esp. 323–26.
27. Beth Irwin Lewis, *George Grosz: Art and Politics in the Weimar Republic* (Princeton, N.J.: Princeton University Press, 1991), 6.
28. Kaes, "Mass Culture and Modernity," 323.
29. For a full analysis of Höch's photomontage *Schnitt mit dem Küchenmesser* [Cut with the kitchen knife], see Gertrud Jula Dech, *Schnitt mit dem Küchenmesser DADA durch die letzte weimarer Bierbauchkulturepoche Deutschlands: Untersuchungen zur Fotomontage bei Hannah Höch* [Cut with the kitchen knife DADA through the last Weimar beer-belly cultural epoch of Germany: Investigations on the photomontage by Hannah Höch] (Münster: Lit Verlag, 1981), and *Schnitt mit dem Küchenmesser dada durch die letzte weimarer Bierbauchkulturepoche Deutschlands* [Cut with the kitchen knife DADA through the last Weimar beer-belly cultural epoch of Germany], Kunststück Series, ed. Klaus Herding (Frankfurt am Main: Fischer Taschenbuch Verlag GmbH, 1989). Many other Höch scholars have subsequently addressed this photomontage as well; Dech's was the first to examine it in detail. For an account of Höch's use of machine imagery in her photomontages, see Maria Makela, "The Misogynist Machine: Images of Technology in the Work of Hannah Höch," in *Women in the Metropolis: Gender and Modernity in Weimar Cul-ture,* ed. Katharina von Ankum (Berkeley: University of California Press, 1997), 106–27.
30. For an illustration of *Und wenn du denkst der Mond geht unter* [And if you think the moon is setting], see Boswell and Makela, *The Photomontages of Hannah Höch,* 40, pl. 16.
31. For an illustration of *Equilibre,* see ibid., 88, pl. 34. Höch referred to the name change in a notebook in which she documented the location of artworks and objects in her estate. In the entry dated May 2, 1962, Höch indicates that during the World War II she changed the title from *Amerika balanciert die Europa* [America balances Europe] to *Equilibre.* My thanks to Maria Makela for providing me with this citation.
32. The caption reads: "Raquel Meller, der Star der Palace Revue, Paris, für die 'Violetten' geschrieben wurde" [Raquel Mellor, the star of the Palace Revue, Paris, written for the "Vio-letten"]; see *Der Querschnitt* 6 (Summer 1925): opp. 512. For an illustration of this page layout in the scrapbook, see Lavin, *Cut with the Kitchen Knife,* 82.
33. Kracauer, "The Mass Ornament," 76.
34. Source unknown; the scrapbook caption reads: "Die Tänzerin als Girltruppe: Senta Born in einem neuartigen Schattentanz in der neuen Nelson-Revue. Idee und Aufnahme: Stone" [The dancer as girl troupe: Senta Born in a new type of shadow dance].
35. Alfred Polgar, quoted by Erhard Schütz, *Romane der Weimarer Republik* (Munich: W. Fink, 1986); cited by Peukert, *The Weimar Republic,* 180; Kracauer, "The Mass Ornament," 75–76.
36. For an illustration of this scrapbook page layout, see Lavin, *Cut with the Kitchen Knife,* 78.
37. Tower discusses this at length in her essay "Ultramodern and Ultraprimitive," 85–104.
38. *Berliner Illustrirte Zeitung* 35, 22 (May 29, 1926): 676. The caption reads: "Interessante Sprungbilder aus dem neuen Film 'Wege zu Kraft und Schönheit, II Teil.' Verschiedene Zeitlupen-Bildchen einer bestimmten Bewegung, die hier in Bergrößerungen aneinanderg-ereigt sind" [Interesting picture of a jump from the new film "Ways to strength and beauty, part II." Various time-lapse pictures of a specific movement which are here enlarged and placed one after the other]. For a reproduction of this scrapbook page, see Lavin, *Cut with the Kitchen Knife,* 83.
39. Hannah Höch and Wolfgang Pehnt, "Interview des Deutschlandfunks mit Wolfgang Pehnt aus der Reihe: Jene Zwanziger Jahre: ein Gespräch mit Hannah Höch" [German Radio

interview with Wolfgang Pehnt from the series Those 1920s: a conversation with Hannah Höch], March 4, 1973; unpublished manuscript of a radio interview, Höch Archives, Berlinische Gallerie, BG/HHC H108/79, 15–16.

40. Eva Noack-Mosse, "Uhu," *Hundert Jahre Ullstein* [A century of Ullstein] (Berlin: Ullstein Verlag, 1977), 181.

41. Lynda J. King, *Bestsellers by Design: Vicki Baum and the House of Ullstein* (Detroit: Wayne State University Press, 1988), 85. In 1927 Ullstein broke its publications down into categories: daily newspapers (*Tageszeitungen*), including *Berliner Morgenpost, Vossische Zeitung, Berliner Allgemeine Zeitung,* and *B. Z. am Mittag;* weekly newspapers (*Wochenzeitungen*), including *Berliner Montagspost, Die Grüne Post, Wohnungs-Tausche-Anzeiger,* and *Die Post aus Deutschland;* traditional magazines (*Zeitschriften*), including *Berliner Illustrirte Zeitung, Blatt der Hausfrau, Die Dame, Zeitbilder;* and the new U.S. magazines, including *Uhu, Die Koralle,* and *Der Querschnitt.* See *50 Jahre Ullstein: 1977–1927* (Berlin: Ullstein Verlag, 1927), 304.

42. Georg Bernhard, "Die deutsche Presse," in *Der Verlag Ullstein: Zum Welt Reklame Kongress Berlin 1929* [The Publishing House Ullstein: To the World Advertising Congress, Berlin 1929] (Berlin: Ullstein Verlag, 1929), 77; Noack-Mosse, "Uhu," 181. *American Magazine* (New York: Colver) was published from 1906 to 1956.

43. Noack-Mosse, "Uhu," 181.

44. "200 Worte Deutsch, die Sie vor zehn Jahren noch nicht kannten" [200 German words that were not known ten years ago], *Uhu* 10 (July 1930); reprinted in Christian Ferber, *Uhu: Das Monats-Magazin* [Uhu: The monthly magazine] (Berlin: Ullstein Verlag, 1979), 231.

45. "Die Wohnstätte von 8 Millionen Menschen: Eine erstaunliche Flugzeug-Aufnahme von New York aus 5000 Meter höhe" [The home of 8 million people: An astonishing aerial photograph of New York from 5000 meters high], *Berliner Illustrirte Zeitung* 40 (October 6, 1929): 40. For a reproduction of this scrapbook page, see Lavin, *Cut with the Kitchen Knife,* 70.

46. "Eine der gewaltigen Feigen-Pflanzungen in Kalifornien, vom Flugzeug aus gesehen" [One of the enormous fig fields in California, seen from an airplane], *Berliner Illustrirte Zeitung* 15 (December 14, 1924): 1477.

47. "Aus der Lande der unbegrenztem Möglichkeiten: Bretterstapel von 25 Meter Höhe in Amerika" [From the country of unbounded possibilities: lumber pile 25 meters high in America], *Berliner Illustrirte Zeitung* 38 (September 18, 1921): 578.

48. "Interessante Flieger-Aufnahmen aus den Vereinigten Staaten: Verlassenes Goldland in Kalifornien. Ein Stück Land am Yuba-Fluß, das von Goldsuchern so umgegraben worden ist, daß es aus der Luft wie eine phantastische Mondlandschaft aussieht" [Interesting aerial photographs of the United States: abandoned gold country in California: a piece of land on the Yuba River so dug up by gold-seekers that from the air it looks like a fantastic moonscape], *Berliner Illustrirte Zeitung* 27 (September 14, 1924): 1061.

49. The sources of these two images are unknown. The captions in the scrapbook read: "Das größte Naturtheater der Welt: Flugzeugaufnahme des gewaltigen Freilich theaters bei Hollywood in Kalifornien. Presse-Pho . . ." [The largest outdoor theater in the world: aerial view of the enormous open-air theater in Hollywood in California. Press-Pho . . .] and "Wo die New-Yorker Schlittschuh laufen: Eisbahn an der 5. Avenue auf dem Centralpark-See" [Where New Yorkers ice skate: ice rink on Central Park Lake on 5th Avenue].

50. "Der Straße entrissen: New-Yorker Straßenkinder auf dem Dachgarten einer Somerschule" [Plucked from the streets: New York street children on the roof garden of their summer school], *Uhu* 11 (August 1929): 15.

51. Thomas J. Saunders, *Hollywood in Berlin: American Cinema and Weimar Germany* (Berkeley: University of California Press, 1994), 1.

52. Ibid., 11.

53. "Amerika-dämmerung. Das begeisterte Europa beginnt die Kehrseit Amerikas zu betrachten" [The twilight of America. Enthusiastic Europe begins to see the wrong side of America], *Uhu*

3 (December 1929): 79. The caption reads: "Das Porträt der amerikanischen Bäuerin, wie sie nicht in Filmen gezeigt wird: Diese Bäuerin aus dem Staate Tennessee hat . . . gelegentlich erfahren, daß vor zehn Jahren ein Weltkrieg stattgefunden hat. Sie kann weder lesen noch schreiben." [Portrait of an American woman farmer who has never been seen in films: This woman, from the state of Tennessee, accidentally learned that ten years earlier there had been a world war. She can neither read nor write.]

54. In a review essay dealing with visual culture, Johanna Drucker clearly articulates the difficulty art historians have had in understanding this relationship; see "Who's Afraid of Visual Culture?" *Art Journal* (Winter 1999): 37.

CHAPTER 8: THE SECRET SCRAPBOOK OF A "SOILED DOVE"

1. The term "soiled dove" is a euphemism for "prostitute." The American Heritage Center is an archival manuscript repository that houses the University of Wyoming archives, more than seven thousand manuscript collections, the fifty-thousand-volume Toppan Rare Book Library, and extensive collections of photographs and maps.
2. University of Wyoming Libraries Accession Log, September 21, 1938.
3. N.d., Early Accession Log, Albany County Historical Society, Laramie Plains Museum, American Heritage Center. The Laramie Woman's Club founded the museum and gathered the items that were later donated to the University of Wyoming.
4. Mary Read Rogers, ed., *Our Heritage: The Wyoming Federation of Women's Clubs* (Cheyenne, Wyo.: Pioneer Printing and Publishing, 1976), 280.
5. News clipping, n.p., n.d., Laramie Woman's Club Collection, American Heritage Center.
6. The date of publication of the notice is not provided, but the clerk of court's order to publish, given in the text, is dated December 29, 1877.
7. Art. 1, Sec. 1–6, and Art. 2, Sec. 1–2, Charter and Ordinances of the City of Laramie of Wyoming Territory, 1887; *Laramie Daily Boomerang,* May 20, 1896.
8. Wyoming Territorial Census for 1880 (Cheyenne: Wyoming State Archives and Historical Department [hereinafter WSAHD]).
9. Specifications and Contract, L. W. Schroeder to Dolly Bailey, October 18, 1880, Probate File 59, WSAHD.
10. Certificate of Marriage, John A. Grover to Christy Finlayson, September 17, 1881, Probate File 59, WSAHD.
11. Policies from the Home Insurance Company of New York, an inventory of the contents of Christy Grover's houses, and account records from Trabing's Grocery, A. Helfferich, Jeweler, and J. Kellner Dry Goods may be found in Probate File 59, WSAHD.
12. Grover-Lambert marriage announcement, October 2, 1883, Monte Grover Scrapbook, 12.
13. Coroner's Inquest, February 20, 1882, WSAHD.
14. Ibid.
15. Probate File 59, WSAHD.
16. Probate File 544, WSAHD.
17. Grover-Lambert marriage announcement.
18. Patricia P. Buckler and C. Kay Leeper, "An Antebellum Woman's Scrapbook as Autobiographical Composition," *Journal of American Culture* 14 (Spring 1991): 1.
19. Patricia P. Buckler, "A Silent Woman Speaks: The Poetry in a Woman's Scrapbook of the 1840s," *Prospects* 16 (1991): 149–54.
20. Anne M. Butler, *Daughters of Joy, Sisters of Misery: Prostitution in the American West, 1865–90* (Chicago: University of Illinois Press, 1985), 27–28.
21. Suzanne L. Bunkers, "'Faithful Friend': Nineteenth-Century Midwestern American Women's Unpublished Diaries," *Women's Studies International Forum* 10 (1987): 14; Buckler and Leeper, "An Antebellum Woman's Scrapbook," 2.

22. Laramie City Council Minutes, November 5, 1895; Gladys B. Beery, *The Front Streets of Laramie City* (Laramie: Albany County Seniors, 1990).
23. Laramie City Council Minutes, July 21, 1891, and September 5, 1893.
24. Ibid., May 6, 1890.
25. Ibid., April 30, 1895.
26. Ibid., November 5, 1895; Beery, *Front Streets of Laramie City*, 145.
27. Ibid., November 5, 1895.
28. Ibid.
29. Probate File 560, April 18, 1914, WSAHD.
30. *Laramie Daily Boomerang,* April 22, 1912.

CHAPTER 9: INVITING NARRATIVES

1. The Willa Cather Pioneer Memorial and Educational Foundation's archive contains letters, photographs, newspapers published during Cather's lifetime, and miscellaneous Cather family items, including several scrapbooks. Among the scrapbooks is one made by Cather, which was given to Bernice Slote, the founder of the foundation, by Helen Cather Southwick, Cather's niece.
2. For a detailed explanation of the Cather family's way of dealing with tuberculosis and other motivations for moving west, see Susan J. Rosowski, *Birthing a Nation: Gender, Creativity, and the West in American Literature* (Lincoln: University of Nebraska Press, 1999), especially the chapter "The Long Foreground to Cather's West."
3. For a complete biography of Cather, see James Woodress, *Willa Cather: A Literary Life* (Lincoln: University of Nebraska Press, 1987).
4. Ibid., 55–56.
5. Cather's use of male narrators has been the subject of much speculation. Sharon O'Brien's *Willa Cather: The Emerging Voice* (New York: Oxford University Press, 1987) and subsequent publications argue for an interpretation of lesbianism. However, Joan Acocella in *Willa Cather and the Politics of Criticism* (Lincoln: University of Nebraska Press, 2000) contends that in advancing political agendas, critics distort Cather's work, which is inspired not by a political program but by a tragic vision of life's complexities.
6. Deborah A. Smith, "Consuming Passions: Scrapbooks and American Play," *Ephemera Journal* 6 (1993): 63.
7. Little is known about the actual creation of Cather's scrapbook. The opening poem is not dated, and there is no other handwritten indication of date inside. Given the copyright dates on some of the advertising cards in the scrapbook and Cather's use of her nickname, Willy, it seems likely that she compiled the scrapbook between 1883, when she arrived in Nebraska at the age of nine, and 1890, when she left Red Cloud to attend the university in Lincoln at the age of seventeen.
8. In *O Pioneers!* Cather demonstrates her knowledge of horticulture by making more than eighty references to specific flowers and plants. Cynthia Briggs argues that Cather uses the "language of flowers," a Victorian code of meaning for specific plants, to create "a unified structure that works as an underground river of imagery and symbol that surfaces systematically to emphasize theme, then retreats to function as an underlying current that connects theme as it moves the novel to resolution." See Briggs, "The Language of Flowers," *Willa Cather Pioneer Memorial Newsletter* 30 (1986): 3, 29–33. Cather was fascinated by all kinds of plants and flowers and tried to learn as much about them as she could.
9. Willa Cather, *My Ántonia,* ed. Charles Mignon with Kari Ronning, with a historical essay and explanatory notes by James Woodress (Lincoln: University of Nebraska Press, 1994), 325.
10. Robert Jay, *The Trade Card in Nineteenth-Century America* (Columbia: University of Missouri Press, 1987), 3; Smith, "Consuming Passions," 65.
11. Sarah Stage, *Female Complaints: Lydia Pinkham and the Business of Women's Medicine* (New York: W. W. Norton, 1979), 27.

12. Barbara Welter, *Dimity Convictions: The American Woman in the Nineteenth Century* (Athens: Ohio University Press, 1976), 32.

13. Ibid., 57.

14. Woodress, *Willa Cather*, 52.

15. Lina and Adelia Beard, *The American Girls' Handy Book: How to Amuse Yourself and Others* (New York: Scribner, 1889), 396–97.

16. Welter, *Dimity Convictions*, 35.

17. Smith, "Consuming Passions," 66.

18. Jay, *Trade Card in Nineteenth-Century America*, 75.

19. Eric Foner and John A. Garraty, eds., *The Readers' Companion to American History* (Boston: Houghton Mifflin, 1991); History Channel, www.historychannel.com/perl/print_book .pl?ID=35211 (accessed November 15, 2000).

20. Cather, *My Ántonia*, 78. Scrapbooks made as substitute picture books for young children served a training function, according to Garvey's essay in this volume, and could be used to influence a child's interests.

21. Ibid., 7–8.

22. James E. Miller Jr., "My Ántonia: A Frontier Drama of Time," *American Quarterly* 10 (1958): 476–84.

23. Cather, *My Ántonia*, 80.

24. Ibid., ix.

25. Ibid., xi–xiii.

26. Rosowski, *Birthing a Nation*, 90–91.

27. Woodress, *Willa Cather*, 290.

28. Cather, *My Ántonia*, xiii; Rosowski, "Romanticism," in *Approaches to Teaching Cather's My Ántonia*, ed. Susan Rosowski (New York: Modern Language Association, 1989), 65.

29. Susan L. Roberson, ed., *Women, America, and Movement* (Columbia: University of Missouri Press, 1998), 4–5.

30. Terence Martin, "The Drama of Memory in *My Ántonia*," *PMLA* 84 (1969): 304–11; Cather, *My Ántonia*, 312.

31. Kate McCullough, *Regions of Identity: The Construction of America in Women's Fiction, 1885–1914* (Stanford, Calif.: Stanford University Press, 1999), 2.

32. Cather, *My Ántonia*, 338, 339.

33. Rosowski, *Birthing a Nation*, 92.

CHAPTER 10: IN THE HANDS OF CHILDREN

1. Maude Cushing Nash, *Children's Occupations* (Boston: Houghton Mifflin, 1920), 124–25. And see Lydia Maria Child, *The American Frugal Housewife* (New York: S. and W. Wood, 1832), 1; Catharine Beecher and Harriet Beecher Stowe, *The American Woman's Home*, ed. Joseph Van Why (Hartford, Conn.: Stowe-Day Foundation, 1975), 220–32.

2. Anne Lundin, introduction to *Defining Print Culture for Youth: The Cultural Work of Children's Literature*, ed. Anne Lundin and Wayne A. Wiegand (Westport, Conn.: Libraries Unlimited, 2003), xi.

3. André Béguin, *Polymetal, Printmaking Equipment: A Technical Dictionary of Print Making* www.polymetaal.nl/beguin/mapc/chromolithography.htm (accessed August 10, 2004). See also Iris Snyder, *Color Printing in the Nineteenth Century: An Exhibition at the University of Delaware Library* (Newark: University of Delaware Library, 1996).

4. Peter Marzio, *The Democratic Art: Pictures for a Nineteenth Century America, Chromolithography, 1840–1900* (Boston: David R. Godine, 1979), xi.

5. Maurice Rickards, *The Encyclopedia of Ephemera: A Guide to the Fragmentary Documents of Everyday Life for the Collector, Curator, and Historian* (New York: Routledge, 2000), 284; Malcolm Warrington, "The Scrap Album," www.scrapalbum.com/pat1.htm (accessed August 10, 2004). For more information see James Mackay, *Childhood Antiques*

(New York: Taplinger, 1976. Scraps were also called Oblaten or Glanzbilder (wafers or gloss pictures).

6. The size of the first scraps were perhaps designed to imitate that of the woodblock print, used to pass on oral traditions and Christian stories before the printed word. See Evelyn Lincoln, *Invention of the Italian Renaissance Printmaker* (New Haven: Yale University Press, 2000), 69–85; *Paper before Print: The History and Impact of Paper in the Islamic World* (New Haven: Yale University Press, 2001), 209–23. Among the first scraps (1800) were those Rudolph Ackermann produced in large sheets, to be cut. See Rickards, *Encyclopedia of Ephemera*, 284–85. Many of the world's scrap experts and enthusiasts reside in the United Kingdom. An exhibit of children's scraps was held at the Museum of Childhood, Edinburgh, in 2003.

7. Warrington, *Scrap Album.*

8. Mary Margaret Sittig, *L. Prang & Company, Fine Arts Publishers* (master's thesis, George Washington University, 1970), 145. See also Larry Freeman, *Louis Prang: Color Lithographer, Giant of a Man* (Watkins Glen, N.Y.: Century House, 1971).

9. Marzio, *Democratic Art*, 99.

10. Katharine Morrison McClinton, *The Chromolithographs of Louis Prang* (New York: Clarkson N. Potter, 1973), 74.

11. Alistair Allen and Joan Hoverstadt, *The History of Printed Scraps* (London: New Cavendish Books, 1983), 149.

12. Ellis A. Davidson, *The Happy Nursery: A Book for Mothers, Governesses and Nurses Containing Games, Amusements, and Employments for Boys and Girls* (London: Cassell, Petter, and Balpin, 1872), 65. See also George Miller and Dorothy Miller, *Picture Postcards in the United States, 1893–1918* (New York: Clarkson N. Potter, 1976).

13. Miller and Miller, *Picture Postcards*, 2.

14. Allen and Hoverstadt, *History of Printed Scraps*, 11.

15. Ibid., 25–32.

16. McClinton, *Chromolithographs of Louis Prang*, 74.

17. Allen and Hoverstadt, *History of Printed Scraps*, 25.

18. James C. Jackson, *Training of Children, or, How to Have Them Healthy, Handsome and Happy* (Dansville, N.Y.: Austin, Jackson, 1872), 74.

19. Lydia Maria Child, *The Little Girl's Own Book* (New York: Edward Kearney, 1843), iii –iv.

20. For more on these cards, see Patricia Fern and Alfred P. Malpa, *Rewards of Merit: Tokens of a Child's Progress and a Teacher's Esteem as an Enduring Aspect of American Religious and Secular Education* (Schoharie, N.Y.: Ephemera Society of America, 1994).

21. All the images in this chapter are from the Marguerite Archer Collection of Historic Children's Materials, Archives/Special Collections Department, J. Paul Leonard Library, San Francisco State University, San Francisco, California.

22. Besides being housed in the Marguerite Archer Collection of Historic Children's Materials, the scrapbook is also available on microfilm in the Bancroft Library, University of California, Berkeley. This and other scrapbooks are cited in the finding aid *Japanese American Evacuation and Resettlement Records, 1930–1974* (reel no. 379). The scrapbook is also described in Vincent Tajiri, ed., *Through Innocent Eyes: Writings and Art from the Japanese American Internment* (Los Angeles: Keiro Services Press and the Generations Fund, 1990).

23. See Tamar Katriel and Thomas Farrell. "Scrapbooks as Cultural Texts: An American Art of Memory," *Text and Performance Quarterly* 11 (January 1991): 1–17.

24. Cathy N. Davidson, *Reading in America: Literature and Social History* (Baltimore: Johns Hopkins University Press, 1989), 2.

CHAPTER 11: PICTURING LOVE AND FRIENDSHIP

1. For "reasonable," see "Editorial Miscellany," *American Journal of Photography* 3 (February 1, 1861): 272. For an illustration of the Rolodex-style stereocard viewer, see Robert Taft,

Photography and the Modern Scene: A Social History, 1839–1889 (1938; repr., New York: Dover, 1964), 172–73.

2. Noah Webster, *An American Dictionary of the English Language* (New York: Harper and Brothers, 1846).

3. For advice to photographers, see *American Journal of Photography* 3 (February 1861): 272. For the Easterner, see "Photographic Albums," *American Journal of Photography* (December 15, 1862): 337. Of the forty-two albums including photographs from the 1860s that I have examined, all the ones for which the owner's class can be estimated belonged to middle- or upper-class families. [Oliver Wendell Holmes], "Doings of the Sunbeam," *Atlantic Monthly* 12 (July 1863): 3. For the Midwestern editor, see "Photographic Albums," *Indiana Daily Journal* (December 24, 1863): 3.

4. Alonzo Lewis, *History of Lynn, Essex County, Massachusetts* (Boston: J. L. Shorey, 1865), 409. Advertisement in James Dabney McCabe, *Behind the Scenes in Washington* (New York: Continental Publishing Company, 1873), 522–23.

5. "The Shecesh," *Vanity Fair* 50 (1862): 163.

6. Joan Jacobs Brumberg, *The Body Project: An Intimate History of American Girls* (New York: Random House, 1997), 3–4. Mary P. Ryan, *Cradle of the Middle Class: The Family in Oneida County, New York, 1790–1865* (Cambridge: Cambridge University Press, 1981), 167–85. See also E. Anthony Rotundo, *American Manhood: The Transformations in Masculinity from the Revolution to the Modern Era* (New York: Basic Books, 1993), 56–74. L[ouisa] C. Tuthill, *The Young Lady at Home and in Society* (New York: Allen Brothers, 1869), 14–15.

7. For the 1862 advertisement, see "Just Received," *Indianapolis Daily Journal* (December 1, 1862): 3. When the Civil War transport ship *Maple Leaf* sank near Jacksonville, Florida, in 1864, the private luggage of the men of Colonel Robert Foster's brigade was lost. Subsequently preserved by anaerobic mud, the luggage is now being examined by archaeologists. Among the items is an ambrotype (photograph on glass) of a woman, presumably a soldier's wife; the ambrotype is artifact no. 164, St. John Archeological Expeditions, Jacksonville, Florida. For the Star Gallery, see the *Indianapolis Daily Journal* (August 8, 1862): 3. The war also contributed to the popularity of celebrity photographs; people collected photographs of leaders such as Abraham Lincoln and Robert E. Lee and installed those images in their family albums.

8. Annie Collins to Richard H. Collins, March 5, 1863, box 1, folder 10, Collins Papers, Special Collections and Archives, University of Kentucky Libraries, Lexington. I am grateful to Scott Stephan for bringing this collection to my attention.

9. "Duprey," photograph-autograph album, Autograph Collection, Cumberland University, Lebanon (Wilson County), Tenn., 1859/60, box 3, Manuscript Section, Tennessee State Library and Archives. Thomas L. Harrison, "Annapolis Album of Photographs" album, 1860, Thomas Locke Harrison Papers, Southern Historical Collection of the Manuscripts Department, University of North Carolina, Chapel Hill (hereinafter SHC). For "Visiting during study," see personal correspondence with Gary A. LaValley, archivist, U.S. Naval Academy, June 18, 1998.

10. Adeline T. Fuller, "Addie Fuller–Lynn, Mass–1866" album, 1866, lot 7060, Prints and Photographs Division, Library of Congress; Mary E. Fuller, "Mary E. Fuller, Lynn, Mass." album [1866], ibid.; Adeline T. Fuller, "ALBUM" [1866], ibid.

11. [Virginia Larwill Miller Ewing], "Sherman-Ewing-Larwill-Miller family album," ca. 1880, box 1, collection P-48, Ohio Historical Society, Columbus. At least two of the young men who posed together graduated from Kenyon.

12. Mary Jane Arnold, "Mollie J. Arnold, Mooresville, Ind." album, 1866, A. O. Mitchell Collection, Indiana Historical Society, Indianapolis. For the newspaper notice, see the October 27, 1874, clipping on page 21 of "Mooresville, Morgan County, Indiana, Scrapbook," Historical Genealogy Collection, Allen County Public Library, Fort Wayne, Ind. Benjamin Dakin also appeared in the album Mollie compiled after her marriage; see A. O. Mitchell and Mol-

lie (Arnold) Mitchell, "Capt. A. O. Mitchell and Lady" album, 1866, A. O. Mitchell Collection, Indiana Historical Society, Indianapolis.

13. For the history of photographers in Mooresville, see Clara S. Richardson, *A Brief History of Mooresville, Indiana, 1824–1974* (n.p.: n.p. [ca. 1977]), 58.

14. Evelyn M. Ludlum, "Annetta," *Overland Monthly and Out West Magazine* 3, 3 (1884): 327.

15. For "long before," see Alexis de Tocqueville, *Democracy in America* (1840; repr., New York: Vintage, 1945), 2:209–10. Auguste Carlier, *Marriage in the United States,* trans. B. Joy Jeffries (Boston: De Vries, Ibarra, 1867), 32. Carlier traveled in the United States from 1855 to 1857, when he was in his fifties; the first edition of his book was published in France in 1860.

16. On nineteenth-century courtship in the United States, see Michael Grossberg, *Governing the Hearth: Law and the Family in Nineteenth-Century America* (Chapel Hill: University of North Carolina Press, 1985); Karen Lystra, *Searching the Heart: Women, Men, and Romantic Love in Nineteenth-Century America* (New York: Oxford University Press, 1989); Ellen K. Rothman, *Hands and Hearts: A History of Courtship in America* (New York: Basic Books, 1984); Rotundo, *American Manhood.*

17. For "more taken" and "rising artist," see Frank Ingersoll to Sister, June 7 [1863], Lilly Library, Indiana University, Bloomington. For "Jane," see Frank Ingersoll to Sister [Mary], November 20, 1861.

18. For "beloved, adored Bettie," see Walter Rogers to Elizabeth Goelet, July 29, 1864, Goelet-Buncombe papers, SHC.

19. "Would fade" quoted in Rothman, *Hands and Hearts,* 125. Fanny Fern, *Ruth Hall and Other Writings,* ed. Joyce W. Warren (New Brunswick, N.J.: Rutgers University Press, 1986), 106.

20. Rogers to Goelet, July 29, 1864.

21. Rogers to Goelet, April 2, 3, 1865.

22. A. O. Mitchell and Mollie (Arnold) Mitchell, "Capt. A. O. Mitchell and Lady" album.

23. Elizabeth Goelet Rogers and Walter H. Rogers, untitled album, late 1860s, Goelet-Buncombe Family collection, SHC.

24. For "must have it," see Rogers to Goelet, January 29, 1867. For "kindly received," see Rogers to Goelet, September 8, 1864. "Walter H. Rogers and Edward Buncombe Goelet" in Goelet-Rogers album.

25. Rogers to Goelet, August 31, 1864.

CHAPTER 12: TELLING PARTICULAR STORIES

1. The idea that revision is at the core of collecting is explored by a number of theorists, notably Susan Stewart in *On Longing: Narratives of the Miniature, the Gigantic, the Souvenir, the Collection* (Durham, N.C.: Duke University Press, 1993). Scrapbooks and albums were favored vehicles for collecting and remembering, and I have written about their creation by girls in "Reading and Re-reading: The Scrapbooks of Girls Growing into Women, 1900–1940," in *Defining Print Culture for Youth: The Cultural Work of Children's Literature,* ed. Anne Lundin and Wayne Wiegand (Westport, Conn.: Greenwood Press, 2003). That middle-class, African American students participated in making such books is not surprising, but their works provide a more pronounced account than do those of white students of revision, of rejecting the images of one culture in favor of another, and of creating memories of a self within various cultures.

2. Each might be called a *memory book,* a term that seems to have been used by the popular press and by publishers, booksellers, and stationers; see, for example, *Times Picayune,* June 13, 1897, 13. Publishers involved in producing such books and often incorporating the phrase *memory book* in titles or in advertisements included Dodd, Mead; Paul Elder; G. W. Dillingham Company; J. P. Lippincott Company; W. L. Bacon; the College Memorabilia Company; W. C. Horn Brothers; Reilly and Lee Company; and C. R. Gibson.

3. Storage of photographs within albums is discussed in Richard Horton, "Photo Album Structure, 1950–1960," *Guild of Book Workers Journal* 32, 10 (Spring 1994): 32–43; Jaap Boerdam and Warna Martinius, "Family Photographs: A Sociological Approach," *Netherlands Journal of Sociology* 16, 2 (October 1980): 95–120; Saundra Gardner, "Exploring the Family Album: Social Class Differences in Images of Family Life," *Sociological Inquiry* 1, 2 (May 1991): 242–51; and Shannon Zachary, ed., *Conservation of Scrapbooks and Albums*, (Washington, D.C.: American Institute for Conservation of Historic and Artistic Works, 2000). See also Elizabeth E. Siegel and Sarah McNair Vosmeier in this volume for a discussion of the album's introduction into many households.

4. Louise Perret and Sarah K. Smith, *The Girl Graduate: Her Own Book* (Chicago: Reilly and Lee, n.d.); *Cumulative Book Index*, 1906–1912, and *The United States Catalog*, 1912–1927 (Washington, D.C.: U.S. Government Printing Office).

5. In my study of some eighty scrapbooks and albums, I found that about one-fourth of them bear an inscription indicating that these books were given as gifts. These scrapbooks are now housed in New Orleans (at Historic New Orleans Collection; Howard-Tilton Library, Tulane University; Amistad Research Center at Tulane University; Long Library, University of New Orleans; and Newcomb Archives, Tulane University); in Denton, Texas (at Texas Woman's University Library and North Texas State University Library); in New York City (at Barnard College Library; New York Public Library; Teachers College Library, Columbia University; and New York Historical Society); and in Virginia (at Sweet Briar College Library and Randolph Macon Woman's College Library).

6. Perret and Smith, *Girl Graduate*, n.p.

7. Martha Banta, *Imaging American Women: Ideas and Ideals in Cultural History* (New York: Columbia University Press, 1987), 136.

8. Ibid., 1–39, 104–11; Shane White and Graham White, *Stylin': African American Expressive Culture from Its Beginnings to the Zoot Suit* (Ithaca, N.Y.: Cornell University Press, 1998), 180–219.

9. Doug Ramsey, "Fletcher Henderson, Discography," disc liner in Henderson's *Tidal Wave* compact disc (New York: MCA Records, 1994), 10.

10. Florence Borders, "Fletcher Hamilton Henderson Papers, ca. 1877–1972: Unpublished Register, Scope, and Content Note," 1985, Amistad Research Center at Tulane University, 1–2.

11. Atlanta University, *The Diamond Hill Chronicle* [senior annual, Atlanta University] 1, 1 (June 1920).

12. See, for example, the images in Helen Lefkowitz Horowitz, *Campus Life: Undergraduate Cultures from the End of the Eighteenth Century to the Present* (Chicago: University of Chicago Press, 1987); and Barbara Schreier, *Fitting In: Four Generations of College Life* (Chicago: Chicago Historical Society, 1991).

13. Walter C. Allen, *Hendersonia: The Music of Fletcher Henderson and His Musicians: A Bio-Discography* (Highland Park, N.J.: n.p., 1973), 1.

14. Charles Garner, "Fletcher Henderson: A Summary of His Career, His Music, and His Influence" (PhD diss., Teachers College of Columbia University, 1991), 20.

15. Margery Dews, *Remembering the Remarkable Henderson Family* (Chicago: Adams Press, 1978), 42.

16. Borders, Henderson Papers, n.p. Dews also provides some photographs of campuses, but these are not identified.

17. In 1916, for example, whites made up only slightly less than half the teachers and workers in Congregational Church schools, according to Thomas Jesse Jones, *Negro Education: A Study of the Private and Higher Schools for Colored People in the United States* (Washington, D.C.: Government Printing Office, 1917), 369. See also Jacqueline Jones, *Soldiers of Light and Love: Northern Teachers and Georgia Blacks, 1865–1873* (Chapel Hill: University of North Carolina Press, 1980).

18. W.E.B. DuBois, *The Souls of Black Folks* (1902; repr., New York: Bantam Books, 1989), 3. For directing me toward thinking of these memory books in terms of DuBois's theories, I thank Arthé Anthony.

19. For information on curriculum choices, see Atlanta University, *The Diamond Hill Chronicle*, June 1920.

20. Allen, *Hendersonia*, 6, 14; Dews, *Remembering the Remarkable Henderson Family*, 23; Garner, "Fletcher Henderson," 31.

21. Allen, *Hendersonia*, 3.

22. The yearbook lists activities, as well as chosen quotes, for each student; see ibid.

23. Allen, *Hendersonia*, 28.

24. Ethel Waters, *His Eye Is on the Sparrow* (Garden City, N.Y.: Doubleday, 1951), 141.

25. Allen, *Hendersonia*, 2.

26. Burton Peretti, *The Creation of Jazz: Music, Race, and Culture in Urban America* (Chicago: University of Illinois Press, 1992), 120–44; Horowitz, *Campus Life*, 118, 126.

27. Biographer Ramsey describes Henderson as "diffident and modest" and never one to push "himself on anyone"; see Ramsey, "Fletcher Henderson, Discography," 8–9. Garner describes him as easygoing; see Garner, "Fletcher Henderson," 14. One can imagine him giving away images of himself when asked.

28. Linda Haverty Rugg, *Picturing Ourselves: Photography and Autobiography* (Chicago: University of Chicago Press, 1993), 1.

29. Françoise Lionnet, *Autobiographical Voices: Gender, Race, and Self Portraiture* (Ithaca: Cornell University Press, 1989), 248.

30. Peretti, *Creation of Jazz*, 120–44.

31. "Collection Description. Juanita Page Johnson Scrapbook," n.d., Amistad Research Center at Tulane University.

32. U.S. Census 1920, Rock Island County, East Moline, Illinois, ed. 162, sheet 10, line 53.

33. See Tucker, "Reading and Re-Reading."

34. In the period 1910–25, only Yazoo City provided a public school for African Americans in Mississippi, according to Jones, *Soldiers of Light and Love*, 408. See also Carole Marks, *Farewell—We're Good and Gone: The Black Migration* (Bloomington: Indiana University Press, 1989), 77.

35. The scrapbooks I have studied are located in collections named in note 5.

36. Chicago Commission on Race Relations, *The Negro in Chicago: A Study of Race Relations and a Race Riot in 1919* (1922; repr., New York: Arno Press, 1968), 245, 253, 255.

37. Ibid., 245, 252. Other sources that present some of the activities, courses, and racial and ethnic makeup of Phillips are Elvira D. Cabell, "Social Activities of Chicago High Schools," *Chicago Schools Journal* 5 (1923): 360–66; and Thomas W. Gutowski, "The High School as an Adolescent-Raising Institution: An Inner History of Chicago Public Secondary Education, 1856–1940" (PhD diss., University of Chicago, 1978).

38. Although I have not been able to find whether a segregated white team existed at Wendell Phillips at the time, it seems unlikely, because African American students accounted for three-fourths of the school population by 1921. See Michael W. Homel, *Down from Equality: Black Chicagoans and the Public Schools, 1920–41* (Chicago: University of Illinois Press, 1984), 14; Alan H. Speer, *Black Chicago* (Chicago: University of Chicago Press, 1967), 44–46.

39. For more information on Wendell Phillips's role in the birth of the Harlem Globetrotters, see Josh Wilker, *The Harlem Globetrotters* (New York: Chelsea House, 1997). For more on the work of Alpha Kappa Alpha Sorority, see Deborah Whaley, "The Cultural and Counterpublic Sphere Work of Alpha Kappa Alpha Sorority" (PhD diss., University of Kansas, 2002).

40. James's hair is upswept, not unlike that of the black teacher featured in Kathleen Thompson and Hilary MacAustin, eds., *The Face of Our Past: Images of Black Women from Colonial America to the Present* (Bloomington: Indiana University Press, 1999), 78, 109.

41. Philip Stokes, "The Family Photograph Album," in *The Portrait in Photography*, ed. Graham Clarke (London: Reaktion Books, 1992), 197.

42. Todd Gernes, "Recasting the Culture of Ephemera: Young Women's Literary Culture in Nineteenth Century America" (PhD diss., Brown University, 1992), 57–109; Starr Ockenga, *On Women and Friendship: A Collection of Victorian Keepsakes and Traditions* (New York: Stewart, Tabori, and Chang, 1993), 40–45.

43. Theodore Weld, *American Slavery as It Is: Testimony of a Thousand Witnesses* (New York: American Anti-Slavery Society, 1839).

44. For information on the scrapbooks of abolitionists, see Thomas C. Leonard, *News for All: America's Coming-of-Age with the Press* (New York: Oxford University Press, 1995), 168–69.

45. Dorothy Porter Wesley, "Black Antiquarians and Bibliophiles Revisited, with a Glance at Today's Lovers of Books and Memorabilia," in *Black Bibliophiles and Collectors: Preservers of Black History*, ed. Elinor Des Verney Sinnette, W. Paul Coates, and Thomas C. Battle (Washington, D.C.: Howard University Press, 1990), 8.

46. Sulayman Clark, "Indexes of the William Dorsey Collection," 1982, Leslie Pinckney Hill Library, Cheyney State College, 8.

47. Ibid., 3; Roger Lane, *William Dorsey's Philadelphia and Ours: On the Past and Future of the Black City in America* (New York: Oxford University Press, 1991), 1–3, 411–12.

48. Tony Martin, "Bibliophiles, Activists, and Race Men," in Sinnette et al., *Black Bibliophiles and Collectors*, 24, 29, 31.

49. W.E.B. DuBois, *The Philadelphia Negro: A Social Study* (Philadelphia: University of Pennsylvania, 1899), iv.

50. Ibid., "DuBois Albums of Photographs of African Americans in Georgia Exhibited at the Paris Exposition Universelle in 1900," Daniel Murray Collection, Rare Book and Special Collections Division, Library of Congress..

51. Arnold Rampersad, "DuBois, William Edward Burghardt," in *Encyclopedia of African-American Culture and History*, ed. Jack Salzman, David Lionel Smith, and Cornel West (New York: Macmillan Library Reference, 1995), 807–9.

52. Shawn Michelle Smith, *American Archives: Gender, Race, and Class in Visual Culture* (Princeton, N.J.: Princeton University Press, 1999), 177–86.

53. Ibid., 158, 182–83.

54. Marianne Hirsh, *Family Frames: Photography, Narrative, and Postmemory* (Cambridge: Harvard University Press, 1997), 215.

55. bell hooks, "In Our Glory: Photography and Black Life," in *Picturing Us: African-American Identity in Photography*, ed. Deborah Willis (New York: New Press, 1994), 49.

CHAPTER 13: MATERNAL RECORDS AND MALE MODERNIST IDENTITIES

Acknowledgments: A research grant awarded by the John F. Kennedy Library, Boston, allowed me to review Grace Hall-Hemingway's albums and other holdings in the library's Hemingway Collection. Professors Holly Laird and Anne Stavney at the University of Tulsa provided helpful criticism at various stages in the preparation of this essay.

1. Michael Levenson, *A Genealogy of Modernism: A Study of English Literary Doctrine, 1908–1922* (Cambridge: Cambridge University Press, 1984). In her study, *Katherine Mansfield and the Origins of Modernist Fiction* (Ithaca, N.Y.: Cornell University Press, 1991), Sydney Janet Kaplan calls attention to and explicitly critiques Levenson's male-centered account of the genesis of literary modernism. Kaplan's book is an important contribution to the well-developed countertradition of feminist criticism and female modernism.

2. Dennis Brown, *Intertextual Dynamics within the Literary Group: Joyce, Lewis, Pound, and Eliot* (London: Macmillan, 1990).

3. Martin Green, *Children of the Sun: A Narrative of "Decadence" in England after 1918* (New York: Basic Books, 1976), 63.

4. See Alec Marsh, "Thaddeus Coleman Pound's 'Newspaper Scrapbook' as a Source for *The Cantos*," *Paideuma* 24, 2/3 (Fall/Winter 1995): 163–93. Marsh describes the scrapbook of Pound's paternal grandfather as consisting almost exclusively of public documents such as newspaper clippings, published poems, and letters to the editors of various newspapers.

5. In *The American Ezra Pound* (New Haven, Conn.: Yale University Press, 1989), Wendy Stallard Flory makes clear Pound's preference for his paternal over his maternal lineage and cites

a passage from the medical files of Pound's statements during his incarceration in St. Eliza-beth's Hospital: "My harmony with my father was unusual. I was my father's son in opposition to my mother. Most sons fight their fathers all their lives. My own case is farthest removed from the Oedipus complex" (22). Affirming references by Pound to his grandfather can be found in *Jefferson and/or Mussolini* ([New York: Liveright, 1935], 33) as well as in "A Visiting Card" (1942): "It was only when my father brought some old newspaper clippings to Rapallo in 1937 that I discovered that T. C. P. had already in 1878 been writing about, or urging among his fellow Congressmen, the same essentials of monetary and statal economics that I am writing about today" (see *Selected Prose: 1909–1965* [New York: New Directions, 1973], 325).

6. Pierre Bourdieu, "The Cult of Unity and Cultivated Difference," in *Photography: A Middle-Brow Art*, ed. Pierre Bourdieu, Luc Boltanski, Robert Castel, Jean-Claude Chamboredon, and Dominique Schnapper, trans. Shaun Whiteside (1965; repr., Stanford, Calif.: Stanford University Press, 1990), 19, 21.

7. Susan Sontag, *On Photography* (1977; repr., New York: Doubleday, 1990), 21, 133.

8. Val Williams, *The Other Observers: Woman Photographers in Britain, 1900 to the Present* (1986; repr., London: Virago Press, 1991), 166. Here, the Polysnappers' critique of family portraiture uses language strongly reminiscent of the early Roland Barthes. Although not directly addressing the institution of the nuclear family, Barthes's short essay on the *Great Family of Man* photography exhibition of 1955 implicitly critiques attempts through photography to naturalize the nuclear family alongside other institutions such as education and work and free it from the "determining weight of History"; see *Mythologies*, selected and trans. Annette Lavers (New York: Noonday Press, 1972), 100–102. The later Barthes is far more ambivalent about the critical tendency to view "the Photograph as family rite, . . . nothing but the trace of a social protocol of integration, intended to reassert the Family"; see *Camera Lucida: Reflections on Photography*, trans. Richard Howard (New York: Hill and Wang, 1981), 7, 74.

9. Bourdieu, "Cult of Unity," 13–72.

10. Ibid., 22, 22–23.

11. Grace Hall-Hemingway, Scrapbooks, Ernest Hemingway Collection, John F. Kennedy Library, Boston.

12. Bourdieu, "Cult of Unity," 19.

13. Marilyn F. Motz, "Visual Autobiography: Photograph Albums of Turn-of-the-Century Mid-western Women," *American Quarterly* 41, 1 (March 1989): 72, 89–90.

14. Kenneth A. Lynn, *Hemingway* (New York: Simon and Schuster, 1987), 40–41, 43.

15. Ibid., 45, 77.

16. Ibid., 57–58, 388–89, 486–88, 542–43.

17. Ernest Hemingway, *For Whom the Bell Tolls* (New York: Charles Scribner's Sons, 1940), 67, 345, 346.

18. Lynn, *Hemingway,* 388n.

19. Ernest Hemingway, *The Complete Short Stories of Ernest Hemingway* (New York: Charles Scribner's Sons, 1987), 515.

20. Ibid., 531.

21. Ibid., 533, 535.

22. Ibid., 344.

23. Ernest Hemingway, *The Garden of Eden* (New York: Charles Scribner's Sons, 1986), 6, 12, 14–15.

24. Ibid., 81–82.

25. Ibid., 82–84.

26. Ibid., 37.

27. Susan Beegel, "Soldier's Home," e-mail to Heming-l@mtu.edu, May 27, 1999.

28. Hemingway, *Complete Short Stories,* 375.

29. Lynn, *Hemingway,* 44.

30. Ibid., 38, 40.

31. In his discussion of "Soldier's Home," Lynn hints at but does not explore possible connections between the mother-son rivalry and the close sibling relationship in Hemingway's piece. "A significant weakness in the story is that its most memorable character, Mrs. Krebs, is not linked in any way to this quasi-incestuous byplay going on in her household between two of her children," Lynn writes. He continues: "For all the determination to achieve self-understanding that Hemingway seems to have brought to the composition of 'Soldier's Home,' he was only able to dramatize the intimacy between Krebs and his kid sister, not account for it"; see Lynn, *Hemingway*, 258–59.

32. Hemingway, *Complete Short Stories*, 111.

33. Ibid.

34. Ann Douglas, *Terrible Honesty: Mongrel Manhattan in the 1920s* (New York: Farrar, Strauss and Giroux, 1995), 220–25.

35. Ibid., 222.

36. Hemingway, *Complete Short Stories*, 114.

37. Ibid.

38. Ibid., 114–15, 39.

39. Ibid., 116.

40. Hemingway, *Complete Short Stories*; Ernest Hemingway, *Islands in the Stream* (New York: Charles Scribner's Sons, 1970); Hemingway, *The Garden of Eden*.

41. Bourdieu, "Cult of Unity," 39, 72.

42. *Re-visioning* is a term coined by Adrienne Rich to describe the task of "seeing with fresh eyes," a task necessary to the reconstruction and recovery of women's literary history. See Adrienne Rich, "When We Dead Awaken: Writing as Revision" (1971), in *On Lies, Secrets, and Silence: Selected Prose, 1966–1978* (New York: Norton, 1979), 33–39. Jonathan Weinberg has discussed how Carl Van Vechten, in his scrapbooks from 1935 onward, similarly "pasted together a history of gay life from the thirties to the fifties." Through Van Vechten's clipped pictures and texts—many of which are arranged in ironic combinations—"the dominant culture's language . . . is made to speak sexual transgression"; see Jonathan Weinberg, "'Boy Crazy': Carl Van Vechten's Queer Collection," *Yale Journal of Criticism* 7, 2 (Fall 1994): 25–49, esp. 31–32.

43. Christopher Isherwood, *All the Conspirators* (London: Jonathan Cape, 1928), 118–19.

44. Claude J. Summers, *Christopher Isherwood* (New York: Frederick Ungar, 1980), 48.

45. Christopher Isherwood, *The Memorial: Portrait of a Family* (1932; repr., Norfolk, Conn.: New Directions, 1947).

46. For a discussion of Isherwood's revision of family ties in his fiction, see James Kelley, "Aunt May, Uncle Henry, and Anti-Ancestral impulses in *The Memorial*," in *The Isherwood Century*, ed. James J. Berg and Chris Freeman (Madison: University of Wisconsin Press, 2000), 141–49.

47. Kathleen Bradshaw-Isherwood, Journal, October 4–November 4, 1909, Department of Special Collections, McFarlin Library, University of Tulsa; Christopher Isherwood Papers 2:11, October 4–November 4, 1909, Department of Special Collections, McFarlin Library, University of Tulsa (hereinafter, Isherwood Papers).

48. Christopher Isherwood, "Jottings from a Holiday Diary," Travel journal, Isherwood Papers 8:1, ca. 1917–18.

49. Bourdieu, "Cult of Unity," 39, 72.

50. Christopher Isherwood, Photograph album: Canary Islands and Spanish Morocco, Isherwood Papers, 10:5, 1934.

51. Motz, "Visual Autobiography," 85.

CHAPTER 14: "MISS DOMESTIC" AND "MISS ENTERPRISE"

1. Nod Patterson, "Two Kinds of Album Pictures," *The Photographer's Friend/Almanac and American Yearbook of Photography for 1872* (Baltimore: R. Walzl, 1872), 45.

2. Ibid., 45.
3. Ibid., 47.
4. The first notice I have seen for albums in the United States occurs in an advertisement for E. & H. T. Anthony on December 22, 1860, in both *Harper's Weekly* and *Frank Leslie's Illustrated Newspaper*. By 1861 carte-de-visite albums seem to have become popular with a broad enough public to strike notice in several trade and general publications.
5. Most current scholarship about family photography tends to focus on more recent—that is, post-Kodak—histories of family pictures, examining the snapshot at the expense of the posed studio portrait; this body of work takes as a given that the conventions of the family album, intricately linked to definitions of family, stem from the snapshot. See Julia Hirsch, *Family Photographs: Content, Meaning, and Effect* (New York: Oxford University Press, 1981); Annette Kuhn, *Family Secrets: Acts of Memory and Imagination* (New York: Verso, 1995); Jo Spence and Patricia Holland, eds., *Family Snaps: The Meaning of Domestic Photography* (London: Virago, 1991); and Marianne Hirsch, *Family Frames: Narrative Photography and Postmemory* (Cambridge: Harvard University Press, 1997). By contrast, I begin with the photograph album's origins: the carte de visite. I have discussed this in greater length in my dissertation, "Galleries of Friendship and Fame: The History of Nineteenth-Century American Photograph Albums" (University of Chicago, 2003), as well as in the article "Talking through the 'Fotygraft Album,'" in *Phototextualities: Intersections of Photography and Narrative*, ed. Alex Hughes and Andrea Noble (Albuquerque: University of New Mexico Press, 2003).
6. The larger cabinet card was introduced in 1866, and albums were produced with slots to accommodate the new size alongside the older carte de visite.
7. "Lay in Your Holiday Stock," *Anthony's Photographic Bulletin* 2, 11 (November 1871): 369–70; an 1872 price list advertised forty-five different albums from $1.00 to $27.00. "Novelties: Albums," *Anthony's Photographic Bulletin* 3, 9 (September 1872): 675–76.
8. The editors delightedly wrote: "Albums have once more claimed their place on 'the Centre-Table;' not those of the persecuting order, that made the visitor tremble as he surveyed the touching tributes of affection therein recorded, lest he should, in turn, be bored for an 'original' contribution, and which robbed Moore and Byron of much of their well-earned fame; but the album photographic, which all delight to honor, inasmuch as few people are averse to seeing their faces or their names in print!" See "Centre-Table Gossip: Photographic Albums," *Godey's Lady's Book* 64 (February 1862): 208.
9. See Sarah McNair Vosmeier, "Picturing Love and Friendship: Photograph Albums and Networks of Affection in the 1860s," in this volume.
10. "Editorial Department," *American Journal of Photography* 5, 13 (January 1, 1863): 312.
11. "Photography and Its Album," *Godey's Lady's Book* 68 (March 1864): 304.
12. Arthur Jerome Dickson, ed., *Covered Wagon Days: A Journey across the Plains in the Sixties, and Pioneer Days in the Northwest; from the Private Journals of Alvert Jerome Dickson* (Cleveland: Arthur H. Clark, 1929), 192.
13. See the *Subject-Matter Index of Patents for Inventions Issued by the United States Patent Office from 1790–1873, Inclusive* (New York: Arno Press, 1976), entries for "Album" and "Photographic Album."
14. John E. Cussans, "The Past and Future of Photography," *Humphrey's Journal* 17, 1 (May 1, 1865): 7.
15. "Keep Your Albums Locked," *Anthony's Photographic Bulletin* 7, 2 (February 1876): 43.
16. "The New Size," *Philadelphia Photographer* 3, 34 (October 1866): 311.
17. George Eastman House International Museum of Photography, Sipley Collection 77:317:1–50.
18. Collecting cartes in albums was an extremely popular pastime for young women, and many female readers were addressed as purchasers of cartes and maintainers of albums in the pages of *Godey's Lady's Book*, *Peterson's Magazine*, and the like. On the carte craze and young women, see "Lady Beggars," *Vanity Fair* 50 (February 22, 1862): 93.

19. "Photography and the Affections," *Humphrey's Journal* 17, 6 (July 15, 1865): 93.
20. This article was originally published in England (hence the servant's cockney slang) but was reprinted for a U.S. audience in *Anthony's Photographic Bulletin*. Such borrowing of articles was not an uncommon practice.
21. "Keep Your Albums Locked," 43.
22. Ibid.
23. I have seen two examples of this particular album, one (1864) at the National Museum of American History, Smithsonian Institution, and another (1865), with slight revisions, at the George Eastman House, International Museum of Photography and Film. My citations are from the revised Eastman House copy.
24. Platt provided a "model register," detailing how one might fill out the personal and physical data of the record. A few examples give some insight into what he thought the typical family to be, along with some facts of life in the nineteenth-century United States: "Descent: English, Irish, Scotch, German, &c."; "No. Bro's and Sis's: Five Brothers and Three Sisters"; "Occupation: Farmer, Lawyer, Mechanic, &c."; "Religion: Methodist, Baptist, Catholic, &c."; Health: Feeble, Average, Good, Vigorous"; "Disease: Consumption, Killed in Battle."
25. The reader should be alerted to a methodological problem in examining old albums, namely that their provenance is sometimes not established and unscrupulous dealers may remove or replace the photographs inside. George Eastman House's album comes from the old Sipley Museum of Philadelphia; little is known about how it came into that collection. The Smithsonian's album, which also has none of the lines filled in and photographs on the wrong pages, can trace its provenance back to a collector but not beyond that. For my purposes, I assume they represent the families' use of the album; even if the photographs have been changed, the written portion is still left blank.
26. John L. Gihon, "Photographic Albums," *Photographic Mosaics* 13 (1878): 69.
27. These conclusions are based on albums I have viewed at the International Museum of Photography, George Eastman House; National Museum of American History, Smithsonian Institution; Chicago Historical Society; Art Institute of Chicago; New-York Historical Society; and Society for the Preservation of New England Antiquities.
28. Anne Higonnet, "Secluded Vision: Images of Feminine Experience in Nineteenth-Century Europe," *Radical History Review* 38 (1987): 22–23, 24.

About the Contributors

〰〰〰〰

Carol Bowers, reference manager of the American Heritage Center, Laramie, Wyoming, is a lecturer in history of the nineteenth-century American West at the University of Wyoming.

Jennifer L. Bradley is associate professor of English and chair of liberal arts and sciences at Mercy College of Health Sciences in Des Moines, Iowa. Recent articles include "'To Entertain, to Educate, to Elevate': Willa Cather Learns the Commodification of Manners at the Home Monthly," in *Willa Cather and Material Culture: Real-World Writing, Writing the Real World* (forthcoming).

Patricia P. Buckler, associate professor of English and director of composition at Purdue University North Central in Westville, Indiana, teaches courses on literature and writing. Besides her research into antebellum scrapbooks, her scholarly interests include composition pedagogy and detective fiction. She was a 2001–2 Mellon Research Fellow in early U.S. history and culture at the Library Company of Philadelphia and the Pennsylvania Historical Society.

Meredith Eliassen is curator of the Marguerite Archer Collection of Children's Materials, San Francisco State University. Her current research, which centers on popular and material culture in the San Francisco Bay Area, includes a study of female boardinghouse operators in San Francisco during the gold-rush era.

Ellen Gruber Garvey, associate professor of English at New Jersey City University, is the author of *The Adman in the Parlor: Magazines and the Gendering of Consumer*

Culture, 1880s–1910, which was chosen best book of 1996 by the Society for the History of Authorship, Reading, and Publishing. She has held the Fulbright Walt Whitman Distinguished Chair in American Literature in the Netherlands and is currently working on a book on nineteenth-century scrapbooks and their relationship to ideas of authorship and recirculation, nineteenth-century reading practices, and present-day artists' books.

Beverly Gordon, a professor in the environment, textiles, and design department at the University of Wisconsin–Madison, is the author of *Bazaars and Fair Ladies: The History of the American Fundraising Fair* and *Shaker Textile Arts*. She is past president of the Textile Society of America.

Melissa A. Johnson is assistant professor of art history at Illinois State University. She wrote her doctoral dissertation on Hannah Höch's Weimar scrapbook and continues to research this topic as well as twentieth-century artists' books.

Jennifer A. Jolly, assistant professor of art history at Ithaca College, teaches courses in Latin American art. Her current research explores postrevolutionary mural and graphic arts in Mexico.

James Kelley is assistant professor of English at Mississippi State University–Meridian. As a Fulbright junior lecturer, he taught courses in U.S. culture and literature in Magdeburg, Germany.

Anne Sinkler Whaley LeClercq is director of the Daniel Library, the Citadel. She is the author of *An Antebellum Plantation Household, Including the Receipts and Remedies of Emily Wharton Sinkler* and *Between North and South: The Letters of Emily Wharton Sinkler*.

L. Rebecca Johnson Melvin, the author of *Self Works: Diaries, Scrapbooks, and Other Autobiographical Efforts*, is associate librarian and coordinator of the Manuscripts Unit, Special Collections, University of Delaware Library. She is active in the Society of American Archivists and the Association of College and Research Libraries.

Katherine Ott is curator in the Division of Science and Medicine at the Smithsonian Institution's National Museum of American History. She is the author of *Fevered Lives: Tuberculosis in American Culture since 1870* and coeditor of *Artificial Parts, Practical Lives: Modern Histories of Prosthetics*. She teaches a course on museums and material culture at Georgetown University.

Elizabeth E. Siegel, assistant curator of photography at the Art Institute of Chicago, wrote her doctoral dissertation on the history of nineteenth-century U.S. family albums. She is coeditor *of Taken by Design: Photographs from the Institute of Design, 1937–71*.

Susan Tucker is curator of books and records at Newcomb College Center for Research on Women, Tulane University. A former Fulbright student to Iceland, she is the author of *Telling Memories among Southern Women: Domestic Workers in the Segregated South.*

Sarah McNair Vosmeier, assistant professor of history at Hanover College in Indiana, teaches courses on women, the family, and the middle class in the United States. Her research centers on family photography and photograph albums.

Index

wwww